To Matthew and the memory of Paulette.

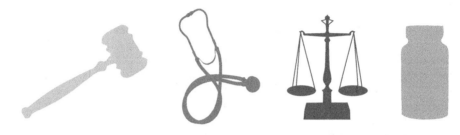

LAW AND ETHICS IN NURSING AND HEALTHCARE

AN INTRODUCTION

GRAHAM AVERY

Los Angeles | London | New Delhi
Singapore | Washington DC

Los Angeles | London | New Delhi
Singapore | Washington DC

SAGE Publications Ltd
1 Oliver's Yard
55 City Road
London EC1Y 1SP

SAGE Publications Inc.
2455 Teller Road
Thousand Oaks, California 91320

SAGE Publications India Pvt Ltd
B 1/I 1 Mohan Cooperative Industrial Area
Mathura Road
New Delhi 110 044

SAGE Publications Asia-Pacific Pte Ltd
3 Church Street
#10-04 Samsung Hub
Singapore 049483

Editor: Susan Worsey
Assistant editor: Emma Milman
Production editor: Katie Forsythe
Copyeditor: Mary Dalton
Proofreader: Clare Weaver
Marketing manager: Tamara Navaratnam
Cover design: Lisa Harper
Typeset by: C&M Digitals (P) Ltd, Chennai, India
Printed by MPG Books Group, Bodmin, Cornwall

Library of Congress Control Number: 2012938113

British Library Cataloguing in Publication data

A catalogue record for this book is available from
the British Library

MIX
Paper from
responsible sources
FSC
www.fsc.org   FSC® C018575

ISBN 978-1-84860-733-0
ISBN 978-1-84860-734-7 (pbk)

LAW AND ETHICS IN NURSING AND HEALTHCARE

SAGE has been part of the global academic community since 1965, supporting high quality research and learning that transforms society and our understanding of individuals, groups and cultures. SAGE is the independent, innovative, natural home for authors, editors and societies who share our commitment and passion for the social sciences.

Find out more at: **www.sagepublications.com**

CONTENTS

ABOUT THE AUTHOR

I am a Lecturer at the University of Essex in the School of Health and Human Sciences, having been here for just over eight years. Prior to this, I worked for 25 years in an acute hospital setting, and the area with which I was most closely associated was surgical nursing. I was instrumental in introducing a variety of initiatives to the workplace: individualised pre-operative fasting, self-administration of medicines, patient group directions, and a no-fault system of drug error reporting. I also studied Medical Law and Ethics at King's College London, and I have undertaken research into non-medical prescribing.

The study of law and ethics in healthcare has gained increasing attention in recent years for a variety of reasons. Firstly, it is a vibrant area of study, for new developments in medicine are constantly presenting new challenges and dilemmas. Secondly, people are now generally more aware of their rights, and we live in an increasingly litigious society. More importantly than either of these, though, is that a grasp of legal and ethical concepts enables healthcare practitioners to fulfil their moral and professional imperative: i.e. to do what is right for the patients in their care.

This book is intended to deliver key concepts in an easy-to-read style, and it should therefore be of especial value to those who are new to this subject. Writing the book has been challenging and, at times, frustrating; but it has reaffirmed and strengthened my passion for this field of study, and I hope that this enjoyment is transmitted to the reader.

INTRODUCTION

When I was invited just over a couple of years ago to write a book on healthcare law and ethics, my initial reaction was that the market had become flooded with such texts in recent years and that there was no space for another one. A more considered approach, however, made me realise three things. First, healthcare law and ethics are dynamic and constantly changing. New developments in medicine create new ethical dilemmas; expansion of the role of nurses and allied health professionals renders them more exposed to the threat of litigation than was previously the case; and politicians always make the National Health Service a central issue in each election. Healthcare law and ethics therefore pervades the public consciousness: they cannot be ignored, and healthcare professionals have an obligation (to the public, their employers and themselves) to ensure that they are familiar with the core principles.

Second, and closely related to the first point, the general public are much more aware of their rights than used to be the case. The image of the passive patient, never questioning and never arguing, is fast fading from memory. In truth, they always had the right to good healthcare and to have their autonomy respected, but they are much more likely to demand such rights today and to complain when they have not been met. When Lord Denning spoke of a 'dagger at the doctor's back' (*Hatcher v Black [1954]*), he envisaged a situation somewhat akin to the United States, where the threat of litigation is ever-present, and where patients are frequently subjected to a battery of unnecessary, expensive and invasive procedures in order to avoid such a threat. For a variety of reasons, this scenario has not been replicated within the United Kingdom; but the *possibility* of litigation is at least more real, and practitioners have a stronger need than ever before to acquaint themselves with legal and ethical principles.

Third, and arguably more importantly than either of the previous two, an understanding of healthcare law and ethics helps to provide practitioners with a model for good practice. While it may be tempting to perceive such issues as the villain hiding in the corner that is ready to pounce whenever standards fall short of perfection, a more professional approach would be to look at them as positive forces for change. Florence Nightingale once said that there is no such thing as standing still: when we believe that there is nothing more to learn or no way in which it is possible to improve our performance, we are actually going backwards, because others will quickly catch up and overtake us. A study of healthcare law and ethics frequently exposes the weaknesses of practice and this inevitably induces discomfort and a defensive attitude; but it is necessary to be able to identify the shortcomings so that they can be addressed.

The definitive textbook on healthcare law and ethics has yet to be written, and this one certainly has no pretensions to be such. My purpose, however, has been to produce a source that provides the reader with a solid foundation of knowledge and understanding, upon which new knowledge can be built by reference to more detailed texts. With this in mind, I have endeavoured to write it in as accessible a form as lies within my abilities, and have interspersed the narrative with a number of examples (real and fictional). The reader will note that the vast majority of legal principles derive from cases involving doctors; this should not come as a surprise, given that medicine carries the potential for doing the most harm, as well as the most good. The principles, however, are applicable to *all* healthcare professionals, and are much more likely to be invoked as other practitioners venture into territory that was formerly the exclusive province of doctors.

The order in which the chapters are read is, of course, entirely at the discretion of the reader, but there was a certain amount of logic behind the book's structure. For those new to this field, I would advise that Chapters 1 and 2 are read first, simply because these are intended to provide a framework for what comes later. In other words, an understanding of the English legal system will help to explain the progress of cases through the courts, whereas a grounding in ethical theory will assist analysis of the moral issues. The next two chapters (Negligence and Consent) are those areas that affect healthcare professionals the most, and are therefore accorded the priority that they deserve. The remaining chapters all cover areas of importance, and it is not intended that they are in any order of merit. It seemed logical to put End of Life Decisions at the end, but their profile has noticeably increased in recent years. There are a number of areas that could have been included, and one thinks of abortion, genetic testing, organ donation and research ethics, to name but a few. Each of these deserves attention, but I was conscious that this book is intended as an Introduction and did not therefore wish it to appear too bulky and overwhelming.

There has been a tendency in texts of the past to assume that the doctor is male and the nurse is female. The patient is also perceived as male, unless circumstances of the illness dictate otherwise. Clearly, this no longer has application in today's society, where the number of women entering medicine is at least as many as that of men, and there are increasing numbers of male nurses. Some writers have sought to redress the balance by continually referring to the doctor as 'she', but this seems to me to be making the same mistake. I have therefore endeavoured to be as gender neutral as possible and have referred to healthcare practitioners and patients as 's/he'. I acknowledge the criticism from a number of authors that this is a clumsy technique, but I believe it to be the best way of escaping from the confines of gender politics.

Finally, I would like to extend my thanks to the reviewers of this book, who have made many helpful suggestions and who have helped me avoid several errors and omissions. Needless to say, any mistakes that remain are entirely my own. I would also like to thank the staff at Sage for their support, especially Susan and Emma, who have shown remarkable tolerance and patience throughout. My own estimation of how quickly I could finish this book was always going to be wildly inaccurate, but their forbearance has been admirable. Last but not least, I must acknowledge the debt that I owe to my students. Not only have they been a pleasure to teach, but also they have stimulated my own thoughts about issues and have frequently furnished me with ideas for scenarios.

Writing this book has been a hard journey, but has often been enjoyable and informative. My hope is that this enjoyment is conveyed to the reader.

April 2012

1

THE ENGLISH LEGAL SYSTEM

Learning Objectives

At the end of this chapter, the reader will:

1   Acknowledge the distinction between the criminal law and the civil law.

2   Be aware of the court system.

3   Have an understanding of the common law and the doctrine of judicial precedent.

4   Be able to locate case law and legislation, and understand the system of citation.

1 INTRODUCTION

At his best, man is the noblest of all animals; separated from law and justice he is the worst. Aristotle, *Politics (Book One: Part II)*

There are many pleasant fictions of the law in constant operation, but there is not one so pleasant or practically humorous as that which supposes every man to be of equal value in its impartial eye, and the benefits of all laws to be equally attainable by all men, without the smallest reference to the furniture of their pockets. (Charles Dickens, *Nicholas Nickleby*)

These two quotations represent the polarity of opinions concerning the law. The first argues that mankind would quickly degenerate into anarchy without its restraining influences; the second contends that 'justice' within the system is dependent upon one's wealth and status. There are enough examples and anecdotes to support either of these two positions, but most would agree that some form of legal system is necessary if society is to thrive. This is true of the most primitive of cultures, but the English legal system has developed over many centuries, and, in the process, has become increasingly sophisticated and complex. My purpose, therefore, in this chapter is not to give a detailed outline of this system, but to illustrate a couple of key distinctions in the hope that the central concepts will be clarified.

We should begin by asking why a book such as this should feel the need to open with a chapter on the English legal system. The answer, quite simply, is that what follows will become more intelligible if there is an understanding of the legislative and court process. We should also note that what we are considering here is an *English* legal system, rather than a United Kingdom legal system. Scotland and Northern Ireland have always had separate jurisdictions, although they remain bound by decisions of the highest court in the land (the Supreme Court). Moreover, they remain under the sovereignty of Parliament in London, although the Scotland Act 1998 and the Northern Ireland Act 1998 granted them powers to create primary legislation. Wales also has some powers of this nature (since 2007), but its legal system is fundamentally the same as that of England.

One final point to make before discussing the key distinctions is that, self-evidently, healthcare professionals are bound by the same laws as any other citizen in the land. In addition, however, they are subject to professional Codes (see Chapter 9), so that penalties can be imposed for offences that might not be considered by the courts (Montgomery, 2003). One thinks, for example, of healthcare professionals who refuse to care for patients with HIV or who arrive for duty in an intoxicated state. Healthcare professionals are also subject to what is known as quasi-law: most commonly, this refers to health service circulars emanating from the Department of Health and elsewhere, which have no legal force, but which are expected to be followed unless there are good reasons for not doing so. Certainly, they have strong persuasive authority in the courts, for they offer guidance upon what is expected of the reasonable practitioner.

None of this need detain us any further, however, for my hope is that it will become clearer in the following chapters. We must therefore move to discussion of the first of the key distinctions to be drawn within the English legal system.

2 THE CRIMINAL LAW AND THE CIVIL LAW

A DEFINITION

The criminal law serves to regulate behaviour that constitutes offences against the public. It is technically possible to initiate a private prosecution (Prosecution of Offences Act 1985, s6 [1]), but this usually requires the permission of the Attorney General or Director of Public Prosecutions, is very expensive, and is consequently very rare. Most prosecutions, therefore, are brought in the name of the State, and are written thus: *R v Danvers [1982]*. Here, 'R' is short for the Latin word *Regina*, meaning Queen (or *Rex* if there is a king on the throne at the time that the case is heard), and is referred to in court as the *Crown*. In this particular example, *Danvers* is the *defendant*, who has been brought to trial to face a criminal prosecution.

The civil law, by contrast, is that which governs the relationship between individuals, and may be written thus: *Donoghue v Stevenson [1932]*. In this example, *Donoghue* is bringing the action and is known as the *claimant* (formerly, the plaintiff). The action is brought against the second-named individual (*Stevenson*), who is known as the *defendant*.

B TYPES OF ACTION

Broadly speaking, the criminal law covers three main areas: offences against the State, against the person, and against property. Thus, offences against the State would include treason and espionage, and are covered by such statutes as the Official Secrets Act 1989 and the Treason Acts of 1351 and 1848. Offences against the Person include murder, grievous and actual bodily harm and sexual assault. There are a range of legislative measures to deal with such matters (e.g. Offences against the Person Act 1861; Sexual Offences Act 2003), but some offences are covered by the common law (of which more later). Offences against property include criminal damage, theft and fraud, and are covered by such laws as the Theft Act 1968. Admittedly, this is a very simplified account of the types of action available in the criminal courts, and some offences (terrorism, for example) could be said to fit into all three of these categories. Nevertheless, it remains helpful in the majority of cases to demarcate offences into one of these three broad headings.

The civil law, however, is less obliging, for the varieties of action are much more extensive. Thus, the list includes Contract law, Property law, Family law, and Company law. This list is by no means exhaustive, but there is one type of action that will recur frequently as this book progresses: that of Tort, meaning civil wrong (or *delict*, as it is known in Scots law). Within Tort, there are a number of sub-categories of action, including Defamation (i.e. libel or slander), Nuisance, Trespass (to land, person, or goods), and False Imprisonment. Again, this list is not exhaustive, but the most important Tort for our purposes is that of Negligence.

C SANCTIONS

The range of sanctions available to the criminal courts include fines (which are paid to the court, not the victim), imprisonment and community service orders. The last of these was introduced by the Criminal Justice Act 1972, and extended by virtue of the Criminal Justice Acts of 1991 and 2003; and their existence is a recognition that imprisonment neither deters crime effectively nor reduces the incidence of crime (Home Office, 1990). Similar thinking would have been behind the introduction of Anti-Social Behaviour Orders (ASBOs), which first appeared in the Crime and Disorder Act 1998, and whose powers were extended by the Anti-Social Behaviour Act 2003. The terms of the ASBO are open to the discretion of the courts, and can include curfews (where the offender is required to remain in a specified place for a prescribed period of time within any 24-hour period), and exclusion orders (where the offender is barred from entering specified areas).

Until 1965, capital punishment (i.e. execution) would have been available as a penalty for murder, as it still is in some countries. Similarly, corporal punishment remains a sanction in some jurisdictions: in Saudi Arabia, for example, conviction of theft may result in the amputation of a hand. The Isle of Man persisted with the birching of offenders (i.e. being beaten with birch rods) until the case of *Tyrer v United Kingdom [1978]* established that the practice constituted inhuman and degrading treatment, and was thereby in contravention of Article 3 of the European Convention on Human Rights 1950.

The Criminal Justice Act 2003 (s142) outlines the key aims of sentencing, which can be summarised thus:

Box 1.1   The aims of sentencing

1 To punish offenders.
2 To compensate the victim(s), which may be an individual or the State.
3 To rehabilitate offenders.
4 To protect the public.
5 To reduce crime.

Whether any of these aims of sentencing are effective or not is a matter of considerable debate, however, and it might be argued that some are in direct conflict with each other. For example, imprisonment of an offender is extremely expensive, imposing a drain upon the resources of the State and the taxpayer; thus, the second of these aims is sacrificed for the sake of the first. Moreover, it is difficult to accept that sentencing is designed to rehabilitate offenders when the incidence of re-offending is so high. Finally, the ultimate deterrent (the death penalty) had no appreciable impact upon the murder rate in the United Kingdom while it was in place: although the rate increased after abolition, this was smaller than for other violent offences, none of which would have been affected by abolition (Easton and Piper, 2005). The truth, of course, is that the causes of crime are numerous and frequently complex (social deprivation, drug and alcohol abuse, psychological disturbances, etc.), and sentencing alone cannot address these. Thus, the argument that crime will be reduced if there are longer prison sentences, increased fines and even the re-introduction of the death penalty is fundamentally flawed.

Having expanded at some length on the sanctions available to the criminal courts, we should now turn to those available in the civil courts, and the fundamental remedy, of course, is that of compensation (or damages) for the aggrieved party. There are, however, occasions when the claimant is not seeking compensation, but rather hopes for what is known as an equitable remedy. Examples of these equitable remedies include *specific performance*, which is essentially an order of the court to someone in breach of contract to fulfil his/her obligations under that contract. Technically, for example, it would be possible for a court to order that a football manager who wished to change clubs mid-contract must remain where he is until the contract expires. In such a situation, however, the court would be unable to ensure that the manager did his best for the club at which he was forced to stay. Therefore, this remedy is usually unenforceable by the courts, and is consequently rarely awarded.

A more common equitable remedy is the use of *injunctions*, which are orders of the court to refrain from activity that is damaging to another. Thus, an injunction can be served upon an abusive husband to prevent him from coming into contact with his wife. In recent years, a number of celebrities have served injunctions on those with whom they have had extra-marital affairs, preventing the latter from selling their stories to the press. If an injunction is breached, this would be a contempt of court, which is a criminal offence and which may be punishable by means of imprisonment.

The final remedy is *rescission*, which is a term used in contract law. Essentially, it means that the parties to a contract are returned to the position they were in before the contract ever existed. Thus, if I were to buy a painting by John Constable and I later discovered that it was a forgery, I would simply return the painting and I would get my money back. Such a remedy, of course, would only be available if the painting remained in its original condition, and if there had not been an unreasonable delay in seeking the remedy (Turner, 2005).

D THE COURT SYSTEM

The criminal court system can be summarised in the following diagram:

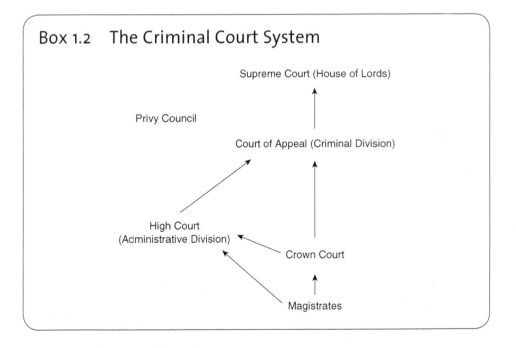

Box 1.2   The Criminal Court System

Supreme Court (House of Lords)

Privy Council

Court of Appeal (Criminal Division)

High Court
(Administrative Division)

Crown Court

Magistrates

From this, we can see that the lowest rung of the ladder is that of the *magistrates*. It is often argued (with a good deal of justice) that the English legal system is very expensive, but it is worth noting that the vast majority of work is done by these people, all of whom are unpaid. Every criminal case brought to court, no matter how serious, must come before the magistrates in the first instance. The vast majority of these cases (98 per cent) can be dealt with directly by the magistrates themselves and are known as *summary offences* (Boylan-Kemp, 2011). Examples of such offences include common assault, motoring offences, and low-level theft, etc. Thus, on the assumption that guilt has been established, they are empowered to impose a fine of up to £5,000, and/ or the full range of community service orders, and/or imprisonment for up to 6 months for a single offence (or 12 months for more than one offence). The Criminal Justice Act 2003 has provisions to enable magistrates to sentence an offender to 12 months in prison for a single offence (s154), but this has not come into force to date.

If the accused is charged with an offence which carries a penalty greater than these restrictions allow, this is known as an *indictable offence* and must be referred to the *Crown Court*. It is not the function of the magistrates to establish guilt in such cases, but simply to confirm that there is a case to answer.

There are some offences that fall midway between these two, and are known as hybrid or either-way offences. They include theft and assault causing actual bodily harm, and the venue for the trial is largely down to the accused. If, for example, s/he pleads guilty, the offence is dealt with by the magistrates and they will impose what they consider to be an appropriate sentence. If the plea is not guilty (or if the magistrates feel that the offence merits a punishment greater than they are permitted to enforce), the case is committed to the Crown Court. The advantage for the accused of being tried in the magistrates' court is that it is dealt with quickly and the sentence is likely to be less severe than that of the Crown Court. The advantage of being tried in the Crown Court, however, is that there is a higher chance of acquittal.

The reason why there is a higher chance of acquittal is that cases in the Crown Court are heard by juries. There have been some cases where trial by judge alone has been allowed (for example, the 'Diplock courts' in Northern Ireland, where conviction of terrorists was hampered because of the fear of reprisals for jurors); but, generally speaking, it has been a long-held fundamental principle of English law that every citizen has the right to be judged by his peers. The difficulties with this system, however, are that jurors are unlikely to have a good knowledge of the law, they may be unable to grasp many of the legal complexities of individual cases, and they may easily be swayed by factors other than the evidence. There are sufficient examples of perverse verdicts (i.e. where the decision of the jury does not accord with either the evidence or the law) to suggest that trial by jury is a flawed system, but alternatives that have been suggested seem equally likely to produce injustice (Boylan-Kemp, 2011).

The Magistrates' Courts Act 1980 (s111) entitles both the prosecution and defence to appeal decisions of the magistrates and Crown Court to the Administrative Division of the *High Court*. Such appeals, however, require permission from the court, and are likely to be denied if they are perceived as being 'frivolous' (i.e. a waste of time and effort). The higher appeal courts include the *Court of Appeal* (criminal division), which is headed by the Lord Chief Justice. Cases are heard before three senior judges, who are known as Lord (or Lady) Chief Justices of Appeal.

The final appeal court is the *Supreme Court*, which was created by the Constitutional Reform Act 2005, and which became established in 2009. Prior to this, the highest court in the land had been known as the House of Lords, but the change was made for one primary reason: namely, that judges sitting in this court would no longer be able to vote upon legislation in the upper chamber of Parliament. To have a role in the legislative process and then to sit in judgement upon cases was seen to represent a conflict of interest, and these powers should therefore be separated (Elliott and Quinn, 2011). For similar reasons, the Lord Chancellor (who was formerly the most senior judge in the land) is no longer able to sit as a member of the judiciary, and his role as head of the Ministry of Justice is a political role, rather than a judicial one. As Boylan-Kemp (2011) notes, the role has now become one in which the holder no longer needs a legal qualification.

The system in Scotland is somewhat similar, but the courts have different nomenclature. Thus, the *District Courts* are the lowest criminal courts and are presided over by a magistrate. Above this, the *Sheriff Courts* hear summary offences and all but the most serious indictable offences. The latter are heard before the *High Court of Judiciary*, which is the highest Scottish criminal court and which also serves as an appeal court. A number of Commonwealth countries (including Crown dependencies, such as the Channel Islands) are able to appeal criminal cases to the *Privy Council*, whose members are justices of the Supreme Court. Whereas this was once the final court of appeal for *all* Commonwealth countries, most have now abolished this right and the relevance of the Privy Council has correspondingly declined.

By contrast, the civil court system can be summarised thus:

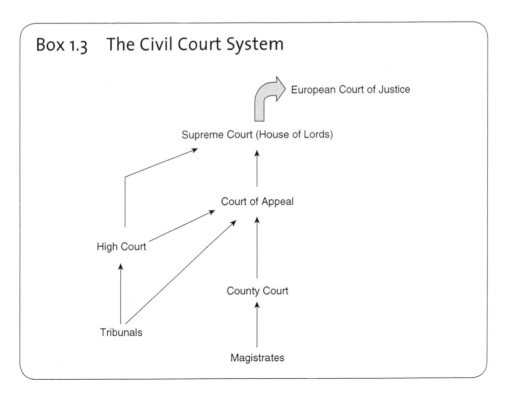

Box 1.3   The Civil Court System

This system is unquestionably more complex than its criminal counterpart, and is largely reflective of the wider variety of possible actions. *Magistrates* have some role to play here, especially in relation to family law matters and the licensing of premises to sell alcohol. In addition, specialised *tribunals* (such as employment, immigration and asylum, and social security tribunals) reduce much of the work-load of the courts by resolving disputes in a fairly quick, efficient and inexpensive manner. Professional Conduct Committees of the various healthcare disciplines (see Chapter 9) can also be seen to fit within this category. Their work, however, is overseen by the High Court, and appeals against their decisions can be made to the Court of Appeal.

Much of the work of the civil justice system, though, is performed by the *County Courts*. In theory, there are no limits to the value of claims being pursued that can be heard in the County Court, except for those pertaining to personal injury dam-ages (where the upper limit is £50,000). In practice, however, the more complicated cases, and those where higher sums of money are involved, tend to be referred to the *High Court*.

The High Court has three main divisions – Queen's Bench, Family and Chancery – each of which has specialist functions. Of these, the Family Division is likely to hear the majority of healthcare legal cases; and, sitting within this Division lies the *Court of Protection*, whose central remit is to protect the interests of the incapacitated adult (see Chapter 4). Appeals against decisions of both the County Court and the High Court are generally heard in the Court of Appeal (civil division), although the High Court can occasionally leap-frog directly to the *Supreme Court*.

At one time, of course, the Supreme Court (or House of Lords, as it was previ-ously known) was the highest court in the land, from which there was no right of appeal. Membership of the European Union, however, entails that there is now a higher court even than this: the *European Court of Justice*. An illustration of its power can be seen in the following case:

Box 1.4   *Marshall v Southampton and South West Hampshire Area Health Authority [1994]*

Mrs Marshall was a dietician, working in a hospital, and who reached the age of 60. Her employers allowed her to work another two years, but then compelled her to retire. She argued that it was very unfair that she should be forced to retire at 60 when her male colleagues had the privilege of being able to carry on working until they were 65. Her attempts to resolve this claim in the courts were destined for frustration as she was bounced from one court to another over a period of 16 years. Eventually, however, the case reached the European Court of Justice, which reached a verdict in her favour. They stated that to discriminate in the workplace on the basis of gender was contrary to principles of European law and was therefore illegal.

Mrs Marshall had evidently long since retired before this verdict was reached, and her only tangible benefit was the compensation that she was awarded. It established an important principle, though, which has subsequently affected the employment conditions of all women. Whether or not she is the most popular member of her gender remains in doubt, but the case identifies one other principle. Any decision made by the High Court, Court of Appeal or the Supreme Court can be overturned in an instant by the European Court of Justice; and this represents a fundamental loss of sovereignty, because it means that control has been largely handed over to a court that consists almost entirely of foreigners (only one of its members is British). The debate about whether or not this is a price worth paying for continued membership of the European Union is not one that we need to concern ourselves with here. Suffice it to say that the courts (when determining cases) and Parliament (when enacting legislation) must be ever-mindful of the power of the European Court.

In Scotland, the civil court system begins with the Sheriff Courts, which are roughly equivalent to County Courts. The next rung up the ladder is the Court of Session: the Inner House hears appeals, whereas the Outer House hears new cases. Above this is the Supreme Court, which is the same court serving England and Wales.

E THE BURDEN OF PROOF

In the criminal legal system, the burden of proof rests with the prosecution, and guilt must be proven *beyond all reasonable doubt*. The old adage that the defendant is innocent until proven guilty remains true, and any change to this position would represent a considerable shift away from the central principles of justice. In the civil legal system, the burden of proof rests with the claimant (i.e. the person bringing the action), but the case need only be proven on the *balance of probabilities*. If one imagines a set of scales being tipped slightly to one side, this will be the side that wins the case. If the scales are evenly balanced, the claimant will lose. As we explore some of the negligence cases later, it may seem that the burden of proof is significantly more onerous than this, but this remains the stated distinction between the two court systems.

At times, the distinction can produce bizarre results, and perhaps the most well-known of these was the American case of O.J. Simpson (*People of the State of California v Orenthal James Simpson [1995]*). He was first tried in the American equivalent of the Crown Court on a charge of the murder of his wife and her lover. Guilt could not be proven beyond all reasonable doubt, and he was acquitted. His wife's family subsequently took out a civil action in the American equivalent of the High Court (the action being trespass against the person), and there his guilt was established on the balance of probabilities. Thus, he was innocent in one court and guilty in another, all because of a difference in the burden of proof.

In theory, the victim of a criminal assault or damage would have to take out a civil action if compensation was required. However, the establishment of guilt in a criminal court would render it inevitable that the offender would be found guilty in a civil court (because the former requires a higher burden of proof); and this would create an unnecessary burden on both the courts and the protagonists. Thus, the

Powers of Criminal Courts (Sentencing) Act 2000 empowers the criminal courts to award appropriate compensation to the victim (s130). This includes the magistrates, although the maximum that they can award is limited to £5,000.

Box 1.5   A summary of the distinction between the criminal law and the civil law

	Criminal Law	Civil Law
Definition	That which regulates behaviour as offences against the public.	The law which governs the relationship between individuals.

Types of action	i Offences against the State.
	ii Offences against the Person.
	iii Offences against Property.
		i Contract.
		ii Property.
		iii Family.
		iv Company.
		v Torts:
		   a Negligence
		   b Defamation
		   c Nuisance
		   d Trespass (to land, person. Goods)
		   e False imprisonment.

Sanctions	i Fines. ii Imprisonment. iii Community Service orders.	i Damages (i.e. compensation). ii Specific performance. iii Injunctions. iv Rescission.
Burden of proof	Beyond all reasonable doubt.	On the balance of probabilities.

3 THE COMMON LAW AND LEGISLATION

The second key distinction to be drawn within the English legal system is that between the common law and legislation.

A DEFINITION

By legislation we mean the law which is made in Parliament in the form of statutes (e.g. Mental Health Act 1983). Not all cases coming before the courts are covered by legislative provisions though, and, in such cases, the judge has to make a decision. In doing so, s/he creates a principle of law, which remains binding on all citizens within the realm until or unless Parliament enacts legislation to overturn it. The reality is a little more complicated than this, as we shall see later; but the essential point to take from this is that the *common law* is that law which has been made by judges.

Originally, the common law had a different definition. Prior to the Norman Conquest of 1066, different parts of England had different systems of law, but the Normans sent out itinerant justices, who eventually ensured that a standardised system of law existed across the land (Elliott and Quinn, 2011). This process took almost 200 years, but the end result was a law that was common to all the people of England.

The influence of Parliament on the development of law has increased immeasurably in recent years, to a point that has been described as 'legislative hyperactivity' (Bingham, 2011: 40). The influence of judges has correspondingly decreased, but we owe much of the law of this land to judicial decision-making. Occasionally, common law principles developed over time are collated and codified into statutes, such as the Mental Capacity Act 2005 (see Chapter 4). Some areas, however, are too controversial to be dealt with by means of legislation, for they polarise opinion and can quickly lose a Government votes at the next election. One thinks, for example, of the withdrawal of nutrition and hydration from people in a permanent vegetative state, the sterilisation of women with learning disabilities, and the separation of conjoined twins. There never has been any statute that addresses these issues, and there probably never will be. All of the law that we have on them, therefore, is that which has been made by judges.

So, how do judges do this? The traditional position, and one that existed for almost two centuries largely unchallenged, was that the judge's role was simply to *apply* the law as it existed (Blackstone, 1769). There is enough evidence to suggest that this is not entirely true, and realist theorists hold that the law 'is only a matter of what the judge had for breakfast' (Dworkin, 1986: 36). Something of this, perhaps, could be seen in the infamous *Oz* trial:

Box 1.6 *R v Anderson and others [1971]*

The editors of a magazine (*Oz*) were charged with conspiracy to corrupt public morals and publishing an obscene article contrary to s2 of the Obscene Publications Act 1959. Their eventual conviction by a jury and draconian prison sentences owed much to the judge, who appears to have formed an opinion long before the first words were spoken in evidence. His direction to the jury was described as 'entirely wrong' by the Court of Appeal, rendering the verdict unsafe.

The judge's stance on this issue may have been the product of his upbringing: by their nature, the judiciary tend to be drawn from a very narrow section of society (public school-educated, Oxbridge graduates). It would not be unreasonable to suggest that this influences their political views, and it certainly distances them from many of those who come before them (Kairys, 1998). This would do a disservice to the majority of them, though, who acknowledge the importance of their role in seeing that justice is done.

Some (such as the positive theorists) believe that judges should focus on what is morally right in each circumstance, rather than allow themselves to be encumbered by unjust legal principles (Doherty, 2006). For Dworkin (1986), though, it is more important that people know what the law is, and they expect judges to treat everybody equally. This suggests that the judiciary should adopt a cautious approach when making new law, rather than take a cavalier and adventurous approach, which might destabilise the law and produce confusion. Not all judges have accepted this position in the past, but the constraining principle has always been that of *judicial precedent*.

B JUDICIAL PRECEDENT

As mentioned earlier, if a case comes before the court and there is no legislation to guide the judge, s/he must make a decision, which then becomes a statement of law. This statement is binding on all lower courts, following the principle of *'stare decisis'* (i.e. let the decision stand), and is unique to English law. It is a system that was taken to all countries within the British Empire, and those countries have retained the concept of judicial precedent. This contrasts with the civil law system in Europe, which was based upon Roman law, and which gives greater weight to legislation as the source of law.

The statement of law contained within a case is known as the *ratio decidendi* (literally, the reason for the decision). It is not, however, printed in bold capitals within the judgment, and it can sometimes be difficult to locate. Nevertheless, it means that a decision taken by the Court of Appeal (civil decision) will be binding on that court and any other court below it. If, therefore, a similar case comes before one of these courts, it must be decided in exactly the same way. The decision would *not* be binding upon the Supreme Court, because this is a higher court, which could overturn the principle and establish a completely different one. Once established, though, this becomes binding on all lower courts. Similarly, decisions of the European Court of Justice have binding authority on all English courts.

Since a Practice Statement of 1966, the Supreme Court is able to escape the bonds of precedent, and can depart from previous decisions that it has made (although it is reluctant to do so, and this has only occurred very infrequently). Moreover, the criminal division of the Court of Appeal is given greater licence to depart from precedent, because the defendant's liberty is at issue. Some lawyers, most notably Lord Denning, have argued that the civil division of the Court of Appeal should also have greater freedom of decision-making. In *Davis v Johnson [1979]*, Lord Denning contended that an unjust principle could only be overturned in the Supreme Court (at the time, the House of Lords), and this was both expensive and time-consuming. The strength of this argument has not gone unnoticed (Boylan-Kemp, 2011), but it was rejected in the strongest terms by Lord Diplock when the case reached the House of Lords.

Why was this? A number of advantages have been cited for the use of judicial precedent, the most important being that it creates certainty and stability within the law. Thus, if a claimant goes to a solicitor with a problem, that solicitor will generally be able to tell him/her whether or not there is a good chance of success (based upon the decisions of earlier cases). If there is little or no chance of victory, the claimant would be best advised to drop the claim. If there is a good chance of success, the defendant would be best advised to settle the claim out of court (and thereby avoid expensive legal costs). Thus, the courts are not crowded out with similar cases, and only those that raise unique questions tend to be litigated. Lord Denning's plea, however well-meaning, would have created considerable instability to this position if it had been accepted.

Despite this, there are several disadvantages of judicial precedent. We have, for example, already noted that precedents can produce injustice: a number of these legal principles were established in cases of many years ago, and circumstances will have changed considerably over time. Moreover, the importance attached to judicial precedent in court means that lawyers will focus heavily on this, so that cases are longer, more complex, and certainly more expensive as each side seeks and cites cases that may strengthen their arguments. The court attempted to limit the number of citations used by lawyers in *R v Erskine [2009]*, but the image of barristers sitting behind tall piles of legal texts remains constant.

There are a number of things that the courts can do to reduce the likelihood of injustice. For example, a higher court can *reverse* the decision of a lower court. It can also *over-rule* a principle established in an earlier case: the decision in that case will remain, but a new precedent will be created. In addition, the court could argue that the precedent is *outdated* and is no longer applicable for modern times. Perhaps, though, the most commonly employed stratagem is that of *distinguishing* between cases. No two cases are exactly the same, and it may be possible to argue that the facts of the case where the precedent was established are significantly different from the case before the court. In such circumstances, the judge will be entitled to hold that the precedent has no applicability in the instant case. An example of this principle in action can be seen in the following:

Box 1.7   'Wrongful birth' cases

In *McFarlane v Tayside Health Board [2000]*, a couple had four children, and the husband underwent a vasectomy to prevent the arrival of any more. This operation was performed negligently, and the wife subsequently gave birth to a fifth child. She claimed the costs of bringing up this child, but her claim was rejected by the court. She was able to recover loss of earnings for the period of time that she was pregnant, and damages for the inconvenience of pregnancy and the pain of childbirth. However, the birth of a healthy child should be seen as a blessing, rather than a burden (per Lord Mustill), and it was therefore unreasonable to expect to be compensated for this. The logic of this

(Continued)

(Continued)

argument has come in for criticism (see Mason and Laurie, 2011), but it established the principle that the birth of a healthy child is not recoverable in terms of compensation, and this principle is binding on all lower courts.

In *Parkinson v St. James and Seacroft University Hospital NHS Trust [2001]*, however, a failed sterilisation resulted in the birth of a *disabled* child. Here, the mother was able to recover the costs associated with the special needs of rearing this child – the decision in *McFarlane* was distinguished because that case had only considered the birth of a *healthy* baby.

In *Rees v Darlington Memorial Hospital NHS Trust [2002]*, a woman gave birth to a healthy child after a negligently performed sterilisation, but she herself had a disability (a severe visual impairment). She was able to recover the costs of child rearing attributable to her disability (e.g. the hiring of a nanny), because *McFarlane* had only considered the position of *able-bodied parents*.

We can see, therefore, that judges have considerable discretionary powers to ensure that justice prevails. The more discretion they use, though, the more unstable the law becomes; and by far the most effective means of avoiding bad precedents is by means of legislation.

C LEGISLATION

As has already been mentioned, legislation is the law made by Parliament in the form of statutes. Because of the sovereignty of Parliament, it has the power to over-rule any principle of common law, even if that principle has existed for many centuries. However, the European Court of Justice has the power to over-rule Acts of Parliament if they are in conflict with the various European treaties, and this has occurred on several occasions (see Chapter 7, where the Mental Health Act 1983 was found to be incompatible with the European Convention on Human Rights and necessitated an amendment to the Mental Capacity Act 2005).

Despite its power, legislation is an extremely slow-moving process (Griffith and Tengnah, 2010), and judge-made law is generally more responsive to the changing circumstances of society. Ministers have a number of powers to update legislative provisions by a process known as secondary (or delegated) legislation. This enables them to respond fairly quickly to changing situations and needs of society without the necessity for the time-consuming process of enacting new legislation, although these powers are restrained and can be challenged in court (see Chapter 6).

Where the wording of an Act is clear and unequivocal, the judge has no choice but to follow it to the letter, even if the end result appears to be the perpetration of injustice. For example, many judges were criticised for imprisoning those who refused to pay the unpopular Community Charge during the Thatcher administration in the 1980s, but the law made it clear that this was the penalty for the offence and there were to be no exceptions. It is often the case, however, that legislation is very far from being clear: it may be poorly worded and obscure (Bingham, 2011), and those drafting the legislation cannot be expected to foresee every eventuality that presents itself before court (Boylan-Kemp, 2011). The Interpretation Act 1978 has gone some way to clarify the meaning and intention of Parliament, as have the Explanatory Notes that have accompanied Acts since 1999. But there will still be many occasions when judges are called upon to decipher legislation, and they do this by referring to one of the following rules of statutory interpretation:

i) The Literal rule: this rule states that the judge will interpret the words of the Act exactly as they are written, even if this produces an injustice. There are many examples of this rule in operation, but one of the most oft-cited is that of Berriman's case:

Box 1.7 *London and North Eastern Railway Company v Berriman [1946]*

The railway company was obliged by law to provide a lookout whenever one of its employees was repairing or relaying the line. Berriman's job was to top up the oil boxes which lubricated the line, but no lookout was provided and a train killed him. His widow sued for damages, but lost the case: Berriman was neither repairing nor relaying the line, but simply *maintaining* it.

This judgment may seem somewhat harsh, and it is the kind of thing people have in mind when they argue that 'the law is an ass' (a phrase attributed to Charles Dickens in *Oliver Twist*, but which is actually much earlier than this). Mindful of the injustice that the literal rule can produce, and of its propensity to weaken public confidence in the law, some judges will resort to the second of the rules of statutory interpretation.

ii) The Mischief rule: this rule asks a simple question – 'what mischief was the law designed to correct?' – and is seen at work in the following case:

Box 1.8 *Smith v Hughes [1960]*

The Street Offences Act 1959 stated that it was illegal to solicit 'in a street or public place'. A prostitute was sitting inside her own house, and invited men to procure her services as they passed by her window. A literal interpretation of this case would have resulted in an acquittal, because she was neither soliciting in a street nor a public place. However, the court held that the Act was designed to correct a specific mischief – namely, that pedestrians should be able to walk along the street without being pestered by prostitutes. The defendant was duly convicted.

The danger with application of the mischief rule, of course, is that it calls upon judges to second-guess the intentions of Parliament, and they may be mistaken. Its use, therefore, is limited, although judges may refer to a hybrid version of the first two rules.

iii) The Golden rule: This rule states that judges will interpret the words of an Act as literally as possible until they produce an injustice. Perhaps the case that is most commonly cited as an illustration of this principle is the following:

Box 1.9   R v Allen [1872]

The Offences against the Person Act 1861 (s57) states that 'whosoever being married shall marry again' is guilty of bigamy. Allen argued that he could not 'marry again', because such a marriage was necessarily invalid while he remained married to his first wife: in other words, it should be impossible to commit the crime of bigamy! The court applied the golden rule, and held that the phrase 'marry again' implied 'going through a ceremony of marriage'.

It should be clear that the result of a case can depend upon the rule that the judge chooses to employ. Moreover, where more than one judge is involved in a case, there may be huge divergences of opinion. A good example of this in a case pertaining to healthcare is provided by the following:

Box 1.10   Royal College of Nursing v Department of Health and Social Security [1981]

The Abortion Act 1967 (s1) permits the termination of pregnancy when it is carried out 'by a registered medical practitioner'. Since this legislation was enacted, however, the technique of early-term abortions has been refined, and now simply requires the woman to take an oral drug (mifepristone), followed by a vaginal pessary two days later. This technique is usually overseen and managed by a nurse, without the presence of a doctor; and the RCN sought clarification that its members were not breaking the law. In the House of Lords, two Law Lords applied the literal rule: in their view, the Act specifically states that a doctor must be in attendance when a woman is undergoing a termination of pregnancy. By contrast, three Law Lords (and hence the majority) applied the mischief rule: the Act was designed to prevent women from seeking the services of back-street abortionists, because this was unhygienic and unsafe. No such problems arose when the procedure was carried out by a qualified nurse within the clinical environment.

The logic of the majority is difficult to resist, but the minority view here identifies a key point. By interpreting the will of Parliament in this way, the judges have essentially created new law and established a precedent that is binding upon all lower courts. This is not really their job, for it should be left to the elected representatives of the people. Thus, the safer (and more democratic) stance to take would be for the judges to say to Parliament: '*Your* law has created this injustice, and it is up to you to correct it'. In practice, however, we have already seen that amendments to legislation are slow and dependent upon the political will of the Government of the day (Elliott and Quinn, 2011). Mindful of this, most judges will endeavour to effect a delicate balancing act, even though this exposes them to criticism from all quarters.

4 FINDING CASE LAW AND LEGISLATION

Before leaving this chapter on the English legal system, it is perhaps worth giving a brief explanation of the methods by which cases are cited. At first glance, the full citation of a case appears very confusing, but it identifies the precise location of where the judgment can be found. Thus, let us take as an example a key case in healthcare law, and which is discussed in Chapter 3:

Bolam v Friern HMC [1957] 2 All ER 118

Here, we can immediately see that *Bolam* is the claimant, because he is the first-named; and that *Friern HMC* are the defendants to this action. If we were to look for this case in a library, we would need to find the *All England Law Reports* (All ER). In a law library, there will be several shelves devoted to this publication, and we would then need to look for the *1957* editions. There may be several volumes for each year, depending upon the number of cases reported; and in this instance, we must look for *Volume 2*. Having done this, we now need to turn to *Page 118* of this volume, and we will find the speech of the judge who adjudicated this case.

The All England Law Reports are but one example of legal publications of cases, and the following list gives the major ones, along with their appropriate abbreviations:

Box 1.11   Citations

1	AC	Appeal Cases
2	All ER	All England Law Reports
3	BMLR	Butterworth's Medical Law Reports
4	EHRR	European Human Rights Reports

(Continued)

(Continued)

5	FCR	Family Court Reporter
6	FLR	Family Law Reports
7	Lloyd's Rep. Med.	Lloyd's Law Reports: medical
8	Med LR	Medical Law Review
9	QB	Queen's Bench Reports
10	SJ	Solicitors' Journal
11	WLR	Weekly Law Reports

This list is by no means exhaustive, and does not include citations of cases from America, Canada, Australia or New Zealand. Nevertheless, it features the main ones that will be found in this book. In addition, some cases are reported by electronic means, and these are given what is known as a neutral citation. Thus, in *Campbell v Mirror Group Newspapers Ltd.* *[2004]* UKHL 22, the case was the *22nd* to be heard in the House of Lords during 2004. Other neutral citations are as follows:

Box 1.12   Neutral citations

1	EWHC	England and Wales High Court
2	EWCA	England and Wales Court of Appeal
3	UKHL	United Kingdom House of Lords
4	UKPC	United Kingdom Privy Council
5	UKSC	United Kingdom Supreme Court

Moreover, any abbreviations not listed here can be found on the following very useful websites: www.acronymfinder.com/ and www.library.qmul.ac.uk/subject/law/abbreviations.

Not all cases will follow the same pattern as *Bolam*, and the following is an illustration of another legal device:

Re F [1990] 2 AC 1

If this were an American case, it would probably be cited as 'In the matter of F', which is more long-winded, but which fully encapsulates the meaning of 'Re'. An initial has been used because anonymity of the subject of the court case is required. This is most commonly because the individual is particularly vulnerable or the material is of a highly sensitive nature. In this case, *F* was a woman with severe learning disabilities, and the court was being asked whether it would be lawful to sterilise her (see Chapter 4).

In Chapter 6, we will come across cases of judicial review, an example of which is cited thus:

R v NW Lancashire Health Authority, ex parte A, D and G [2000] 2 FCR 525

We have already noted that 'R' here means 'The Crown', and 'v' is always expressed as 'and' or 'against'. In this particular case, three protagonists (A, D and G) claimed that their local health authority was failing to provide a service to which they felt entitled (gender reassignment surgery), and asked the court to declare that this omission was illegal. Judicial review cases may also be cited thus: *R (on the application of Burke) v General Medical Council [2004]* EWHC 1879.

On the assumption that not everybody has access to a law library, it is possible to view cases online. Students at universities which run law courses will undoubtedly have access to databases such as Lexis Nexis and Westlaw UK. Although it is possible to access these sites without being a university student, it would be extremely expensive to do so and is not to be recommended. However, there are a number of free resources, which can be located on the following websites:

Box 1.13   Web-based resources

Name	Website	Content
British and Irish Legal Information Institute	http://www.bailii.org/	Case law judgments and Acts of Parliament
House of Lords	http://www.publications. parliament.uk/pa/ld/ ldjudgmt.htm	An archive of House of Lords judgments
Supreme Court	http://supremecourt.gov.uk/ decided-cases/index.html	Judgments of the Supreme Court
Office of Public Sector Information	http://www.legislation.gov. uk/ukpga	Acts of Parliament

---

Although these websites contain a lot of useful information, those reporting case law (i.e. the first three) give the neutral citations for the cases. This means that a number of cases will not be present on the sites, and the student would need to look elsewhere. A further advantage of reading material directly from the texts or from Lexis Nexis / Westlaw UK is that the latter frequently contain a shortened version of the case at the beginning. This is known as the headnote and is a summary of the facts of the case, the key legal arguments, the decision, and the reason(s) for that decision. Perhaps this is best illustrated by using an example:

Box 1.14   A worked example

[1988] Q.B. 481
[COURT OF APPEAL]
GOLD v. HARINGEY HEALTH AUTHORITY
1987 March 10, 11, 12; April 14

Watkins, Stephen Brown and Lloyd L.JJ.

Medical Practitioner - Negligence - Duty to inform - Sterilisation operation - Failure to give warning of possibility of fertility being restored - Subsequent pregnancy - Claim in negligence for non-disclosure of risk - Body of medical opinion against giving warning as to risk of pregnancy - Whether accepted professional standard test applicable to non-therapeutic advice

During the course of her third pregnancy in 1979, the plaintiff, after indicating that she did not wish to have any more children, was advised to undergo a sterilisation operation at the defendants' hospital after the birth of her child. The operation was duly carried out but the plaintiff later became pregnant and gave birth to a fourth child. She brought an action for damages for negligence against the defendants alleging, inter alia, that she had not been warned of the failure rate of female sterilisation operations and that if she had been warned her husband would have undergone a vasectomy instead. Medical evidence was adduced at the trial that there was a substantial body of responsible doctors who would not have given any such warning in 1979. The judge however held that the test whether there existed a substantial body of medical opinion who would have acted as the defendants had done applied only to advice given in a therapeutic context and did not apply to advice given in a contraceptive context. Applying his own view as to what information should have been given, he found that the defendants had been negligent in not warning the plaintiff that the operation might not succeed.

On the defendants' appeal: -

Held, allowing the appeal, that for the purposes of ascertaining the test as to the duty of care owed by a doctor to a patient there was no distinction to be made between advice given in a therapeutic context and advice given in a non-therapeutic context; that, accordingly, the judge erred in holding that advice given in a contraceptive context was not to be judged by the contemporary standards of a responsible body of medical opinion; and that, on the evidence, there was a substantial body of responsible doctors who would not in 1979 have warned the plaintiff of the failure rate of female sterilisation operations (post, pp. 489F - 490C, 491B-D, 492C-E).

Bolam v. Friern Hospital Management Committee [1957] 1 W.L.R. 582 and Sidaway v. Board of Governors of the Bethlem Royal Hospital and the Maudsley Hospital [1985] A.C. 871, H.L.(E.) applied.

Decision of Schiemann J. reversed.

The first few lines of the headnote tell us that the case was heard in the Court of Appeal before three Lord Justices of Appeal (Watkins, Stephen Brown, and Lloyd) over the course of three days in March 1987. The decision was delivered on 14th April, but the case was not reported until the following year, appearing in the 1988 volume of the Queen's Bench reports on page 481. Immediately below the names of the judges, there are a few key words to illustrate certain facets of the case, and which facilitates cross-referencing between cases.

Following this, the essential facts are outlined, together with the main arguments of both the plaintiff (or claimant) and the defending health authority. Finally, the decision of the court is summarised in the paragraph beginning *Held*. We can see too that the precedents of two earlier cases (*Bolam v Friern Hospital Management Committee [1957]* and *Sidaway v Board of Governors of the Bethlem Royal Hospital and the Maudsley Hospital [1985]*) have been applied to this case; and, in the process, the decision of the High Court judge (Schiemann, J.) – who had distinguished *Gold* from these cases – has been reversed.

The strength of the legal reasoning behind this decision might be called into question, and it has to be seen in the context of its day. Therefore, whether or not the decision would be the same if the case were heard today is open to question (see Chapter 3). Nevertheless, this headnote offers a concise and accurate synopsis of the case and can be a valuable time-saver. For those who would like more detail than this, the full judgment has to be read, and this follows immediately after the headnote.

REFERENCES

TEXTS

Bingham, T. (2011) *The Rule of Law*. London: Penguin Books.

Blackstone, W. (1769) *Commentaries on the Law of England, Vol. 1*. London: Clarendon Press.

Boylan-Kemp, J. (2011) *English Legal System: the Fundamentals*, 2nd edn. London: Sweet & Maxwell.

Doherty, M. (2006) *Jurisprudence: the Philosophy of the Law*, 3rd edn. London: Old Bailey Press.

Dworkin, R. (1986) *Law's Empire*. Oxford: Hart Publishing.

Easton, S. and Piper, C. (2005) *Sentencing and Punishment: the Quest for Justice*. Oxford: Oxford University Press.

Elliott, C. and Quinn, F. (2011) *English Legal System*. London: Longman.

Griffith, R. and Tengnah, C. (2010) *Law and Professional Issues in Nursing*, 2nd edn. Exeter: Learning Matters Ltd.

Home Office (1990) *Crime, Justice and Protecting the Public: the Government's Proposals for Legislation*. Cm. 965. London: HMSO.

Kairys, D. (1998) *The Politics of Law: a Progressive Critique*. New York: Basic Books.

Mason, J.K. and Laurie, G.T. (2011) *Mason and McCall Smith's Law and Medical Ethics*, 8th edn. Oxford: Oxford University Press.
Montgomery, J. (2003) *Health Care Law*, 2nd edn. Oxford: Oxford University Press.
Turner, C. (2005) *Contract Law*, 2nd edn. London: Hodder Arnold.

CASES

Bolam v Friern Hospital Management Committee [1957] 2 All ER 118.
Campbell v Mirror Group Newspapers Ltd. [2004] UKHL 22.
Davis v Johnson [1979] AC 264.
Donoghue v Stevenson [1932] AC 562.
F, Re [1990] 2 AC 1.
Gold v Haringey Health Authority [1988] QB 481.
London and North Eastern Railway Company v Berriman [1946] 1 All ER 255.
Marshall v Southampton and South West Hampshire Area Health Authority [1994] 1 All ER 736.
McFarlane v Tayside Health Board [2000] 2 AC 59.
Parkinson v St. James and Seacroft University Hospital NHS Trust [2001] 3 All ER 97 (CA).
People of the State of California v Orenthal James Simpson [1995] Case No. BA 097 211.
Practice Statement [1966] 3 All ER 77.
R v Allen [1872] LR1CC 367, CCR.
R v Anderson and others [1971] 3 All ER 1152.
R v Danvers [1982] Crim LR 680.
R v Erskine [2009] EWCA Crim. 1425.
R v North West Lancashire Health Authority, ex parte A, D and G [2000] 2 FCR 525.
R (on the application of Burke) v General Medical Council [2004] EWHC 1879.
Rees v Darlington Memorial Hospital NHS Trust [2002] EWCA Civ. 88.
Royal College of Nursing v Department of Health and Social Security [1981] 1 All ER 545.
Sidaway v Board of Governors of the Bethlem Royal Hospital and the Maudsley Hospital [1985] AC 871 (HL).
Smith v Hughes [1960] 1 WLR 830.
Tyrer v United Kingdom [1978] 2 EHRR 1. Appl. No.: 5856/72.

LEGISLATION

Abortion Act 1967
Anti-Social Behaviour Act 2003
Constitutional Reform Act 2005
Crime and Disorder Act 1998
Criminal Justice Act 1972
Criminal Justice Act 1991
Criminal Justice Act 2003
European Convention on Human Rights 1950
Interpretation Act 1978
Magistrates' Courts Act 1980

Mental Capacity Act 2005
Mental Health Act 1983
Northern Ireland Act 1998
Obscene Publications Act 1959
Offences against the Person Act 1861
Official Secrets Act 1989
Powers of Criminal Courts (Sentencing) Act 2000
Prosecution of Offences Act 1985
Scotland Act 1998
Sexual Offences Act 2003
Street Offences Act 1959
Theft Act 1968
Treason Act 1351
Treason Act 1848

2

AN INTRODUCTION TO HEALTHCARE ETHICS

Learning Objectives

At the end of this chapter, the reader will:

1 Be aware of a structured framework for the analysis of ethical dilemmas.

2 Have a broad-based understanding of the main ethical theories and be able to apply them to healthcare situations.

3 Understand ethical principlism and acknowledge its relevance to healthcare.

1 INTRODUCTION

A simple definition of ethics is that it is the study of what is right and of how we should live our lives (Buka, 2008). Applied to healthcare, it represents an attempt 'to unravel the rights and wrongs of different areas of health care practice in the light of philosophical analysis' (Campbell et al., 2005: 2). This, of course, is no easy task, requiring 'a broadly informed, systematic and deeply experienced approach to thinking about the issues at stake and how best to resolve them' (Johnstone, 2004: 34). And yet, despite the mental effort required of ethical analysis, its importance to healthcare cannot be understated. As we explore the issues relevant to practice, we will find ethical dilemmas at every turn. For example, should artificial nutrition and hydration be withdrawn from people in a permanent vegetative state? Should women with learning disabilities be sterilised to prevent them from having children? How can we ensure that resources are allocated fairly and justly? Many of these issues have been played out in the courts, but the judgments have been informed by moral reasoning. In other words, it is the lawyers who can frame the strongest moral argument that will win the day. Philosophical analysis, however, is dynamic and evolving, meaning that a winning argument one day may be discredited at some time in the future.

This, therefore, is the appeal of healthcare ethics as well as its importance. As medical technology advances, new ethical dilemmas arise, which require analysis and judgement. Moreover, not only is it vibrant and ever-changing, but it represents for me the ultimate in freedom of speech. In other words, it is permissible to be as outrageous as possible when expressing an opinion, but the challenge for opponents is to defeat your position with logical argument (rather than resorting to violence). Hope (2004) cites the example of a debate between two men, in which one protagonist lost his temper and threw a glass of wine into the face of the other. The victim simply said: 'This, sir, is a digression: now, if you please, for the argument.' Perhaps this is a naïve view, and it is conceivable that freedom of speech never truly exists. Equally, though, the person who resorts to violence (verbal or physical) has run out of ideas and has subsequently conceded defeat to his/her debating partner.

We, by contrast, ought to be able to do better than this. Ethical analysis requires, as we have said, depth of thinking and a clear expression of the issues. It also requires humility, for one should be prepared to modify (and even radically alter) one's opinions if they are successfully challenged by a stronger argument. Humility, in turn, will help to avoid the trap of believing that one can ever develop true expertise in this area. As Seedhouse (2005) has said: 'no one can be an ethics expert if being an ethics expert means knowing for certain how to live right' (p. 120). Thus, we start with the premise that ethical solutions are largely illusory and unknown. Indeed, we may even be tempted to throw up our hands in despair and claim that moral beliefs 'are all just a matter of opinion'. This *moral relativism*, as it is known, has a certain appeal, but Pattinson (2009) exposes its inherent contradiction: we can only hold that morality is down to individual conscience if we also believe that tolerance itself is a matter of opinion.

The reality is that moral relativism offers no assistance to the healthcare practitioner, who generally has to make moral decisions on a daily basis. We need, therefore, a structured framework to help us analyse ethical dilemmas. More of this shortly, but before doing so, it might be useful to consider one such dilemma:

Box 2.1   The case of Liz Buttle

In 1997, Liz Buttle of Wales gave birth to a son after receiving fertility treatment. She was 60 years old at the time, but had told her doctors that she was 49 in order to be eligible. The ovum came from a donor and was fertilised with sperm from her husband.

Worldwide, there have been several similar cases. In 1996, Arceli Keh of California gave birth to a daughter when aged 63; Jeanine Salomone, a French retired teacher, gave birth at the age of 62 in 2001; Adriana Iliescu, a Romanian, gave birth to a daughter in 2005 at the age of 66; and Carmela Bousada had twins in 2006 a few days short of her 67th birthday. At the time of writing, the current record is 73 years old and goes to a woman in North India. There are at least two things that unite all of these cases, and which make this an ethical dilemma. First, all the women were post-menopausal and required the eggs of donors before becoming pregnant: it was therefore the advances of medical technology that made this situation possible at all. Second, all the women lied about their age to the fertility clinics. Jeanine Salomone even compounded the lie by telling the doctor that the sperm donor was her husband, when in fact he was actually her brother. Had they been honest, they would have been rejected before treatment could ever begin.

Our first and most natural response when faced with this dilemma is an *intuitive* one. In other words, we make no attempt to intellectualise our support for, or our objections to, Liz Buttle's actions, but instead make a simple recourse to our gut feeling. Moral philosophers, by and large, tend to have great respect for intuition, for it is believed that it comes from a deep-seated moral code that has served us well in the past. Their purpose, therefore, is to attempt to explain why we feel the way that we do, rather than to challenge those beliefs.

But intuition, by itself, is not a reliable moral guide (Hendrick, 2010). We all like to think we have made some sense of this world, especially as we grow older; and the framework of understanding we construct may become more and more rigid as the years go by. Thus, anything that falls outside of this framework is likely to destabilise it, and this will induce anxiety. Moreover, there are countless examples from history to denote that intuition can be horribly wrong at times. In Nazi Germany, for example, there was a widely held intuitive belief that Jews were a sub-species of the human race and that their extermination would solve most of the nation's problems. This is an obviously extreme example, but it serves as an illustration of the potential consequences of unchecked intuition.

The evidence suggests that the strongest intuitive response to Liz Buttle's actions has been that they were wrong. Not all agree, though, and we must therefore examine the conflicting arguments to determine which are the more cogent. The following toolkit for analysis of ethical dilemmas is an eclectic mix of the thoughts of numerous authors (Hendrick, 2010; Mason and Laurie, 2011; Markkula Center, 2009; Beemsterboer, 2010; etc.). These writers will undoubtedly acknowledge their debt to others, as I do to them. It is to be hoped, though, that the end-point of our deliberations will be a clearer understanding of the issues at stake, even if we remain unable to provide a definitive solution.

2 THE FRAMEWORK

A CLARIFY THE FACTS AND IDENTIFY THE MORAL PROBLEM

It is a statement of the obvious to declare that an informed decision cannot be made without a full appraisal of the facts (Beemsterboer, 2010), but it can sometimes be difficult to distinguish facts from opinions or values. There is also a danger of select-ing only those 'facts' which support one's original intuitive feeling. Nevertheless, we know that it is against State law in some countries to offer fertility treatment to post-menopausal women. Indeed, the French lady (Jeanine Salomone) had to go to the USA to receive in vitro fertilisation (IVF) because the law in France prohibited such therapy. It is not technically illegal in the United Kingdom, but the Human Fertilisation and Embryology Act 1990 stipulates that:

A woman shall not be provided with treatment services unless account has been taken of the welfare of any child who may be born as a result of the treatment... (section 13 [5]).

The clear implication from this is that treatment would almost certainly be denied to an older woman in this country, for there is an assumption that a child's best interests are not served by being born into this situation. The assumption is open to challenge, of course, and we shall examine the arguments shortly; but its existence, as we have already seen, forces women to lie in order to receive treatment. It has been estimated that nearly half of British fertility clinics are treating patients who have used false identities to secure the service (Mail Online, 2006), and this decep-tion will be perpetuated for as long as the current policy remains.

But is the policy correct? Some would argue that fertility treatment given to post-menopausal women is contrary to principles of *natural law*. In other words, modern medicine is creating a situation that could not exist if the rules of Nature were allowed to govern. A similar argument can be found in those who believe that such treatment is 'against God's will'. The natural life cycle, it is contended, has been pre-ordained by a higher authority, and advances in medical technology represent a challenge to this authority (and, by extension, are sacrilegious). One might argue, of course, that the charge could be levelled against *all* medicine (Smajdor, 2010); but fertility treatment for post-menopausal women is somewhat different from insulin injections for diabet-ics, for the former 'lacks any reference to disease or illness... [and] ... has very little in common with the traditional gamut of a physician's work' (Bittner and Eichinger, 2010: 744).

In answer to such claims, it is unclear about what is 'unnatural'; and, even if a therapy can be labelled as such, this does not automatically condemn it as being morally wrong (Hope, 2004). Moreover, we cannot be certain of whether we are usurping God's will or, in fact, carrying it out. Whether one believes in God or not does not detract from the fact that Mankind has been given the intelligence to create such technology. Above all else, arguments from natural law and God's will perspectives are heavily value-laden and based upon faith rather than empiri-cal data. Admittedly, they cannot be disproved, but nor for that matter can they be proven.

We might be on slightly more solid ground when assessing the physical risks of pregnancy to the older woman and the potential for birth defects of children born by virtue of this technology. Unfortunately the evidence is inconclusive and con-tradictory. Bittner and Eichinger (2010) cite studies which suggest that there is an increased risk of complications during pregnancy (e.g. hypertension, gestational diabetes, etc.), but Edwards (1993) claims that these risks are no greater in older women than they are in the younger age group. It is true that the oldest European woman to give birth (Carmela Bousada) died just over two years later, but there was no suggestion that this was directly related to the stresses of pregnancy and the traumas of childbirth. It is equally true that children of older parents run a higher risk of developing birth defects, but the technology enables defective embryos to be screened before implantation (Powell, 2004).

The facts, such as they are, have contributed to a broader understanding of the issues, but have not delivered a solution. Had they done so, we would have had to say that this is not an ethical dilemma, for it would simply be a case of right and wrong (Beemsterboer, 2010). We are left, though, with a moral question: 'Should post-menopausal women be able to access fertility treatment?' To help us answer this question, we need to move on to the next stage of the framework.

B HOW WILL ETHICAL THEORY HELP IN RESOLVING THIS ISSUE?

There are four main ethical theories that have developed through the ages, and each contains useful insights that might help us to answer our question. Each, however, also has weaknesses, and we need to be aware of these. A focus on these shortcomings has frequently left each theory 'irreparably wounded' (Beauchamp and Childress, 2001: 337), but this should not impel us to dismiss the central arguments out of hand. Moreover, despite their apparent differences, the theories often converge to produce a broad level of agreement about certain issues.

Utilitarianism   Utilitarianism (sometimes known as teleological theory or Consequentialism) owes its origins to the work of two British philosophers – Jeremy Bentham (1748–1832) and John Stuart Mill (1806–1873). Its fundamental principle is that an action is right 'if, and only if, it promotes the best consequences' (Hope et al., 2008: 22). Thus, when faced with a choice between two or more possible actions, we should choose the one that produces the best overall result (or 'the greatest happiness of the greatest number').

As the theory has become more sophisticated, varying types of Utilitarianism have been proposed. Thus, *hedonic Utilitarianism* seeks to maximise happiness and minimise pain; *preference Utilitarianism* seeks to obtain the quality of life that a person would wish for; and *ideal Utilitarianism* seeks to maximise the lives of others. In its most basic form, however, Utilitarian principles could potentially be used to permit apparently immoral actions. Beauchamp and Childress (2001), for instance, offer the example of a young healthy individual who is murdered in order to harvest his internal organs for the benefit of those on the transplant waiting list. There is no question that this action would benefit many, while sacrificing only one, but this is not a course of action that we would seriously contemplate.

Perhaps a more telling criticism is that it insists that majority interests should almost always over-ride the rights of minorities. When Mr Spock (of *Star Trek* fame) uttered his mantra of 'The needs of the many outweigh the needs of the few', he was giving expression to an idea that dominates the thinking of those responsible for resource allocation. If one were to choose between allocating funds for a heart transplant unit or cataract surgery, the latter has the potential to enhance the quality of life of many thousands more than the former. For those waiting on the transplant list, however, this decision marks the difference between life and death.

Campbell et al. (2005) argue that 'good' has to be measured in *qualitative* terms, as well as in *quantitative* terms. Thus, a treatment which prolongs life, but does so at the expense of intense pain and misery, cannot be considered to have utility in any meaningful sense. Moreover, an estimation of the likely consequences of any action is fraught with difficulty and cannot account for all eventualities. Bear in mind that the Utilitarian must consider the *long-term* consequences as well as the short-term, and this reduces the accuracy of prediction even further.

Notwithstanding these criticisms, Utilitarianism is based upon the idea that we should increase human happiness whenever possible, and this is clearly a worthy aim. Moreover, whether one accepts its central tenets or not, it is equally clear that one cannot approach a moral dilemma without giving some consideration to the likely consequences of one's decisions (Beauchamp and Childress, 2001). So, how would a Utilitarian approach the question of post-menopausal pregnancies?

There are several competing interests here: that of the post-menopausal woman, of society in general, and of any children that result from fertility treatment. To take the first of these, it seems evident that the happiness of the woman will be increased by such measures. Not all parents consider the birth of a child to be a blessing, but this woman certainly will, given the time, trouble and expense that she will have invested in order to become pregnant. We have already noted that the perceived risks to her health are inconclusive, although each case would need to be assessed on its own merits. Moreover, Bittner and Eichinger (2010) contend that, with successful anti-aging measures, it is possible for a 60-year-old woman to have the mind and body of a 40-year-old. The therapy also represents an egalitarian measure, for it enables women to have the same career ambitions as men. In other words, the barrier to career aspirations that is created by the biological window of fertility is removed.

It is arguments of this nature that would suggest to a Utilitarian that society will ultimately benefit from such treatment, for the woman's productivity in the workplace will be increased and the economy will correspondingly be stimulated. It is not entirely clear that the latter is an inevitable consequence, but it is difficult to see how society is 'harmed' by post-menopausal pregnancies in any tangible way. As Hope (2004) notes, the State is not funding this treatment, and the woman cannot therefore be considered a burden upon the taxpayer. In addition, it is not as though her treatment is preventing another couple from receiving therapy, for there is potentially an inexhaustible supply of gametes.

A slightly stronger argument might be found when considering the notion of the 'slippery slope'. The concept of a slippery slope is that, when one sets foot on it, it becomes impossible to get off, and one slides inexorably to the bottom. The idea has found favour with those opposed to euthanasia (see Chapter 10), where it is assumed that the legalisation of voluntary active euthanasia will inevitably lead to non-voluntary and even involuntary euthanasia. It could also be applied to post-menopausal fertility treatment, where societal acceptance would ultimately lead to a free-for-all. In other words, clinics offering this therapy will no longer concern themselves with a full assessment of the health risks to the mother or the social situation of resulting children, but will instead be solely motivated by economic concerns. Those who can pay for the treatment will receive it, and the caring ethos that was always intended to dominate the thinking of healthcare professionals will be lost forever. Some, of course, would argue that this is an overly pessimistic prediction of consequences and that it also fails on a number of analytical grounds (Smith, 2005a, 2005b). Moreover, Hope (2004) suggests that the slope could fairly easily be converted into a stairway: if clear guidelines were drawn up for the administration of this therapy, practitioners would know that there were certain lines that could not be crossed without fear of prosecution. Whether one accepts this argument or not may be a matter of personal choice, but it illustrates the difficulties for the Utilitarian of predicting consequences when empirical data is largely absent.

The interests of the child may hold the key to answering this question. Perhaps the main argument put forward in opposition to post-menopausal pregnancy is that there is an increased chance that the parents may die before the child reaches maturity. There are, of course, no guarantees of longevity for any of us, and the deaths of younger parents (in a road traffic accident, for example) would often mean that the child was subsequently cared for by grandparents. Would we have moral misgivings about this? Having said that, the deaths of parents while the child is still young is going to have a devastating impact, and the Utilitarian may see this as a consequence that should be avoided.

A balancing act needs to be achieved here. Experience suggests that older mothers are more nurturing, because their child is seen as a special gift (*St. Louis Times*, 1997). Moreover, it is likely that older parents will be more mature, wiser, wealthier, and have more time to spend with their children (Edwards, 1993). Adopting a Utilitarian perspective therefore requires us to weigh up the possibilities of early parental demise alongside the possibilities of a child being born into a loving and happy family.

There is one final thing that the Utilitarian would wish to address in our scenario, and this involves the telling of a lie to procure treatment services. If we accept that the birth of a healthy child to a loving mother is a good consequence, then a Utilitarian might argue that telling a lie was justified in these circumstances. It might also be possible to argue, though, that the long-term consequences may be more harmful, because it sends out a clear message that deceit is permissible, that it is rewarded, and that it should become the norm in all social interactions. The difference between these two positions is known as the distinction between Act Utilitarianism and Rule Utilitarianism, where the latter holds that certain rules should be followed even if the short-term consequences are adverse (because the long-term consequences are even worse). Beauchamp and Childress (2001) suggest that there may be a middle way between the two perspectives: i.e. that lying may be acceptable in *some*, but not all, situations. The difficulties of establishing a uniform approach to what is acceptable are obvious, but it is nevertheless true that an inflexible adherence to the truth can often produce more problems than it solves.

The little 'white lie', or at least the withholding of truth, also frequently demonstrates compassion and respect for others.

Application of Utilitarian theory does not appear, on balance, to rule out the possibility of post-menopausal pregnancy, but it is only one of several such theories, and we must now turn to the second of these.

Deontology   Rule Utilitarianism, as described above, was designed to avoid some of the worst excesses of pure Act Utilitarianism, but it can become difficult to distinguish this from Deontology, a moral theory developed by a German philosopher, Immanuel Kant (1724–1804). Its fundamental tenet can be expressed thus: 'I ought never to act except in such a way that I can also will that my maxim become a universal law'. In other words, if an action is morally right, it must be right in all circumstances, *regardless of* the consequences. Kant called this the 'categorical imperative', denoting at once that such actions were not up for debate. It has echoes of the Christian principle of 'Do unto others as you would have them do unto you', but it is essentially a restraining philosophy: it tells us what *not* to do (as opposed to Utilitarianism, which tells us what we *should* do (Beauchamp and Childress, 2001)). Thus, we should never treat people as a means to an end (unless they agree to be treated this way, as a fully informed and consenting research subject would), and we should never sacrifice individual interests for the benefit of others.

For some, Deontology is far too rigid and uncompromising to stand alone as a model for living our lives. Not only would one have to be a moral saint to continue as a pure Deontologist; it is equally clear that it is too impersonal a system for use with family and friends (Melia, 2004). Moreover, if two obligations conflict (e.g. honesty and confidentiality), the Deontologist is unable to effect a compromise solution, and seems to suggest that we should do both (Beauchamp and Childress, 2001). Seedhouse (2005) also argues that a consistency of approach – which is demanded by Deontology – is only justifiable if the original principle is correct. Thus, if the maxim that we hold to be a universal law is flawed in some way, consistency of application would only serve to compound our error.

Despite these criticisms, we should remember that Deontological principles have been the cornerstone of healthcare ethics. When a Code of Professional Conduct states that a healthcare professional *must* treat all people with respect, regardless of race, religion, colour, age, gender or sexual orientation, it gives expression to a categorical imperative (Newham and Hawley, 2007). Such an imperative countenances no exclusions, thereby clearly implying that those who cannot adhere to the principle have no place in the healthcare professions. So, how would a Deontologist approach our scenario?

The Deontologist would probably first be struck by the inconsistency of approach. In Italy, for example, adoption laws prevent couples from adopting when the mother (but not the father) is more than 40 years older than the child (Benagiano, 1993). Similarly, some would argue that it is hypocritical to allow abortion but to prevent pregnancy. The fact that such anomalies exist suggests that we have not found a universal law to govern the ethics of reproduction. Perhaps more significantly, though, the relationship between client and healthcare professional does not always appear to be based upon mutual respect. The woman who lies about her age in order to procure fertility treatment is thinking about the long-term consequences; but, if lying is wrong, then it must be wrong in all circumstances. Equally, it is clear that her deception is using the healthcare professionals as a means to an end, which a Deontologist would also see as morally wrong.

The healthcare professionals do not escape unscathed from such situations either. Who, for example, are the people who are donating the eggs to enable post-menopausal women to conceive? If they are from poorer countries and are being exploited, they too will have been used as a means to an end. Moreover, there are suspicions that some doctors are using post-menopausal women deliberately to demonstrate their skill and expertise in reproductive technology. As Benagiano (1993) states: 'The fallacy ... lies with the implicit consequence that anything medically or technically possible has to be good and therefore to be encouraged' (p. 1345).

Thus, if the *motive* of the doctors here is primarily to 'make a name for themselves', this would make their actions morally wrong. We have noted that Deontology has much in common with Christian principles (and Kant himself was a very religious man), and we may be tempted to suppose that post-menopausal pregnancies would be seen to be against God's will. We have also mentioned, though, that we cannot be certain that such technology is against God's will, and a Deontologist would probably be reluctant to use such arguments. It is not inevitable that a Deontologist would be opposed to post-menopausal pregnancies, but there are sufficient doubts about the motives of the interested parties to make this action morally suspect.

Rights-based ethics   The concept of a duty-based ethical system (which is what Deontology essentially is) automatically entails that others have a claim upon us to insist that certain duties are performed. In other words, we have *rights*, and these should not be withheld or interfered with by others. The close correlation between duty and rights has led some to conflate the two ethical systems, but the language of human rights has gained increasing prominence in recent years, suggesting that it is worthy of separate attention.

Certainly, it would appear that, with every right, there comes a duty. Thus, we all have a *right* to be treated with respect, but equally, we have a *duty* to treat others with respect. If we fail in our duty, it can be reasonably said that we have forfeited our right. Whether there is any such thing as an absolute right (i.e. one that cannot be over-ridden in any circumstances) has been debated by many over the years, but in truth it is difficult to think of any. The right to life is forfeitable in some circumstances (for example, in self-defence), and the right to practise one's own religion would be constrained if such religion involved human or animal sacrifice. The right to freedom is obviously forfeited when one commits a serious criminal offence, but has also been over-ridden in other circumstances. If, for example, an infectious patient refuses to be isolated in hospital, the wider needs of the public demand that this person's liberty should be restricted. Thus, virtually all of the claims that we may assert have been handed down by God are forfeitable and can also be over-ridden by stronger moral claims. They are not, therefore, absolute rights, but are instead *prima facie* rights (Johnstone, 2004).

The major difficulty of a rights-based theory is that people's rights frequently conflict with each other. The smoker, for example, may claim a right to smoke in a restaurant, but the non-smokers will claim a right to eat their meal in a smoke-free environment. Currently, the latter's rights hold sway in this country, but it was not very long ago that the opposite was the case. Therefore, our perception of 'rights' may frequently be little more than an expression of one pressure group's political and cultural philosophy. Notwithstanding these criticisms, though, it is equally clear that a failure to acknowledge people's rights has led to dreadful injustice and inhumanity in many areas of the world (Beauchamp and Childress, 2001). The argument that the suspension of human rights is justifiable in the interests of the community has been a recurring feature of totalitarian dictatorships, and has done little more than increase the sum of human misery.

So, how would a rights-based theorist perceive our dilemma? The first thing to notice here is that there are a variety of competing rights: namely those of the post-menopausal woman, of society, and of any children born into this situation. For example, does every woman have a fundamental right to have a child? Some have suggested that this is so, but the implications of accepting this position are that society would have a duty to ensure that all infertile women receive appropriate treatment free of charge if they request it. It would be difficult to gain acceptance for this viewpoint, particularly when one considers the other demands for healthcare resources. Rejection of it, however, inevitably means that the technology required to render a post-menopausal woman pregnant is restricted to those who can afford it. Without even trying, it has become socially unjust, and possibly racially discriminatory also. Where the exercise of (or claim upon) a 'right' is determined by the size of one's bank balance, the morality of post-menopausal motherhood may be called into question.

Equally, though, the biological nature of reproduction appears to discriminate against women. Kahn et al. (2010), for example, have provided evidence to show that women who had children in their early to mid-twenties did not fare as well economically as those who delayed childbirth until a later age. Similarly, the ability of men to father children well into their seventies and beyond does not incur the same societal disapproval or legal sanctions (Vaidya and Shah, 2010). Benagiano (1993) suggests that 'such a different reproductive pattern is created (or shall I say, wanted) by nature: motherhood is biologically at a different level than fatherhood' (p. 1345); but this may be intellectualising a prejudice against women that has been received through the ages and reinforced by organised religion.

A child cannot claim a right to be conceived, and current abortion laws also deny a right to be born. S/he may, however, argue that there is a right to be raised by a loving family, but there is little to suggest that the post-menopausal mother is unable to provide this. Moreover, if such a right existed, we might consider the sterilisation of women who were drug addicts, alcoholics, or abusers of children. The fact that we do not do this suggests that the 'right' to have a child exists only when technology is not required: once it is needed, society claims a right to put constraints upon its exercise. Finally, the child may claim a right to be raised by parents who will survive at least until s/he reaches maturity. We have already noted, though, that such an expectation can never be guaranteed, although admittedly its chances are significantly reduced when the parents are in an older age group.

Virtue ethics   Virtue ethics owes its origins to Aristotle in the 4th century BC, but has enjoyed a revival in recent years and has particular application to healthcare. It can be defined as the quality and practice of moral excellence (Johnstone, 2004), in which the agent's character is the focus of moral concern (Campbell et al., 2005). Virtues such as care, compassion, empathy and courage all have their place in health-care practice and are necessary for the alleviation of human suffering, but Hope et al. (2008) also remind us that virtue is its own reward: helping others enables an indi-vidual to develop personally.

Of crucial importance is the *motive* of the individual. A cat burglar, for example, may demonstrate courage, but his motives are immoral. Similarly, the nurse who gives care out of a sense of duty rather than genuine compassion may still be of value to the service, but does not demonstrate the virtue expected of him/her. Melia (2004) notes that the drive for the professionalisation of nursing and the desire to make it a competence-based profession is not necessarily in opposition to virtue eth-ics, because competency equates with excellence, and excellence in care is a virtue. It would become less of a virtue if increasing skill and competence distanced practi-tioners from patients, and the healthcare professional should always ensure that the virtues are in balance.

Perhaps one of the main advantages of virtue ethics is that it can provide 'solu-tions' to apparently impossible dilemmas. For example, Harris (2003) cites Hart's (1968) example of the lorry driver who is trapped in the cab of his vehicle. As the flames begin to engulf the cab and it becomes increasingly obvious that there is not going to be time to rescue him, the driver pleads with a policeman to shoot him so that he is spared the agony of being burned alive. The Deontologist would undoubtedly refuse such a request, for if killing another human being is wrong, it must be wrong in all circumstances. The Utilitarian may also have doubts, for the shooting of the driver may have adverse consequences for the policeman. Finally, the rights-based ethicist will declare that the driver cannot claim a right to be killed, whereas the policeman has a right to protect himself from possible prosecution for murder. The virtue ethicist, though, will quickly see that shooting the driver is an act of compassion, and this must be the motivating force (rather than consideration of one's own personal safety).

Harris (2003) suggests that the policeman would be justified in shooting the driver even if the latter did not (or was unable to) request it. Such was the case during the San Francisco earthquake of 1906, where an eye witness reports:

When the fire caught the Windsor Hotel at Fifth and Market Streets there were three men on the roof, and it was impossible to get them down. Rather than see the crazed men fall in with the roof and be roasted alive the military officer directed his men to shoot them, which they did in the presence of 5,000 people' (*The San Francisco Earthquake 1906*).

If virtue ethics are not constrained by the rigidity of Utilitarianism and Deontology (Melia, 2004), it is nevertheless also the case that their lack of clear guiding principles can lead to bad outcomes. A person can exhibit all of the virtues, but still perform wrong actions because of a lack of knowledge, education or information. Thus, despite the importance of virtuous character, this system of philosophy cannot be relied upon to the exclusion of all others.

How, then, would a virtue ethicist perceive our dilemma? Perhaps the first thing that stands out is the dishonesty exhibited by the post-menopausal woman in order to secure treatment. We have already noted the factors compelling this dishonesty, but truthfulness (in common with Deontological principles) is a virtue that cannot be compromised unless a higher virtue requires it. The withholding of secrets from an enemy of the State, for example, would serve to protect the interests (and possibly lives) of many innocent people; and the virtues of courage, loyalty and compassion would clearly outweigh the virtue of honesty.

Leaving this aside, the key issue for a virtue ethicist is going to be that of motive. If the woman is motivated solely by a desire to give love and care to a child, this alone would be sufficient to sanction the treatment. For a virtue ethicist, the ability to care is of much greater importance than the age of the mother, and anything that increases the sum total of love and compassion in this world has to be seen as a good thing. Similarly, even if the medical team were fully aware of the woman's age, they would be justified in offering the treatment on this basis. If, however, their motive for acting was founded upon a desire to test the limits of technology and/or to secure fame and wealth, they would lack the virtues of integrity and humility and their actions would correspondingly be immoral.

We have now explored the dilemma from the perspectives of four main ethical theories, and the 'answer' can be different in each one. Even within each theory, we may come to a different conclusion depending upon the circumstances. There are other theories that could have been discussed, such as care ethics (which owes much to virtue ethics) and Communitarianism (which has a number of similarities with Deontology); but it is time to try a different approach. The arguments from both sides are now a little clearer, but ethical theory can probably do little more than this. We must therefore move on to the next stage of the framework.

C HOW WILL ETHICAL PRINCIPLISM HELP IN RESOLVING THIS ISSUE?

Ethical principlism is most closely associated with Beauchamp and Childress (2001), for they have become the most influential of its proponents. They do not, however, claim to be the originator of the principles, for they acknowledge the work of earlier writers (Frankena (1973), for example), and indeed, argue that the principles have existed since the dawn of civilisation. It is simply that they have given the principles their most articulate expression and have related them directly to the field of healthcare. Essentially, there are four principles to be taken into account when considering a moral issue:

1   *Autonomy*, which can be defined as the right of self-determination or the right to make one's own choices. It is closely allied to the concepts of Liberty and Freedom, but its exercise is constrained by two main conditions: first, the autonomous individual must be competent to make decisions affecting his/her life and welfare. Thus, the severely depressed individual should be prevented from committing suicide because this action would be the product of a deranged mind. Second, the actions of an individual should not impinge upon the autonomy of others. The mugger may be competent in any meaningful sense of the term, but his/her crimes have an adverse impact upon the lives of the victims. Notwithstanding these constraints, Autonomy remains a key feature of healthcare ethics, for it underpins the concepts of informed consent, privacy and dignity, and confidentiality (among others).

2   *Non-maleficence*, which can be defined as the obligation to avoid doing harm to others. It is a negative obligation in that it can prevent apparently beneficial treatment if such treatment creates more harm than good. For example, in Chapter 6, the case of *R v Cambridge Health Authority, ex parte B [1995]* is discussed, where a hospital was faced with the decision of whether or not to give chemotherapy to a young girl suffering from leukaemia. The hospital decided that, on balance, the best option was not to treat, because the chances of success of the chemotherapy were very small, but it would also induce a lot of suffering for the girl. In other words, the avoidance of doing harm was of greater importance than the possibility of doing good in this instance. This, of course, is not always the case, and it could be argued that virtually every patient is harmed in some way by the healthcare team. Despite this, the principle of Non-maleficence is a fundamental tenet of healthcare: it features in the Hippocratic oath, it can be found in all the professional Codes of Conduct, and it was expressed by Florence Nightingale in 1863 when she said: "It may seem a strange principle to enunciate as the very first requirement in a hospital that it should do the sick no harm".

3   *Beneficence*, which is a positive obligation to do good to others. Some have doubted that Beneficence can ever be considered a 'duty' when it is impossible to do good to everyone at the same time (Clouser and Gert, 1990), and there are no obligations to provide a benefit to others if our own interests are compromised as a result. Thus, most would accept that there is no duty upon us to rescue someone from a burning building if, in doing so, our own lives are endangered. Such a duty, however, would lie with members of the Fire Service, just as healthcare practitioners have a legal, moral and professional obligation to serve the best interests of those in their care.

4   *Justice*, which equates with fairness and as an equal distribution of benefits and burdens. For healthcare professionals, the concept is of crucial importance when considering the question of how limited resources are to be distributed fairly. It would be reasonable to assume that most practitioners have little direct influence on such matters, but time is also a resource, and each individual must decide how this is to be allocated when faced with competing demands from patients. Who gets our attention first? – the patient who shouts the loudest? Or the patient who has the most charming smile? Or the patient who has the greatest need? The professional approach is to adopt the last of these, but it is rarely as simple as this. Many years ago, Stockwell (1972) identified that nurses are heavily influenced by the nature and character of the patient and will allocate their time accordingly. Most of

this operates at a subliminal level, but it runs counter to the ethics of healthcare. Moreover, it can be very difficult to assess patient 'need' in a truly objective sense: for example, we can see that a patient is in pain, but we cannot know exactly how much. If two patients are screaming for analgesia at the same time, the practitioner has to make a judgement call as to which will receive it first, and such decisions are inevitably error-prone. All of this suggests that Justice is not a simple concept, although the public have a right to demand that healthcare professionals have it at the forefront of their minds.

As mentioned earlier, principlism has had an enormous influence upon healthcare ethics, although it has not been without its critics. Clouser and Gert (1990), for example, have launched a particularly scathing attack, in which they argue that principlism confuses the issue by rejecting moral theory but being unable to replace it with any clear guidelines:

[Ethical theories] are reduced to four principles from which agents are told to pick and choose as they see fit, as if one could sometimes be a Kantian and sometimes a Utilitarian and sometimes something else, without worrying whether the theory one is using is adequate or not (p. 223).

In their defence, Beauchamp and Childress (2001) state that they have never attempted to produce a general ethical theory, and have doubts that such a thing is possible. Similarly, they contend that the study of ethics is destined to be confusing and we should be prepared to face up to that:

we regard disunity, conflict and moral ambiguity as pervasive features of the moral life. Untidiness, complexity, and conflict may be perplexing, but a theory of morality cannot be faulted for realistically incorporating those dimensions of morality (p. 390).

Walker (2009), on the other hand, has less of a problem with the idea of ethical principles, but contends that the four outlined by Beauchamp and Childress are simply not enough. He cites the example of bestiality, which we recognise as being morally wrong, even though it does not appear to transgress any of the four principles. Similarly, it is conceivable that the principles cannot capture cultural differences, so that guidance may miss things that are important for certain people. Beauchamp and Childress have not had an opportunity as yet to answer this claim, although they might argue that most of the other principles that Walker has in mind can be subsumed within at least one of the four main principles. For example, truthfulness is respectful of another person's Autonomy and may also be Beneficent.

Whatever the strengths of these criticisms, the four principles can provide a useful framework for discussing ethical dilemmas. Frequently, of course, these principles are in conflict with each other. Thus, the adult Jehovah's Witness who refuses a life-saving blood transfusion presents a conflict between Autonomy (his right to determine what happens to his body) and Beneficence (the healthcare professionals' obligation to serve his best interests). In such circumstances, Autonomy will prevail (at least in this and other English-speaking countries), for the right to make one's own decisions is considered more important than the right to health. It would be a different matter if the Jehovah's Witness had a three-year-old child who needed the blood transfusion. Here, the child is unable to exercise his/her own Autonomy, and therefore, Beneficence will prevail (thereby over-riding the parent's refusal).

So, which principles are at issue in our dilemma, and which should take priority? As we consider them, we find that much of the foregoing discussion is revisited. Thus, one might be able to argue that the post-menopausal woman has an Autonomous right to determine what happens to her body, and this will include the right to have a child. She does not, however, have a right to impinge upon the Autonomy of others, and we might feel that she has done this by lying to the healthcare professionals. The healthcare team might have an Autonomous right to refuse this treatment, but only if they can provide a solid justification for doing so. One such justification would be that it could be potentially damaging to the woman if she were to experience pregnancy and childbirth at an advanced age. In other words, the principle of Non-maleficence will outweigh all other considerations. Once again, though, the healthcare team would need to provide evidence that this is actually the case, and such evidence can be difficult to locate. It may well be that *some* women are in greater danger from pregnancy, but this cannot be used as an excuse to impose a blanket ban on fertility treatment for all post-menopausal women. In short, each case deserves to be treated on its own individual merits.

The healthcare team have an obligation to consider the interests of any child born as a result of this treatment, but it is difficult to identify the harm that would be done to him/her. We cannot say that a child is harmed by being born, because the alternative is non-existence (Johnstone, 2004). Perhaps existence is a harm if the life is short, debilitating and extremely painful, but it ought to be possible to identify such congenital abnormalities long before birth occurs. Similarly, the argument that the child will become an orphan before s/he reaches adulthood is little more than an assumption, and we have already noted that no child has a guarantee that his/her parents will live for at least 20 years.

We might see fertility treatment for the post-menopausal woman as a Beneficent act, in that it gives her the child that she craves, and a child is born into a loving, caring and nurturing family. As mentioned earlier, however, any good done by this treatment must outweigh the potential for harm. Thus, the woman who was unlikely to withstand the strain of pregnancy and the traumas of childbirth would not be benefited by this treatment.

Finally, we have seen that Justice plays a key role in discussions on the merits and demerits of post-menopausal fertility treatment. There is strength in the argument that women are disadvantaged in the workplace by virtue of their biological clocks. This would not have been seen as an issue worthy of consideration in years gone by, but it is no longer something that we can ignore. Genuine equality of the sexes demands equality of opportunity, and this is significantly reduced when the reproductive years coincide with a woman's most creative and productive period. Equally, though, we have noted that this treatment is reserved only for those who are able to fund it, and this too may be seen to be unfair.

D MAKE A DECISION, JUSTIFY IT, EVALUATE IT, AND LEARN FROM THE CONSEQUENCES

We began this discussion with an intuitive suspicion that post-menopausal fertility treatment was morally wrong, and some will undoubtedly adhere to that view. An exploration of ethical theory and ethical principlism, however, has at least cast some doubt upon the strength of that position, and Antinori et al. (1993) probably sum it up best when they ask:

> is it right or justifiable for a menopausal woman to want a child? And to such a couple seeking a pregnancy a doctor might paradoxically respond by saying: 'The possibility of having one exists, but you must not have it.' However, if the couple were then to ask: 'Why mustn't we have it?', the doctor would not be in a position to answer.

This is not to say that post-menopausal fertility treatment is right in all circumstances, but that the onus must fall upon those who would deny such treatment to provide a solid justification for their decision. Or, as Smajdor (2010) puts it: 'we need to decide whether our dislike of squirming is a reasonable basis for establishing a maximum age for fertility treatment'.

Equally, though, this chapter began with an acknowledgement that moral debate is dynamic, vibrant and ever-changing. In other words, arguments omitted from the foregoing discussion might sway the decision in a different direction. When all is said and done, we are most likely to identify the strengths and weaknesses of an argument by the consequences of any action or inaction that we take. Nevertheless, an application of ethical theory and ethical principlism can help to avoid some of the more catastrophic of those consequences.

REFERENCES

TEXTS

Antinori, S., Versaci, C., Hossein Ghalami, G., Caffa, B. and Pauci, C. (1993) 'A child is a joy at any age', *Human Reproduction*, 8 (10): 1542.

Beauchamp, T.L. and Childress, J. F. (2001) *Principles of Bio-medical Ethics,* 5th edn. Oxford: Oxford University Press.

Beemsterboer, P.L. (2010) *Ethics and Law in Dental Hygiene*, 2nd edn. St. Louis, MI: Saunders Elsevier.

Benagiano, G. (1993) 'Pregnancy after the menopause: a challenge to Nature?' *Human Reproduction*, 8 (9): 1344–5.

Bittner, U. and Eichinger, T. (2010) 'An ethical assessment of post-menopausal motherhood against the backdrop of successful anti-aging medicine', *Rejuvenation Research*, 13 (6): 741–7.

Buka, P. (2008) *Patients' Rights, Law and Ethics for Nurses*. London: Hodder Arnold.

Campbell, A., Gillett, G. and Jones, G. (2005) *Medical Ethics*, 4th edn. Oxford: Oxford University Press.

Clouser, K.D. and Gert, B. (1990) 'A critique of principlism', *The Journal of Medicine and Philosophy*, 15: 219–36.

Edwards, R.G. (1993) 'Pregnancies are acceptable in post-menopausal women', *Human Reproduction*, 8 (10): 1542–4.

Frankena, W. (1973) *Ethics*, 2nd edn. Englewood Cliffs, NJ: Prentice-Hall.

Harris, J. (2003) 'Consent and end of life decisions', *Journal of Medical Ethics*, 29: 10–15.

Hart, H. (1968) *Punishment and Responsibility*. Oxford: Oxford University Press.

Hendrick, J. (2010) *Law and Ethics in Children's Nursing*. Chichester: John Wiley & Sons.

Hope, T. (2004) *Medical Ethics: a Very Short Introduction*. Oxford: Oxford University Press.

Hope, T., Savulescu, J. and Hendrick, J. (2008) *Medical Law and Ethics: the Core Curriculum*, 2nd edn. London: Churchill Livingstone.

Johnstone, M-J. (2004) *Bio-ethics: A Nursing Perspective*, 4th edn. Sydney: Churchill Livingstone.

Kahn, J.R., Garcia-Manglano, J. and Bianchi, S.M. (2010) 'The motherhood penalty at midlife: the long-term impact of birth-timing on women's careers'. Available at: http://paa2010.princeton.edu/download.aspx?submissionld=10153.

Mail Online (2006) Thousands lie to IVF clinics in desperation to have a baby. Available at: www.dailymail.co.uk/health/article391606/Thousands-lie-IVF-clinics-desperation-baby.html

Markkula Center (2009) A framework for thinking ethically. Available at: www.scu.edu/ethics/practicing/decision/framework.html.

Mason, J.K. and Laurie, G.T. (2011) *Mason and McCall Smith's Law and Medical Ethics*, 8th edn. Oxford: Oxford University Press.

Melia, K. (2004) *Health Care Ethics*. London: Sage Publications.

Newham, R.A. and Hawley, G. (2007) 'The relationship of ethics to philosophy', in G. Hawley (ed.), *Ethics in Clinical Practice: An Interprofessional Approach*. Harlow: Pearson Education.

Nightingale, F. (1863) *Notes on Hospitals*, 3rd edn. London: Longman Green, Longman, Roberts and Green.

Pattinson, S.D. (2009) *Medical Law and Ethics*, 2nd edn. London: Sweet & Maxwell.

Powell, K. (2004) 'There is no place for ageism in reproductive medicine', *Nature*, 432: 1.

Seedhouse, D. (2005) *Values-based Decision-making for the Caring Professions*. Chichester: John Wiley & Sons.

Smajdor, A. (2010) 'Time to put a stop to post-menopausal mothers?' Available at: www.bionews.org.uk/page_54017.asp.

Smith, S.W. (2005a) 'Evidence for the practical slippery slope in the debate on physician-assisted suicide and euthanasia', *Medical Law Review*, 13 (Spring): 17–44.

Smith, S.W. (2005b) 'Fallacies of the logical slippery slope in the debate on physician-assisted suicide and euthanasia', *Medical Law Review*, 13 (Summer): 224–53.

St. Louis Times (1997) Motherhood at mid-life — a medical and ethical dilemma. May 31. Available at: www.infertile.com/inthenew/lay/midlife.htm.

Stockwell, F. (1972) *The Unpopular Patient*. London: Royal College of Nursing.

The San Francisco Earthquake 1906. www.eyewitnesstohistory.com/sfeq.htm:

Vaidya, R. and Shah, R. (2010) '"Brave old" motherhood: beyond biological boundaries', *Journal of Mid-life Health*, 1 (1): 3–4.

Walker, T. (2009) 'What principlism misses', *Journal of Medical Ethics*, 35: 229–31.

CASES

R v Cambridge Health Authority, ex parte B [1995] 25 BMLR 5 (HC); 2 All ER 129 (CA).

LEGISLATION

Human Fertilisation and Embryology Act 1990

3

NEGLIGENCE

Learning Objectives

At the end of this chapter, the reader will:

1   Have an understanding of the elements of negligence.

2   Be aware of a variety of cases that have helped to shape the law of negligence.

3   Acknowledge the possible defences to a charge of negligence.

4   Identify some of the weaknesses of the tort system, and be aware of potential solutions to the problems.

1 INTRODUCTION

In 2008/9, a total of £769 million was paid in compensation for clinical negligence claims, and this represented a rise from £633 million in the previous year (NHS Litigation Authority, 2009a). This rise cannot be explained simply in terms of inflation, for the year saw a rise in clinical claims of more than 11 per cent, and the NHSLA is unable to account for any particular factor that may have triggered this rise. We could speculate and argue that the range of clinical procedures is becoming more invasive and that the likelihood of long-term damage is increased. We might also be able to argue that we are living in a more litigious society, where patients are more likely to assert their rights if their treatment does not work out as well as had been hoped.

Whatever the reasons, it is an unarguable fact that negligence claims represent a considerable drain on the resources of the NHS. Moreover, although the vast majority of claims are directed towards medicine, nursing has not been exempt. A total of £11 million has been paid by the Clinical Negligence Scheme for Trusts since April 1995 in matters related to nursing (NHS Litigation Authority, 2009b), and this figure excludes those claims that were lower than the excess (usually £50,000) and which were handled by Trusts alone. As the range of nursing skills continues to expand, it is not unreasonable to assume that this figure will continue to rise.

These statistics help to explain why the threat of a negligence claim exercises the thoughts of most healthcare professionals at some time or another. Healthcare is a risky business and the potential for disaster is ever-present. Despite this, however, the purpose of this chapter is to show that the claimant faces a series of obstacles before being awarded compensation, and that the route to litigation is a tortuous path. By way of introduction, consider the following scenario:

Box 3.1   *Gow v Harker [2003]*

Miss Gow had a thyroid condition, which required her to have periodic blood tests. In 1995, she visited her GP for one such test, but the doctor had difficulty in obtaining the blood. The GP was eventually successful when she tried the right wrist, but Miss Gow claimed that the needle had been inserted at an angle of 90° and that she immediately felt pain in her fingers and hand. Over the weekend, she complained of numbness in a couple of fingers of the right hand and she was unable to move her right arm.

   This case eventually came to the High Court in 2002, but the doctor had long lost confidence in taking blood and referred all such patients to the practice nurse. When she heard that the claim was going to court, she immediately resigned from the practice and gave up medicine altogether, claiming that 'she could not cope with someone feeling that she had been negligent'.

   Although the claimant was originally successful in the High Court, the Court of Appeal reversed this decision, arguing that Miss Gow's testimony could not be considered reliable. They also stated that it was conceivable that injury to the radial nerve had occurred, but this could have happened in a non-negligent manner.

In itself, this case is neither remarkable nor of great significance to anybody other than the chief protagonists. It did not create new law, nor did it even extend existing law. Nevertheless, it is a good illustration of several factors that are often associated with negligence cases:

1   You will notice the time span of eight years between the incident and the court's final judgment. This is by no means uncommon and it suggests that the claimant has to be very single-minded and determined to pursue such claims. Unless s/he is left with permanent disability, it is likely that most will have given up long before the case finds its way to court; and the anger that the claimant felt at the time of the incident will often dissipate with the passage of the years. An added complication is that one's recollection of events becomes increasingly hazy or embellished as time goes on, ensuring that doubts can be cast upon the reliability and veracity of the claimant's testimony.

2   Closely related to this last point is the realisation that negligence claims can be extremely difficult to win, even where there is clear evidence that the patient has come to harm. The burden of proof rests with the claimant, and the Court generally requires conclusive evidence of negligence before it will find against a healthcare professional. Some of the possible reasons for this will be discussed later, but suffice it to say at this stage that the claimant faces a difficult struggle.

3   The final point is that the case provides a graphic illustration of the fact that nobody emerges as a clear winner in negligence claims (unless you count the lawyers!). The patient's claim may be successful, but it is likely that s/he will have been left with a permanent disability. Even if the court finds for the defendant, the damage to the healthcare professional's confidence and reputation may be irreversible (as indeed it was in this case). Thus, the psychological impact upon the patient, the healthcare professionals involved and the service cannot be under-estimated.

For a claimant to win an action in negligence, the following three elements have to be in place:

a   A duty of care is owed to the claimant.
b   There has been a breach in the standard of the duty of care owed.
c   The breach has caused reasonably foreseeable harm.

Note that the claimant must be able to show, on the balance of probabilities, that all three elements are present and that they all exist at the same time. If the case falls down on one of these elements (or even one part of an element), it will be dismissed in favour of the defendant. Thus, let us take each one of them in turn and examine them in more detail.

2 DUTY OF CARE

A ORIGINS OF THE CONCEPT

When speaking of the concept of a 'duty of care', the following case is usually cited as being of seminal importance:

Box 3.2   *Donoghue v Stevenson [1932]*

A friend bought a bottle of ginger beer from a retailer and gave it to the claimant. The drink came in an opaque bottle, meaning that the latter was unable to visualise its contents. She poured out the first half of the ginger beer and drank it; but when she poured out the second half, out plopped the decomposing remains of a dead snail. She claimed to have subsequently suffered shock and severe gastro-enteritis.

As the law stood at this time, there appeared to be no cause of action for Mrs Donoghue. The Sale of Goods Act 1893 imposed a duty upon manufacturers and retailers to supply goods that were of 'merchantable quality' (s14 [2]), but this duty was a contractual arrangement and therefore existed only with the purchaser. Similarly, the civil law states that a contract only exists between buyer and seller: Mrs Donoghue was neither. Nevertheless, the case came before the courts and went all the way to the House of Lords. The decision ultimately turned in her favour, but only by a majority of 3:2, illustrating the dilemma faced by the court and the uncertain legal position at the time. Its primary significance, however, is that it extended the scope of a duty of care to those outside a contractual relationship. To this end, the most-quoted passage from the case comes from Lord Atkin (at 581):

> You must take reasonable care to avoid acts or omissions which you can reasonably foresee would be likely to injure your neighbour. Who, then, in law is my neighbour? The answer seems to be – persons who are so closely and directly affected by my act that I ought reasonably to have them in contemplation as being so affected when I am directing my mind to the acts or omissions which are called in question.

B WHEN DOES A DUTY OF CARE ARISE?

The principle enunciated by Lord Atkin has application across a broad range of disciplines, but it is of particular relevance in healthcare. It means that whenever a patient crosses the threshold of a healthcare premises, the professionals therein have a duty of care to him/her. It means, equally, that when a community nurse attends a patient in his/her home, a duty of care is automatically established. The patient has a right to expect that healthcare professionals will offer the appropriate treatment and/or advice; and the healthcare professionals have a legal obligation to provide it. Of the three elements constituting negligence, therefore, this will almost always be the easiest hurdle to overcome for any potential claimant.

There are, however, a range of situations where it is not entirely clear whether or not a duty of care exists:

When the healthcare professional is off-duty   Dimond (2008) cites the example of the nurse who comes upon a road traffic accident victim in her off-duty hours, and asks whether she has a duty of care to this individual. One could certainly argue that she has a *moral* obligation to assist, and it is also possible to claim that she has a *professional* duty (more of which later); but there is no *legal* duty to rescue in the United Kingdom (see *Stovin v Wise [1996]*; *Vellino v Chief Constable of Greater Manchester [2001]*). A duty of care exists in some other countries, most notably France (French Criminal Code, s63 [2]) where a potential penalty exists of five years in prison and a fine of €100,000, and also in Germany (German Criminal Code, s323c). But, even here, the duty does not go beyond contacting the emergency medical services.

In the UK, the healthcare professional would have a duty of care to an accident victim if s/he had *caused* the accident. Moreover, having started to administer first aid, s/he would be expected to continue to provide assistance until there were compelling reasons to desist. Until first aid is given, there is no duty of care; once first aid has commenced, however, a duty of care automatically becomes established. Finally, the healthcare professional would have a duty of care if there was a pre-existing professional relationship with the person requiring assistance (for example, if a community nurse came upon a victim who was already her patient).

At no time, though, is anybody expected to administer assistance if their own life is thereby endangered. Your own children could be burning to death in a building, but there would be no legal duty upon you to go in and rescue them.

It would seem, therefore, that the healthcare professional who refuses to assist at the scene of an accident is offered greater protection from the law than the person who is more morally virtuous, for the latter exposes him/herself to the threat of litigation if something goes wrong with the efforts to administer first aid. To this charge, there are perhaps three points to be made:

i   The courts tend to be very reluctant to allow successful lawsuits against what we might call the 'good Samaritan', for this would be sending out an unfortunate signal. It would be tantamount to saying: 'Do *not* assist at the scene of an accident or you are likely to get sued for it'. Clearly, this is not the kind of message that the courts want to convey, and therefore, they are likely to reserve such actions for those who do something completely unreasonable (for example, trying to walk somebody who has a broken back). Bear in mind, too, that this standard will apply to ordinary members of the public; the fact that the rescuer is a healthcare professional does not, of itself, impose a noticeably higher standard. In addition, the courts will recognise that there are serious limitations to what a rescuer can do in a situation removed from the workplace. In the absence of equipment, medication and manpower resources, the best that the rescuer can hope to achieve is to keep the patient as safe as possible until the paramedics arrive.

ii The position of the Nursing and Midwifery Council (NMC) is that nurses have a professional responsibility to provide care in an emergency, both in and outside the work setting (NMC, 2008b). Whether failure to assist at the scene of an accident would result in disciplinary proceedings remains doubtful. One version of the Code of Conduct (NMC, 2004) stated categorically that this duty existed (s8.5), but it is interesting to note that this was removed from the most recent edition (NMC, 2008a). When the NMC states that 'if a nurse or midwife chooses to walk away from an emergency situation they could be called to account for this' (NMC, 2008b), it does not specify who will do the calling. There is a chance that the NMC may consider that such an individual was bringing the reputation of the profession into disrepute, but the more likely scenario is that the nurse/midwife's employer will initiate disciplinary action. Even here, though, such action is doubtful unless a storm of adverse publicity has arisen from the healthcare professional's inactivity.

iii There is an increasing body of opinion which suggests that healthcare professionals should be liable in negligence if they fail to assist at the scene of an accident. Williams (2001) makes this argument very forcefully and highlights two cases which seem to imply that a higher standard is expected of healthcare professionals than of others. The first is *Kent v Griffiths [2000]*, where an ambulance service was held liable for failing to attend an emergency in a reasonable time (meaning that a pregnant woman who was experiencing an asthmatic attack subsequently suffered a respiratory arrest, serious brain damage and a miscarriage). The defendant sought to rely on earlier judgments where liability was rejected when the police failed to respond to an alarm that had been triggered by a burglary (*Alexandrou v Oxford [1993]*), and when the fire service failed to attend a fire in response to a 999 call (*Capital & Counties plc v Hampshire County Council [1997]*). However, the court held that there was a significant difference between an ambulance service and the services provided by the police or fire service (per Lord Woolf at 45). This might be considered a debatable viewpoint, but the fact that the court holds it strongly suggests that it considers that the public have the right to expect more from healthcare professionals than from other public services.

The second case is that of *Lowns v Woods [1996]*, where a doctor was held liable for failing to attend an 11-year-old boy who was in *status epilepticus* (and who subsequently suffered brain damage and quadriplegia). The fact that the boy was not a patient of the doctor is significant, for this means that there was no prior existing relationship between the two. One cannot escape the conclusion that the court imposed a higher moral standard upon this case: in other words, there was no practical reason why the doctor could not attend the patient, and consequently, it was immoral of him not to do so. We should note that this is an Australian case and does not therefore have authority in the UK. It could, however, be cited in a future case in this country, and the arguments may well be considered highly persuasive.

One final point to make is that GPs are already under a contractual agreement to provide services to all those in their practice area who are in need of care following an accident or emergency, regardless of whether or not the victim is a patient on their lists (NHS [General Medical Services Contracts] Regulations 2004, s15 [6]). There are no obvious signs that this clause will be built into the contracts of other healthcare professionals, and it does not currently apply to midwives who may come across a woman giving labour while on holiday (Dimond, 2006); but it remains a possibility for the future.

When the healthcare professional is on duty, but the accident occurs outside of the healthcare premises Some years ago, a man collapsed in the street just outside a hospital. The people who were with him rushed into the hospital to ask for assistance, but the staff refused to go to the man's aid. One of their arguments was that they were not insured (which, as it turned out, was not strictly accurate); but the main argument was that they did not have a duty of care to the person lying in the street. They *did*, however, have a duty of care to the patients within the hospital. Therefore, if they abandoned those patients to go to the aid of the man in the street, and something subsequently happened to those patients, the staff might be held liable in negligence.

The moral of this story appears to be that, if you see somebody collapse outside a hospital, call an ambulance: the staff within the hospital are obligated to remain at their posts and cannot therefore be relied upon to answer the call for assistance. In practice, one suspects that most healthcare professionals would feel very uncomfortable about adopting this position, but it is important to realise that their primary duty lies with those already in their care. Therefore, if the call for help is to be answered, they must first ensure that the safety of those patients has been secured.

When it is not entirely clear to whom the duty of care is owed   In *Caparo Industries v Dickman [1990]*, the court endeavoured to give some guidance for when it was unclear whether or not a duty of care arose. Thus, a three-stage test was developed, all three of which needed to be proven by the claimant:

i   There must be foreseeability of damage.
ii There must be proximity between the parties.
iii It must be just and reasonable to impose a duty of care.

Application of this test is illustrated clearly in the case of *Goodwill v British Pregnancy Advisory Service [1996]*:

Box 3.3   *Goodwill v British Pregnancy Advisory Service [1996]*

The claimant became pregnant after having unprotected intercourse with her partner, the latter having been given assurances by BPAS that his vasectomy had been success-ful. She therefore sued for the costs of raising the child and other expenses incurred as a result of the pregnancy.

It is arguable that this case fails all three limbs of the *Caparo* test, for BPAS could only be held liable to those patients that they treated. Any departure from this principle would potentially render them liable to the whole world. Interestingly, however, the claimant might have had a course of action if she had sought assurances from BPAS herself and the latter gave her the same information. In such circumstances, proximity would have been established and the defendant would be aware of an identifiable individual who could potentially be harmed by their actions.

Other applications of *Caparo* can be seen in two cases heard together by the House of Lords:

Box 3.4   *X v Bedfordshire CC [1995]*

Five claimants had alleged that they were experiencing parental abuse and neglect. The council knew of these allegations but failed to investigate the matter. In consequence, the claimants continued to suffer abuse, and they sued the council when they had reached maturity.

Box 3.5   *M v Newham LBC [1995]*

A psychiatrist diagnosed sexual abuse of a child and mistakenly identified the abuser as the mother's co-habitee. The psychiatrist felt that the mother was unable to protect the child, and so, the latter was removed from her care. Both mother and child sued the council for the psychological damage caused by the pain of separation.

In both cases, it was held that the social workers and the psychiatrist had been retained by the local authorities to advise *them* and not the claimants. Therefore, they could have no duty of care to either the children or the parent. Whereas the claimants might have been able to argue that the first limb of the *Caparo* test had been established, their actions foundered on the second and third elements.

Despite this, one is left with an uncomfortable suspicion that injustice has been committed in these cases. People have been damaged by the actions or inactions of local authorities, but there is no opportunity for them to obtain any form of redress. Pattinson (2009) suggests that this is because the courts are constantly aware of public policy considerations, and they must consider whether the interests of a small minority should be allowed to outweigh those of the majority. This argument states that public bodies (whether they be governmental departments, local authorities, emergency services or healthcare institutions) have difficult jobs, and it would not serve the interests of the public if those bodies were continually exposed to the threat of litigation. Thus, the *Caparo* test is not a scientific formula for calculating the likelihood of success of an action; rather, 'the result is an anti-academic, pragmatic approach in which we can only be certain that there is a duty of care when the courts have held this to be so' (Pattinson, 2009: 71).

If this is so, it follows that a better chance of success lies with the European Court, for this is less likely to be encumbered by the constraints of public policy. Some evidence for this contention comes in the case of *RK & AK v UK [2008]*:

Box 3.6   *RK & AK v UK [2008]*

A couple had a daughter who, when she was three months old, sustained a fractured femur. The medical personnel involved in this child's care were in no doubt that this was a non-accidental injury, and the court removed the child from the parents and placed her in the care of an aunt. Some months later, the child sustained another injury, and this time she was diagnosed with brittle bone disease. The parents sued for the pain and suffering incurred as a result of the nine months' separation from their daughter.

It is worth noting that all three English courts (the High Court, Court of Appeal, and the House of Lords) all found for the defendants, for earlier precedents *(X v Bedfordshire CC [1995]*, etc.) had established that there was no duty of care to the parents. Moreover, the European Court held that there had been no breach of Article 8 (the right to family life), for the authority's primary duty was to protect children, and it was acknowledged that it would have been very difficult to diagnose brittle bone disease in a three-month-old baby. Nevertheless, the Court also held that there had been a breach of Article 13, because the English legal system had failed to guarantee an effective remedy for this injustice: in consequence, the claimants were awarded €10,000.

Intuitively, this seems a fair decision, but it has served to introduce some confusion to the law. In theory at least, Article 13 should only apply when there has been a breach of another Article: where this is not the case, the claimants should not be entitled to a remedy. Bailey-Harris (2009) suggests that this is precisely how an English court would continue to see it, even in the presence of the Human Rights Act 1998. Nevertheless, the European Court felt that the parents' complaints were sufficiently 'arguable' to justify the award of compensation, even though they had failed to establish a breach of Article 8. This is not exactly how English courts have been programmed to function, for it is more a question of 'all or nothing'. Either the claimants prove their case (when they will be given the appropriate compensation) or they do not (when they will leave with nothing).

Notwithstanding the fact that this case is unsettling, it suggests that the law in this area is evolving. English courts are obliged to follow the precedents established in the European Court, and the principle enunciated in *X v Bedfordshire CC [1995]* now seems outdated. What this means, in practice, is that healthcare professionals may soon find that their duty of care extends to a wider class of people than was formerly the case.

In conclusion, we have seen that there are a variety of situations where the duty of care is unclear or non-existent, but no such ambiguity exists in the vast majority of healthcare situations. This, therefore, brings us onto the second element of negligence.

3 STANDARD OF CARE

One of the most important cases in the field of healthcare law is that of *Bolam v Friern Hospital Management Committee [1957]*, the facts of which are stated below:

Box 3.7 *Bolam v Friern Hospital Management Committee [1957]*

A patient underwent electro-convulsive therapy for treatment of depression, but the anaesthetist did not administer any muscle relaxant drugs. In consequence, as the shock waves passed through his brain, his body went into such severe spasm that he dislocated both hips and fractured his pelvis on each side.

It is reasonable to assume that this incident would not have improved his mental state, and it is equally unsurprising that he sued the hospital for damages. At the trial, he was able to produce an expert witness who stated categorically that he always used relaxant drugs on patients undergoing electro-convulsive therapy. The defendants, however, produced their own experts, who accepted that the use of relaxants was gaining in popularity, but contended that it was not yet common and universal practice. Or, to put it another way, 'some give relaxants, some don't'.

The judge presiding over this case was therefore faced with a conflict of opinion, and his method of resolving it can be summarised in one of the most quoted passages in English legal jurisdiction:

> A doctor is not guilty of negligence if he has acted in accordance with a practice accepted as proper by a responsible body of medical men skilled in that particular art (per McNair, J. at 122).

In other words, a doctor accused of negligence can escape liability simply by finding another doctor who is prepared to stand up in court and say that he considers the actions of the defendant to have been reasonable. As we shall soon see, this is an overly simplistic interpretation of the 'Bolam test' (as it has come to be known), and it has undergone some modifications in recent years. Nevertheless, it has two major implications: first, it gives doctors a level of protection within the law which few other professions enjoy. For example, in *Edward Wong Finance Company Limited v Johnston, Stokes and Master [1984]*, a solicitor was unable to defend his negligent practice by stating that nearly everybody else in the profession was doing the same thing. Despite this, a later case affirmed that *Bolam* is not specific to the medical profession:

> Counsel [for the claimant] did his best to argue that the Bolam test is confined to doctors ... [but] ... I cannot accept that argument. I can see no possible ground for distinguishing between doctors and any other profession or calling which requires special skill, knowledge or experience (*Gold v Haringey Health Authority [1987]*, per Lloyd, L. J. at 894).

Even allowing for this, however, there are strong suspicions that doctors are considered a special case in the civil law, and the possible reasons for this will be explored later.

Second, and more importantly, the effect of *Bolam* is that it can make it extremely difficult for claimants to win actions in negligence against the healthcare professions.

It is worth noting that the 'standard' being referred to here is not a particularly exacting one. It is simply what the reasonable practitioner would do in the same or similar circumstances. Clearly, therefore, if one practises as a brain surgeon, one's performance will be judged alongside that of the competent brain surgeon. To take a more down-to-earth example, let us consider the skill of cannulation: the healthcare professional would not be expected to insert the cannula in the vein every time, because nobody can achieve this and it would therefore be an unreasonable expectation. S/he would, however, be expected to use the right equipment, conform to the principles of asepsis, and administer the correct technique. Anything less than this would be considered as falling below an acceptable standard of care.

One other point about *Bolam* is that McNair, J.'s speech was not the delivery of a judgment, but was rather an address to a jury, who could (in theory at least) have decided to reject his advice. In all likelihood, the case would have gone to appeal, and a higher court would probably have overturned the decision; but it remains a tantalising possibility that the *Bolam* principle could have been strangled at birth. As things transpired, it was another 24 years before it gained official approval by the House of Lords, since which time it has been cited in virtually every medical negligence case thereafter. We need to examine, therefore, the possible reasons for the predominance of *Bolam*, of which Montgomery (2003) suggests there are three:

A THE COURTS LACK THE NECESSARY EXPERTISE TO MAKE A JUDGMENT IN THE FIELD OF HEALTHCARE

The courts have certainly in the past been extremely reluctant to challenge medical clinical judgement, and it is widely assumed that this is because they feel unable to comprehend medical practice. The increasing complexity of medical care has ensured that this fact remains as true today as it ever was, for the judiciary have been unable to keep pace with it. Had they done so, it is possible that they would have built up a specialist body of knowledge which would have enabled them to take a more objective view of cases brought before them. It is clearly in the interests of the medical profession that this situation should continue; Foster (1998) gives voice to the fear of doctors if the courts were to adopt a more interventionist approach:

> We are to be judged by laymen who know nothing at all about medicine. Our professional reputations are liable to be ruined because someone whose scientific education stopped at fifth form biology in the 1950's thinks that our practices, hallowed by experience and adopted by many eminent clinicians, could be improved upon. The courts will tell us that there is only one way to do things. Dogmatic clinicians, perhaps in the minority, but supported by a few publications and a persuasive court manner, will use the courts to impose their clinical views on the rest of the profession.

This rather emotive language reflects the strong sense of clinical freedom that is guarded so jealously by the medical profession, but which is not a feature of other healthcare professionals. Whether or not the courts will feel more confident in judging non-medical practice within healthcare is a difficult question to answer, for the limited evidence neither supports nor refutes this contention. In *Clarke v Adams [1950]*, a physiotherapist was found negligent for failing to give a proper warning to a patient of the risks of being burnt during treatment, even though an expert from the Chartered Society of Physiotherapists had argued that the defendant had not fallen below an acceptable standard of practice. This case might suggest that the courts do not consider the practice of nurses and allied healthcare professionals to be as esoteric as that of doctors, but it pre-dated *Bolam* and there is therefore no guarantee that the decision would have been the same today. A slightly better example is *Penney, Palmer & Cannon v East Kent Health Authority [2000]*, the facts of which are stated below:

Box 3.8   *Penney, Palmer & Cannon v East Kent Health Authority [2000]*

A screener examining cervical smears failed to identify abnormal slides from three patients, with the result that these women went on to develop invasive cervical cancer, necessitating extensive surgery. There was a conflict of opinion between the experts of both sides as to what constituted acceptable practice, and the judge preferred the testimony of the claimants' experts. This decision was subsequently upheld by the Court of Appeal.

By itself, this case does not prove that the courts limit the application of *Bolam* to cases involving doctors, but it is difficult to escape the conclusion that the decision might have been different if the defendants had been medical practitioners. There are a number of medical cases where the experts have differed, but the courts have demurred from balancing the evidence. Equally, however, there is growing evidence that the courts are prepared to question the testimony of experts. This is a point to which we will return shortly, but we should now look at the second possible reason for the predominance of *Bolam*.

B THE COURTS ARE RELUCTANT TO FIND NEGLIGENCE IN HEALTHCARE PROFESSIONALS BECAUSE OF PUBLIC POLICY CONSIDERATIONS

The issue of public policy considerations acting as a powerful constraint on medical negligence claims may have pre-dated Lord Denning, but they were given their most eloquent expression by him in *Hatcher v Black [1954]*, in which he said:

> a doctor examining a patient, or a surgeon operating at a table, instead of getting on with his work, would be forever looking over his shoulder to see if someone was coming up with a dagger — for an action for negligence against a doctor is for him like unto a dagger.

He returned to this theme several years later in *Whitehouse v Jordan [1980]*:

> If [doctors] are to be found liable whenever they do not effect a cure, or whenever anything untoward happens, it [i.e. a negligence claim] would do a great disservice to the profession itself. Not only to the profession but to society at large. Take heed of what has happened in the United States. 'Medical malpractice' cases there are very worrying,

especially as they are tried by juries who have sympathy for the patient and none for the doctor, who is insured. The damages are colossal... In the interests of all, we must avoid such consequences in England (at 658).

Thus, Lord Denning considered that the public interest was best served by protecting doctors from litigation, for the alternative might result in the practice of 'defensive medicine'. Moreover, he was concerned that an opening of the floodgates to litigation would produce a situation to rival that of the USA. Some have argued that the evidence to support this 'nightmare scenario' is unconvincing and is only anecdotal in nature (Jones, 1991). Nevertheless, notwithstanding the strengths or weaknesses of these arguments, it should be clear that if these considerations act as a powerful force inhibiting successful litigation, then they must apply to *all* healthcare professionals. There is, for example, no reason to suspect that nurses would be more vulnerable than doctors, for they form the largest single working group within the National Health Service. An attack on them would represent an attack on a public institution just as much as if the courts decided to allow an increasing number of successful claims against doctors.

While this might suggest that nurses and allied healthcare professionals are as protected by the law as doctors, it should not be forgotten that the courts are often called upon to effect a delicate balancing act. A secure and stable Health Service might well be in the best interests of the general public (even if this means sacrificing the individual interests of a few); but it is not in the public interest for negligent healthcare professionals to continue to practise without censure. As Rougier, J. said in *Barker v Nugent [1987]*:

I can think of only one thing more disastrous than the escalation of defensive medicine and that is the engendering of a belief in the medical profession that certain acts or omissions which would otherwise be classed as negligence can, in a sense, be exonerated.

The outcome of a case, therefore, will continue to rest upon the presentation of the evidence, and the importance of public policy considerations should not be over-estimated.

C THE COURTS FEEL THAT THE MEDICAL PROFESSION IS OWED A SPECIAL DEFERENCE

This is the most contentious of the possible reasons and is impossible to prove. Nevertheless, in an earlier edition, Montgomery (1997) felt that there was sufficient evidence to raise the suspicion, and cited Farquharson, L. J. (a Court of Appeal judge in the case of *Bolitho v City & Hackney Health Authority [1993]*), who appeared to accept the medical evidence because of the *status* and *credibility* of the witnesses, rather than an assessment of the reasonableness of the content of their views. If there is any substance to this assertion, it would seem unlikely that a nurse or allied health professional would enjoy the same protection, and that s/he would find it more difficult to gain acceptance of his/her views.

That the courts are aware of this criticism levelled at their practice can be seen in a paper written by Lord Woolf (the Lord Chief Justice, as he then was) in 2001 (Woolf, 2001). In this paper, he accepts that the charge has been a fair one in the past, but that times have changed and the courts are slowly changing with them. The reasons cited for this change include, among others, the recognition of the difficulties for claimants in winning cases (and the inherent injustice that this produces), an increasing awareness of patients' rights, and the fact that the general public no longer feel quite the same reverence for the medical profession (particularly as the reputation of the profession itself has been damaged in a series of scandals). Only time will tell if Lord Woolf's optimism for the prospects of future claimants is well-founded; but, on the assumption that it is, its effects will be to *reduce* medical protection rather than *increase* that of nurses and allied health professionals.

Having outlined some of the possible reasons for the predominance of *Bolam*, it is now necessary to trace its evolution over the years. We have noted that the case was heard in 1957, but its decision could not be considered a binding principle of common law until it had been accepted by a higher court. This did not happen until 24 years later in the case of *Whitehouse v Jordan [1981]*. In the years that followed, *Bolam* took on a life of its own, and the courts adopted an increasingly passive approach to its implementation. Examples of this can be seen in the following two cases:

Box 3.9   *Maynard v West Midlands RHA [1985]*

The claimant had symptoms suggestive of tuberculosis, but there were suspicions that she might have Hodgkin's disease. The doctors sought to eliminate the latter as a possible diagnosis by performing a mediastinoscopy. However, the claimant's vocal cords were damaged during this procedure, and it transpired that she had tuberculosis.

Her argument in court was that her injuries were sustained as the result of an unnecessary procedure, and she was able to produce expert witnesses who concurred with this opinion. The defendants, however, produced their own experts who argued that the doctors were perfectly justified in ensuring that the patient did not have Hodgkin's disease. Faced with this conflict of opinion, the judge in the High Court decided that he was more impressed by the testimony of the claimant's experts, but his decision was overturned by both the Court of Appeal and the House of Lords. In a much-quoted passage, Lord Scarman said:

I have to say that a judge's 'preference' for one body of distinguished professional opinion to another also professionally distinguished is not sufficient to establish negligence in a practitioner whose actions have received the seal of approval of those whose opinions, truthfully expressed, honestly held, were not preferred... For in the realm of diagnosis and treatment, negligence is not established by preferring one respectable body of professional opinion to another (at 639).

In other words, it was not the strength of the testimony that was important, but rather the fact that one body of medical opinion supported the defendant's actions. This is seen even more graphically in the next case:

Box 3.10   *De Freitas v O'Brien [1993]*

The claimant complained of severe back pain, which adversely affected her mobility. The defendant undertook exploratory surgery of her spine, during which her cerebro-spinal fluid became infected.

Her argument, confirmed by experts, was that this was unnecessarily hazardous surgery, and that it should not be performed unless a definite diagnosis was present. The defendant's experts, however, said that the risks associated with this procedure were acceptable, provided that it was performed by those with the appropriate expertise. Not surprisingly, the court adopted the approach taken in *Maynard* and found for the defendants. The remarkable thing about this case, however, is that the defendant's experts constituted a tiny minority of opinion: they represented just four or five neurosurgeons (out of a population of 250) who dealt exclusively with the spine. If the courts were ever going to prefer one body of medical opinion to another, this would have been their opportunity; but they held that these four or five specialists were sufficient to constitute a respectable body. Newdick (2005) suggests that statistical evidence from such a small group cannot be considered reliable, and argues that the courts should have been more willing to challenge them. That they did not is a clear illustration of how passively they were prepared to accept medical evidence at this time.

There are other cases relating to consent which emphasise this point further, but which will be reserved for the next chapter. The important thing to take away from these cases is that they represent the 'high point' of *Bolam* (or 'low point', if you prefer). The passivity of the courts' approach to medical decisions could not survive for long in an age that increasingly emphasised the equality of individual rights. The bubble eventually burst in the following case:

Box 3.11   *Bolitho v City & Hackney Health Authority [1998]*

A two-year-old boy was admitted to hospital with respiratory difficulties. His condition subsequently deteriorated and the nurse called the doctor, but the latter did not attend. The child eventually went into cardiac and respiratory arrest; and, although he was resuscitated, he suffered severe brain damage and died a few years later.

The doctor admitted negligence in failing to attend the patient, but she argued that she would not have intubated him at this point in any case, for the procedure carried too many risks in a child of this age. Expert opinion differed, and, true to the spirit of *Maynard,* the court found in favour of the defendant. On the face of it, therefore, this case is just one more in a long line of cases protecting the medical profession. However, its primary significance is the speech by Lord Browne-Wilkinson, who stated:

> [I]n my view, the court is not bound to hold that a defendant doctor escapes liability for negligent treatment or diagnosis just because he leads evidence from a number of medical experts who are genuinely of opinion that the defendant's treatment or diagnosis accorded with sound medical practice... If, in a rare case, it can be demonstrated that the professional opinion is not capable of withstanding logical analysis, the judge is entitled to hold that the body of opinion is not reasonable or responsible (at 243).

What this means, in effect, is that the courts are reclaiming their power to make decisions in healthcare cases. Therefore, it is no longer sufficient for an expert witness to claim simply that s/he would have done exactly the same as the defendant in similar circumstances. His/her testimony must stand up to logical scrutiny; and, if it does not, the court is entitled to reject it.

This judgment has led a number of leading commentators to suggest that the back of *Bolam* has been broken (Grubb, 1998; Brazier and Miola, 2000), but they too acknowledge that *Bolitho* will not open the floodgates of medical litigation. For one thing, it will be 'a rare case' when a court decides to reject medical testimony, and it will only occur when that testimony is patently 'not reasonable or responsible'. Lord Browne-Wilkinson felt unable to hold that this was the case in *Bolitho,* and he was unable to envisage many situations when it would hold true.

Despite this, however, the judgment represents a significant change in philosophy and offers increasing hope to claimants. Evidence that the courts are prepared to take a more proactive approach when interpreting medical testimony can be detected in the following cases:

1   *Marriott v West Midlands Health Authority [1999]:* the claimant fell and sustained head injuries. The hospital discharged him, but he remained unwell and the GP visited eight days later. The GP prescribed painkillers, but the claimant collapsed four days later. At the hospital, it was discovered that he had a fractured skull and an extradural haematoma, which left him paralysed. At the trial, there was a conflict of opinion between the experts on each side, but the judge held that the GP had failed to satisfy an appropriate standard of care. This decision was subsequently upheld by the Court of Appeal.

2   *Reynolds v North Tyneside Health Authority [2002]:* a woman had not been examined properly during childbirth, resulting in asphyxiation of her baby and subsequent cerebral palsy. The judge found for the claimant, and, in a clear application of *Bolitho,* stated: 'Where the sole reason relied upon in support of a practice is untenable, it follows...that the practice itself is not defensible and lacks a proper basis' (per Gross, J.).

3   *Lillywhite and another v University College London Hospitals NHS Trust [2005]*: a pregnant
    woman underwent a series of ultrasound scans by three experienced doctors (including
    a Professor of Obstetrics and Gynaecology, and a radiologist). All three failed to identify
    foetal malformation of the brain, and the claimants sued the Trust. The High Court judge
    refused to find negligence, holding that it was not unreasonable to miss this diagnosis
    in the circumstances. The Court of Appeal, however, reversed the decision, stating that
    the defendants had not offered plausible explanations for failing to identify the abnor-
    mality. (See also *Conway and another v Cardiff & Vale NHS Trust [2004]* for a similar case,
    with the same result.)

4   *Manning v King's College Hospital NHS Trust [2008]*: a young woman was diagnosed with
    tongue cancer and was treated with radiotherapy. In the following years, she had several
    biopsies, but the pathologist said that they were all negative. She subsequently had a recur-
    rence of her cancer, necessitating the complete removal of her tongue, and she later died.
    At the trial, the judge found in favour of the woman's husband, for (despite some evidence
    to the contrary) the pathologist had not acted in a 'reasonably competent' manner.

There have been other cases where the courts have rejected medical opinion, but it
would be mistaken to think that this is now a common feature of healthcare law.
In both *A v Burne [2006]* and *Wisniewski v Central Manchester Health Authority
[1998]*, the High Court judges' confidence in rejecting medical testimony was held
to be misplaced by the Court of Appeal. In the latter case, especially, it has been
noted that the court will be impressed by the eminence of the expert witness
(Brazier and Cave, 2007). As Brook, L.J. stated: 'It is quite impossible for a court
to hold that the views sincerely held by doctors of such eminence cannot logically
be supported at all' (at 237).

Therefore, we have seen that the first element of negligence is usually a relatively
simple obstacle for the claimant to overcome, but that the second element can pose
a number of difficulties. On the assumption that s/he manages to get this far, there is
one more hurdle to jump – that of causation.

4 CAUSATION

When considering this third arm of negligence, there are three sub-elements that all
need to be satisfied. First, harm must be caused. Compensation is awarded for damage
caused and endeavours to be commensurate with the degree of harm. Consequently,
if there is no damage, then there is nothing to compensate. An example of this would
be if a patient received the wrong drug: he would be able to satisfy the first two elements of negligence (duty of care and standard of care), but would only be able to
secure compensation for this error if he could show that the drug had caused him
harm. Similarly, you will recall the case of *Donoghue v Stevenson [1932]* mentioned
earlier in this chapter: if the ginger beer had come in a clear bottle, the claimant would
have been able to see the decomposing snail before she consumed the drink. In such
circumstances, the most that she would have been able to hope for is an apology and
another bottle of ginger beer.

Second, any harm caused must be 'reasonably foreseeable'. A classic illustration of this principle in practice can be seen in the following case:

Box 3.12   *Roe v Minister of Health [1954]*

A patient underwent surgery for a repair of a hydrocoele and he was given a spinal anaesthetic. He subsequently became paraplegic and sued for damages.

The defence offered by the anaesthetist (and accepted by the court) was that the glass ampoules of cinchocaine (i.e. the anaesthetic) had been stored in phenol. There had presumably been some mishandling of these ampoules during transport and the ampoules sustained invisible cracks, through which the phenol seeped. The fact that these cracks were 'invisible' meant, by definition, that they could not be seen. Logically, therefore, if they could not be seen, nobody could have known that they were there. Despite the devastating consequences for the patient, he could not win this case, because the harm was not 'reasonably foreseeable'. Bear in mind that the burden of proof rests with the claimant, and he must establish all the elements of negligence to win the case. If it fails on one of these elements, or even on *one part* of an element, the case is dismissed.

As a matter of interest, some evidence came to light many years later, suggesting that this case had been wrongly decided (Maltby et al., 2000). The 'cracks' were never more than just a theory, and were never conclusively proven. Even if they had existed, it is doubtful that enough phenol would have seeped through to cause the paralysis. However, this was the only evidence produced before the court, and therefore, the only evidence that it could rule upon. A more plausible explanation is that, at the time, needles, syringes and surgical instruments would all be boiled before use in a sterilising water boiler. We know now that this was not true sterilisation, but it was the best that could be achieved at the time. However, when there is boiling water, it is inevitable that there will be a build-up of limescale (as in a kettle). Periodically, therefore, an acidic descaler would be inserted into the boiler; having been left there for a while, it would then have been drained off and the machine would have been flushed out with water before it could be used again.

What appears to have happened is that somebody forgot to drain off the descaling agent, with the result that the needles, syringes and instruments were all boiled up in this, rather than just water. This, it is contended, would have been sufficient to cause the paralysis. Further evidence to support this claim emerged when it was discovered that the person who was responsible for maintaining the boiler (the theatre sister) was unwell on this day – she had violent headaches and vomiting, and subsequently underwent surgery for the removal of a pituitary tumour.

Had this evidence been given in court, one would have to say that all three elements of negligence have been satisfied. Anybody in theatres at the time would have known that the descaling agent must be drained off before the boiler is re-used to sterilise instruments. The harm caused here, therefore, is unquestionably foreseeable. Nevertheless, notwithstanding the fact that this case may have been wrongly decided, it serves as an illustration of the principle that there must be foreseeability of harm.

It is important to note here that this defence can usually be used only once, for, when an incident occurs, it automatically becomes foreseeable for all future generations. Thus, one is unlikely to see glass ampoules stored in phenol any more. Having said this, the courts will acknowledge that new information generally needs a little time to permeate through the profession. For example, in *Crawford v Board of Governors of Charing Cross Hospital [1953]*, a patient sustained brachial palsy as a result of his arm being extended for a long time during an operation. This risk had been identified in an article in *The Lancet* six months earlier, but the court held that it would be unreasonable to expect practitioners to read every article in the healthcare press. Generally speaking, it often appears that the most effective way of disseminating information is by means of a court case! It therefore requires an unfortunate patient to have suffered debilitating injuries and a healthcare professional standing before a court to justify his/her actions or inactions. This may seem a little cynical, but it is by far the most efficient method of getting people to sit up and take notice. It should not be forgotten that many of the advances in healthcare have been at the expense of a series of victims.

The third and final sub-element in causation is that any harm caused must flow as a direct result of a breach in the standard of care. To illustrate this, consider the following case:

Box 3.13   *Barnett v Chelsea & Kensington HMC [1968]*

Three night-watchmen attended Casualty with abdominal pain, having drunk tea unknowingly contaminated with arsenic. The nurse called the doctor, but the latter was unwell himself and sent a message to ask the men to contact their GPs. One of them (Mr Barnett) subsequently died a few hours later, and his widow sued the hospital.

If we analyse this case according to the three elements of negligence, the first question we must ask is: 'Was a duty of care owed to this man?' Our answer must be in the affirmative, because a duty of care is owed to *anybody* who comes through the Casualty doors. The only way to avoid this duty is either to close the doors, or to put a sign outside stating that the hospital does not accept emergencies (Kennedy and Grubb, 1994).

The second question to ask is: 'Did the doctor breach a reasonable standard of care expected of him by deciding not to examine this man?' Once again, we must answer in the affirmative, for the reasonable practitioner in the same or similar circumstances would have seen these patients. His reason for not examining the men was that he too was unwell, although the fact that this incident happened on the morning of January 1st led some to suspect the nature of this illness. In fairness, the doctor strenuously denied that he had been drinking; but, even allowing for the fact that his illness was not self-inflicted, he had a duty to ensure that all the patients coming into Casualty were appropriately seen and treated (even if this meant arranging cover for his shift). The fact that he did not do so meant that he had fallen below an acceptable standard of care expected of someone in his position.

Thus, we have now jumped two hurdles and there is only one more to clear before compensation is awarded. The third question to ask is: 'Did the fact that the doctor failed to examine the patient inevitably mean that the latter was destined to die?' To answer this, we must try to imagine that the doctor is on top form and that he sees the patients as soon as they come through the Casualty doors. Clearly, he is unaware at this stage that the patients have ingested arsenic, for even they did not know this. Therefore, he would have had to arrange a series of tests and investigations to establish the cause of the vomiting before he could administer the appropriate antidote. The earliest that he could have known the results of these tests would have been 2 p.m., by which time Mr. Barnett had already died.

What we have here, therefore, is what is known as a break in the chain of causation. Although there has been a breach in the standard of care, and although the patient has come to harm, these two facts are not intimately related; because, even if there had been *no* breach, the patient would still have died. This case is commonly cited as a classic illustration of the 'but for' test: in other words, *but for* the defendant's negligence, would the claimant have come to harm? Unfortunately for Mr Barnett's widow, the answer to this question was in the negative. The doctor's negligence did not cause the harm, because the patient's death was inevitable.

Despite the ease with which the decision in this case is accepted by many texts, it nevertheless leaves one with an uncomfortable feeling. Certainly, the doctor could not have been expected to diagnose arsenic poisoning quickly, but it is conceivable that Mr Barnett might have been kept alive for longer if he had received appropriate monitoring and supervision. For example, hospitalisation would have helped to ensure that side-effects could be managed; and this might have given him sufficient time to survive until the diagnosis had been confirmed. The case also graphically illustrates the dangers of making assumptions: if a patient comes in on the morning of January 1st complaining of vomiting, the automatic response is to assume that he has been over-indulgent with alcohol. There is clear evidence that both the Casualty nurse and doctor made this very assumption and that they were not prepared to consider other possibilities. They made a mistake, but a legal loophole allowed them to escape without punishment. Other practitioners who make diagnoses in the absence of empirical evidence may not be so lucky.

Notwithstanding the dissatisfaction that the *Barnett* case may engender, the 'but for' test is clearly an important element of the law of negligence. It would unquestionably be unfair to hold healthcare professionals liable for the harm experienced by a patient if there was nothing that they could have done to avoid that harm. Before we imagine that this is an insuperable obstacle for a claimant to overcome, however, the following two cases suggest otherwise:

Box 3.14 *Rhodes-Hampton v Worthing & Southlands Hospital NHS Trust [2007]*

The claimant, a midwife, sustained injuries from an aggressive patient who was emerging from anaesthetic after an emergency Caesarean section. The court held that the Trust had a duty to arrange for more staff to help in such circumstances and/or to fit cot sides: *but for* this failure to act, the claimant would not have been injured.

Box 3.15 *Oakes v Neininger & others [2008]*

The claimant sought medical attention for back pain, which eventually developed into cauda equina syndrome. He eventually had an operation, but the effects of the cauda equina syndrome were irreversible, leaving him with poor balance, impaired walking, faecal and urinary incontinence, and erectile dysfunction. The court held that the doctor could not be held responsible for the development of cauda equina syndrome, but his delay in making a diagnosis meant that the patient was left with irreversible injuries: *but for* this delay, the patient would have made a full recovery.

The 'but for' test becomes slightly more complicated when negligence can reduce or eliminate a claimant's chances of recovery. Consider the following case:

Box 3.16 *Hotson v East Berkshire AHA [1987]*

A 13-year-old boy fell out of a tree and injured his hip. He was taken to hospital, but his injuries were not properly diagnosed, and he went on to develop avascular necrosis of the epiphysis. This entailed that he was left with a permanent degree of disability and a virtual certainty that he would go on to develop osteo-arthritis in later life.

His argument in court was that he would have had a 25 per cent chance of a full recovery if he had been properly diagnosed when first seen at the hospital. This was accepted by the High Court judge, who awarded him 25 per cent of the damages. The decision, however, was subsequently overturned by the House of Lords. If the claimant was to be successful, he would have to show that, *but for* the defendant's negligence, he would have had at least a 51 per cent chance of recovery (i.e. he would have tilted the balance of probabilities in his favour); *or* that he was among the 25 per cent who would have recovered. If he had been able to prove either of these two possibilities, he would have been awarded 100 per cent of the damages.

This principle was re-affirmed in *Gregg v Scott [2005]*, where the loss of chance was even higher:

Box 3.17   *Gregg v Scott [2005]*

The claimant went to his doctor complaining of a lump under his arm. The doctor initially diagnosed it as being benign, but it was later discovered to be cancerous. Mr Gregg therefore had to undergo chemotherapy, and his chances of surviving more than 10 years had now been reduced from 42 per cent to 25 per cent.

The majority of the House of Lords (3:2) held that the rule in *Hotson* must apply to this case, for the alternative would introduce confusion to the law. A minority, however, felt that a 42 per cent chance of recovery was significant and that Mr Gregg should be allowed to recover damages. This suggests that, if a 25 per cent chance was not significant (in *Hotson*), but a 42 per cent chance was (in *Gregg*), there must be a cut-off point some way between these two figures. Their Lordships did not venture to suggest what this figure would be, and the fact that their opinions were in the minority meant that they did not have to. Nevertheless, one senses within this case a subtle change in philosophy that is becoming more patient-friendly.

One such illustration of this can be seen in the following case:

Box 3.18   *Bailey v The Ministry of Defence and another [2008]*

The claimant underwent an ERCP (endoscopic retrograde cholangio-pancreatography), which caused heavy bleeding. However, her fluid replacement was inadequate, as a result of which she had to undergo a further three procedures. She subsequently developed pancreatitis, inhaled her vomit, had a cardiac arrest, and was left with permanent brain damage.

The court acknowledged that the development of pancreatitis was not the fault of the defendant, and that this could have been the cause of the cardiac arrest. However, the court was also convinced that the defendant's negligence in failing to provide adequate fluids after the first procedure made a *material contribution* to the patient's weakness, thereby increasing the chances of a cardiac arrest. Thus, there are two possible causes of this catastrophe (one negligent, one non-negligent), but the court is not addressing itself to which is the most important; it is simply stating that *both* contributed to the harm, and the patient should therefore recover damages.

If this case leads one to suspect that the law has undergone a fundamental change, we should bear in mind that it is possible to distinguish *Bailey* from *Hotson* and

Gregg (Turton, 2009). In the latter two cases, the defendants did not introduce another source of harm, whereas they did so in *Bailey*. In other words, the defendants did not *cause* the injury to Hotson's leg, nor did they create the malignant lump under Gregg's arm. They did, however, negligently induce a weakened state in Bailey, which rendered her more likely to suffer serious consequences.

We have now analysed all three elements of negligence and discussed their application in a range of different situations. There remain a few loose ends to tie up and a few unanswered questions. One such question is the *nature* of the harm:

A DOES THE HARM HAVE TO BE PHYSICAL, OR CAN IT ALSO BE PSYCHOLOGICAL?

The courts acknowledge that negligence can induce psychological distress and are prepared on occasions to award damages, but they make a distinction between primary victims and secondary victims. Primary victims are those who are directly involved as participants in a shocking event; they may be the patient upon whom a negligent act has been performed, or they may be required to treat those who are the victims of negligence. Secondary victims, on the other hand, tend to be those who become distressed upon learning about negligence performed on another person (most commonly, a close relative). Perhaps the best-known illustration of this principle can be found in the following case:

Box 3.19   *Alcock and others v Chief Constable of South Yorkshire Police [1992]*

During the course of the Hillsborough football disaster in 1989, many of the relatives of the dead and dying victims witnessed the events unfold on TV, listened to the radio, or were later informed of the catastrophe by friends. They brought an action for the psychological distress induced by this episode.

The High Court initially allowed the claim for those relatives who were at the ground or saw the events live on TV, but excluded all other claimants. Both the Court of Appeal and the House of Lords, however, held that *none* should be awarded damages. Why should this be? There was never any doubt that all the claimants suffered psychological harm, and they were all therefore 'victims' in a very real sense. However, whereas a primary victim only needs to show that the harm was reasonably foreseeable, the criteria for secondary victims are much more stringent. In order to win an action, the secondary victim must show that all five of the *Alcock* criteria have been satisfied:

a   The victim was not unduly susceptible to psychiatric illness.
b   The harm occurred through a sudden shock.

c   The victim was in close proximity to the event or its immediate aftermath.
d   The victim had close personal or family ties with the injured person.
e   The victim perceived the event through his/her own unaided senses.

It is conceivable that *some* of the relatives would have satisfied all of these criteria (particularly those who were at the ground), but the court argued that each case would have to be heard individually, rather than as a block. Arguably, the police officers who were present at the disaster, and who suffered subsequent psychological damage, had a stronger case when measured against these criteria *(White v Chief Constable of South Yorkshire Police [1999])*. Their claim too was ultimately dismissed, however, although one Law Lord (Lord Hoffman) felt the necessity to introduce the concept of 'distributive justice' (at 510). By this, he was tacitly acknowledging that the police officers qualified for compensation, but that it would be perceived as unfair if they were successful when the relatives of the deceased had failed.

Some have argued that the court's reluctance to allow claims for psychological damage stem from a fear that the floodgates of litigation will be opened (Brazier and Cave, 2007; Pattinson, 2009). The courts themselves have often strenuously denied this, but the evidence frequently suggests otherwise. For example, in *Sion v Hampstead HA [1994]*, a man stayed by his son's bedside for 14 days, while the latter steadily deteriorated and died as the result of a motorcycle accident. His claim for psychological harm was rejected because his illness did not result from the sudden appreciation of a horrifying event. Chico (2006), however, notes that the shock requirement is not supported by psychiatric opinion, which contends that this is not how mental illness is caused. If it is the accumulation of events over a prolonged period of time that is of more significance in the development of psychiatric illness, the courts would appear to have taken it upon themselves to ignore medical opinion.

Some recognition of the inconsistencies of this approach can be seen in the following case:

Box 3.20   *North Glamorgan NHS Trust v Walters [2002]*

The claimant's 10-month-old son became unwell and he was taken to hospital. It was later discovered that he was suffering from acute hepatitis, which led to liver failure, but there was a delay in this diagnosis. The child subsequently had a seizure one night, but his mother was told that he had suffered no brain damage, and he was transferred to another hospital for a liver transplant. It was at this hospital, however, that it was discovered that he had sustained severe brain damage: the liver transplant was therefore cancelled, the ventilator was switched off, and the baby died.

The mother in this case is a secondary victim, but the court held that she satisfied the *Alcock* criteria because the period of time of these events (36 hours) could be seen as a single unifying episode.

There are other examples where the courts have found for the claimants. In *Briody v St. Helen's & Knowsley HA [2001]*, for example, a woman had to undergo an emergency Caesarean section, her baby was stillborn, and a subtotal hysterectomy was performed. She was awarded £66,000 after the court accepted that these events induced post-traumatic stress disorder. Similarly, in *Froggatt and others v Chesterfield & North Derbyshire Royal Hospital NHS Trust [2002]*, the husband and son of a woman who had been mistakenly diagnosed with breast cancer (and who subsequently had a mastectomy) were awarded compensation as secondary victims: they had proximity to the primary victim, they experienced a sudden shock, and they developed psychiatric illness as a result.

This last case has been perceived as exceptionally generous in the light of earlier cases (Brazier and Cave, 2007; Herring, 2008; Jackson, 2010), and some might argue that it suggests a more claimant-friendly approach by the courts. Others, however, would argue that it is an illustration of the confusion and arbitrariness of this aspect of the law (Pattinson, 2009). If we are to look for consistency, there are probably two facts that stand out. First, the cases in which claimants win actions for psychological damage are rare. Thus, when they occur, they cause a lot of excitement within the legal profession and tend to be widely publicised. Second, the claimant has to be able to show that s/he has suffered *real* psychological damage, requiring ongoing treatment. In the *Walters* case, for example, the victim suffered from insomnia, anorexia, alcohol abuse, suicidal feelings, flashbacks and relationship problems with her partner, and needed to be prescribed tranquillisers. In short, she had a diagnosable psychiatric condition that was a direct result of the negligence of the defendant hospital, and she had no difficulty in supplying an expert witness in court who would testify to that fact.

B IS POOR COMMUNICATION ACTIONABLE IN NEGLIGENCE?

Box 3.21   *Coles v Reading & District HMC [1963]*

A young man crushed his finger when a lump of coal fell on him. He went to the cottage hospital and a nurse dressed the wound, but she did not explain about the need for a tetanus injection. Subsequently, he went to his GP, but the latter simply re-dressed the wound and made no mention of the injection. The patient later died of tetanus.

This action, brought by the young man's father, was successful, because it was clearly shown that there had been a complete breakdown in communication all the way along the line. Certainly, the nurse was implicated in this episode, and so too was the GP. As the judge who presided over this case stated: 'Any system which failed to provide for effective communication was wrong and negligently wrong'.

Thus, communication can be actionable in negligence if it falls below an acceptable standard of care. Another example of poor communication can be seen in *Prendergast v Sam & Dee Ltd. [1989]* (discussed below), but the *Coles* case raises a couple of interesting points. First, it is not entirely certain that the nurse failed to explain the importance of a tetanus injection. Perhaps she did and the patient either failed to absorb the information or chose to ignore it. The burden of proof falls upon the claimant, and it is generally his/her word against that of a healthcare professional. One would expect the latter to win on most occasions, but these days it is acknowledged that verbal information alone is insufficient, for it tends to be poorly retained (Calkins et al., 1997; Kitching, 1990). This is not because patients are unintelligent, but simply because they are in a stressful environment and situation, and it can be very difficult to absorb information in such circumstances. Therefore, it needs to be supplemented with written information: opinions vary as to the appropriate reading age that the information should be aimed at, some arguing for nine (Griffin and Griffin, 1996), while others suggest that twelve is the most suitable (Albert and Chadwick, 1992). All agree, though, that the information should be simple to understand, clearly written and unambiguous.

If a patient came into Casualty with a head injury, they too should be discharged with written information, but this should be handed to somebody who is going to be caring for them. The same principle will apply if the patient is a child, has learning disabilities or dementia, is blind, or is illiterate. This is what the reasonable practitioner would do, and anything less must be construed as negligence.

The second point to make about *Coles* concerns the concept of *contributory negligence*. Let us assume, for argument's sake, that the patient *was* told to get a tetanus injection, but he failed to act on this information. Would that make him responsible for his own injuries? For the reasons stated above, it would not have been a factor in this case, but claimants are expected to mitigate their losses as much as possible. For example, if a nurse bandages a patient's leg too tightly, the patient would be expected to seek medical attention before his/her leg went gangrenous. If s/he had dementia, however, it would not be reasonable to expect him/her to do this. Where the concept of contributory negligence applies, the claimant still receives compensation, but his/her award will be reduced depending upon how much s/he could have prevented the worst of his/her injuries (Law Reform [Contributory Negligence] Act 1945, section 1). An example of this can be seen in the following case:

Box 3.22 *Egan v Central Manchester & Manchester Children's University Hospitals NHS Trust [2008]*

A nurse was using a mechanical hoist to transfer a patient into the bath, but the hoist's wheels jammed, and she was injured as a result.

The Trust had not carried out a risk assessment on this piece of equipment, and was therefore in breach of the positive duty imposed upon it by the Manual Handling Operations Regulations (SI 1992, No. 2793) and the Work Equipment Regulations (SI 1998, No. 2306). However, the court held the accident could also have been avoided if the claimant had taken proper care too. Because the court was unable to distinguish the blame-worthiness of each party, the claimant was awarded 50 per cent of the damages.

C CAN A TEAM BE HELD COLLECTIVELY LIABLE FOR A NEGLIGENT ACT?

Box 3.23   *Wilsher v Essex AHA [1988]*

A baby was born three months prematurely and was treated in the Special Care Baby Unit. Because the lungs have not fully developed in a child born this early, it is necessary to monitor the arterial level of oxygen in the blood; and this is done by means of cannulating the umbilical artery and then connecting it to a pulse oximeter. Unfortunately, the doctor cannulated the vein rather than the artery, but failed to see his mistake. The oximetry reading was inevitably low, because it was the *venous* level of blood that was being monitored. Believing it to be the arterial level, however, the child was then exposed to high levels of oxygen. He subsequently developed retrolental fibroplasia, resulting in near-blindness.

The novel argument raised by the defence can be paraphrased thus: 'We are a multi-disciplinary team and we all function together as a cohesive unit. Therefore, if one member of the team makes a mistake, we feel that the whole team should accept collective responsibility for it.' This 'all-for-one, one-for-all' approach found little favour with the court, however, for it was felt that it would be extremely unfair if a junior staff nurse should be expected to take his/her share of the blame for the mistakes of a senior Consultant.

Thus, the concept of *team liability* (or collective liability) was born and died in the same case, and the courts generally prefer to focus on the individual responsible for the error. There is, however, a concept known as *joint and several liability*, where more than one person can be called to account, depending upon their part in the negligent act. An example of this is illustrated in the following case:

Box 3.24   *Prendergast v Sam & Dee Ltd. [1989]*

A GP wrote a prescription for Amoxil (an antibiotic), but his handwriting was illegible and the pharmacist assumed that it was Daonil (a hypoglycaemic agent given in diabetes). The patient duly took these Daonil tablets three times a day, went into a hypoglycaemic coma, and suffered irreversible brain damage.

This case did not come before the court to establish negligence, because this was obvious: the patient was certain to be compensated for this error. The question before the court was: Who pays? Should it be the doctor for writing an illegible prescription, or should it be the pharmacist for dispensing the wrong drug? The answer, of course, is that both were held liable, although the pharmacist was considered to be more to blame, for there were other signs that should have alerted him to the possibility of an incorrect prescription. His proportion of the costs, therefore, was put at 75 per cent, compared to the GP's 25 per cent. It is reasonable to assume that this case would have provided a strong stimulus to the introduction of computerised prescribing within the community, thereby eliminating illegible handwriting as a possible source of error.

Returning to the *Wilsher* case, there was another defence raised by the Trust:

D IS INEXPERIENCE AN EXCUSE FOR NEGLIGENCE?

The doctor who put the cannula in the vein rather than an artery was a Senior House Officer and had only been on the unit a couple of weeks when this incident happened. His argument was that he had not had the time or opportunity to develop all the skills necessary to function as a fully competent professional, and therefore, some allowances should be made for his lack of experience. On the face of it, this argument has a certain appeal, but it was fairly swiftly rejected by the court. The reason for its rejection was that every patient has the right to a reasonable standard of care, regardless of who is giving that care. Therefore, one is not judged by the level of experience, but by the task that one is performing. If a healthcare professional takes on a new skill, s/he is expected to conform to a reasonable standard the very first time that it is performed. The best way of avoiding liability in these circumstances, of course, is to ask a senior colleague to check one's work, and this is precisely what the junior doctor did in *Wilsher*. The registrar, unfortunately, made exactly the same mistake.

The precedent for inexperience not being a defence came from a case completely unrelated to the practice of healthcare:

Box 3.25   *Nettleship v Weston [1971]*

Mrs Weston asked a friend of hers (Mr Nettleship) to give her driving lessons. On one of these lessons, however, she became gripped by a panic attack: she mounted the kerb, hit a lamp-post, and eventually ground to a halt. Mr Nettleship sustained a fractured patella during this episode and sued for damages.

Her argument in court can be paraphrased thus: 'I am a learner driver. By definition, therefore, I am not competent to drive. In consequence, you cannot expect the same level of driving ability from me as from somebody who has passed their test and had years of experience on the roads.' Once again, this is not a totally unreasonable argument, and it was certainly enough to convince the High Court judge and one of the judges in the Court of Appeal. The majority opinion in the Court of Appeal, however, was that anybody who gets behind the wheel of a car is expected to exercise a certain amount of caution. By extension, too, we might add that the general public should feel able to walk along the pavement without cars coming careering towards them!

Thus, we have seen that the defence arguments in *Wilsher* of team liability and inexperience were both destined to fail. Ultimately, however, the claimant was unable to win the case because it failed on an issue of causation. Although it is known that too much oxygen can cause retrolental fibroplasia, the same condition can be caused by a number of other factors associated with prematurity. Remember that the burden of proof rests with the claimant, and s/he must prove his/her case on the balance of probabilities. Clearly, there has been a serious mistake here, and it is equally evident that the child has come to harm. It is not entirely clear, however, that the harm has been caused by the negligence. Although the House of Lords ordered a re-trial (because this issue of causation had not been discussed in the earlier trials), the two parties eventually reached an out-of-court settlement.

5 CRIMINAL NEGLIGENCE

For negligence to tip out of the civil law and into the criminal law, a patient inevitably has to die, and the conduct of the healthcare professional has to be so bad that it made a significant contribution to this death (gross negligence manslaughter). Bear in mind that there is no *intention* to cause harm here (in which case the crime would be that of murder); it is simply that the actions of the healthcare professional have made this harm a likely eventuality. If, for example, I drive my car down the High Street at 80 mph, I would not necessarily have it in mind to kill anybody, but this reckless behaviour has made it a distinct possibility.

It has been noted that the number of prosecutions against doctors for manslaughter has shown an increase in recent years (Ferner and McDowell, 2006), although not many are successful. An example of one such successful action can be seen in the following case:

Box 3.26   *R v Adomako [1995]*

An endotracheal tube became disconnected from a patient during the course of an operation, which meant that he was starved of oxygen. Although an alarm sounded, the anaesthetist failed to acknowledge it (and there was some suspicion that he was actually out of the Theatre at the time). The patient had a cardiac arrest and died.

The Court of Appeal endeavoured to clarify when criminal negligence applied *(R v Adomako [1994])*, and gave four examples:

1   Where the healthcare professional is indifferent to an obvious risk of injury to his patient.
2   Where the healthcare professional recklessly decides to run a risk.
3   Where the healthcare professional's attempts to avoid a risk are particularly poor.
4   Where the healthcare professional displays no effort to avert a serious risk.

Adomako clearly failed at least one or two of these tests, and the case has since been applied in a number of other instances (e.g. *R v Misra [2004]*). As mentioned earlier, however, successful actions against doctors for manslaughter are rare, for the courts are mindful that the nature of medicine compels it to be an error-ridden activity and that it would seem overly harsh to punish those whose primary intention is to serve the public. One such illustration of this can be found in the following case:

Box 3.27   *R v Prentice [1993]*

A 16-year-old boy was being treated for leukaemia and required the administration of two drugs: Vincristine (which was to be given intravenously) and Methotrexate (which was to be given intrathecally). Unfortunately, both were given intrathecally and the patient died.

The Crown Court initially convicted the two doctors responsible for this error, but the conviction was subsequently overturned in the Court of Appeal. The rationale for the latter's decision was that the jury had not been advised to consider mitigating circumstances that may have contributed to the error (e.g. a lack of supervision). If this fails to convince, however, there is another possible line of defence: the patient in this case was already seriously ill and had a life-threatening illness. Therefore, it might be difficult to prove beyond all reasonable doubt that it was the drug which killed him rather than the disease.

The same incident, involving the same drugs, has occurred on a number of occasions since (DH, 2008), but the Crown Prosecution Service has desisted from bringing an action because it recognises the difficulties of obtaining a conviction. Moreover, the fact that this incident is recurrent suggests that there is a *system failure*, and that individuals should not be called to account in these circumstances (see Chapter 9).

6 VICARIOUS LIABILITY

The good news for healthcare professionals is that a claimant is unlikely to sue the individual allegedly responsible for his injuries, but will instead sue the employing authority. It is said that we exist in a master–servant relationship: our employer is our master and we are its servants, and the master takes responsibility for the actions of its servants. This clearly has benefits for claimants, because they will be keen to sue those who have got the money; the chances of recovering substantial compensation from any individual practitioner are going to be extremely limited.

However, if a healthcare professional is found to be negligent, s/he will be in breach of contract. The employer is therefore empowered to take disciplinary action against the employee, which may result in dismissal, depending upon the severity of the offence. It is also technically possible for the employer to try and recover some of the damages paid out in compensation from the negligent employee; although this has never been done, and the NHS has stated that it has no intention of doing so in the future (NHS Executive, 1996).

In addition, the NHS Trust may be *directly* liable if it can be shown that it has created a system where mistakes are inevitable. There are one or two cases that have touched upon this concept, perhaps the most notable being the following:

Box 3.28   *Bull v Devon AHA [1993]*

Mrs Bull was pregnant with twins and went into labour, but she experienced difficulties with the birth of her second child. Medical assistance was summoned, but the medical services operated across two sites (one mile apart), and there was a delay before the doctor could attend. As a result, the child was deprived of oxygen, and sustained severe brain damage.

The court was convinced that it was the system, rather than any individual's negligence, that was to blame for this tragedy, and accordingly held the hospital to be directly liable. Such cases are rare, however, and the courts are generally reluctant to tell health authorities how to manage their Trusts. This is an issue to which we will return when discussing judicial review (Chapter 6).

7 PRINCIPLES OF COMPENSATION

The purpose of compensation is restorative, rather than punitive. In other words, it is not intended to punish the individual or organisation responsible for the negligence, but is instead intended to put the victim back into the position s/he occupied before the incident. Clearly, a patient left completely paralysed by a medical error will never return to his/her former position, but compensation can help to ensure that s/he enjoys as reasonable a quality of life as possible. Thus, this will probably require a complete refurbishment of his/her house and s/he may require 24-hour nursing care.

In addition to these costs, the patient will be able to claim for any loss of earnings (both currently and in the future), and for loss of amenity. If, for example, his favourite hobby was playing rugby on a Saturday afternoon, he will be able to claim more than somebody who has similar injuries but who rarely engaged in physical activity of any kind. At this point, the quantification of damages becomes notoriously arbitrary and susceptible to the charge of injustice. Whereas the courts have made an effort to be equitable by imposing a tariff to determine the value of a limb or organ (Kemp, 1994), it becomes much more difficult to estimate any pain or suffering experienced by the victim. In cases of bereavement, the figure to compensate for grief is set by the Fatal Accidents Act 1976 and is currently £11,800 (as of January 2008), and no attempt is made to distinguish between different cases. Consider, for example, the recently bereaved widow who is totally devastated by the loss of her life-partner, and compare her with a woman in a similar position who has been released from a violent and abusive relationship. Both will receive the same money, even though the second woman may have cause to be grateful for the hospital's negligence.

It is unfair to expect the court to make these kinds of calculations, for they can never be accurate. There are, though, certain elements that remain constant. First, the greater the level of disability, the higher the award will be. Second, the longer the patient has to live with his/her injuries, the greater the sum of compensation to be agreed. With these two principles in mind, it quickly becomes obvious that the higher awards (running into seven-figure sums) will be given to children who have been left severely and permanently disabled as the result of medical negligence.

This raises the further thorny issue of determining how long a patient is likely to live. At best, this can only be a rough estimate and will almost certainly be inaccurate. It became an issue in the case of Hollie Calladine (Dyer, 1997), who was born with brain damage as the result of an anaesthetist's error. It took nine years for this case to come to court, after which she was awarded £700,000. One week later, Hollie died and the Trust asked for its money back. The Trust eventually backed down from this position following some very adverse publicity, but there was a certain amount of merit in their arguments. For example, the money was not awarded to the parents, but to Hollie herself; it was intended to be used for *her* care, and was therefore no longer needed by the parents. Second, the Trust argued that this money could be used for the benefit of other patients.

One way of avoiding this situation is to make a *staged* award. The patient receives an annual sum of money for as long as s/he lives, but which ceases automatically when s/he dies. These have rarely been popular with either the claimant or the defendant, and in the past they required the agreement of both parties before they could be implemented. However, since 2005, the courts have been able to over-ride the objections of either party if they feel that this is an appropriate arrangement (Damages [Variation of Periodical Payments] Order 2005).

There remain further difficulties in calculating a lump sum award. In three cases heard together (*Page v Sheerness Steel Company Limited, Wells v Wells, and Thomas v Brighton Health Authority [1999]*), the House of Lords were asked to consider this question. Lord Lloyd considered the hypothetical example of a claimant who needed £10,000 per year and who was expected to live for 20 years. A quick calculation would suggest that the final sum should be £200,000, but this is not what s/he will get. Let us assume that s/he receives all of this money in one go. What is s/he going to do with it? It is conceivable that s/he could stuff it under a mattress, but it is more likely that s/he will put it in a place of safety (i.e. a bank or building society), wherein it will gain interest. For argument's sake, let us assume that the rate of interest is 5 per cent. How much money will be left at the end of 20 years? The answer, of course, is that *all* of it will be there, because 5 per cent of £200,000 is £10,000. Therefore, s/he will only ever need to spend the interest.

This is not the purpose of compensation awards, for the money should have run down to zero at the end of 20 years. Therefore, some calculation has to be made to account for this, but the question before the court concerned how the money should be invested. The defendants argued that it was incumbent upon the claimant to invest the money in high-return equities and bonds; this would ensure that the final award was lower. The claimants' argument, however, was that such investments were inherently risky and that they were unlikely to take such gambles with their only source of income. The House of Lords accepted this argument, and made the assumption that the claimants would invest the money in the most secure place (index-linked Government securities). Inevitably, this carries a low rate of interest, and it means that compensation awards have to be higher to account for this.

There are two further points to be made about compensation. The first is that the Limitation Act 1980 imposes an obligation upon a claimant to make a claim within three years of the injury (or three years from the time that s/he realised that a claim could be brought). This is obviously to ensure that cases are dealt with as quickly as possible and that health authorities do not have the threat of claims hanging over them for many years. For children, however, the limitation period does not begin to run until they reach 18; and so, an injury at birth could result in a claim 21 years after the event.

The second point is that all NHS Trusts are protected from paying out the highest sums by means of their membership of the Clinical Negligence Scheme for Trusts (CNST). This is administered by the NHS Litigation Authority, which in turn was established by the NHS and Community Care Act 1990 (s21[3]). It operates in much the same way as any insurance scheme. Therefore, there will be an excess (usually £50,000), and any claim that is below this figure will be met by the Trust alone. Moreover, in order to reduce the premiums, the CNST insist upon fairly rigid risk management standards: failure to reach these standards may also induce the scheme to withhold payment in a successful claim.

8 PROBLEMS WITH THE TORT OF NEGLIGENCE

The fact that the tort of negligence has existed for so many years without major change may lead us to suspect that it is a fundamentally flawless system. There are, however, at least a couple of major problems with it, and some reference has been made to them in the foregoing.

First, we have seen that the negligence system makes it extremely difficult for claimants to win. The average time between launching an action and seeing the case come before the court is approximately seven to eight years, meaning that claimants need to be single-minded, determined, and prepared to traverse the many obstacles that will be put in their path. Those who meet these criteria appear to have about a 30 per cent chance of success in court (NHSLA, 2007), but success is not dependent upon level of harm caused. The following case illustrates this graphically:

Box 3.29   *Joyce v Merton, Sutton & Wandsworth HA [1996]*

The claimant (aged 49) underwent a brachial cardiac catheterisation, but the doctor inadvertently created an arterial occlusion when he sutured the incision. A clot eventually dislodged from this site, resulting in upper brain stem infarction. Mr Joyce was left in a permanent locked-in state, his only movement being a slight lateral shift of the eyes.

Although initially successful in the High Court, the Court of Appeal reversed the decision, holding that the doctor had acted reasonably and responsibly. Thus, the patient's life was in ruins, but he was left with no form of redress against those who had caused his injuries.

Paradoxically, however, it may be that far less deserving candidates have a better chance of success. For example, where the injury is a minor one, NHS Trusts may consider that it is cheaper to pay off the patient, rather than take the case to court. Lawyers who operate a 'no win, no fee' system frequently encourage litigation, and it is clear that the costs to the NHS are rising each year (Pattinson, 2009). These costs would somehow be easier to bear if they were apportioned equitably, but the evidence suggests that the converse is true.

Second, the law tends to focus on the individual responsible for the error, whereas current thinking acknowledges that it is more likely to be a system failure that is the cause. Thus, on the one hand, the Government (DH, 2000) is stating that the only way to avoid errors is to examine the system that helped to create them, and that the healthcare professional accused of negligence is more a victim than a culprit. On the other hand, the law appears to make few allowances for this, but instead seeks to lay the blame squarely at the feet of an individual practitioner.

This conflict hampers the efforts of the National Patient Safety Agency (NPSA) to eliminate the blame culture within the NHS. Instead, the threat of litigation and public disgrace encourage an atmosphere of secrecy and subterfuge, where efforts are made to cover up mistakes rather than learn lessons which will prevent their recurrence (Bristol Royal Infirmary Inquiry, 2001). The rhetoric of the NHS usually echoes that of the NPSA, but the reality for those working within it frequently tells a different story.

POSSIBLE SOLUTIONS

The problems of the negligence system are well recognised, both by those within and outside the legal profession. Solutions, however, tend to be thin on the ground, although some efforts have been made to simplify the system. The Woolf reforms (Woolf, 1996) represent one such effort, their purpose being to speed up the process of resolving claims, ensuring greater equity, and reducing costs to the NHS. Thus, the Civil Procedure Rules 1998 (enacted under the Civil Procedure Act 1997) insist upon alternative dispute resolution before a case comes before the court; the number of expert witnesses in court is limited only to those necessary to assist in the judgment; and the courts are empowered to insist on periodical payments (i.e. staged awards, mentioned earlier).

The NHS Redress Act 2006 is another attempt to speed up claims and reduce costs. It applies only to negligence claims in NHS hospitals, and is limited to claims below £20,000. Claimants are still entitled to use the court system, but not once they have accepted payment under the Act. There has not been enough time to assess the effectiveness of this legislation as yet, and one suspects that its primary measure of success will be the volume of savings to the NHS. Therefore, if the savings are impressive, one would confidently expect the system to be rolled out to primary care. If they are negligible, or if they actually increase, the Act may find itself confined to the dustbin of history.

It must be considered doubtful that either the Woolf reforms or the NHS Redress Act make significant inroads into addressing the problems of the negligence system, for inequities will continue to exist. A more radical solution would be the introduction of a 'No-fault' system of compensation. Such schemes are to be found in Scandinavia and, most notably, in New Zealand; and their purpose is to award compensation for personal injury without the need to prove fault. Under such a scheme, for example, one would expect *Joyce* (Box 3.29) to be compensated, even though the doctor has not been found to be negligent.

The advantages of such schemes are that they tend to be quicker, simpler and much more equitable (for more people are compensated). The primary disadvantage, and the main reason why they have consistently been rejected in the UK, is that they are more costly. A weaker argument is that they discourage the deterrence element of negligence actions: i.e. practitioners are less likely to take care in their practice once they realise that they will not be called to account. Not only is this an overly simplistic interpretation of what actually happens in healthcare, it also makes the mistake of assuming that error can be prevented by threatening to punish employees (Merry and McCall Smith, 2001). Given that errors can occur as the result of a variety of factors (excessive work demands, staff shortages, inadequate training and supervision, etc.), it must remain doubtful that the deterrence element has much impact upon the volume of errors. Although resistance to such schemes remains as strong as ever in the UK, it is equally unlikely that New Zealand will return to the tort system.

CONCLUSION

This chapter has outlined the elements of negligence, identified some of the problems with this system, and has briefly looked at possible solutions to these problems. Clearly, it is a system that has flaws and its genesis occurred in an age that is very different from that of today. However, although the law moves very slowly, there are encouraging signs that it is beginning to reflect a stronger emphasis on patients' rights.

The language used by Lord Browne-Wilkinson in the *Bolitho* case, for example, strongly suggests that the excessive deference given to the medical profession in the past is now outdated. One could argue that there is a moral imperative to reduce costs wherever possible, for this will mean that there are greater resources to treat all of the public. But it cannot be morally right to withhold compensation from those who are the innocent victims of healthcare mistakes. A much more effective and ethical way of reducing costs is to focus on eliminating the causes of error. Specific problems may exist within the NHS to prevent this from happening, but the fact that it has been possible in the aviation industry (DH, 2000) should provide some encouragement to continue working on it.

SUMMARY

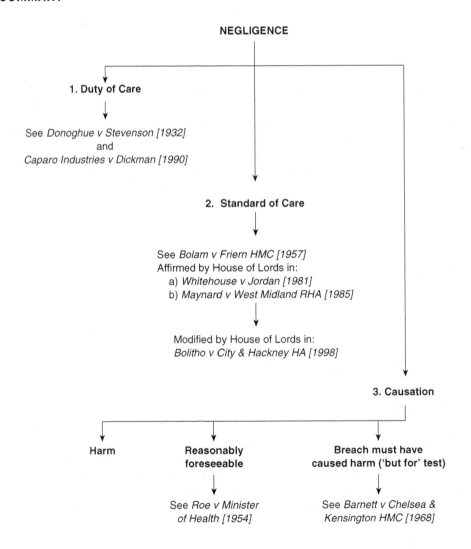

REFERENCES

TEXTS

Albert, T. and Chadwick, S. (1992) 'How readable are practice leaflets?' *British Medical Journal*, 305: 1266–7.

Bailey-Harris, R. (2009) Case reports. *Fam. Law 9*.

Brazier, M. and Cave, E. (2007) *Medicine, Patients and the Law*, 2nd edn. London: Penguin Books.

Brazier, M. and Miola, J. (2000) 'Bye-bye Bolam: a medical litigation revolution', *Medical Law Review*, 8: 85.

Bristol Royal Infirmary Inquiry (Kennedy Report) (2001) *Learning from Bristol: the Report of the Public Inquiry into Children's Heart Surgery at the Bristol Royal Infirmary 1984–1995*. Command Paper Cm 5207, July.

Calkins, D.R., Davis, R.B. and Reiley, P. (1997) 'Patient–physician communication at hospital discharge and patients' understanding of the post-discharge treatment plan', *Arch. Intern. Med.*, 157: 1026–30.

Chico, V. (2006) 'Saviour siblings: trauma and tort law', *Medical Law Review*, 14: 180–218.

Department of Health (2000) *An Organisation with a Memory*. London: Department of Health.

Department of Health (2008) *Updated National Guidance on the Safe Administration of Intrathecal Chemotherapy*. London: Department of Health (HSC 2008/001).

Dimond, B. (2006) *Legal Aspects of Midwifery*, 3rd edn. London: Elsevier.

Dimond, B. (2008) *Legal Aspects of Nursing*, 5th edn. London: Pearson Education.

Dyer, C. (1997) 'Health authority tries to reclaim £700,000 settlement', *British Medical Journal*, 314: 1781 (21 June).

Ferner, R.E. and McDowell, S.E. (2006) 'Doctors charged with manslaughter in the course of medical practice', *Journal of the Royal Society of Medicine*, 99: 309–14.

Foster, C. (1998) 'Bolam: consolidation and clarification', *Health Care Risk Report*, April: 5–8.

Griffin, J.P. and Griffin, J.R. (1996) 'Informing the patient', *J. R. Coll. Physicians London*, 30: 107–11.

Grubb, A. (1998) 'Negligence, causation and Bolam', *Medical Law Review*, 6: 378.

Herring, J. (2008) *Medical Law and Ethics*, 2nd edn. Oxford: Oxford University Press.

Jackson, E. (2010) *Medical Law: Text, Cases, and Materials*, 2nd edn. Oxford: Oxford University Press.

Jones, M. (1991) *Medical Negligence*. London: Sweet & Maxwell.

Kemp, D. (ed.) (1994) *Kemp and Kemp on the Quantum of Damages*. London: Sweet & Maxwell.

Kennedy, I. and Grubb, A. (1994) *Medical Law: Text with Materials*, 2nd edn. London: Butterworths.

Kitching, J.B. (1990) 'Patient information leaflets – the state of the art', *J. R. Soc. Med.*, 83: 298–300.

Maltby, J.R., Hutter, C.D.D. and Clayton, K.C. (2000) 'The Woolley and Roe Case', *British Journal of Anaesthesia*, 84 (1): 121–6.

Merry, A. and McCall Smith, A. (2001) *Errors, Medicine and the Law*. Cambridge: Cambridge University Press.

Montgomery, J. (1997) *Health Care Law*, 1st edn. Oxford: Oxford University Press.

Montgomery, J. (2003) *Health Care Law*, 2nd edn. Oxford: Oxford University Press.

NHS Executive (1996) *NHS Indemnity: Arrangements for Clinical Negligence Claims in the NHS*.

NHS (General Medical Services Contracts) Regulations 2004/291.

NHS Litigation Authority Claims Factsheet (2007). Available at: www.nhsla.com.

NHS Litigation Authority (2009a) Report and Accounts. 7 July 2009. HC 576.

NHS Litigation Authority (2009b) Factsheet 3: information on claims. November 2009.

Newdick, C. (2005) *Who Should We Treat?* 2nd edn. Oxford: Oxford University Press.

Nursing and Midwifery Council (2004) *The NMC Code of Professional Conduct: Standards for Conduct, Performance and Ethics*. July 2004. London: NMC.

Nursing and Midwifery Council (2008a) *The Code: Standards of Conduct, Performance and Ethics for Nurses and Midwives*. May 2008. London: NMC.

Nursing and Midwifery Council (2008b) *Providing Care in an Emergency Situation Outside the Work Environment*. October 2008. London: NMC.

Pattinson, S.D. (2009) *Medical Law and Ethics*, 2nd edn. London: Sweet & Maxwell.

Turton, G. (2009) 'A case for clarity in causation?' *Medical Law Review*, 17, Spring: 140–7.

Williams, K. (2001) 'Medical Samaritans: is there a duty to treat?' *Oxford Journal of Legal Studies*, 21 (3): 393–413.

Woolf, Lord (1996) *Access to Justice: Final Report to the Lord Chancellor on the Civil Justice System in England and Wales*. London: HMSO.

Woolf, Lord (2001) 'Are the courts excessively deferential to the medical profession?' *Medical Law Review*, 9, Spring: 1–16.

CASES

A v Burne [2006] EWCA Civ. 24.

Alcock and others v Chief Constable of South Yorkshire Police [1992] 1 AC 310.

Alexandrou v Oxford [1993] 4 All ER 328.

Bailey v The Ministry of Defence & another [2008] EWCA Civ. 883.

Barker v Nugent [1987] 3 MLJ 182.

Barnett v Chelsea & Kensington HMC [1968] 1 All ER 1068.

Bolam v Friern HMC [1957] 2 All ER 118.

Bolitho v City & Hackney HA [1993] 13 BMLR 111 (CA).

Bolitho v City & Hackney HA [1998] AC 232 (HL).

Briody v St. Helen's & Knowsley HA [2001] EWCA Civ. 1010.

Bull v Devon AHA [1993] 4 Med. LR 117.

Caparo Industries v Dickman [1990] 2 AC 605.

Capital & Counties plc v Hampshire County Council [1997] QB 1004.

Clarke v Adams [1950] 94 SJ 599.

Coles v Reading & District HMC [1963] 107 SJ 115.

Conway and another v Cardiff & Vale NHS Trust [2004] EWHC 1841 (QB).

Crawford v Board of Governors of Charing Cross Hospital [1953] The Times, 8 December, CA.

De Freitas v O'Brien [1993] 4 Med. LR 281 (CA).

Donoghue v Stevenson [1932] AC 562.

Edward Wong Finance Company Ltd. v Johnston, Stokes and Master [1984] AC 296, PC.

Egan v Central Manchester & Manchester Children's University Hospitals NHS Trust [2008] EWCA Civ. 1424.

Froggatt and others v Chesterfield & North Derbyshire Royal Hospital NHS Trust [2002] All ER (D) 218.

Gold v Haringey HA [1987] 2 All ER 888.

Goodwill v British Pregnancy Advisory Service [1996] 2 All ER 161.

Gow v Harker [2003] EWCA Civ. 1160.

Gregg v Scott [2005] UKHL 2.

Hatcher v Black [1954] The Times, 2 July.

Hotson v East Berkshire AHA [1987] 2 All ER 909 (HL).
Joyce v Merton, Sutton & Wandsworth HA [1996] 7 Med. LR 1.
Kent v Griffiths [2000] 2 WLR 1158.
Lillywhite and another v University College London Hospitals NHS Trust [2005] EWCA Civ. 1466.
Lowns v Woods [1996] Aust. Torts Reports 81-376.
M v Newham LBC [1995] 2 AC 633.
Manning v King's College Hospital NHS Trust [2008] EWHC 1838 (QB).
Marriott v West Midlands HA [1999] Lloyd's Rep. Med. 23.
Maynard v West Midlands RHA [1985] 1 All ER 635.
Nettleship v Weston [1971] 3 All ER 581 (CA).
North Glamorgan NHS Trust v Walters [2002] EWCA Civ. 1792.
Oakes v Neininger and others [2008] EWHC 548 (QB).
Page v Sheerness Steel Company Ltd., Wells v Wells, and Thomas v Brighton HA [1999] 1 AC 345 (HL).
Penney, Palmer & Cannon v East Kent HA [2000] Lloyd's Rep. Med. 41 (CA).
Prendergast v Sam & Dee Ltd. [1989] 1 Med. LR 36.
R v Adomako [1994] QB 302 (CA)
R v Adomako [1995] 1 AC 171 (HL).
R v Misra [2004] EWCA Crim. 2375.
R v Prentice [1993] 4 All ER 935.
Reynolds v North Tyneside HA [2002] Lloyd's Rep. Med. 459.
Rhodes-Hampton v Worthing & Southlands Hospital NHS Trust [2007] EWCA Civ. 1202.
RK & AK v UK [2008] ECHR 38000/05.
Roe v Minister of Health [1954] 2 All ER 131.
Sion v Hampstead HA [1994] 5 Med. LR 170.
Stovin v Wise [1996] 3 All ER 801.
Vellino v Chief Constable of Greater Manchester [2001] EWCA Civ. 1249.
White v Chief Constable of South Yorkshire Police [1999] 2 AC 455.
Whitehouse v Jordan [1980] 1 All ER 650.
Whitehouse v Jordan [1981] 1 All ER 267.
Wilsher v Essex AHA [1988] 1 All ER 871 (HL).
Wisniewski v Central Manchester HA [1998] Lloyd's Rep. Med. 85.
X v Bedfordshire CC [1995] 2 AC 633.

LEGISLATION

Civil Procedure Act 1997
Damages (Variation of Periodical Payments) Order 2005, SI 2005/841
Fatal Accidents Act 1976
Human Rights Act 1998
Law Reform (Contributory Negligence) Act 1945
Limitation Act 1980
Manual Handling Operations Regulations (SI 1992, No. 2793)
NHS and Community Care Act 1990
NHS Redress Act 2006
Sale of Goods Act 1893
Work Equipment Regulations (SI 1998, No. 2306)

Scenarios (answers at back of book)

1   A neighbour discovers that you are a healthcare professional and rings you one evening to ask for some advice. He went out earlier and ate a curry in a nearby restaurant, and is now complaining of abdominal pain. You suspect that it might be
indigestion, and suggest that he takes an antacid. It subsequently transpires that
he is rushed to hospital with a perforated gastric ulcer.

Does he have a claim in negligence against you?
[For some assistance with this question, see Hedley Byrne & Co. Ltd. v Heller & Partners
Ltd. [1964] 2 All ER 575.]

2   A patient has recently been discharged from hospital, having had a major abdominal
operation, and you are a Community Nurse performing a routine visit. He complains
of soreness in his mouth and you notice that he has some white spots on his tongue
and palate. You suspect that this may be oral thrush (candidiasis), and you mention it to the doctor, who accepts your diagnosis without question and prescribes
Nystatin. It later transpires that the spots were pre-cancerous lesions, and their continued growth means that the patient eventually has to undergo radiotherapy and
extensive maxillo-facial surgery.

Does he have a claim in negligence against you?

3   A young woman requires fairly extensive dental work and receives treatment from a
dental hygienist every three months, in which sealants are used on a frequent basis.
However, six years after the onset of treatment, she develops breast cancer. She
has read a report on the Internet, linking breast cancer to exposure to bisphenol-A
(a plastic resin used in some sealants), and claims that this is the cause of her
condition.

Does she have a claim in negligence?

4   A physiotherapist is helping a patient get up from the bed, but the electronic mechanism for raising the bed is not working. She suddenly feels a sharp pain in the top of
her neck, radiating down the spine, arms, and left leg. She subsequently undergoes
investigations which reveal a disc bulge and which requires surgery. She argues that
this injury was caused by deficiencies in the bed, and that the Trust had a responsibility to ensure that it was in good working order. The Trust contends that the
physiotherapist suffered the injury as a result of the unavoidable requirements of
the job, and that she is responsible for her own injuries.

Does she have a claim in negligence?

4

CONSENT

Learning Objectives

At the end of this chapter, the reader will:

1 Have an understanding of the elements of a valid consent, and be able to distinguish between Battery and Negligence.

2 Have an awareness of the test for competence when assessing a patient's ability to consent on his/her own behalf.

3 Be aware of the level of information that a patient needs to give a valid consent.

4 Acknowledge the criteria necessary for a valid Advance Decision to refuse treatment.

5 Have an understanding of the legal basis for treating the adult incompetent patient without consent.

6 Acknowledge some of the ethical issues pertaining to consent.

1 INTRODUCTION

It might be argued that a knowledge of the law will tell us the minimum that we can get away with, whereas a study of ethics guides us towards the best that we can achieve. If this is true, the distinction has probably been most apparent in the field of Consent, although recent history has shown that the two are coming closer together. As they merge, the law has become increasingly complex, but it is the intention of this chapter to try and de-mystify some of the central concepts. It does not consider the special issues related to the consent of children (covered in Chapter 8), nor does it address specifically those issues pertaining to the mentally ill (covered in Chapter 7) unless they have featured in cases that have helped to frame the law. Thus, this chapter is essentially an exposition of the law as it pertains to *adults* (i.e. anybody above the age of 18), and concludes with a consideration of some of the ethical concepts.

2 CONSENT: THE LEGAL PERSPECTIVE

Consider the following situation:

Box 4.1

A woman discovers a lump in her breast and seeks medical attention. She undergoes a biopsy which confirms that she has cancer, and she is then invited to see the breast care surgeon. The surgeon explains the alternative forms of treatment, but does not seek a decision from the patient at this time. Instead, she is referred to a Breast Care Counsellor, who goes over the information in greater detail and gives her as much time as she needs to ask questions. She is then sent home, armed with a variety of information leaflets to which she can refer at her leisure. At home, she is able to discuss the disease and the treatment options with her family so that they are given maximum opportunity to be supportive. Moreover, this time period enables both she and her family to come to terms with the diagnosis. She will be admitted to hospital within one to two weeks and will see the same surgeon and Breast Care Counsellor, at which point she will be asked her decision.

This rather idyllic scenario represents the paradigm of what constitutes a valid informed consent. It respects the patient's autonomous right to make her own decisions regarding her treatment, it has furnished her with all the relevant information to enable her to make that decision, and it has given her the appropriate amount of time to consider the options thoughtfully and to discuss them with her family. However, anybody who has had any dealings with healthcare (either as patient or professional) will know that it is difficult to re-create this paradigm in other settings. The patient admitted as an emergency does not have the time to weigh up the alternatives, nor is it likely that s/he will be able to absorb and retain too much information if s/he is in pain. Moreover, as a percentage, few patients have the services of specialist counsellors who will give them the time and information that they need.

We begin, therefore, with the assumption that truly valid informed consent is only possible in comparatively rare circumstances. This does not mean, though, that the concept should be abandoned completely, for the law acknowledges a right of action for patients whose rights have been ignored. As long ago as 1914, an American judge stated the position, with which few would now disagree:

Every human being of adult years and sound mind has a right to determine what shall be done with his own body; and a surgeon who performs an operation without his patient's consent commits an assault (*Schloendorff v New York Hospital [1914]*).

The law in the UK was a little slow to catch up, but the case of *Chatterton v Gerson [1981]* re-affirmed this tenet and went a long way towards clarifying fundamental principles.

Box 4.2   *Chatterton v Gerson [1981]*

The claimant suffered severe pain from a post-operative scar in her right groin, and the doctor performed a sensory nerve block. There was some dispute between claimant and doctor about whether warnings of numbness in the right leg had been given; but the pain relief was only temporary, and the claimant underwent a second operation ten months later. This time, the doctor admitted that no warning of risks had been given because he assumed that the patient was aware of these after the first operation. The claimant lost sensation in her right leg, but was still left with severe pain in the scar area. She sued for trespass and negligence.

Trespass to the person (or Battery) occurs in healthcare when a competent adult patient's refusal of treatment is over-ridden, *or* if treatment is given to that patient without first seeking consent, *or* if the patient has no idea what s/he has consented to. In this case, the claimant failed because she had given her consent to the operation and the doctor had explained its nature and purpose 'in broad terms'. She might have had a stronger case in Negligence if she had been able to show that the information she received from the doctor was insufficient to enable her to give a valid consent, but here too she failed.

The distinction between Battery and Negligence in consent may be a fine one, but can perhaps be illustrated by the following theoretical example:

Box 4.3

A woman goes to Theatre having consented for 'breast surgery', but later discovers to her horror that she has had a mastectomy.

She would not be able to sue for Battery in this instance, because she has consented to the broad nature and purpose of the treatment (i.e. breast surgery). She might, however, be able to sue in Negligence, because she has not been sufficiently informed about the precise nature of that surgery.

In truth, actions in Battery are extremely rare in healthcare, and the judge in *Chatterton* was keen to emphasise that it would not be in the public interest if they were more common. Kennedy (1986) has suggested that patients' rights might be better protected if such actions had a wider application, but this seems unlikely to happen. Moreover, when a Battery occurs, it is usually so obvious that there is little need for the claimant to take the action to court. The outcome is inevitable and the offending healthcare provider will avoid legal costs by settling the compensation claim out of court. Thus, if a surgeon amputates the wrong leg, this will be a Battery, because the patient has not consented to removal of the healthy leg. Jones (1999) notes that once the initial shock of having amputated the wrong leg sinks in, there comes the slowly dawning realisation that the other leg still has to come off. In such circumstances, neither the patient nor the doctor has a leg to stand on!

There have, however, been a few cases of Battery that have reached the courts, and the following is one of the most notorious:

Box 4.4   *Appleton v Garrett [1995]*

Eight patients brought an action against a dentist, who was found to have conducted large-scale restorative dental work upon them, even though they did not need it. This work included large fillings, root canal treatment, and crowns, but radiographs confirmed that the teeth were perfectly healthy.

The court was forced to conclude that this case fell squarely into the arms of Battery rather than Negligence, for the patients' consent had been secured on the basis of false information. Had the dentist been honest with them, they would never have consented to this invasive, painful and expensive treatment. It is, however, a little depressing to point out that the main reason he was caught was that he was not very good at performing the procedures. Therefore, patients would continue to suffer pain following the work and would then seek the services of another dentist. If he had been more skilled, the chances of his wrongdoing coming to light would have been considerably reduced.

In *R v Richardson [1998]*, another dentist continued to practise whilst suspended from the dental register. This case came before the criminal court and ultimately failed, because the court considered that the dentist was not acting fraudulently. Her patients knew that she was a dentist and they were fully informed about the treatment that they were receiving. The court did, however, argue that a *civil* claim for damages in Battery might succeed, suggesting that the criminal law is more reluctant to find liability in such cases (Pattinson, 2009).

Another criminal court was less reluctant to find fault in *R v Tabassum [2000]*, where a man posed as a doctor and claimed to be conducting research into breast cancer. A number of women therefore allowed him to examine their breasts. Despite their willingness to be examined, their consent had been obtained as the result of a deception, and this subsequently rendered that consent invalid.

A case such as this seems fairly straightforward and does not require too much consideration. Things become a little more complicated, however, if the doctor operating upon a patient is not the same professional that the patient saw earlier. In other words, if a patient has seen a Consultant in the Out-Patients' Clinic, had the options explained to him/her by that doctor, and then consented to the procedure, does the patient have a right to expect that this will be the person who performs the operation? Or, if the operation is performed by a junior, would this invalidate the consent? Brazier and Cave (2007) suggest that an action in Battery would be unlikely to succeed *unless* there had been a clear understanding beforehand that the Consultant would perform the procedure (as would be the case in private medicine). Nevertheless, notwithstanding the fact that the law would almost certainly protect healthcare professionals in these instances, it makes good sense to ensure that patients are aware that the person who operates on them is not necessarily going to be the same one that they saw in clinic.

Before moving on to a consideration of the key elements constituting a valid consent, it is necessary to clarify a couple of issues. The first is that consent does not have to be written. In fact, the vast majority of healthcare interventions do not require a written consent, verbal consent being considered perfectly acceptable. There is also a concept known as *implied* consent, where the actions of the patient suggest that they have consented to a procedure even though no verbal communication has taken place. The most frequently cited case illustrating this principle is as follows:

Box 4.5   *O'Brien v Cunard [1891]*

A lady was bound for America on a ship, when she joined a queue, held out her hand, and received a smallpox vaccination. She argued that she had not expressly consented to this procedure, and that this therefore constituted a Battery. The defendants argued that the fact that she held out her hand was a clear implication that she had consented to the vaccination.

The full facts of this case appear to have been somewhat lost in the mists of time, but suffice it to say that the court found for the defendants. We probably have to see this in the context of the age in which it occurred, where the concept of human rights was poorly developed. It seems doubtful that the woman knew what she was queuing for, and it seems equally possible that she held out her hand to shake that of the doctor. Therefore, whether the case would meet with the same result today must be open to doubt, and it is unwise for healthcare professionals to rely upon implied consent as a defence. The fact that a patient enters a hospital seeking medical attention does not automatically imply that s/he is prepared to accept anything that that the healthcare professionals throw at him/her. Similarly, the frequently cited example of the patient who holds out his arm as the nurse approaches him with a blood pressure cuff (Dimond, 2008; Griffith and Tengnah, 2008) serves as a useful illustration of implied consent, but it would represent poor nursing practice if no form of communication took place.

Surgical operations generally require written consent, but it is important to note that a signature does not automatically imply that a valid consent has been given. If the patient has been given inadequate information to enable him/her to make a decision, the consent form ceases to be worth the paper that it is written on (*Chatterton v Gerson [1981]*). In between the two extremes of taking a blood pressure and performing a surgical operation, there are a range of procedures that carry serious risks. One thinks of urinary catheterisation, for example, where there exists the potential for severe trauma. Similarly, the patient undergoing radiotherapy and/or chemotherapy will doubtless experience a number of unpleasant side-effects, some of which could prove fatal. Technically, it could be argued that written consent is not required here, but the General Medical Council (1998) suggests that it would be good practice. In section 28, for example, written consent is advised where:

> The treatment or procedure is complex, or involves significant risks and/or side-effects; [and/or]

> There may be significant consequences for the patient's employment, social or personal life.

Whether catheterisation or the insertion of a naso-gastric tube can be said to satisfy the first of these criteria is debatable. The risks unquestionably exist, but they are extremely rare. The side-effects of chemotherapy, by contrast, are certainly not rare, and it would seem that the advice given by the GMC in this instance is sound. Once again, a written consent does not by itself imply that the patient has received adequate information, and the healthcare professional is best advised to keep a record of the communication that has taken place.

Another issue pertaining to consent is that it is largely age related, and the following diagram illustrates this principle:

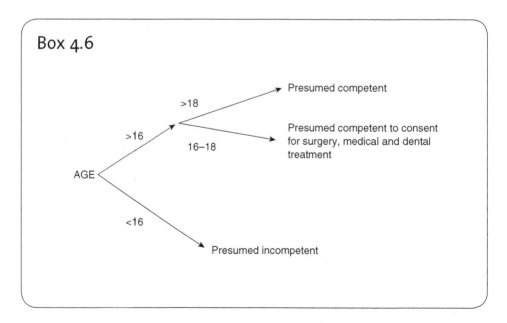

Box 4.6

AGE
- >16
  - >18 → Presumed competent
  - 16–18 → Presumed competent to consent for surgery, medical and dental treatment
- <16 → Presumed incompetent

Thus, if a patient is 18 or above, s/he is presumed in law to be competent to make a decision; s/he can both consent to and refuse treatment, and this decision must be respected by the healthcare professionals. Conversely, if the patient is below the age of 16, s/he is presumed in law to be incompetent to make a decision, and somebody must make that decision on his/her behalf (normally a parent or legal guardian). Both of these presumptions, however, are rebuttable: therefore, just as an adult patient can be declared incompetent, then so too can a child be declared competent, but the onus will fall upon the healthcare professional to justify why these presumptions have been overturned. As mentioned earlier, the issue of consent in children will be examined in a later chapter, as will the Family Law Reform Act 1969, which entitles 16–18-year-olds to consent on their own behalf, provided they are competent to do so.

We are concerned at this stage with those elements that constitute valid consent, namely:

a   The patient must be *competent* to make a decision.
b   The patient must be sufficiently *informed* prior to making a decision.
c   Any decision made must be given *voluntarily*, and therefore free from the duress or undue influence of others.

The law in this area is now largely governed by the Mental Capacity Act 2005 (and by the Adults with Incapacity (Scotland) Act 2000 in Scotland), but this Act is essentially a codification of common law principles that had already existed long before the legislation was passed. It gives those principles statutory authority, however, and it makes some additions to the law, but it is worth examining the key cases to understand how the law developed.

3 COMPETENCE

Given that a pre-condition of being able to give a valid consent is that the patient should be competent to make that decision, we need some method of determining whether or not s/he passes the test. Some might argue that anybody who rejects the advice of healthcare professionals is, by definition, incompetent; but this would represent a fundamental assault on patient autonomy, transferring all power to the professionals and rendering the concept of informed consent obsolete (Kennedy and Grubb, 1998). Therefore, a more patient-friendly test is required. Consider the following two cases:

Box 4.7   *Re C [1994]*

C had paranoid schizophrenia and was a resident of Broadmoor Hospital. He subsequently developed gangrene in his foot and his doctors felt that amputation was warranted, but C refused. He accepted that he had a condition which would probably result in his death if left untreated, but he preferred to die as a whole man. The doctors, however, argued that C suffered from delusions (including the belief that he was an international surgeon), and that he was therefore unable to make a competent decision.

Box 4.8   *Re T [1992]*

T was 20 years old and 34 weeks pregnant when she was involved in a road traffic accident. She had previously been a Jehovah's Witness, but her faith had lapsed. She recovered this faith, however, after speaking to her mother, and signed a form refusing blood transfusions. Following the stillbirth of her baby, her condition subsequently deteriorated and she required ventilation. The doctor, father and boyfriend asked the court to over-ride her refusal to have a blood transfusion.

In both of these cases, an adult patient is refusing consent to treatment. In one of them, the court overturned the refusal as being invalid; while in the other, it upheld the refusal as the decision made by a competent person. But, which one is which?

The answer is that the court upheld the refusal in *Re C*, but overturned it in *Re T*. How, though, is it possible to reconcile these two decisions? To all intents and purposes, C would fail most people's assessments of what constitutes competence in an individual. He was a paranoid schizophrenic, a patient of Broadmoor hospital, and had a series of bizarre delusions. However, when it came to the matter of his leg, he knew exactly what was wrong with it, and what the consequences of his refusal would be. Moreover, he was not blaming anybody for his condition, so that it could not be said that his refusal was a feature of his paranoia.

Therefore, the court was forced to conclude that, although incompetent in most aspects of his life, C was able to make a competent decision regarding his leg. The fact that his leg subsequently recovered would have done little to dispel the delusion that he was an international surgeon; but it is an excellent illustration of the fact that having a mental illness does not automatically preclude someone from being able to give a valid consent. Nor does it necessarily preclude people with learning disabilities from being considered competent. In *Re JT [1998]*, the learning disability was apparently quite severe, but the patient was able to convince the court that her refusal to accept dialysis treatment was calm, rational and consistent. In short, everything depends on the individual circumstances of each case.

In *Re T*, it should be obvious that the High Court is not going to allow a young woman to die if it can possibly avoid it. However, it needs a reason for overturning the refusal of an adult, and it found the necessary loophole in the behaviour of T's mother. In other words, T had been exposed to the undue influence of another whilst in a highly vulnerable state. In such circumstances, therefore, the court held that T was not in a position to make a competent decision.

One senses a certain desperation in *Re T* to find a mechanism for overturning the presumption of competence, and the cynic might argue that there is a more disturbing distinction between these cases: namely that C and JT had no prospects of ever providing a useful service to society, whereas T's life had unlimited potential. This would, however, be unfair, for there were other possible ways of over-riding T's refusal, but they were rejected by the court. For example, the fact that her faith had lapsed had no relevance, for an individual is entitled to reclaim his/her religious beliefs at any moment in time. Similarly, the fact that T subsequently became unconscious did not invalidate her earlier refusal, and this case established the legality of Advance Decisions (to which we shall refer later in this chapter). Finally, the court refused to accept that a Jehovah's Witness who declined a life-saving blood transfusion was, by definition, incompetent. Had the case been heard in France or Germany, this alone would have been sufficient to over-ride the patient's refusal (Lewis, 2006), but this is not a feature of the law in this country.

For our purposes, the main significance of *Re C* was that it established a test of competence (the so-called C-test). Therefore, if a healthcare professional wishes to establish that a patient is incompetent, s/he must be able to show that the patient fails *at least one* of the following elements:

a   He must be able to understand the information.
b   He must be able to retain it.
c   He must be able to weigh it in the balance to arrive at a decision.

This test underwent a slight modification from the original by the Court of Appeal in a later case (*Re MB [1997]*), and was eventually given statutory authority by the Mental Capacity Act 2005, which added one further clause (section 3):

d   He must be able to communicate his decision by any means.

A good illustration of the application of this test can be seen in the following case:

Box 4.9   *Re MB [1997]*

A 23-year-old woman was 40 weeks pregnant, but her foetus was in a breech position. It was evident, therefore, that a Caesarean section would be necessary in order to save the life of the foetus. The woman understood and accepted this information, but she had a needle phobia, thereby preventing her from agreeing to the induction of anaesthesia.

An application of the C-test demonstrated that the patient passed elements (a) and (b) (and she would have passed (d) too if the case had been heard following enactment of the Mental Capacity Act). However, she was unable to weigh the information in the balance, because her phobia was preventing her from doing so. Having failed one of the elements, the court felt justified in holding that she was incompetent and that her refusal could be over-ridden.

There have been a number of cases involving women who have refused Caesarean sections, and the history suggests that the courts have stretched the interpretation of what it means to be competent to its limit in order to preserve the lives of both mother and foetus (Lewis, 1997). In *Rochdale Healthcare NHS Trust v C [1997]*, for example, the judge held that a woman in the throes of labour was unable to weigh information in the balance (and was therefore incapable of making a competent decision) because she was in too much pain and under too much stress. He may have a point, but the logical extension of this argument is that every pregnant woman must be stripped of her autonomy (Herring, 2008). *Norfolk and Norwich Healthcare NHS Trust v W [1996]* is another example, where a woman was considered to be 'incapable of weighing up the considerations that were involved' (at 272): there were stronger indications here that she had a mental illness, but the judge re-emphasised the difficulties of making a competent decision when in pain.

A unifying factor among all these cases is that the judicial decision has had to be made quickly. In *Rochdale*, for example, the judge was told that he only had 15 minutes to make his judgement; any later than this, and the foetus would be dead. Without the luxury of hearing representations from both parties in detail, and without the opportunity to reflect at length upon the case before making a pronouncement, it is inevitable that some of these decisions are going to be ill-considered. In *Re S [1993]*, the judge went one step too far and over-rode a woman's refusal to have a Caesarean section. She (and her husband) made this refusal on religious grounds, and there could be no doubt that she was competent. The judge, however, ignored this fact, despite being unable to find English legal authority for his decision. His judgment was ultimately criticised by the Court of Appeal in *Re MB [1997]*, and they confirmed the legal position in the following case:

Box 4.10   *St. George's Healthcare NHS Trust v S [1998]*

S was 35 weeks pregnant and was suffering from pre-eclampsia. Her doctors considered that a Caesarean section was warranted, but she refused, stating that she wanted the child to be born naturally, even if this meant her own death and that of the baby. The High Court over-rode her refusal, and S then sought judicial review of this decision.

The Court of Appeal held that the operation had been performed illegally, because the refusal of a competent adult had been ignored. In the words of Lord Justice Judge:

> She is entitled not to be forced to submit to an invasion of her body against her will, whether her own life or that of her unborn child depends on it. Her right is not reduced or diminished merely because her decision to exercise it may appear morally repugnant (at 692).

In making this judgment, the Court of Appeal was doing little more than reiterating the doctrine expounded in earlier cases. Thus, in *Re T [1992]*, Lord Donaldson stated:

[The] right of choice is not limited to decisions which others might regard as sensible. It exists notwithstanding that the reasons for making the choice are rational, irrational, unknown or even non-existent (at 865).

The Jehovah's Witness who refuses a life-saving blood transfusion may not appear to many of us to be acting rationally, but the law recognises his/her right to follow his/her religious beliefs without the interference of others. However, that the issue of autonomy in pregnancy took so long to catch up with the prevailing doctrine clearly has much to do with the fact that *two* lives are at stake here: that of the mother and the foetus. Lord Donaldson himself appears to have been instrumental in creating this confusion when he acknowledged (in *Re T*) that the issue of a viable foetus produces a different and more complex dilemma. Nevertheless, this confusion now appears to have been put to rest, and the autonomy of the pregnant woman has been restored to its proper place.

Before moving on, there is one final point to be made about competence. It is one thing to apply the test of competence to a patient and be able to justify that s/he is unable to make a decision; but the Mental Capacity Act 2005 states that one's responsibilities do not end there. Thus, healthcare professionals have a duty to take all measures to enhance decision-making capacity (section 4, iv). In many cases, it will not be enough simply to transmit key points and it may be necessary to develop imaginative methods for assisting patients to understand. For example, Gunn et al. (1999) have noted that patients with learning disabilities are often capable of a higher level of understanding than many have given them credit for, providing that the information is conveyed in a pictorial format. The NMC Code of Conduct (2008) makes a similar point, arguing that every patient should be given as much opportunity as possible to influence decisions pertaining to his/her treatment. Providing that all reasonable attempts have been made to enhance understanding, the healthcare professional will find that the law will look upon him or her with favour.

4 INFORMATION

On the assumption that an adult patient is competent, it follows that s/he must be given sufficient information to enable him/her to make a decision. But how much information should the healthcare professional divulge? Consider the following two scenarios:

Box 4.11 *Sidaway v Bethlem Royal Hospital Governors [1985]*

Mrs Sidaway suffered from persistent pain in her neck and shoulders, and was advised by her surgeon to have an operation on her spinal column to relieve this pain. He did not, however, warn her of the possibility of damaging the spinal cord, because this risk

(Continued)

(Continued)

was very small (less than 1 per cent). Needless to say, this risk materialised and she was left severely disabled. She was unable to claim for negligent performance, because there was little doubt that the operation had been carried out correctly. Therefore, she based her claim upon the contention that she had not been fully apprised of the facts before the operation and, in consequence, was not in a position to give a valid consent.

Box 4.12   *Rogers v Whitaker [1992]*

Mrs Whitaker had been nearly blind in her right eye from an early age as the result of a penetrating injury. At the age of 47, her doctor suggested that he could remove scar tissue from this eye, thereby improving its appearance and possibly improving its sight. Unfortunately, Mrs Whitaker developed the post-operative complication of sympathetic ophthalmia – a rare auto-immune condition, where infection or trauma in one eye is mimicked by the other eye. She therefore became totally blind in her left eye, but with no improvement in the right eye. Her doctor admitted that he had not warned her of this risk before the operation, but this was because he considered it too small to be worthy of mention (approximately 1 in 14,000).

Thus, what we have here are two patients, both of them arguing that they did not receive enough information before their operations to enable them to give a valid consent. One of them wins and the other loses, but which one is which?

The answer is that Mrs Whitaker won and Mrs Sidaway lost, but how is it possible to reconcile these two decisions? Admittedly, the risk in *Sidaway* was small (less than 1 per cent), but this is considerably higher than the risk in *Rogers* (1 in 14,000). So, why should the court look with less favour on Mrs Sidaway than it did with Mrs Whitaker?

There are, in fact, two ways to reconcile these decisions. The first is that *Sidaway* is an English case, whereas *Rogers* is an Australian case. Australian courts are not bound by the decisions made in English courts (and English courts are not bound by the decisions made in Australian courts); but they have to take account of them in the interests of justice. Thus, the real reason why these decisions differed was that the two courts used different tests. In *Sidaway*, the court used the *Bolam* test (from *Bolam v Friern HMC [1957]*), which asks the question: 'What would a responsible body of medical men do in this situation?' In other words, would they warn the patient of a risk that was less than 1 per cent? The answer to this question was unequivocally in the negative; if patients were to be told of every conceivable risk before an operation, none of them would ever consent to treatment again, because they would all be too terrified.

In *Rogers*, the Australian court abandoned the *Bolam* test in the field of information-giving, substituting it instead with the *reasonable patient* test. This asks the question: 'If this patient had been informed of the risk before the operation, would she still have consented to surgery?' Mrs Whitaker was able to convince the court that she would not have agreed to the operation: it is one thing to be blind in one eye, but it is completely different to be blind in both.

For many years, *Sidaway* has remained the leading English case in the field of information-giving, and it is difficult to escape the conclusion that it is protective of doctors to the detriment of patient rights (Jones, 1999). This may be a little unfair, however, for a number of Law Lords took the opportunity to remind healthcare professionals of their responsibilities to patients. Lord Bridge, for example, stated that, when a patient asks a specific question about risks, 'the doctor's duty must ... be to answer both truthfully and as fully as the questioner requires' (at 661). Moreover, he was prepared to over-ride accepted medical opinion if a practice was inconsistent with rational judgement. Thus, a doctor who did not warn of a 10 per cent risk of a stroke from surgery could not expect the court to apply *Bolam* in these circumstances.

Even allowing for these limitations placed upon a doctor's power, though, the over-riding impression for *Sidaway* is that it must be a professional judgement as to how much information is revealed to a patient. Lord Diplock was the most forceful in stating this position when he said:

> To decide what risks the existence of which a patient should be voluntarily warned ... is as much an exercise of professional skill and judgement as any other part of the doctor's comprehensive duty of care to the individual patient, and expert medical evidence on this matter should be treated in just the same way. The Bolam test should be applied (at 659).

There was, however, one Law Lord who questioned the applicability of *Bolam* in this context. To paraphrase Lord Scarman, he acknowledged that *Bolam* should be applied in the fields of diagnosis and treatment, because doctors are experts on these matters and judges could not be expected to evaluate conflicting medical opinion in the absence of this specialist knowledge. But, why should a doctor be in a better position than anybody else to know how much information a patient can tolerate? There is nothing in their medical training that equips them to do this, and the whole premise rests upon the assumption that the doctor is in possession of the most intimate details of each of his/her patients' lives. Even the patients' closest relatives will not have this information, and therefore, any judgement to withhold information because it may have a detrimental effect on the patient's psychological health is, at best, a guess.

Lord Scarman did actually support the defence of 'therapeutic privilege' (i.e. that information can be withheld from patients if it is thought that it may cause them undue stress); but he suggested that *Bolam* should be abandoned in cases such as *Sidaway*, to be replaced by the reasonable patient test. He was, of course, in a minority of one, but it is interesting to note that Mrs Sidaway would still have lost her case if this test had been applied. If she had been warned of the risks before the operation, she would almost certainly still have consented to surgery, because she was in so much pain.

As mentioned earlier, *Sidaway* has had a lasting influence upon how such cases are dealt with in this country, and Lord Diplock's position was adopted in the earlier ones as being the least complicated (*Blyth v Bloomsbury HA [1987]*; *Gold v Haringey HA [1988]*). However, as Kirby (1995: 8) has stated:

> Times have changed. The reasons for the changes are easy enough to see. They include the general advance of education of the population at large and thus of patients; the decline of the awe of professionals and indeed of all in authority; the termination of unquestioning acceptance of professional judgement; the widespread public discussion of matters concerning health, including in the electronic media, and the growing recognition in medical practice of the importance of receiving a full input from the patient so that the whole person is treated, not simply a body part.

As one might expect, judicial movement in the UK towards this position has come by increments rather than in a revolutionary fashion (Brazier and Cave, 2007), and those cases which have stressed patients' rights to information tend to be noticeable because they are so rare. One such case was the following:

Box 4.13   *Smith v Tunbridge Wells HA [1994]*

A young man underwent surgery to repair a prolapsed rectum and subsequently became impotent and faecally incontinent. The surgeon was aware of this risk, but chose not to tell the patient because he thought the chances of it materialising were too small.

Even the leading textbook of the day did not mention this as a risk, and an application of *Bolam* should have vindicated the surgeon. However, the judge held that the patient should have been informed of the risk prior to surgery, because it was of such importance to him. It is interesting to speculate upon whether or not the outcome would have been the same if the patient was *older*. If not, this might suggest that the courts have abandoned all hope of laying down guiding principles and will treat each case on its own merits.

McAllister v Lewisham & North Southwark HA [1994] is another example, where a court held that a doctor was negligent for not informing the patient of a risk of sensory loss in her arm following brain surgery. An expert witness provided testimony in support of the defendant, but this testimony was subsequently found to be contradictory and inconsistent with the evidence of other experts.

These, of course, are both High Court cases, and therefore have limited authority, for the decisions are not binding upon higher courts. A case which had higher authority was the following:

Box 4.14   *Pearce v United Bristol Healthcare NHS Trust [1998]*

Mrs Pearce was pregnant with her sixth child and was 14 days beyond term. She asked her Consultant if she could be induced or have a Caesarean section, but he disagreed for he felt that both options were too risky. He therefore suggested that a natural birth was the safest option, but did not warn her of the possibility that the child would be stillborn.

The Court of Appeal found in favour of the defendant, but the case is of importance because there is clear judicial approval of the concept that patients have the right to be told of significant risks. If they are not, the courts are therefore entitled to conclude that the healthcare professionals are acting unreasonably and irresponsibly.

The case which really demonstrated a shift in judicial thinking, however, was the following:

Box 4.15   *Chester v Afshar [2004]*

Miss Chester suffered from repeated episodes of low back pain, and it was discovered that some of her vertebral discs protruded into the spinal canal. She was referred to a neurosurgeon (Mr Afshar), who operated on her, but did not warn her of the 1–2 per cent risk of cauda equina syndrome. This risk subsequently materialised and she was left with a permanent disability.

The House of Lords found, by a majority of 3 to 2, for the claimant, but their mechanism for doing so is rather complicated and has led to some confusion in the law. The claimant's argument was that, if she had been informed of this risk, at the very least she would have postponed the operation and might have cancelled it altogether. By contrast, the defendant's argument was that Miss Chester's symptoms suggested that she would almost certainly have had the operation at some point, when she would have been exposed to exactly the same risk. Thus, the surgeon cannot be said to have *caused* the patient's injuries, for there was never any question that his performance was substandard; nor could it be said that his failure to warn of the risks made any difference to the claimant's decision.

Failure of the causation element of negligence should automatically imply that the action fails; but not in this case, where Lord Steyn argued that the facts demand 'a modest departure from traditional causation principles' (at para. 24). For some, this departure was rather more than 'modest', and the two dissenting Law Lords voiced their objections very forcefully. If the doctor has not been negligent, the claimant should not be able to claim for any damages. However, the majority argued that she had been denied the loss of an opportunity to make an informed decision. This would not normally be actionable, but to award her nothing would be tantamount to showing a lack of respect for her autonomy. Interestingly, she was awarded full damages for her physical injuries, suggesting that she may have been over-compensated (Jackson, 2010). Notwithstanding this, however, the case is significant because it demonstrates judges using the language of human rights: in other words, patients have a *right* to information, and healthcare professionals have a *duty* to give it to them. The provision of information is therefore no longer an optional extra.

Clearly, this represents a significant departure from the doctor-friendly judgment in *Sidaway*, and it shows the courts moving more closely to the position in *Rogers v Whitaker [1992]*. It is also the kind of decision that sends shock waves through the healthcare professions. Whether it opens the floodgates to a host of similar claims remains to be seen, although Foster (2004) is convinced that it will. There are probably enough specific elements of this case that would enable future courts to distinguish it from other cases, but this is by no means certain. Sher (2003), for example, notes that Miss Chester was a private patient, and compensation would not therefore come out of the public purse, thereby encouraging the court to take a more generous line. The precedent established in the case, however, is applicable to NHS patients too, but a court may be less content to find liability in such cases.

One subsequent case that has cited *Chester* in its judgment is the following:

Box 4.16   *Birch v University College Hospitals NHS Foundation Trust [2008]*

Mrs Birch had a suspected brain aneurysm and she underwent a cerebral catheter angiogram to confirm this diagnosis. However, she suffered a stroke and brought an action against the doctor. The court held that the doctor was not negligent in choosing to perform the angiogram, for this was considered an acceptable and reasonable course of action to take. He *was* negligent, though, in failing to inform Mrs Birch of an alternative investigation – an MRI scan might have been able to do the same job as the angiogram, but carried no risk of stroke.

Here, the court appears to have extended the principle in *Chester*, arguing that not only do healthcare professionals have a duty to warn patients about the risks of treatment, but also they must inform them of alternatives so that they can make a considered decision. As Heywood (2009) notes, there may be occasions when no alternatives exist or those alternatives are not practical, in which case the healthcare professional will have a valid defence. But it is clear from *Birch* that the courts are now much more protective of patient autonomy than they ever were in the past.

All of this is calculated to create a level of anxiety within the healthcare professions, and there is a perception that the courts have removed practitioners' rights to exercise clinical discretion (Heywood et al., 2010). I have already suggested that the estimation of how much information a patient can tolerate is fraught with difficulties and is certainly not an exact science. Some might argue that extensive experience has enabled them to make this judgement with accuracy, but it is equally possible that they are deceiving themselves. The ethical perspective will be discussed in a little more detail later on, but there is one more direction that the law can take. If a doctor informs a patient that a certain procedure carries a 1 per cent risk of serious complications, he is quoting *national* (and possibly international) statistics. What he is unlikely to say, however, is: 'When *I* perform this procedure, the risk of complications is more like 10 per cent'. Veerapen (2007) therefore suggests that the level of experience (and the level of skill) of the practitioner performing the procedure is a risk factor that should be disclosed to patients before obtaining their consent.

This is not a feature of English law at present, although it has featured in the Australian case of *Chappel v Hart [1998]*, where the claimant argued successfully that she would have delayed surgery to her throat if she had been informed of all the risks and would probably have sought the services of a more experienced surgeon. The momentum created by *Chester* suggests that this may well be the next step, and the courts may feel encouraged by guidance emanating from the General Medical Council (2008), in which it is stated that the patient should be informed about 'the benefits or risks affected by which organisation or doctor is chosen to provide care' (para. 9e). The very title of this booklet (*Consent: Patients and Doctors Making Decisions Together*) sends out a clear signal that the medical profession itself no longer considers the paternalistic tradition of 'Doctor knows best' as a suitable mantra for the modern age, and the courts cannot fail to be influenced by this.

5 VOLUNTARY

Quite obviously, consent cannot be considered valid if it is obtained following coercion of the patient or subjecting him/her to undue influence. Consider, for example, the patient who is wheeled down to Theatre on a trolley. As he lays prostrate in his surgical gown in the anaesthetic room, the surgeon (gowned and masked) leans over him and asks him to sign the consent form. In such circumstances, this signature will be worthless, for it was obtained at a time when the patient was completely vulnerable. This is not to say that his consent is necessarily invalid, for a lot will depend upon conversations that took place between doctor and patient when the latter was in the Out-Patients' Clinic or the ward. It is simply that the signature itself would offer no legal protection whatsoever for the healthcare professional.

Cases coming before the courts that have raised the issue of coercion or undue influence are rare; and when they have occurred, the decision has invariably fallen in favour of the healthcare professionals. One such case was the following:

Box 4.17   *Freeman v Home Office (No. 2) [1984]*

A prisoner serving a life sentence was prescribed Serenace, Modecate and Stelazine by the prison doctor, and he claimed that these drugs induced depression and suicidal tendencies. He further claimed that he had resisted administration of the medication and had been forced to take them by the prison officers.

We will probably never know whether or not he was compelled to take the medication, and the claimant himself appears to have recognised the difficulties of proving it in court. He therefore dropped this charge, and argued instead that his position as a prisoner invalidated true consent because he was in too vulnerable a position. The court disagreed, stating that only forcible restraint could have invalidated the consent, although it was acknowledged that prisoners are in a special situation and that the potential for abuse is very real.

Another case where undue influence was a feature is as follows:

Box 4.18   *Centre for Reproductive Medicine v U [2002]*

Mr U had had a vasectomy some years earlier, but he and his wife decided that they wanted children. An attempted reversal of the vasectomy was unsuccessful, but Mr U then underwent a surgical operation to retrieve his own sperm. The Sister of the unit, in keeping with the policy of the centre, advised Mr U to withdraw his consent to storage of the sperm if he died or became incapacitated. When he unexpectedly died, his wife wanted to use the sperm, and argued that her husband's withdrawal of consent had been subject to the undue influence of the nurse.

The court dismissed Mrs U's claim, holding that it defied credibility that a young, fit, and intelligent person could be easily manipulated.

Perhaps not unexpectedly, the one case where undue influence was held to be a major factor occurred when a patient's relative was the perpetrator. The case of *Re T [1992]* has already been discussed in the section on Competence, but it is the best illustration that we have of the principle that patients' decisions are invalidated if they are obtained as the result of pressure from others. It has been suggested that this case would not have come to court if the mother had pressurised her daughter into *accepting* a blood transfusion (Feldman, 2002), and this leads one to suspect that the standard for refusing treatment is much higher than it is for consenting to it. Notwithstanding this criticism, though, the case is of enduring importance because it established the legality of Advance Decisions.

6 ADVANCE DECISIONS TO REFUSE TREATMENT

Before discussing this concept, it is necessary to make a brief note about terminology. The terms Advance Directives, Living Wills, and Advance Decisions all mean exactly the same thing and they are frequently used interchangeably. However, the last of these is the more accurate, for it denotes that the patient's power rests in his/her ability to *refuse* treatment only. That the patient is unable to *demand* specific treatment from healthcare professionals was clearly established in the following case:

Box 4.19 *Burke v General Medical Council [2005]*

Mr Burke suffered from a degenerative brain condition and it was inevitable that his condition would ultimately deteriorate to a point where he would require artificial nutrition and hydration. He asked the court to give him assurances that his doctors would not withdraw this treatment, even if they felt that his condition warranted such an action.

Mr Burke initially won his case in the High Court, for the judge felt that he was protected by the Human Rights Act 1998 – Article 2 (the right to life), Article 3 (freedom from inhuman or degrading treatment), and Article 8 (the right to family life). However, the Court of Appeal, while acknowledging that healthcare professionals have a duty to preserve life where possible, rejected the idea that they should be forced to provide treatment that serves no useful purpose or is against the best clinical interests of the patient. As Lord Phillips stated (at 191): 'Ultimately ... a patient cannot demand that a doctor administer a treatment which the doctor considers is adverse to the patient's clinical needs.' Thus, this is the first criterion of a valid Advance Decision – that it can only be used to refuse treatment. *Re T [1992]*, however, established other criteria, all of which have to be satisfied if the decision is to be respected by healthcare professionals:

a The patient must be competent at the time of the decision (and be aged 18 years or over when the refusal was made).
b The decision must be made while free from duress or undue influence.
c The patient must be sufficiently informed.
d The patient must intend his/her refusal to apply to the circumstances which subsequently arise.

You will recall that T's decision to refuse a blood transfusion failed to satisfy (b) because of the influence of her mother, and there was also some doubt that she was well enough at the time to make a competent judgement. Nevertheless, the important point to note here is that, if all the criteria are met, the Advance Decision remains valid even if the patient subsequently becomes incompetent. Perhaps the best illustration of this comes from a Canadian case:

Box 4.20   *Malette v Shulman [1991]*

A husband and wife, both Jehovah's Witnesses, were involved in a road traffic accident. The husband was killed and the wife was taken to Casualty in an unconscious state. The doctor decided to give her a blood transfusion, even though he knew that she would refuse it if conscious.

The doctor effectively saved this woman's life, but the court held that he had committed a Battery and awarded her C$20,000. His single-minded determination to meet her physical needs had ignored her spiritual needs, and the latter were of far more importance to her. This case was cited with approval in *Re T*, suggesting that the result would have been exactly the same if the case had been heard in this country. Moreover, the criteria laid down in *Re T* have now been incorporated into the Mental Capacity Act 2005 (sections 24–6), thereby giving them statutory authority.

The card carried by Jehovah's Witnesses is probably the best example of a valid Advance Decision, and yet it is not a complex legal document. It simply says that the carrier refuses to have a blood transfusion at any time and under any circumstances. It is clear, straightforward and unequivocal, satisfying all of the criteria established by *Re T* and the Mental Capacity Act. The Act does, however, provide a defence for the healthcare professional if s/he is unaware of the existence of the decision (section 26 [2]), but one must question the likelihood of this. The Jehovah's Witness is most likely to carry the card around with him/her at all times, and it ought to be common practice to check the clothing of an unconscious patient (to search for evidence that s/he is a diabetic or epileptic, or is on steroids or anti-coagulants).

Despite the recognition of both the courts and Parliament of the importance of Advance Decisions as exercises in autonomy, there is a common perception that they have limited value because they are so easily over-ridden (Pattinson, 2009). For example, it is not difficult to argue that a patient was insufficiently informed when they made the decision unless that patient is an experienced healthcare professional. Moreover, the last criterion (that the decision must apply to the circumstances that arise) often provides the most difficulties for patients. Suppose, for example, that a man writes an Advance Decision stating that he would not wish to receive artificial nutrition and hydration if he was ever in a permanent vegetative state (PVS). Let us now suppose that he subsequently develops locked-in syndrome. The patient is in much the same position as he had envisaged when he made the decision, but it will not apply – by specifically mentioning PVS, he has excluded all other conditions.

There may also be a change in the patient's *social* circumstances after the signing of an Advance Decision, and the following case is an illustration of this:

Box 4.21 *HE v A Hospital NHS Trust [2003]*

The patient was born and brought up a Muslim, but her parents separated while she was still a child, and she and her mother became Jehovah's Witnesses. As an adult, she required cardiac surgery for a congenital defect, but she developed septic shock secondary to bacterial endocarditis. Her condition began to deteriorate and it became clear that she would die within 36 hours without a blood transfusion.

As with *Malette v Shulman [1991]*, the patient's Advance Decision to refuse blood transfusions should have been valid, but there were important differences with this case. For example, the patient had not attended any Jehovah's Witness meetings for about three or four months, casting serious doubt upon the strength of her faith. More significantly, she was currently engaged to a Muslim and had promised to convert back to his faith when they were married. Thus, there has been an important change in the patient's *social* circumstances, rendering her Advance Decision invalid.

In *Re AK [2001]*, a 19-year-old man had motor neurone disease and was able to communicate only by moving his eyelids. He asked the doctors to discontinue ventilation so that he would be allowed to die, and the court accepted that this was a valid Advance Decision. The fact that the patient's refusal of treatment came when his illness was well advanced, however, does not make this the best example of an Advance Decision in operation. It would not, for example, provide a model for the patient who has been diagnosed in the early stages of Alzheimer's Disease or Huntington's Chorea. In both cases, the patient is competent to make a decision, but has a limited window of opportunity to exercise some control over how s/he is to be treated in the future.

What all of this means is that the drafting of an Advance Decision is not a task to be undertaken lightly if healthcare professionals and the courts are to take them seriously. They have to be written with care, clarity and specificity, for any loopholes will enable them to be ignored with ease. But Parliament would not have incorporated them within the Mental Capacity Act if it was thought that they were useless. Above all else, they represent a chance for people to exert some control over their own destinies even when they are no longer able to vocalise their wishes. Johnstone (2004) has argued that their use is likely to become more common in the future, and that healthcare professionals should become accustomed to them. As they become more popular, it is reasonable to expect that the expertise with which they are drafted will develop commensurately.

7 THE INCOMPETENT ADULT

We have seen that the elements of a valid consent are that the patient must be competent, s/he must be sufficiently informed to make a decision, and that decision should be freely given. But what of the adult patient who is unable to make a decision? Those patients sectioned under the Mental Health Act 1983 can be treated without their consent (s63), but it is important to note that this applies only to treatment of the mental illness itself. It would be illegal to invoke the Mental Health Act to impose any other form of treatment. So, what happens in all other cases? The leading case dealing with this issue is as follows:

Box 4.22   *Re F (mental patient: sterilisation) [1990]*

A 36-year-old woman had severe learning disabilities and it was estimated that she had the mental age of a 6-year-old child. She was a resident of a care home, but her mother and the staff were concerned that she might be having a sexual relationship with one of the male residents. They contended that it would not be a good idea for her to become pregnant, but all forms of contraception were considered impractical. They therefore asked the court for the legal authority to sterilise her so that pregnancy was avoided.

It is well known that non-consensual sterilisation of women with learning disabilities was carried out in the past (Park and Radford, 1998), but this was the first time that the court was faced with this situation. The dilemma here is that the patient is unable to consent for herself, but nobody can legally consent on her behalf: not her doctors, carers, mother or even the court itself. But, if nobody can consent for her, the logical consequence is that she could be denied life-saving treatment. Or, as Kennedy (1988) has said, such patients could 'die with their rights on'.

The court resolved this dilemma by resorting to what is known as the 'best interests' test; but *whose* interests are being considered here? There were four candidates:

a   *Society:* The argument here is twofold. First, sterilising this woman would spare the taxpayer the burden of another mouth to feed. Although it is not inevitable that any child born to her will be disabled, the fact that her male partner has also got disabilities makes this a strong probability. Second, it might be argued that society has an interest in maintaining a strong gene pool; or, in other words, to rid itself of defective genes. This latter argument is known as *eugenics*, and it is worth remembering that it was a popular philosophy in late nineteenth- and early twentieth-century Britain, Europe and America. It reached its most extreme expression in Nazi Germany, and is therefore no longer considered morally acceptable. The eugenic argument can be seen as having an influence on an old American case, where the judge had no hesitation in authorising the sterilisation of a mildly retarded woman who had herself been born to a mother who was equally afflicted, and who had given birth to an allegedly retarded child:

'It is better for all the world, if instead of waiting to execute degenerate offspring for crime, or to let them starve for their imbecility, society can prevent those who are manifestly unfit from continuing their kind. The principle that sustains compulsory vaccination is broad enough to cover cutting the Fallopian tubes ... Three generations of imbeciles are enough' (*Buck v Bell [1927]* per Holmes, J. at 207).

Such comments are unlikely to be heard in a court today; but Montgomery (2003) suggests that the underlying philosophy may never be far from the surface, and points to the decisions in *Re M [1988]*, *Re P [1989]* and *Re HG [1993]* as evidence that eugenic arguments 'have been introduced through the backdoor' (2003: 400). In all of these cases, it appeared that the courts were very quick to authorise sterilisation and used arguments in justification that could not have been applied to women who were mentally competent. Notwithstanding this, the courts have declared that arguments for non-consensual sterilisation based upon the wider interests of society cannot be sustained from an ethical perspective. If they could, it is easy to see sterilisation being forced upon drug addicts, alcoholics and a range of other individuals who have limited abilities to look after children.

b   *The Carers:* An argument in favour of the carers is supported by the fact that this woman will be very difficult to manage while she is pregnant. Moreover, we have already established that there is a very high chance that any child born to her will have severe disabilities also, and will therefore require long-term residential care. A counter-argument to this might be that this is what the carers are employed to do, and they cannot have a legitimate right of complaint. But would it make a difference if the primary carer of the child was going to be the woman's aging mother? Here, we might have a little more sympathy for the individual who has been saddled with this onerous responsibility. However, this was precisely the situation in a famous Canadian case (*Re Eve [1986]*), where the interests of the mother were argued in court but were rejected by the judge. Essentially, his rationale for rejection of the argument was that nobody should have to undergo bodily mutilation for the sake of another. If we were to accept this principle, the implications are too horrible to contemplate. Imagine, for example, a patient with Alzheimer's Disease who is being nursed on a ward, but he is a wanderer and the staff keep having to chase after him to return him to his bed. In the interests of the carers, the logical thing to do here would be to amputate both of his legs!

c   *The Child:* On the face of it, an argument for sterilisation that considers the interests of the child has a little more force. Assuming that s/he will be born with severe disabilities, s/he will need to spend the whole of his/her life in an institution, and will certainly never know his/her mother (for s/he will be removed into care as soon as s/he is born). There are, however, at least two problems with this argument. The first is that nobody is guaranteed to lead an unhappy and unproductive life, even if born into the most extreme of circumstances. Were this to be the case, for example, there would have been a strong argument for terminating the pregnancy of Beethoven's mother! Moreover, even if born with disabilities, the child could still have a happy life. The second counter-argument is that we cannot say that a child is better off by not being born, because it is impossible to know what 'not being born' is like. In other words, we would be trying to compare something with nothing.

d   *The Patient:* What all of this leaves us with is the patient herself; and this is considered the only morally acceptable justification for administering treatment to somebody who is unable to consent on his/her own behalf. In *Re F*, it was not too difficult to make this judgement: she was an unstable epileptic and pregnancy would have destabilised this further; moreover, she would not have been able to understand or cope with the pain of a normal vaginal delivery and so would have required invasive treatment (i.e. a Caesarean section).

The importance of *Re F*, however, is that the principle of 'best interests' will apply in a wide range of situations. Thus, it will apply if the patient is *temporarily* incompetent (e.g. unconscious), *permanently* incompetent (e.g. learning disability, dementia), or in certain *emergencies* (e.g. if the patient is haemorrhaging or in severe pain and is unable to make a decision regarding treatment). At all times, though, the healthcare professional must be able to justify, first, that the patient is genuinely incompetent (using the test of competence outlined in the Mental Capacity Act 2005); and second, that any treatment given is in the patient's interests and nobody else's.

The common law principle outlined in *Re F* has now been incorporated within the Mental Capacity Act 2005 (section 4), and there are a number of considerations that the healthcare professional must take into account. Thus, for example, the practitioner must make an estimation of whether or not the patient is likely to regain competence: if so, it may be possible to delay the decision until then. If s/he is unlikely to regain competence, or the decision must be made quickly, consideration should also be given to any beliefs, values, wishes or feelings that the patient had when competent. Above all else, the practitioner must not make assumptions about a patient; thus, the fact that a person is old does not automatically imply that s/he would refuse major surgery if able to make this judgement.

Clearly, the determination of a patient's best interests is frequently going to be a judgement made with insufficient information, and will therefore necessitate the use of guesswork and intuition. The Mental Capacity Act (2005) Code of Practice (2007) gives some fairly extensive guidance on how to make this judgement (section 42 [4]), and how to maximise a patient's decision-making capacity (sections 2 and 3). Suffice it to say at this point that 'best interests' relate not merely to physical interests, but also to social, psychological, cultural and spiritual interests. As we have already seen, the administration of a life-saving blood transfusion would serve the *physical* interests of a Jehovah's Witness, but would fail to serve his/her *spiritual* interests (the latter being of more importance in this situation).

There are a number of specific legal and ethical issues arising from *Re F*, but there is one question that may be worth considering here. Why was it never suggested that the *male* partner of F should be sterilised? Some might argue that the fact that it was never raised as a possibility is the product of a male-dominated judiciary, and there may be an element of truth in this. However, the one recorded case that dealt with this issue is an excellent illustration of the principle of 'best interests' in practice.

Box 4.23 *Re A (Medical treatment: male sterilisation) [2000]*

A man with learning disabilities was living with his mother, but she was getting to an age when she knew that she would have to put him in residential care. She also knew that he was attracted to women and that it was likely that he would form an attachment to one of the female residents. However, she believed that, if a child was born of

> the union between man and woman, then the man should accept a strong sense of responsibility for the raising of that child. Upon the realisation that her son would never be able to accept this responsibility, she asked the court for permission to have him sterilised so that this outcome would never materialise.

The court *refused* permission for this sterilisation; and its reasons for refusal were exactly the same as their reasons for allowing it in *Re F*. In other words, the sterilisation would not be done in the best interests of A, but instead would be done in the interests of others.

The fact that the court will be guided by the best interests of the patient essentially means that it is freed from the shackles of the *Bolam* test. Medical opinion will undoubtedly have relevance in the case, but the judge is not compelled to accept it as conclusive if it appears to conflict with the interests of the patient. In *Re SL [2000]*, for example, a 28-year-old woman had severe learning disabilities, and her mother and doctors felt that she should be sterilised. The High Court judge had applied the *Bolam* test and declared the sterilisation to be lawful, but the Court of Appeal rejected this approach, for they felt that the insertion of a coil was less invasive and carried fewer risks. As Dame Elizabeth Butler-Sloss said (at 465):

> the principle of best interests as applied by the court extends beyond the considerations set out in Bolam. The judicial decision will incorporate broader ethical, social, moral and welfare considerations.

Once it is established that treatment is in a patient's best interests, it becomes lawful to administer it even if the patient resists. How much force is permitted is not an easy question to answer, but the Mental Capacity Act 2005 states that it should be 'a proportionate response' (section 6 [3]). Or, to put it another way, the level of force should be the minimum required to achieve the desired objective. This had, in fact, been the court's position before the Mental Capacity Act (see *Norfolk & Norwich Healthcare NHS Trust v W [1996]*), but there is a responsibility upon healthcare professionals to balance the patient's physical interests with his psychological interests. Consider the following scenario:

Box 4.24

A patient with learning disabilities has recurrent balanitis and is admitted to a surgical ward for a circumcision. While on the ward, he appears very happy; but when the porters come to take him to Theatre, he begins to scream in terror and becomes very aggressive.

Technically, the healthcare professionals would be justified in imposing this treatment upon the patient and in employing appropriate forms of restraint to enable them to do so. However, it is not a life-threatening emergency, and it is necessary to ask whether the psychological trauma experienced by the patient is worth it. Each case will be different, of course, and it is impossible to formulate clear guiding principles on this. But any conflict between the patient's physical interests and his psychological interests must be weighed carefully in the balance before restraint is imposed. Moreover, the healthcare professional will need to ascertain whether or not treatment remains a feasible option even if the physical interests would appear to outweigh the psychological. In *Re D [1998]*, for example, it was held that haemodialysis could be withdrawn from an incompetent patient, because his resistance made it impossible for the treatment to be given.

When an incompetent adult patient undergoes surgery, there is a space on the consent form for the signature of the relatives. It is important to note, though, that this signature does not imply that these relatives have consented on behalf of the patient. It simply means that they have been involved in the decision-making process – the decision itself has been made by the healthcare professionals. This is not the case in some countries, where relatives do consent on behalf of their aging parents, but it is not a feature of the law in the United Kingdom. Brazier and Cave (2007) suggest that this is because it is not always easy to identify the most appropriate person to seek consent, and that relatives may have vested interests in exposing a patient to the risks of surgery. We might add a third reason, however: namely, that it would impose a huge burden upon these relatives. If the patient were to die following surgery, for example, the guilt experienced by the relatives may be intolerable. Having said this, the Mental Capacity Act 2005 has created an opportunity for others to consent on behalf of a patient in the form of a Lasting Power of Attorney.

8 LASTING POWERS OF ATTORNEY

A Lasting Power of Attorney (LPA) occurs when an individual confers decision-making authority onto another. The individual must be 18 or over and must be competent when the LPA is created. Moreover, this decision-making power only becomes activated when the individual becomes incompetent. To be valid, the document conferring LPA onto another must satisfy legal criteria, and the person on whom this power has been conferred must be registered with the Office of the Public Guardian. On the assumption that it does meet all these criteria and the individual has become incompetent, the person with LPA has the authority to make decisions concerning both the patient's property and affairs and his health and welfare (s9).

Thus, the LPA can give or refuse consent to treatment of the patient (s11 [7c]). As the Mental Capacity Act worked its way through Parliament, and especially upon receiving the Royal Assent, the media frequently interpreted this provision as opening the gateway to euthanasia. It was envisaged that a host of grasping relatives, keen to get their hands on the patient's inheritance, would insist upon the withdrawal of medication and intravenous fluids so that death was hastened. There are, however, sufficient safeguards to prevent this from happening. First, the LPA must always act (and be seen to act) in the patient's best interests (s11). If the healthcare professionals have reason to suspect that this is not the case, they can delay following the instructions of the LPA to withdraw treatment and challenge him/her in court. The court itself would have the power to revoke the LPA if there was evidence to suggest that s/he was not operating in the interests of the patient. Second, the LPA does not have the power to refuse life-sustaining treatment, unless the document conferring power specifically mentions this (s11 [8a]).

Some have argued that the 'power' of an LPA is more of an illusion than a reality (Herring, 2008), and that conflicts between LPAs and healthcare professionals will invariably be decided in favour of the latter. Perhaps because of this, the concept of LPAs has not yet captured the public's imagination, although the Office of the Public Guardian reports a growing interest (John, 2010). It does, though, represent one more step away from the paternalistic tradition of healthcare, and is a recognition of the increasing rights of autonomy for patients.

9 CONSENT: THE ETHICAL PERSPECTIVE

This chapter began with an assertion that the legal standard for consent is lower than that of its ethical counterpart. Any distinction between the two, however, is bound to be artificial, because the law is generally informed and shaped by prevailing ethical beliefs, and we have seen that there has been an evolution in the way that both the courts and Parliament have approached the issue of patient rights. Nevertheless, many ethical issues remain contentious and unresolved, and it is the intention of this section to bring some of them into focus. As with all ethical debates, the chances of finding answers remain elusive, but the alternative is much worse: an absence of a questioning attitude ensures that injustices and anomalies will never be corrected.

Let us begin this discussion by considering the Devil's Advocate position:

Box 4.25

Why should decision-making power lie with the patient, given that his lack of knowledge, fear and illness may prevent him from making the 'right' decision?

We have seen that a valid consent requires three elements: the patient must be *competent*, s/he must have sufficient *information*, and the decision should be a *voluntary* one. Therefore, we need to examine each of these in a little more detail.

A COMPETENCE

Autonomy may be defined as the right of self-determination, or the right to act 'freely in accordance with a self-chosen plan' (Beauchamp and Childress, 2001: 58). It follows, therefore, that mental competence is a necessary pre-condition of being

able to exercise one's autonomy; but is this ever truly possible in a healthcare setting? One's illness and/or pain, the medication that one may be taking, and being in
an unfamiliar environment are all likely to have a detrimental impact on one's cognitive abilities. Even if these things are absent, it is almost inevitable that the patient
will have a level of anxiety or fear about the illness and its treatment, which will
also reduce his/her ability to think clearly.

In these circumstances, there may be an argument for taking a *paternalistic* stance,
where the healthcare professional adopts the position of a parent-figure and does
what is best for the patient, regardless of the latter's wishes. Jackson (2006) distin-
guishes between *soft* paternalism and *hard* paternalism: the former exists when we
stop people from doing things that they would not choose if fully competent (e.g.
exercising some form of restraint over the confused patient); while the latter exists
when we prevent people from making choices, simply because we think that they
are wrong. She argues that the former is morally acceptable and that the latter is
not. Thus, we can accept that the liberty of a seriously mentally ill patient should be
curtailed if this is in the interests of his/her own health and safety; sectioning him/
her under the Mental Health Act enables the enforced administration of medication
which will, hopefully, alleviate the mental symptoms so that s/he is given a better
chance of exercising his/her own autonomy. Neither the law, nor current ethical
thinking, however, would allow the enforced administration of a life-saving blood
transfusion on a Jehovah's Witness. The fact that we may think that the patient has
made a wrong choice has no relevance to this situation.

But why should one's right of autonomy over-ride all other factors? The answer
seems to be that the right of self-determination is considered more important than the
right to health; but, as Herring (2008) notes, this is essentially a western cultural tradition and is not necessarily a feature of other cultures. Consider the following scenario:

Box 4.26

An Asian woman attends a GP surgery, accompanied by her husband. It is clear that she
has a breast lump, and the GP proceeds to explain the implications of this condition
and the range of possible treatments. However, the woman speaks no English and the
GP has to communicate via the husband, who translates for her.

The dilemma for the GP here is that he cannot be sure that the information he conveys
is being translated fully and correctly, for the husband may be being selective in the
information that he chooses to pass on. A possible solution would be to make use of
the services of an independent translator, but this would still fail to acknowledge the
dynamics of the cultural differences between East and West. A strongly patriarchal
society, where the husband makes all decisions for his wife, may be anathema to western women, who have striven for equality over many years; but it would be a mistake
to assume that eastern women automatically feel the same way. Does the GP, therefore,
have the right to attack this cultural dynamic? It could be argued that the couple should

embrace western traditions if they choose to live here, but this would be to accept that we should be prepared to sacrifice our own culture if we were to move abroad.

Moreover, even within our own society, there will be occasions when the autonomy of competent patients will be over-ridden in the cause of the greater good. The case of Mary Mallon (otherwise known as 'Typhoid Mary') is probably the best example of this. She was an Irish immigrant to America who worked as a cook, but was found to be a healthy carrier of typhoid. Although not suffering from the disease herself, she was in an ideal position to infect others – a conservative estimate puts the number at 53, at least three of whom died (Bourdain, 2001). When she was identified as being the carrier, she was quarantined in hospital for three years, but was eventually released on condition that she never worked as a cook again. Incredibly, she then got a job as a cook in a New York hospital (working under the name of Mary Brown) and continued to infect others. This was enough to satisfy the authorities that the public deserved to be protected from this woman, and she was exiled to an island, where she remained until her death in 1938.

Her actions seem irresponsible to us, and her continued protestations that she was not the carrier despite all the evidence seem unreasonable; but she was not incompetent in the truest sense of the word. Her autonomy was restricted, therefore, because her decisions impacted adversely upon other people – not because she was unable to make those decisions herself.

In the United Kingdom, the Public Health (Control of Disease) Act 1984 empowers authorities to forcibly remove sufferers of certain contagious diseases (e.g. cholera, plague, smallpox, typhus) to hospital, even if such patients refuse treatment. Brazier (2006) also argues that the law should acknowledge that the concept of patient rights is of questionable value if it is not accompanied by a sense of responsibility. Thus, the person who refuses life-saving treatment may be exercising his right of autonomy, but his death will have an adverse impact upon those to whom he has obligations (i.e. his wife and children). Similarly, the person with HIV might be said to have moral obligations to inform any sexual partners of his medical status. Neither of these obligations is enshrined in law, and the obvious implication is that the pendulum may have swung too far in the interests of patients' rights. Perhaps, however, it is better that it swings this way than the other.

Another point to consider regarding competence is whether or not it can ever be truly measured in any meaningful sense. We have previously mentioned the test of capacity laid down in the Mental Capacity Act (section 3 [1])EQ, but how can one be sure that a patient has understood the information given to him/her? How, too, do we know that the information has been retained, or that the patient has been able to weigh it in the balance to arrive at a decision? It is probably easier to tell when a patient is *unable* to do these things; but a nod of the head at an appropriate time is not, of itself, evidence of competence. Clearly, a proper assessment of competence will involve a two-way dialogue between patient and healthcare professional. Moreover, the healthcare professional has a responsibility to ensure that decision-making capacity is enhanced as much as possible (Hope et al., 2008). Thus, the environment should be optimised so that the patient makes decisions without distractions, and discussions should take place at a time of day when the patient is at his/her best. Similarly, the patient should be allowed the necessary time, and explanations should be given as simply and as clearly as possible. The pace and pressure of healthcare delivery may make this look like an impossible ideal, but it is a standard to which practitioners should be striving to reach (even if they fall some way short of it).

B INFORMED

The argument that patients have a right to be provided with information before they consent to a medical procedure is unlikely to find many prepared to contest it these days. Thus, if patients have rights to information, it follows that healthcare professionals have a *duty* to provide it. Grubb (2004) has suggested that it may be difficult to find a legal basis for this duty, but that the courts have circumvented this problem by turning it on its head: if the healthcare professional fails to inform the patient adequately, s/he will have *omitted* to perform to a reasonable standard of care.

It is apparent, however, that the term 'reasonable' is open to interpretation. It does not, for example, require the healthcare professional to divulge detailed information (Pattinson, 2009); and there is merit in the contention that too much information could induce fear, depression and confusion. Certainly, the disclosure of all risks can shift attention away from understanding, and it is important to re-visit one's reasons for providing this information. Is it given in recognition of the patient's rights; or is it given to reduce the risk of litigation? If the latter, a curious paradox is created. As the law comes increasingly to acknowledge the patient's rights to be fully involved in decision-making and to be an equal partner in the relationship with healthcare professionals, the latter come to see the patients as potential adversaries, and their practice is guided by self-protection rather than endeavouring to create a therapeutic partnership (McMillan, 1995).

The concept of therapeutic privilege – where a healthcare professional is entitled to withhold information from a patient if it is felt that such information will have damaging psychological effects – is recognised in law (see *Sidaway v Bethlem Royal Hospital Governors [1985]*); but there are risks that healthcare professionals may abuse this privilege. Harris (1985) argues that healthcare decisions should be made by the patient and that the healthcare professional should not bear the responsibility for these. Therefore, the occasions when therapeutic privilege is invoked should be rare, and practitioners should be able to provide strong justification for withholding information.

But, what if the patient expressly states that s/he does not wish to be provided with information? Beauchamp and Childress (2001) have argued that the patient is exercising his right of autonomy not to know, and that this should be respected by healthcare professionals. Harris (1985), however, is less convinced, 'for even those who don't wish to know have no right to remain in ignorance' (p. 212). There is, perhaps, a middle way, to which both would probably agree. If the patient genuinely does not wish to be informed about his/her treatment, risks or side-effects, it would be both pointless and cruel to force this knowledge upon him/her. The Department of Health (2009) acknowledges this, but advises that this should be recorded carefully in the notes and that patients may change their minds over the course of time. Moreover, there are some treatments which demand that a patient be given information, regardless of the fact that s/he has waived the right to know. Imagine, for example, a man who comes into hospital with a gangrenous leg and says to his surgeon: 'I have no wish to know what treatment you are proposing. Just do whatever you have to do'. It will undoubtedly come as something of a shock when he awakes from the anaesthetic to discover that he has had an amputation.

The problem for healthcare professionals is that it is impossible to predict how much information a patient wants or needs, and different generations may have vastly different attitudes. Thus, elderly patients belong to a generation that was highly deferential to members of the healthcare professions and who neither expected nor requested detailed knowledge of their treatment. By contrast, the younger generation are generally less deferential and are able to access information for themselves via the Internet. These are, of course, appalling generalisations and it would be a mistake to assume that one's age determines which category one fits into. Nevertheless, the differences between patients make it very difficult to formulate clear guidelines for practice.

There are, in addition, numerous constraints preventing the transmission of high-quality information to patients. One of these is the lack of time available. But, if one says 'I do not have the time to provide my patients with full information', what one is really saying is 'I do not consider this as one of my priorities'. There may be good justification for making this claim, but the healthcare professional would need to examine what s/he is doing that is of greater importance. It is conceivable that the organisation of one's workload requires some improvement (including a willingness to delegate to others); but equally it is conceivable that a level of rationalisation is present here. Clearly, if a healthcare professional allocates the necessary time for this aspect of work and encourages the patient to ask questions, there is a real danger that the interaction could become highly emotional. In such circumstances, one's counselling skills will be called upon; but, if they are inadequate, there is a danger that things could be made worse. Thus, the healthcare professional may seek to avoid such scenes, not only from a personal point of view, but also from a desire to avoid inducing harm to the patient. If this is true, the solution would be to improve one's counselling skills, rather than hide behind the excuse of a heavy workload.

C VOLUNTARY

While it would be difficult to find examples where the competent patient has been coerced into accepting treatment, manipulation is much more common. Consider the following hypothetical situation:

Box 4.27

A woman has a cancerous breast lump, and her surgeon explains the possible options to her thus: 'I can perform a lumpectomy, but I cannot be certain that I will have removed all of the cancerous tissue. I can perform a wide excision, but this will leave you with a mis-shaped breast. What I would prefer to do, however, is a mastectomy, so that I can be more confident that the cancer has been excised.'

Has the surgeon done anything wrong here? He has provided his patient with the alternatives and has offered her the choice. However, he has accentuated the risks of two of these alternatives, while making his own preference very clear (even though the evidence base for this may be non-existent). In such circumstances, patient 'choice' is illusory: figuratively speaking, she has been poked with a cattle-prod until she enters the field of the surgeon's choosing.

This is rather an obvious and extreme example of manipulation, but undoubtedly more subtle examples exist. The reason is that no matter how much we like to think of the relationship between patient and healthcare professional as a partnership, the reality is that there is an unequal power balance. Many patients, for example, will have concerns about the implications for their care if they reject their surgeon's opinion. While under anaesthetic, the doctor quite literally has the patient's life 'in his hands': to upset somebody with this power is rarely a wise move.

CONCLUSION

We can accept, both legally and morally, that patients have rights of autonomy and that they should be fully involved in the decision-making process. This does not completely answer the question set at the beginning of this section, though. If a patient is sick, frightened and has limited medical knowledge, it is doubtful that much information will be retained, no matter how seriously the healthcare professional takes his/her responsibilities. Similarly, it is not unreasonable that a patient in such circumstances will revert to a childlike state of dependence upon those whom s/he trusts to alleviate his symptoms.

Savulescu (1995) suggest that the model of informed consent may be both impractical and unfair if applied to a large section of patients. They are not in a position to absorb large amounts of information and they cannot be expected to make clear choices. He argues, therefore, for a middle way: a 'rational non-interventional paternalism', where the healthcare professional outlines what s/he believes is the right course of action to take and seeks to persuade the patient by means of rational argument. Note, however, that despite the paternalistic nature of this interaction, Savulescu continues to uphold the patient's right to reject the advice given.

This will not work in all situations, of course, and it has potential for abuse. There is a sense, however, that many patients will appreciate being given clear directions, for they will frequently enter the interaction feeling very confused. What is equally important, though, is that the healthcare professional should establish a climate that encourages the patient to ask questions. In this way, they will seek information that is important to them, and this will inevitably enhance their understanding. Mason and Laurie (2011) contend that the term 'informed consent' is a tautology (because consent must be informed if it is valid), and they suggest that 'valid' consent would be a better term to use. Similarly, O'Neill (2003) argues that the concept should be called *genuine* consent: 'Genuine consent is apparent where patients can control the amount of information they receive, and what they allow to be done' (2003: 5). Therefore, the patient should not be bombarded with information or informed of every conceivable risk, but should feel comfortable about asking questions that are of particular relevance to them.

Finally, we should note that obtaining patient consent does not need to be a one-off event performed by one healthcare professional (except in emergencies). It should be a *process*, where all the members of team can contribute to patient understanding, and where the patient is not pressurised to make an instant decision (General Medical Council, 2008; DH, 2009). In this way, the reality will begin to approach the ideal.

SUMMARY

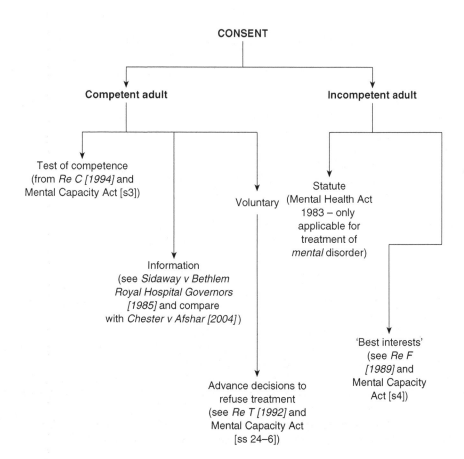

REFERENCES

TEXTS

Beauchamp, T.L. and Childress, J.F. (2001) *Principles of Bio-medical Ethics*, 5th edn. Oxford: Oxford University Press.

Bourdain, A. (2001) *Typhoid Mary: An Urban Historical*. New York: Bloomsbury.

Brazier, M. (2006) 'Do no harm – do patients have responsibilities too?' *Cambridge Law Journal*, 65 (2), July: 397–422.

Brazier, M. and Cave, E. (2007) *Medicine, Patients and the Law*, 4th edn. London: Penguin Books.

Department of Health (2009) *Reference Guide to Consent for Examination or Treatment*, 2nd edn. London: Department of Health. August 2009.

Dimond, B. (2008) *Legal Aspects of Nursing*, 5th edn. London: Pearson Education Limited.

Feldman, D. (2002) *Civil Liberties and Human Rights in England and Wales*. Oxford: Oxford University Press.

Foster, C. (2004) 'It should be, therefore it is', *New Law Journal*, 154 (7151), 5 November.

General Medical Council (1998) *Seeking Patients' Consent: the Ethical Considerations*. London: GMC (November).

General Medical Council (2008) *Consent: Patients and Doctors Making Decisions Together*. London: GMC.

Griffith, R. and Tengnah, C. (2008) *Law and Professional Issues in Nursing*. Exeter: Learning Matters.

Grubb, A. (2004) 'Consent to treatment: the competent patient', in A. Grubb and J. Laing (eds), *Principles of Medical Law*, 2nd edn. Oxford: Oxford University Press.

Gunn, M.J., Wong, J.G., Clare, I.C.H. and Holland, A.J. (1999) 'Decision-making capacity', *Medical Law Review*, 7 (3): 269–306.

Harris, J. (1985) *The Value of Life*. London: Routledge.

Herring, J. (2008) *Medical Law and Ethics*. Oxford: Oxford University Press.

Heywood, R. (2009) 'Medical disclosure of alternative treatments', *Cambridge Law Journal*, 68 (1), March: 30–2.

Heywood, R., Macaskill, A. and Williams, K. (2010) 'Informed consent in hospital practice: health professionals' perspectives and legal reflections', *Medical Law Review*, 18, Spring: 152–84.

Hope, T., Savulescu, J. and Hendrick, J. (2008) *Medical Ethics and Law*, 2nd edn. London: Churchill Livingstone.

Jackson, E. (2010) *Medical Law: Text, Cases and Materials*, 2nd edn. Oxford: Oxford University Press.

Jackson, J. (2006) *Ethics in Medicine*. Cambridge: Polity Press.

John, M. (2010) www.publicguardian.gov.uk/docs/May_12th_2010_Update_note_to_stake holders_on_operational_issues.pdf. Accessed 29/6/10.

Johnstone, M-J. (2004) *Bio-ethics: A Nursing Perspective*. Sydney: Churchill Livingstone Elsevier.

Jones, M.A. (1999) 'Informed consent and other fairy stories', *Medical Law Review*, 7, Summer: 103–34.

Kennedy, I. (1986) 'The fiduciary relationship and its application to doctors', in P. Birks (ed.), *Wrongs and Remedies in the Twenty-first Century*. Oxford: Clarendon Press.

Kennedy, I. (1988) *Treat Me Right*. Oxford: Oxford University Press.

Kennedy, I. and Grubb, A. (1998) *Medical Law: Text with Materials*. London: Butterworths.

Kirby, M. (1995) 'Patients' rights – why the Australian courts have rejected Bolam', *Journal of Medical Ethics*, 21: 5–8.

Lewis, P.J. (1997) 'Law notes', *Dispatches*, 8 (1), Winter, King's College London.

Lewis, P. (2006) 'Assisted dying in France. The evolution of assisted dying in France: a third way?' *Medical Law Review*, 14, Spring: 44–72.

Mason, J.K. and Laurie, G.T. (2011) *Mason and McCall Smith's Law and Medical Ethics*, 8th edn. Oxford: Oxford University Press.

McMillan, R.C. (1995) 'Responsibility *to* or *for* in the physician–patient relationship', *Journal of Medical Ethics*, 21: 112–15.

Mental Capacity Act (2005) Code of Practice (2007). London: HMSO.

Montgomery, J. (2003) *Health Care Law*, 2nd edn. Oxford: Oxford University Press.

Nursing and Midwifery Council (2008) *The Code: Standards of Conduct, Performance and Ethics for Nurses and Midwives*. London: NMC.

O'Neill, O. (2003) 'Some limits of informed consent', *Journal of Medical Ethics*, 29: 4–7.

Park, D.C. and Radford, J.P. (1998) 'Reconstructing a history of involuntary sterilisation', *Disability and Society*, 13: 317–42.

Pattinson, S.D. (2009) *Medical Law and Ethics*, 2nd edn. London: Sweet & Maxwell.

Savulescu, J. (1995) 'Rational non-interventional paternalism: why doctors ought to make judgements of what is best for their patients', *Journal of Medical Ethics*, 21: 327–31.

Sher, J. (2003) 'The triumph of logic over common-sense? A commentary on Chester v Afshar', *Medico-Legal Journal*, 70 (188), 6 January.

Veerapen, R.J. (2007) 'Informed consent: physician inexperience is a material risk for patients', *Journal of Law, Medicine and Ethics*, 35 (3): 478–85.

CASES

A (medical treatment: male sterilisation), Re [2000] 1 FLR 549.

AK, Re [2001] 1 FLR 129.

Appleton v Garrett [1995] 34 BMLR 23 (QBD).

Birch v University College Hospitals NHS Foundation Trust [2008] EWHC 2237 (QB).

Blyth v Bloomsbury HA [1987] [1993] 4 Med. LR 151.

Bolam v Friern HMC [1957] 2 All ER 118.

Buck v Bell [1927] 274 US 200.

Burke v General Medical Council [2005] 3 FCR 169.

C (an adult: refusal of treatment), Re [1994] 1 All ER 819 (FD).

Chappel v Hart [1998] 195 CLR 232.

Chatterton v Gerson [1981] QB 432.

Centre for Reproductive Medicine v U [2002] EWCA Civ. 565.

Chester v Afshar [2004] UKHL 41.

D, Re [1998] 2 FCR 178.

Eve, Re [1986] 2 SCR 388.

F (mental patient: sterilisation), Re [1990] 2 AC 1, sub nom F v West Berkshire HA [1989] 2 All ER 545.

Freeman v Home Office (No. 2) [1984] QB 524 (CA).
Gold v Haringey HA [1988] QB 481.
HE v A Hospital NHS Trust [2003] EWHC 1017.
HG, Re [1993] 1 FLR 588.
JT, Re [1998] 1 FLR 48 (FD).
M, Re [1988] 2 FLR 497.
Malette v Shulman [1991] 2 Med. LR 162.
MB, Re [1997] 2 FLR 426.
McAllister v Lewisham & North Southwark HA [1994] 5 Med. LR 343.
Norfolk & Norwich Healthcare NHS Trust v W [1996] 1 FCR 269.
O'Brien v Cunard [1891] 28 NE 266.
P, Re [1989] 1 FLR 182.
Pearce v United Bristol Healthcare NHS Trust [1998] EWCA Civ. 865.
R v Richardson [1998] 43 BMLR 21 (CA).
R v Tabassum [2000] Lloyd's Rep. Med. 404 (CA).
Rochdale Healthcare NHS Trust v C [1997] 1 FCR 274.
Rogers v Whitaker [1992] 109 ALR 625.
S, Re [1993] Fam. 123.
SL, Re [2000] 2 FCR 452.
St. George's Healthcare NHS Trust v S [1998] 3 All ER 673.
Schloendorff v New York Hospital [1914] 105 NE 92.
Sidaway v Bethlem Royal Hospital Governors [1985] 1 All ER 643.
Smith v Tunbridge Wells HA [1994] 5 Med. LR 334.
T, Re [1992] 4 All ER 649.

LEGISLATION

Adults with Incapacity (Scotland) Act 2000
Family Law Reform Act 1969
Human Rights Act 1998
Mental Capacity Act 2005
Mental Health Act 1983
Public Health (Control of Disease) Act 1984

Scenarios (answers at back of book)

1   An elderly patient has been admitted for an abdomino-perineal excision of rectum (APR), and has signed the consent form. However, as you prepare her for Theatre, it becomes clear to you that she has not understood the treatment that is being proposed for her. She states that there is no point in giving her information, because she has a short-term memory and will therefore forget it very quickly. In addition, she says that she has always trusted healthcare professionals, and believes that the surgeon will do whatever is necessary.

What would you do in this situation?

2   A patient has been involved in a road traffic accident and has sustained a head injury, rendering him unconscious. It is also clear that he has internal injuries and will require a laparotomy to prevent any further haemorrhage. The surgeon has mentioned in the medical notes that a blood transfusion is going to be necessary if this patient is to have any chance of survival. However, as you undress him, you notice that he is carrying a card that identifies him as a Jehovah's Witness and that he is obliged to refuse all blood transfusions.

What would you do in this scenario?

3   An 85-year-old woman has been admitted to the ward with a urinary tract infection, incontinence, anaemia and confusion. She is lying in a wet bed one morning, but becomes very aggressive (verbally and physically) when the nursing staff attempt to clean her and change the bed. She believes that she is in her own home, and strongly objects to people touching her or telling her what to do.

What would you do in this situation?

5

CONFIDENTIALITY

Learning Objectives

At the end of this chapter, the reader will:

1 Have an understanding of the moral basis for confidentiality.

2 Be aware of the legal basis for confidentiality.

3 Acknowledge the legal, employment and professional sanctions available for breaches of confidentiality.

4 Have an understanding of those circumstances where confidentiality can be breached without fear of penalty.

1 INTRODUCTION

One week after the death of French President François Mitterrand in 1996, his doctor (Claude Gubler) published a book about his illness while in office. The book (*Le Grand Secret*) gave details of the President's diagnosis of prostate cancer with bone metastases ten years earlier, and claimed that he 'was no longer capable of carrying out his duties' during his last few months in office (Gorman and Sancton, 1996).

If Gubler harboured any thoughts that this book would lead to fame and fortune, he was soon to be cruelly disabused of this notion. The book was immediately withdrawn from sale by the authorities, he was given a four-month suspended prison sentence, his name was erased from the medical register, he was stripped of the honours conferred upon him (National Order of Merit and National Order of the Legion of Honour), and a court ordered him to pay 340,000 francs (approximately 51,833 euros) in damages to Mitterrand's family.

We can marvel at the severity of these sanctions and speculate that they were politically motivated – would they, for example, have been anywhere near as draconian if the subject of the breach had not been a senior politician? Indeed, in 2004, the European Court of Human Rights declared that France had been in clear breach of Article 10 (freedom of expression), and ordered the ban on the book to be lifted. Nevertheless, the authorities (political and medical) were able to justify their actions by arguing that Gubler had violated professional secrecy; and, by extension, had damaged the honour and integrity of the medical profession.

What is it, then, about confidentiality that makes it so sacrosanct that it applies even when a patient is no longer able to be harmed by its breach? The professional bodies all make confidentiality a central and fundamental principle underpinning healthcare ethics. For example, the General Medical Council (2006) states in section 37:

> Patients have a right to expect that information about them will be held in confidence by their doctors. You must treat information about patients as confidential, including after a patient has died.

Similarly, the Nursing and Midwifery Council's Code of Professional Conduct (NMC, 2008) states (at paragraph 5.1): 'You must treat information about patients and clients as confidential and use it only for the purposes for which it was given'. Finally, the Department of Health (2003) declares that confidentiality binds *everyone* who works within the NHS, regardless of whether or not they belong to a professional body. In consequence, the student nurse is bound by this duty on the very first day of his/her training (Hope et al., 2008). From this, therefore, we can extrapolate that there is a *professional* duty and a *contractual* duty to maintain confidentiality. There is also a *legal* duty, and this is something to which we shall return shortly. The *moral* duty, however, is founded upon a variety of principles, each of which could lay claim to precedence at any given time.

2 THE MORAL BASIS FOR CONFIDENTIALITY

Hope et al. (2008) suggest that there are four possible grounds:

1 *Respect for patient autonomy.* In other words, a person has the right to determine whether or not personal information is shared with others. Moreover, in acknowledging this right, we are demonstrating that we value an individual's dignity and that s/he has equal value (Hendrick, 2010). However, the exercise of autonomy is predicated on the understanding that the patient is mentally competent to make a judgement.
2 *Implied promise.* In other words, the healthcare professional has 'promised' to maintain the patient's confidentiality, and the patient has sought treatment on the understanding that this 'promise' will be kept. Whether or not this reflects the reality of practice is open to doubt, but it seems reasonable to assume that the majority of patients believe in the existence of this 'promise', and this can be evidenced by the sense of betrayal that they experience whenever it is broken.

3   *Virtue ethics.* In this view, trustworthiness is considered a cardinal virtue of healthcare profes-
    sionals, and this will include respecting the confidentiality of their patients. Certainly, a thera-
    peutic relationship between healthcare professional and patient demands that the latter
    should be able to trust the former, and that the former should demonstrate that s/he is worthy
    of that trust. In certain circumstances, however, there may be other virtues (for example,
    beneficence) which can over-ride this one, although such conflicts are often difficult to resolve.

4   *Consequentialism.* This theory suggests that actions should be determined by their conse-
    quences, and that the practitioner should be guided towards the decision that produces
    'the greatest happiness of the greatest number' (see Chapter 2). Thus, it could be argued
    that a breach of confidentiality will damage patients' confidence in healthcare profes-
    sionals and that they will subsequently be reluctant to seek medical advice for any future
    health-related problems. Conversely, however, a *failure* to breach confidentiality could
    potentially result in dire consequences for the patient and/or others.

Thus, each one of these four bases for confidentiality has merits, but each one can be
overturned. Given, therefore, that the moral basis represents a set of guiding principles, rather than hard and fast rules, it might now be worth examining the legal
justification for confidentiality.

3 THE LEGAL BASIS OF CONFIDENTIALITY

A GENERAL PRINCIPLES

The legal right to confidentiality has been recognised for a long time, and was
acknowledged in *Wood v Wyatt [1820]*, where the publication of George III's diaries
was restrained. It has, however, become more of an issue as the methods of mass
communication have evolved, and as the media have become more intrusive. A definition of confidentiality was offered by Lord Goff (in *AG v Guardian Newspapers
Ltd. (No. 2) [1990]*):

> A duty of confidence arises when confidential information comes to the knowledge of a
> person (the confidant) in circumstances where he has notice, or is held to have agreed,
> that the information is confidential, with the effect that it would be just in all the cir-
> cumstances that he should be precluded from disclosing the information to others.

Clearly, this definition allows communication of a patient's medical information
between members of the healthcare team, provided that this is done in good faith
and in a professional manner (DH, 2003, s38). But, as Mason and Laurie state, it
does not allow for 'irresponsible gossip' (2011: 204). A major part of the problem
surrounding confidentiality, however, is that the law has developed in a haphazard
manner, and there is a need for clarity (Toulson and Phipps, 2006). Thus, there is a
potential cause of action for a claimant under any, or all, of the following headings:

a   The common law.
b   The Data Protection Act 1998.
c   The Human Rights Act 1998.

There are (or, at least, may be) remedies for the claimant in each of these categories, and these will be discussed later. At this juncture, though, it is worth considering those situations in which confidentiality can be breached without fear of reprisal:

1 When an individual *consents* to his/her information being shared with others. In a health-care setting, this would arise when a patient authorises his/her medical details to be given to his/her relatives. Disclosure of this nature is predicated on the assumption that the patient is competent to make this decision and that s/he does so voluntarily.

2 When a *court of law* requires information to be disclosed to ensure that justice prevails. As Brazier and Cave state: 'Any breach of confidence made as a witness in court is absolutely privileged' (2007: 87). Moreover, refusal to disclose when asked would amount to a contempt of court, which would bring its own sanctions.

3 When certain *statutes* require it. There is an obligation to record details of the number of:
   i Abortions performed (Abortion Regulations 1991, reg. 4);
   ii Notifiable diseases (Public Health (Control of Disease) Act 1984); and
   iii Sexually transmitted infections (NHS (Venereal Diseases) Regulations 1974).

Note, though, that none of these legislative measures require disclosure of the *names* of individuals affected, for their purpose is purely statistical. In addition, no citizen is under any obligation to inform the police of a crime (Criminal Law Act 1967, s5 [5]), although s/he would be prosecuted if s/he accepted money to conceal criminal activity (s5 [1]). There are, however, a couple of statutes that compel the release of information. The first is the Terrorism Act 2000 (s19), which imposes a duty upon citizens to reveal evidence of terrorist activity. The second is the Road Traffic Act 1988 (s172), which requires healthcare professionals to identify a driver involved in an accident to the police (if they request this information). Confirmation of this requirement had been established in a case heard several years earlier:

Box 5.1 *Hunter v Mann [1974]*

A man and a girl had been involved in a road traffic accident, but fled the scene and later presented themselves at Casualty for treatment. A police officer then asked the doctor who treated them to reveal their identity, but he refused. He argued that this information was confidential, but the court disagreed and found him guilty of failing to comply with the Road Traffic Act 1972 (s168 [2] [b]).

4 When it is in the *public interest*. Clearly, this is always going to be the most contentious of the possible justifications for breaching confidentiality, largely because the 'public interest' defies a satisfactory definition. This is, in essence, a judgement call, and may be influenced by individual conscience, personal moral or religious beliefs, and a whole host of other intangible factors. The healthcare professional must always remain aware that any decision to breach confidentiality (however well-meaning or driven by conscience) may bring him/her into conflict with his/her employer and/or the professional body.

The Department of Health (2010) has, however, produced some guidelines, which should serve as a defence to both criminal/civil action and disciplinary proceedings. The healthcare professional *would*, for example, be expected to reveal details of serious crime to the police (defined, in s12, as murder, manslaughter, rape, treason, kidnapping and child abuse). Disclosure would be less justifiable, on the other hand, in instances of theft, fraud or damage to property (s13). This is not to say that the healthcare professional would necessarily be condemned for breaching confidentiality in such cases, but s/he is asked to consider any potential damage to the therapeutic relationship following such disclosure (s20).

These guidelines go some way towards clarifying when it would be acceptable to breach confidentiality in the public interest, but there remain large areas of obscurity. In fairness, it was always destined to be so, but it may be possible to tease out some guiding principles by discussing a few real and fictional scenarios. Before moving on, it is important to identify a crucial distinction: namely, that the 'public interest' is not the same as 'of interest to the public' (DH, 2010, s19). This distinction is perhaps most clearly seen in the following celebrated scandal:

Box 5.2   The Profumo affair

In 1961, the Secretary of State for War (John Profumo) began an affair with a 19-year-old dancer by the name of Christine Keeler. In itself, this was of no major significance and would probably never have come to light had it not been for the fact that Keeler was also sleeping with a Russian military attaché (Eugene Ivanov). The implication was clear (although never confirmed) that Profumo could reveal State secrets to Keeler, who would subsequently transmit them to a Soviet agent. In other words, national security was being put at risk, and it was in the public interest that this affair was publicised (Profumo affair: www.britannica.com).

B THE PUBLIC INTEREST

Having established this distinction, we can look at a variety of situations where the public interest may be a factor:

The mentally ill

Box 5.3   *W v Egdell [1990]*

W was a patient in a secure hospital, and he applied to a mental health tribunal to be discharged or transferred to a regional unit. His solicitors asked a psychiatrist (Dr Egdell) to examine him, intending to use this report as supporting evidence for their client at the tribunal. After examining W, however, Dr Egdell came to the conclusion that he continued to represent a danger to the public and that he should remain in a secure unit. Knowing that his report would damage their client's case, the solicitors refused to show it to the tribunal. Dr Egdell, in contrast, was determined that the tribunal should be fully aware of all the facts, and he forwarded his report to the Secretary of State. W sought an injunction to restrain the tribunal from using the report, and claimed damages for breach of confidence.

Although initially successful in the High Court, W subsequently lost in the Court of Appeal, these judges holding that it was essential that a mental health tribunal should have all the facts about a patient's mental condition before making decisions concerning his future. This is one of the most important cases in English law pertaining to confidentiality, for the judicial rationale for the decision embraced a number of guiding principles, one of which is the following:

Information may be disclosed in the public interest, provided that the 'risk' is real rather than fanciful, and that it should involve the danger of physical harm to the public.

The case of *Cornelius v de Taranto [2001]* offers an interesting contrast to *W v Egdell*. Here, a schoolteacher suffered from severe stress and wanted to bring a claim for constructive dismissal against her employer. She was seen by a consultant psychiatrist, who sent a report to the defendant (a senior registrar in forensic psychiatry). The latter subsequently transmitted this report to a variety of individuals (including another psychiatrist, the claimant's GP and her solicitor), and Cornelius alleged that she had not consented to this. The court found in her favour: in contrast to *Egdell*, there was no danger to the public, and her written consent was required before transmission of the report.

Let us imagine for a moment, though, that Dr Egdell decided to uphold the sanctity of the principle of confidentiality and did not transmit his concerns to the Secretary of State. Let us further imagine that the tribunal, in the absence of this information, decides to discharge the patient, who subsequently goes on to murder a number of people. Would Dr Egdell be held liable in negligence for these crimes? One would expect him to have a few sleepless nights, but Morris and Adshead (1997) suggest that it would be difficult to establish liability in such cases, particularly as there are likely to be a number of intervening events between discharge and the crime (thereby negating the issue of causation).

Some evidence to the contrary, however, comes from the following American case:

Box 5.4   *Tarasoff v Regents of the University of California [1976]*

A patient confided to a psychiatrist that he intended to kill a young woman (Tatiana Tarasoff). The psychiatrist informed the police, but did not warn the woman, nor did he detain the patient. The latter subsequently went on to murder Miss Tarasoff, and the parents alleged negligence.

In a decision that sent shock waves through the American psychiatric profession, the court found for the parents, holding that the relationship between a psychiatrist and his/her patient was (at least in part) for the safety and benefit of others. If the woman *had* been given this information, though, it is not entirely clear what she could be expected to do with it. Could she have taken the necessary measures to protect herself against someone obsessed with her murder, or was she destined to lead the rest of her life in a permanent state of fear? Equally unclear is whether or not the case would be decided in exactly the same way in an English court. The perceived wisdom is that, by informing the police, the American psychiatrist would have discharged his duty in the UK (Herring, 2010), but that he may be liable if this was not the case.

The closest English equivalent to *Tarasoff* is the following:

Box 5.5   *Palmer v Tees Health Authority [1999]*

A psychiatric patient was released from care, whereupon he abducted a small girl, sexually abused and then murdered her. The parents argued that the Health Authority was responsible for her murder.

This is clearly a tragic and highly emotive case, but negligence still has to be established. In contrast to *Tarasoff*, there was no reasonable prospect of identifying the victim in advance, so the psychiatrist cannot be said to have had a duty of care to her. In other words, she was in the wrong place at the wrong time; and, if she had not been the victim, it is likely that the patient would have found somebody else.

It might be argued that the psychiatrist still fell below an acceptable standard of care by discharging such a patient into the community, but this presupposes that psychiatry is an exact science. Moreover, it has been argued that an extension of liability to psychiatrists for such events might result in defensive practices (Morris and Adshead, 1997). In other words, patients may be detained for much longer than is actually necessary. Such an argument found favour in the court when applied to the police in *Osman v Ferguson [1993]*. Here, a teacher had formed an unhealthy attachment to a 15-year-old male pupil and continually harassed him. He eventually shot and injured the boy and killed the father. The court acknowledged that the police had a duty to this family, for they had been made aware of the teacher's earlier harassment. However, the court also held that it would be against public policy to impose a higher standard of care upon the police, for this would result in defensive practices and the diversion of resources from the investigation and suppression of crime. The European Court (*Osman v UK [1998]*) did not argue against this logic, although they did find that the English jurisdiction had failed to insist that the police account for their actions and omissions. In consequence, the claimants were awarded £10,000 each.

The risk of unintentional harm The above cases have all dealt with deliberate acts of physical harm done to members of the public (albeit by people who have a deranged psychological state). But there may be other situations where the risk of physical harm remains, even though there is no malicious intent. Consider the following case from New Zealand:

Box 5.6 *Duncan v Medical Practitioners' Disciplinary Committee [1986]*

Mr Henry was a bus driver who had had a coronary artery bypass graft. His licence to drive was renewed after the surgeon issued him with a certificate, but his GP felt that he was unfit to drive. The GP then informed the passengers and tried to organise a petition to have Mr Henry barred from driving. Mr Henry complained to the Committee that he was being victimised by the GP, and that the latter had breached confidentiality.

Dr Duncan appealed to the court for review of the disciplinary measures invoked against him by the Committee, but the court upheld this decision. It was accepted that his actions had not been driven by any selfish motives, and that he genuinely had the best interests of the public at heart. However, there are more appropriate methods of raising concerns than standing at a bus stop and disclosing confidential medical information to anybody within earshot. This, then, leads us to a second guiding principle:

> Disclosure should be made only to those whom it is necessary to tell so as to protect the public interest.

An illustration of this principle in action is when a newly diagnosed epileptic patient continues to drive. Should his doctor be concerned about the potential risks to the public; and, if so, to whom should he report these concerns? The Department of Health (2010) has suggested that disclosure would be acceptable in these circumstances (section 11), although there are a few conditions. First, the patient should be encouraged to surrender his licence voluntarily: only if he refuses to do so would the doctor be entitled to breach confidentiality, but s/he should report the information only to the Driver and Vehicle Licensing Centre (DVLC). Moreover, the patient should be informed of the doctor's intention to report.

This, of course, represents guidance, and the doctor is therefore under no legal duty to report. If the doctor did *not* report and the patient went on to cause a serious accident, would s/he be liable in negligence? Both the Department of Health and the General Medical Council appear to be of the opinion that the reasonable practitioner would (and indeed, should) inform the DVLC. Moreover, the doctor could reasonably have foreseen that driving with epilepsy was likely to result in a road traffic accident (although a claimant would have to show that the accident was directly attributable to the patient having an epileptic seizure). Whether or not the doctor has a legal duty of care to all other road users, however, is more difficult to establish. It would seem, therefore, that such an action would be destined to fail, although the doctor would not emerge with an unblemished reputation.

Possession of illegal substances   If reporting somebody with epilepsy to the DVLC is relatively unproblematic, there are other situations that are less straightforward. Consider the following fictional scenario:

Box 5.7   The patient with illegal substances

A patient is admitted unconscious to Casualty following a road traffic accident. Upon checking his belongings, it is noticed that he has a small quantity of cannabis in one of his pockets. Should the police be informed?

It seems reasonable to assume that most practitioners would not consider this worthy of disclosure to the police. A small quantity suggests that the cannabis is for his personal use, and it is doubtful that the police would demonstrate much interest in the case. But what if the quantity was much larger so that it is clear that the patient is a supplier of this substance? Similarly, would it make a difference if the substance was cocaine or heroin?

From a legal perspective, the courts are unlikely to enforce a duty of confidence where the subject matter is iniquitous (*Gartside v Outram [1856]*) or immoral (*Stephens v Avery [1988]*). The Department of Health (2010, s2) and the professional bodies both appear to give some protection to the healthcare professional who discloses information of this nature, although they do not deal specifically with this situation. The practitioner therefore must be satisfied in his/her own mind that the public interest is served by disclosure; and this leads us to our third guiding principle:

> If confidentiality is to be breached, the public interest in disclosure must outweigh the public interest in non-disclosure.

It ought to be possible to justify disclosure of drug-dealing activities to the authorities – not only is it illegal, but also it is potentially harmful to a large number of people (including, possibly, children). There is, however, a price to pay for this breach of confidentiality, in that the patient will inevitably lose trust in all healthcare professionals. If one's judgement is that this is a price worth paying, then the elements of the guiding principle are satisfied.

HIV and genetic disorders   The principle was also seen at work in the following case:

Box 5.8   *X v Y and another [1988]*

Some employees of a Health Authority supplied Y (a newspaper reporter) with information obtained from medical records which identified two doctors who were carrying on general practice having contracted HIV. The Health Authority sought an injunction to restrain the newspaper from publishing the identity of the doctors. The newspaper argued that it was in the public interest to disclose this information.

The court held, in this instance, that the balance tipped towards *non*-disclosure, for it was in the public interest that the confidentiality of these GPs should be preserved. If confidentiality was not maintained, patients with HIV would be reluctant to come forward for treatment, and the disease would escape our best efforts to contain it (Wacks, 1988).

In essence, the principle highlights a conflict between Article 8 of the Human Rights Act (the right to privacy) and Article 10 (the right to free expression). The latter Article is intended to embrace the freedom of the press, which is considered of major importance in a democratic society. The courts are therefore generally very reluctant to impose what many would perceive as censorship, and the balance will frequently tip towards disclosure (see *R (on the application of Stone) v South East Coast SHA [2006]* and *In Re Attorney General's Reference (No. 3 of 1999) [2009]*). Moreover, in *X v Y*, the balance might have favoured disclosure if the doctors had been surgeons, rather than GPs. As GPs, they represented little danger of transmitting the virus to their patients; but this risk is increased when the doctor is a surgeon, where there is always the possibility of cutting him/herself with the scalpel and dripping his/her own blood into the patient's open wound (see *Faya & Rossi v Almarez [1993]*: an American case, where the patients sued successfully for psychological damage following the knowledge that the surgeon who operated on them was HIV positive).

There have, apparently, been only three reported incidents worldwide of HIV transmission from healthcare professionals to patients (a French orthopaedic surgeon, a Florida dentist and a Spanish gynaecologist) (DH, 2005; Pattinson, 2009). This suggests that the risk is extremely low, but it is sufficient to ensure that the HIV positive surgeon should be barred from practice (DH, 2005, para. 4.9).

A further complication arises when one considers the following fictional scenario:

Box 5.9   The patient with HIV

A patient attends a minor injuries unit with abrasions sustained following a fall from a ladder at home. As the nurse takes a medical history, he confides to her that he has recently been diagnosed as HIV positive. His work frequently takes him abroad, and it was on one such trip that he felt particularly lonely and sought the services of a prostitute. He says that he has not informed his wife, but she is a close personal friend of the nurse, and she has made it known that she is keen to start a family soon.

The primary responsibility for informing the patient's wife, of course, lies with the patient himself; and failure to do so could result in criminal prosecution if she subsequently contracts the infection. In *R v Dica [2005]*, a man was convicted of inflicting grievous bodily harm (under the Offences Against the Person Act 1861, s. 20) by infecting a woman with HIV. His actions were held to be reckless; and the woman's consent to intercourse did not provide him with a defence, for she had not consented to run the risk of transmission. This case effectively overturned an earlier decision (*R v Clarence [1888]*), where a man was acquitted of infecting his wife with gonorrhoea.

There have been other cases since *Dica* (e.g. *R v Konzani [2005]*), and even a couple where the woman was the offender (BBC News, 2006). But the question remains as to whether the healthcare professional has a duty to inform the infected patient's partner if the patient refuses to disclose this information.

In practice, the healthcare professional should make every effort to encourage the patient to tell his/her partner. If these efforts fail, however, GMC guidance (2004) suggests that doctors would be permitted to disclose confidential information of this nature to a patient's partner (although they would also be expected to inform the patient of this beforehand). Brazier and Cave (2007) contend that the courts are unlikely to *enforce* this duty, for there is no duty to rescue; although Herring (2010) argues that Article 2 of the Human Rights Act 1998 (the right to life) might impose such a duty. Certainly, if the patient's partner was also a patient at the practice, it might be easier to claim that a duty of care exists towards him/her. Conversely, the healthcare professional might be absolved from a duty to inform the partner if the patient agrees to abstain from intercourse or take precautions (Beauchamp and Childress, 2001), although this is less sustainable (given that the patient's promise has no contractual authority). Johnstone (2004) cites an Australian case, where a woman sued a medical practice for not informing her that her husband was HIV positive, and was awarded $727,000 when she subsequently contracted the infection. Whether or not an English court would have settled this case in the same way, however, is open to question.

If the courts would not enforce a duty of disclosure, though, would they penalise the healthcare professional for breaching confidentiality in these circumstances? The perceived wisdom is that this would be unlikely; and some authority for this position comes from *R v Dica [2005]*, where the court suggested an additional guiding principle:

> Disclosure is more likely to be justified when an infected patient is in a relationship with another, and the partner is at risk of contracting the infection.

Perhaps Johnstone (2004) summarises this position best when she says (at p. 162):

> the principle of confidentiality can never be used morally to protect those who would impose their incompetence, their diseases and their malevolence on to innocent and uninformed victims.

Does this principle extend to disclosure of information about genetic disorders? Gilbar (2004) draws a distinction between this situation and that of the patient with HIV. Here, if the clinician does not tell the partner of the disorder, that clinician does not put him/her at risk of contracting that disorder, but simply prevents him/her from being informed. This is a tempting argument, and appears to have been adopted by the British Medical Association (2009), who contend that patient confidentiality in these instances will usually outweigh the interests of the family. It seems unlikely, though, that this will be of much consolation to the partner who has been denied the opportunity to make a considered decision on whether or not to start a family.

Occupational Health   The example of the HIV positive surgeon has been discussed earlier, and how such an individual will pose a potential risk to patients. The nurse who is a carrier of the Hepatitis B virus and who works in a haemodialysis unit would be another example. It might be possible to re-locate both practitioners to other areas of healthcare, where the risk that they pose is eliminated. But what of the healthcare professionals who have a mental (rather than a physical) disorder, which impacts upon their ability to function safely and effectively? Would, for example, Occupational Health have an obligation to disclose this information to an employer?

The Royal College of Nursing (2005) states clearly that the medical information obtained from employees is strictly confidential and should be restricted to the Occupational Health department. Conversely, the Clothier Report (1994) made a recommendation that Occupational Health should inform the employer whenever an employee poses a risk to others. The Clothier inquiry was initiated following the activities of Beverly Allitt, a nurse working on a paediatric ward, who had a psychiatric condition known as Münchausen syndrome by proxy. This led her to inject large doses of insulin into children in her care, causing the death of four of them and grievous bodily harm to six others.

There were a number of opportunities to avoid this catastrophe, and Occupational Health was by no means the only department implicated. Nevertheless, it is clear that

Allitt's mental condition should have precluded her from working in a healthcare setting, and concerns about her health should have been relayed to her employer. The RCN (2005) fully acknowledges this, but goes on to stipulate that the employee should be fully informed that this disclosure is to take place. An illustration of this principle in action comes from the following court case:

Box 5.10　*Re L [2000]*

A paediatric nurse suffered from a severe personality disorder, and sought an injunction to prevent information about her mental health problems being passed on to her professional body. The court held that the injunction would not be granted, for the public interest dictated that her right to confidentiality should be breached.

Similarly, in *Woolgar v Chief Constable of Sussex Police [1999]*, the claimant (a registered nurse and matron) was arrested following the death of a patient in a nursing home. Although she was not charged, the police felt that details of the interview should be transmitted to her professional body. Ms Woolgar refused, but the court held that the police were free to disclose this information, even in the absence of consent. They should, however, inform the individual that this is being done, to enable him/her time to seek assistance from the court.

Child abuse　Although the Clothier Report was instigated as a direct result of outrages on a paediatric ward, its recommendations are intended to be applied more widely than this. In other words, public safety is of paramount importance, and Occupational Health personnel are expected to keep this in mind when determining whether or not to disclose confidential information to employers. Where there is suspected child abuse, the individual who discloses information to the authorities enjoys special protection from the law, as can be seen from the following case:

Box 5.11　*D v NSPCC [1978]*

The NSPCC were informed that D's 14-month-old daughter had been ill treated. Upon investigation, this was found to be untrue, but D was badly affected by the accusation and demanded to know the name of the informant. Although the Court of Appeal initially ordered discovery, this was subsequently overturned by the House of Lords. Their reasoning was that the public interest required anonymity of the informants: if this were not the case, people would be reluctant to report incidents of child abuse, and children would thereby be made more vulnerable.

There is, of course, no mandatory *duty* to report child abuse (Hendrick, 2010), but the above case identifies another guiding principle:

> The public interest (and, in particular, the interests of children) dictates that those who report child abuse to the authorities should be guaranteed anonymity and freedom from litigation (providing that disclosure is done in good faith and without malicious intent).

If the confidentiality of the informant is to be protected, is a duty of confidentiality also owed to the abuser (or spouse of the abuser)? We might think that this question should obviously be answered in the negative, but the following case would suggest otherwise:

Box 5.12   *C v Cairns [2003]*

C brought an action in negligence against her GP, because the latter did not tell the police or social services that she was being sexually abused by her stepfather when she was a child. The GP's defence was that he was acceding to a request from the mother to keep this information confidential.

Astonishingly, the court accepted this defence, together with his assertion that he could not be held liable for the criminal action of a third party. Before we read too much into this, however, a note of caution must be added: the incidents of child abuse occurred in the 1970s, and it would only be fair to judge the GP's performance alongside the standards of medical practice of the time. It was held that the GP had, indeed, acted in accordance with those standards; *but*, the standards of today would expect the reasonable practitioner to report abuse of this nature. Therefore, the GP who protected the interests of the mother in preference to those of her child would almost certainly be liable in negligence today if the child was to come to harm.

4 THE INCOMPETENT PATIENT

A CHILDREN

The case of *Gillick v West Norfolk and Wisbech Area Health Authority [1986]* made it clear that the same duty of confidence owed to adults extends to children, provided that the latter are able to understand what this entails (see Chapter 8). The potential adverse consequences of breaching a competent child's confidentiality are just as likely as if an adult's rights had been ignored (if not more so). Indeed, in *R (on the application of Axon) v Secretary of State for Health [2006]*, the judge quoted statistics suggesting that the number of teenage girls who sought contraceptive advice fell dramatically after the Court of Appeal decision in *Gillick* (in which the court found in Mrs Gillick's favour); and that these figures only rose again some time after the House of Lords' decision (which overturned the verdict in the Court of Appeal).

The question remains as to whether children who are *not* competent also have a right to confidentiality. Herring (2010) outlines the argument that an incompetent child, by definition, lacks autonomy, and is therefore unable to enter into a relationship of confidence. The obvious implication, in consequence, is that disclosure of medical information to the child's carers would be justifiable. There are two riders to this principle: first, disclosure would only be justifiable if it was in the *child's* best interests; and second, disclosure should be limited only to those who have a need to know, and who are therefore in a position to serve those interests. The second of these conditions suggests that children have general privacy rights, and that their inability to enter into a relationship of confidence does not automatically imply that their medical details can be broadcast to the whole world. Support for this position comes from the following case:

Box 5.13   *In Re C (a minor) (wardship: medical treatment) (No. 2) [1990]*

C had irreversible brain damage and was terminally ill. The court made an injunction to prevent the disclosure of her identity, but a national newspaper sought to overturn this injunction so that the public interest issues could be fully debated. The court held that it would be possible to debate those issues *without* disclosing the identity of C; and that her welfare might be adversely affected if those caring for her were exposed to publicity.

B ADULTS

The position of incompetent adults is much the same as that of the non-Gillick competent child, and their general rights of privacy were acknowledged in the following case:

Box 5.14   *R (on the application of S) v Plymouth City Council [2002]*

C was 27 years old and had serious learning and behavioural problems. His mother wished to challenge a social services authority's recommendation regarding her child's welfare, but needed access to his medical notes in order to present a stronger argument. The authority refused her access to these notes, and she sought judicial review of this decision.

The court held that disclosure was justified in this instance, for the mother needed this information in order to serve her son's interests fully. As Hale, L.J. stated (at para. 49):

> There is a clear distinction between disclosure to the media with a view to publication to all and sundry and disclosure in confidence to those with a proper interest in having the information in question.

Similar situations arise in Intensive Care Units, where patients are frequently unconscious and are thereby unable to consent to disclosure of their medical information to relatives. The relatives will understandably be very anxious, and this anxiety will be increased if they are kept behind a veil of secrecy. Indeed, it should come as little surprise to learn that a lack of communication is one of the leading causes of complaints about healthcare (Siyambalapitiya et al., 2007; Payne, 2009). Let us imagine, though, that information *is* given to the relatives of the unconscious patient; but, when he recovers, he is very angry about this breach and threatens to sue. In defending such an action, the staff may be able to argue that they were entitled to assume that the patient, if conscious, would have been willing to allow release of his medical details to ease the distress of his relatives (DH, 2003, para. 13). Indeed, it has been argued that patients may even have a moral (though not a legal) duty to consider the interests of their relatives in such situations (Gilbar, 2011).

The staff would, however, be expected to ascertain (as far as was reasonably practical) that those to whom information was divulged were, indeed, the relatives/carers of the patient. Moreover, such situations illustrate another guiding principle:

> Where a decision has been made to breach a patient's confidentiality, only the minimum information necessary to serve that patient's interests should be divulged.

There may be other occasions, though, when an adult patient is competent, but is unable to communicate. Consider the following fictional scenario, a version of which was considered in Chapter 4:

Box 5.15   Communication difficulties

A 50-year-old Muslim woman attends a dental practice, accompanied by her husband. She speaks no English, and her husband translates for her. Upon inspection of her mouth, it becomes clear that she will need extensive dental work, requiring numerous visits to both dentist and dental hygienist. The dentist explains this to the husband, outlining the nature of the treatment, the long-term complications of leaving her mouth untreated, and the costs of the therapy. Upon hearing the last of these, the husband appears visibly shocked. Moreover, when he translates this information to his wife, he does so very quickly, and the dentist is convinced that he has not given her all the information. These suspicions are given added strength when the husband says that his wife is refusing the treatment and does not want to discuss it any further.

The battle for equality of women's rights in the UK has been hard fought, lasting over a century and is ongoing. A patriarchal society, therefore, is in direct conflict with this, and produces a clash of cultures. However, do we have a right to impose our cultural beliefs upon others? There is, at this point, no evidence to suggest that the wife is unhappy about her husband making decisions for her; and an insistence that she should assume greater control may only serve to increase her anxiety. Her refusal, moreover, may be genuine: the costs of treatment may impose an intolerable burden upon her family, and she may be frightened of dental treatment.

Perhaps the best compromise in this situation is to insist that the practice's policy is to use an independent interpreter service when translating information to patients who are unable to speak English. In this way, the practice can be assured that full information can be given to the patient by an individual with no vested interests. Such a service may be costly and time-consuming, and the patient's decision may still be heavily influenced by the husband; but at least the practice will have done all that could be reasonably required of it.

A patient's poor oral health is not normally a life-threatening emergency, but the picture would become more complicated if the wife in our scenario had attended a GP surgery with a breast lump. The husband now has to be very careful that his influence upon her is not preventing her from accessing life-saving treatment. The *No Secrets* document (DH, 2000) does not deal specifically with this situation, but represents the best available guidance. It identifies a vulnerable adult as someone who is 'unable to protect him or herself against significant harm or exploitation' (s2.3); it acknowledges that abuse can be 'an act of neglect or an omission to act' (s2.6); and it recognises that 'harm' includes 'the impairment of, or an avoidable deterioration in, physical or mental health' (s2.18). Taken together, all three of these can be applied to our fictional scenario, and the document goes on to emphasise the responsibilities of healthcare professionals to pass on their concerns to the appropriate authority (most commonly, Social Services) (s6.2). Statutory protection for disclosure of this nature comes from the Public Interest Disclosure Act 1998, in which it is stated that one of the criteria is when 'the health or safety of an individual has been, is being or is likely to be endangered' (s43B [d]). It needs hardly be said, however, that this should always be the last resort: only when all measures to reason with the husband have been exhausted should recourse be taken to the involvement of others.

C THE DEAD

This chapter began with an illustration of the legal and disciplinary consequences that befell Dr Gubler when he disclosed medical details of the late French President, François Mitterrand. This was clearly an extreme example, and there must be doubt that a legal cause of action would be open to the family in the UK (unless they themselves had suffered economic loss as a result of the breach). Disciplinary procedures, however, remain a strong option, and Pattinson (2009) suggests that this is a manifestation of the consequentialist position. In other words, people may be discouraged from seeking treatment while alive if they believe that their medical details will be divulged after death. Despite this, death certificates are public documents, meaning that anybody can obtain access to them, providing that they are willing to pay for a copy (Mason and Laurie, 2011). The only exception to this would be if a court had served an injunction upon release of this information, as can be seen in the following case:

Box 5.16   *Re C (adult patient: restriction of publicity after death) [1996]*

A young man (aged 27) suffered anoxic brain damage during the extraction of wisdom teeth, and entered a permanent vegetative state. Artificial nutrition and hydration were discontinued four years later, and the patient died. The court ordered that the identity of the patient, his family, and the hospital staff should remain secret, for the purpose of restricting publicity (i.e. protection of the family and the hospital) endured after the patient's death.

An interesting contrast to this case can be seen in the following:

Box 5.17   *Lewis v Secretary of State for Health and another [2008]*

A number of individuals who had worked in the nuclear industry in Sellafield had died, and tissues were removed from their bodies for analysis of radionuclide content. The Secretary of State for Health wished to conduct an investigation and requested disclosure of the medical records. The doctor in charge of these records was willing to accede to this request, but was concerned that he would be in breach of his duty of confidentiality. The court accepted that a duty of confidence survives death, but the public interest in this case fell on the side of disclosure.

Attempts to see a pattern in these two cases may be destined to fail, for each situation is individual and unique. The court is therefore faced with a delicate balancing act: between the rights of privacy of the individual and his/her family, and the interests of the public in ensuring that information is disclosed. The decision, therefore, will be influenced by those who make the strongest argument in court, suggesting that the outcome in these cases is determined by the skill of the lawyer, rather than any universal system of principles.

It has, moreover, been suggested that confidentiality provides healthcare staff with a shield to hide behind when disclosure would expose their incompetence (Johnstone, 2004). Something of this may be detected in the case of *Re C [1996]*, discussed earlier, although the court was keen to emphasise the rights of the family in this instance. Unquestionably, it can be seen in *A Health Authority v X and others [2001]*, where a doctor refused a request from a health authority to examine the medical records of his patients. His argument that his duty of confidentiality prevented such disclosure was clearly an attempt to avoid an investigation into his unprofessional conduct, and the court was quick to acknowledge this.

Thus, we have covered a range of situations where confidentiality is a central issue, although there are certainly many more. We have, in addition, outlined the key guiding principles for the courts and practitioners. However, if confidentiality is breached, what are the remedies available for those wronged by such disclosure?

5 REMEDIES

A THE COMMON LAW

There are two possible remedies open to the courts under the common law. The first is that they could serve an *injunction*, prohibiting release of the information (see *Re C [1996]*, discussed earlier). If confidential information was disclosed in breach of this injunction, this would be a contempt of court, which is a criminal offence and which is subject to imprisonment or a fine (Contempt of Court Act 1981). If the information has already been disclosed, however, the second possible remedy is that of *negligence*.

The difficulty for the aggrieved party is that all of the elements of negligence have to be satisfied in order to win such an action (see Chapter 3). It would not normally be difficult to establish that the perpetrator owed a duty of care to the subject of the disclosure, nor would it be too problematic to determine that s/he had fallen below an acceptable standard of care. However, the breach must also have caused harm to the claimant, and this is usually much more difficult to prove.

Economic loss caused by the breach would be one instance where damages were recoverable. Thus, for example, if it was disclosed to the general public that the owner of a restaurant had recently undergone the formation of a colostomy, and his business collapsed as a direct result of this breach, there may be a cause of action here. Moreover, the case of *Cornelius v de Taranto [2001]*, discussed earlier, suggests that psychological damage is also compensable. However, such instances are rare, and the understandable anger and annoyance experienced by the victim of an unauthorised disclosure is unlikely to qualify as psychological harm. Thus, the common law does not represent a fruitful avenue for claimants to follow, and they would be well advised to seek alternative forms of redress.

B THE DATA PROTECTION ACT 1998

This Act covers any confidential information that has been recorded, either in a written or computerised form. In particular, a health record is defined as 'any record which:

a consists of information relating to the physical and mental health or condition of an individual, and
b has been made by or on behalf of a health professional in connection with the care of an individual' (s68 [2]).

Note that it does not apply to *verbal* information, and the victims of a breach of this nature would need to seek alternative sources of redress. Note also that it applies only to *living* patients and does not therefore protect the records of the deceased. It enables the release of information (or data to be 'processed', to use the terminology of the Act) in the following circumstances:

Box 5.18 *Data Protection Act 1998 (Schedule 2)*

1 When the patient consents.
2 When it is necessary to protect the vital interests of the patient.
3 When the court demands it.
4 When the data controller (i.e. the person in charge of the records) needs information to pursue legitimate professional interests (e.g. for the purposes of clinical audit).

If the information is particularly sensitive, it may still be released, but at least one of the following conditions must be satisfied:

Box 5.19 *Data Protection Act 1998 (Schedule 3)*

1 The patient consents.
2 It is in the vital interests of the patient (even though consent cannot be obtained).
3 For the protection of the vital interests of another person (and where consent has been withheld unreasonably).
4 When it is necessary for medical purposes.
5 When it is in the public interest.

Mason and Laurie (2011) note that the term 'fair processing' is open to interpretation, and is thereby open to abuse. Nevertheless, the Act does provide a wider range of remedies than the common law: it can enforce the prevention of further disclosures (s10); an aggrieved party can apply to the court to correct inaccurate health records (s14); and compensation is available to the victim of an unauthorised disclosure (s13). Such compensation is available for 'damage' (s13 [1]), which would include physical and economic categories; but is also available for 'distress' (s13 [2]) caused by contravention of the Act.

The Act stipulates that damage must be 'substantial' (s55A) for compensation to be payable, and this might suggest that such penalties are rarely invoked. Nevertheless, the Information Commissioner has powers to impose a fine of up to £500,000 and/or a prison sentence (for deliberate or negligent leaks of information) (Information Commissioner's Office, 2011). In November 2010, a County Council was fined £100,000 when its employees faxed information relating to child sexual abuse and care proceedings to the wrong people. Similarly, a £60,000 fine was issued to an employment services company, which lost an unencrypted laptop containing personal information on 24,000 people who had accessed community legal advice centres (Information Commissioner's Office, 2010).

Section 7 of the Act relates to patients' rights of access to their medical notes: the completion of appropriate documentation (a subject access form), and the payment of a fee (to a maximum of £50) will entitle the patient to see his/her records, and the health authority has an obligation to comply with this request within 40 days. There are limits to disclosure, though: for example, the data controller is entitled to withhold access if the patient or any other person might be harmed by the information, and/or disclosure would reveal information pertaining to a third person who has not consented to the release of that information. Moreover, the Data Protection Act only applies to *living* patients: thus, if the executors of a dead person's estate needed access to that person's records, their request would be covered by the Access to Health Records Act 1990.

C THE HUMAN RIGHTS ACT 1998

The concept of a personal right to privacy as a cause of action has only comparatively recently been acknowledged by the courts (Toulson and Phipps, 2006), and the enactment of the Human Rights Act was clearly the catalyst. The first case which invoked this principle was the following:

Box 5.20   *Campbell v Mirror Group Newspapers [2004]*

The model Naomi Campbell had earlier denied that she took drugs, but was photographed entering a drug rehabilitation clinic. A newspaper published this photograph, and Miss Campbell sued on the grounds that her right to a private life (Article 8 of the Human Rights Act) had been denied. The newspaper countered that Article 10 of the same Act entitled them to freedom of expression.

We have noted earlier that freedom of expression (and freedom of the press in particular) is a fundamental and inalienable right within a democratic society. Nevertheless, there are limits to this freedom, and Baroness Hale (in common with the other Law Lords) felt that the balance tipped in Miss Campbell's favour when she said (at para. 149):

> The political and social life of the community, and the intellectual, artistic or personal development of individuals, are not obviously assisted by poring over the intimate details of a fashion model's private life.

Or, in other words, those who commit themselves to the arduous journey of drug rehabilitation deserve our respect and the right to do this outside of the public gaze. The significance of this case, however, is more wide ranging. Until this point, information was only protected if there was a confidential relationship between the parties, but *Campbell* demonstrates that this relationship is no longer necessary (Pattinson, 2009). Thus, the person who comes across a set of medical notes mistakenly left on a train has no relationship of confidence with the subject of those notes, but would have an obligation to respect that person's privacy and ensure that the notes were returned to their rightful place.

If *Campbell* acknowledged the limits to freedom of expression, it is important to note that the Human Rights Act does not confer an unqualified right to privacy. Article 8 (2) states that this right can be over-ridden if it is necessary 'in the interests of national security, public safety or the economic well-being of the country, for the protection of disorder or crime, for the protection of health or morals, or for the protection of the rights and freedoms of others'. An illustration of this can be seen in the following case:

Box 5.21   *Z v Finland [1997]*

X was HIV positive and had intercourse with a number of women. The prosecutor wished to bring a charge of manslaughter against him, but it was unclear whether or not he was aware of his diagnosis. His wife (Z) was also HIV positive, and the prosecution seized her files in order to gain evidence. X was subsequently convicted, but Z claimed that her rights of privacy had been violated.

The European Court of Human Rights held that disclosure of her medical records was necessary in the public interest, for it enabled the detection of a serious crime. However, the identification of Z in the press reporting of the case was unnecessary, and represented a violation of Article 8.

Those seeking compensation under the Human Rights Act, moreover, may be destined for disappointment. Miss Campbell's monetary award for the established breach of her privacy amounted to £3,500, which barely seems worth the effort, and is possibly representative of the lack of sympathy that she excited in the court (Herring, 2010). Nevertheless, the defendant was left with the legal costs for both sides, which exceeded £1 million, and this should serve as a significant disincentive to press intrusion upon individual rights of privacy.

D PROFESSIONAL PENALTIES

If efforts to seek monetary recompense seem tortuous and uncertain, the aggrieved party may be able to exact revenge in a different format. Unauthorised disclosure of medical information exposes the perpetrator to two lines of assault. First, the requirement to uphold confidentiality is written into the contract of every health service employee; and breach constitutes a summary offence. What this means, in practice, is that an offence could result in instant dismissal (although, obviously, the severity of that offence would be taken into account).

Second, as has been mentioned earlier, the necessity for upholding and protecting the confidentiality of patients forms a clause within all professional Codes of Conduct. Transgression, therefore, provides the professional bodies with an opportunity to exert a range of penalties against the perpetrator, one of which is removal from the register. As Pattinson (2009) notes, these penalties are generally greater than the courts can impose, and have much more long-term impact upon the healthcare professional than would a financial burden.

6 CALDICOTT

Given the importance attached to confidentiality of medical information by the Department of Health, the professional bodies, and employers, it seems only logical that efforts should be made to protect it. No amount of rules and regulations will prevent wilful or grossly negligent disclosure; but equally, it is acknowledged that breaches can occur by accident or because of faults within the system. With this in mind, the Caldicott Report (1997) recognised that not only did each individual within the organisation have a personal duty to uphold confidentiality, but also that the NHS has a *corporate* responsibility. An obligation is therefore imposed upon every organisation within the NHS to adhere to the following principles:

Box 5.22   The Caldicott Principles

1 If confidential information is required, there should always be a justification for this purpose.
2 Patient-identifiable information should only be used when it is absolutely necessary.
3 When patient-identifiable information is required, only the minimum necessary to achieve the desired purpose should be used.
4 Access to patient-identifiable information should be on a strict need-to-know basis.
5 Everyone who has access to this information is under a duty of confidence.
6 Everyone should understand and comply with the law.

The person charged with coordinating the efforts of the Trust to comply with these principles is known as the Caldicott Guardian. Given the importance attached to these principles by the Department of Health (and embodied in the Code of Practice on Confidentiality [DH, 2003]), it follows that the Guardian should be a senior member of the Trust's management executive. It is doubtful that any Trust manages to comply fully with the principles, but the Department of Health expects to see a year-on-year improvement. It is therefore a dynamic and progressive concept, in which no Trust is ever allowed to become complacent.

CONCLUSION

We have seen that the concept of confidentiality is taken very seriously within healthcare, and the reasons for this have been outlined. Although it may be very difficult for a victim of a breach to secure redress within the courts, employers and professional bodies have no reluctance to impose severe penalties upon a transgressor. Despite this, it has become equally clear that the duty of confidentiality is not absolute and that disclosure of information may be justifiable in certain circumstances. The onus, however, will always fall upon the person disclosing the information to defend this action, and the rationale should stand up to logical scrutiny. In our exploration of confidentiality, the following guiding principles have emerged:

Box 5.23   Guiding principles pertaining to confidentiality

1   The default position is that healthcare professionals owe their patients a duty of confidence, and should not divulge information to anybody outside of the team caring for them.
2   Information may be disclosed in the public interest, provided that there is a real risk of physical harm to the public.
3   If information is to be disclosed, it should be given only to those whom it is necessary to tell so as to protect the public interest.
4   If confidentiality is to be breached, the public interest in disclosure must outweigh the public interest in non-disclosure.
5   Disclosure of a patient's sexually transmitted infection is more likely to be justified when that patient is in a relationship with another, and the partner is at risk of contracting the infection.
6   The public interest dictates that child abuse should be reported to the appropriate authorities, and that the informant should be guaranteed anonymity and freedom from litigation (unless s/he is acting out of malice and with an express desire to cause mischief).
7   If patient confidentiality is to be breached, only the minimum information necessary to achieve the desired objective should be divulged.

Adherence to these principles should provide the healthcare professional with the necessary protection, although there will always be situations that do not appear to fit within the criteria. Perhaps the fundamental point to be made is that those in receipt of confidential medical information should endeavour to retain a professional attitude at all times. Moreover, such issues require an ability to empathise with other individuals: in other words, if *you* were the patient, how would you expect healthcare professionals to handle your medical details?

REFERENCES

TEXTS

Beauchamp, T.L. and Childress, J.F. (2001) *Principles of Biomedical Ethics*, 5th edn. Oxford: Oxford University Press.

Brazier, M. and Cave, E. (2007) *Medicine, Patients and the Law*, 4th edn. London: Penguin Books.

BBC News (2006) Woman jailed for giving lover HIV. Monday 19 June 2006. Available at: http://news.bbc.co.uk/1/hi/5094708.stm.

British Medical Association (2009) *Medical Ethics Today: The BMA's Handbook of Ethics and Law*, 2nd edn. London: BMJ Books.

Caldicott, F. (1997) *Report of the Review of Patient-identifiable Information*. London: Department of Health.

Clothier Report (1994) *The Allitt Inquiry: an Independent Inquiry Relating to Deaths and Injuries on the Children's Ward at Grantham and Kesteven Hospital during the period February to April 1991*. London: HMSO.

Department of Health (2000) *No Secrets: Guidance on Developing and Implementing Multi-agency Policies and Procedures to Protect Vulnerable Adults from Abuse*. London: Department of Health (March).

Department of Health (2003) *Confidentiality: NHS Code of Practice*. London: Department of Health (November). Available at: www.dh.gov.uk.

Department of Health (2005) *HIV Infected Health Care Workers. Guidance on Management and Patient Notification*. London: Department of Health (July).

Department of Health (2010) *Confidentiality: NHS Code of Practice. Supplementary Guidelines: Public Interest Disclosures*. London: Department of Health (November).

General Medical Council (2004) *Confidentiality: Protecting and Providing Information*. London. General Medical Council (April).

General Medical Council (2006) *Good Medical Practice*. London: General Medical Council (November).

Gilbar, R. (2004) 'Medical confidentiality within the family: the doctor's duty reconsidered', *International Journal of Law, Policy and the Family*, 18 (2), August: 195.

Gilbar, R. (2011) 'Family involvement, independence, and patient autonomy in practice', *Medical Law Review*, 19, Spring: 192–234.

Gorman, C. and Sancton, T. (1996) 'Mitterrand's deadly secret', *Time*, January 29. Available at: www.time.com/time/magazine/article/0,9171,984025,00.html.

Hendrick, J. (2010) *Law and Ethics in Children's Nursing*. Oxford: Wiley-Blackwell.

Herring, J. (2010) *Medical Law and Ethics*, 3rd edn. Oxford: Oxford University Press.

Hope, T., Savulescu, J. and Hendrick, J. (2008) *Medical Ethics and Law: The Core Curriculum*, 2nd edn. London: Churchill Livingstone Elsevier.

Information Commissioner's Office (2010) *Press release: first monetary penalties served for serious data protection breaches*. Available at: www.ico.gov.uk.

Information Commissioner's Office (2011) *Guidance About the Issue of Monetary Policies*. Available at: www.ico.gov.uk.

Johnstone, M-J. (2004) *Bioethics: A Nursing Perspective*, 4th edn. Sydney: Churchill Livingstone.

Mason, J.K. and Laurie, G.T. (2011) *Mason and McCall Smith's Law and Medical Ethics*, 8th edn. Oxford: Oxford University Press.

Morris, F. and Adshead, G. (1997) 'The liability of psychiatrists for the violent acts of their patients', *New Law Journal*, 147 (6788): 558.

Nursing and Midwifery Council (2008) *The Code: Standards of conduct, Performance and Ethics for Nurses and Midwives*. London: Nursing and Midwifery Council.

Pattinson, S.D. (2009) *Medical Law and Ethics*, 2nd edn. London: Sweet & Maxwell.

Payne, J. (2009) *Reducing complaints through daily nurse-led communication rounds*. NHS Institute for Innovation and Improvement. Available at: www.institute.nhs.uk.

Profumo affair. Available at: www.britannica.com/EBchecked/topic/932575/Profumo-affair.

Royal College of Nursing (2005) *RCN Guidance for Occupational Health Nurses. London.* Royal College of Nursing (October).

Siyambalapitiya, S., Caunt, J., Harrison, N., White, L., Weremczuk, D. and Fernando, D.J.S. (2007) 'A 22 month study of patient complaints at a National Health Service hospital', *International Journal of Nursing Practice*, 13: 107–10.

Toulson, R.G. and Phipps, C.M. (2006) *Confidentiality*, 2nd. edn. London: Sweet & Maxwell.

Wacks, R. (1988) 'Controlling AIDS: some legal issues – Part 2', *New Law Journal*, 138 (6353): 283.

CASES

A Health Authority v X and others [2001] All ER (D) 132.
AG v Guardian Newspapers Ltd. (No. 2) [1990] 1AC 109.
C, Re (adult patient: restriction of publicity after death) [1996] 1 FCR 605.
C v Cairns [2003] Lloyd's Rep. Med. 90.
Campbell v Mirror Group Newspapers [2004] UKHL 22.
Cornelius v de Taranto [2001] EWCA Civ. 1511.
D v NSPCC [1978] AC 171.
Duncan v Medical Practitioners' Disciplinary Committee [1986] 1 NZLR 513.
Faya & Rossi v Almarez [1993] 620 A 2d 327.
Gartside v Outram [1856] 26 LJ Ch. 113.
Gillick v West Norfolk and Wisbech Health Authority [1986] AC 112.
Hunter v Mann [1974] QB 767.
In Re Attorney General's Reference (No. 3 of 1999) [2009] UKHL 34.
In Re C (a minor) (wardship: medical treatment) (No. 2) [1990] Fam. 39.
L, Re (Care proceedings: disclosure to a third party) [2000] 1 FLR 913.
Lewis v Secretary of State for Health and another [2008] EWHC 2196 (QB).
Osman v Ferguson [1993] 4 All ER 344.
Osman v UK [1998] The Times, 5 November 1998.
Palmer v Tees Health Authority [1999] Lloyd's Rep. Med. 351.
R v Clarence [1888] 22 QBD 23.

R v Dica [2005] All ER (D) 405.
R v Konzani [2005] EWCA Crim. 706.
R (on the application of Axon) v Secretary of State for Health [2006] EWHC 37 (Admin.).
R (on the application of S) v Plymouth City Council [2002] EWCA Civ. 388.
R (on the application of Stone) v South East Coast SHA [2006] EWHC 1668 (Admin.).
Stephens v Avery [1988] 2 All ER 477.
Tarasoff v Regents of the University of California [1976] 131 Cal. Rptr. 14.
W v Egdell [1990] 1 All ER 835.
Wood v Wyatt [1820], unreported.
Woolgar v Chief Constable of Sussex Police [1999] 3 All ER 604.
X v Y and another [1988] 2 All ER 648.
Z v Finland [1997] ECHR 22009/93.

LEGISLATION

Abortion Regulations 1991, SI 1991/499
Access to Health Records Act 1990
Contempt of Court Act 1981
Criminal Law Act 1967
Data Protection Act 1998
Human Rights Act 1998
NHS (Venereal Diseases) Regulations 1974, SI 1974/29
Offences Against the Person Act 1861
Public Health (Control of Disease) Act 1984
Public Interest Disclosure Act 1998
Road Traffic Act 1972
Road Traffic Act 1988
Terrorism Act 2000

Scenarios (answers at back of book)

1   A 70-year-old male patient has had major abdominal surgery earlier in the day, in which a bowel resection was performed for colonic cancer, and evidence of liver metastases was also discovered. He is currently sleeping, when the staff receive a telephone call from a woman claiming to be his sister. She states that her brother had told her that he was going to have an operation, but was unsure of what was going to be done. The sister says that she lives 200 miles away and is therefore unable to come and see him within the next few days. In consequence, she requests information about her brother's operation, diagnosis, prognosis and current condition. She goes on to argue that any attempt to fob her off with 'he is comfortable at the moment' will simply make her more anxious.

What would you do in this situation?

2   A 19-year-old male limps into Accident and Emergency late one night, complaining of a severe laceration to his leg. He claims that he sustained this while jumping over a barbed wire fence, and it has been bleeding heavily. While the wound is being treated, two police officers enter the department, stating that they are investigating a burglary committed earlier in the night. They have a general description of the suspect, given to them by the farmer who chased him off the premises; and they also have samples of blood and torn clothing found on a fence. They demand access to the medical notes of all those who have entered Accident and Emergency in the last three hours.

What would you do?
[For some assistance in answering this question, see the Police and Criminal Evidence Act 1984 (ss8–14 and Schedule 1).]

3   A new patient administration system has been loaded onto the computers of a hospital, and all the qualified staff have been given access to it. One Sunday afternoon, the staff are taking advantage of a quiet period and are amusing themselves by looking up the clinical details of members of staff (including senior management and medical staff). They discover that one such individual (a Matron) has visited a particular Consultant recently, who specialises in breast surgery.

What are the legal and ethical issues associated with this scenario?
[For some assistance in answering this question, see the Computer Misuse Act 1990.]

6

RESOURCE ALLOCATION

Learning Objectives

At the end of this chapter, the reader will:

1 Have an understanding of the judicial review process.

2 Be aware of the ways in which the courts have approached issues of resource allocation.

3 Be able to identify a number of ethical issues associated with resource allocation.

4 Acknowledge some of the ideas generated for resolution of resource dilemmas.

1 INTRODUCTION

Lord James Bryce (a British politician, historian and jurist of the nineteenth and early twentieth century) once suggested that Medicine is the only profession that seeks to destroy the reason for its own existence. Certainly, Beveridge appears to have had this in mind when he envisaged that the costs of a National Health Service (NHS) would eventually decline as the health of the nation increased (The Beveridge Report, 1942). It is clearly apparent, however, that both contentions are false: as medical progress increases the range of available treatments, the level of demand for services has increased commensurately. The fact that the costs of the NHS were always going to outstrip the resources allocated to it became obvious almost as soon as it came into being (Newdick, 2005), and this pattern has continued to the present day. Largely because of this, the NHS has become heavily politicised: it is of enormous importance to the general public, and any attempt by Government to limit the range of its activities loses votes; and yet, without some attempt to restrain NHS spending, costs will quickly spiral out of control.

It is not difficult to accept that there should be some limit to the allocation of resources to the NHS, but it is less easy to decide what those limits should be. Many ideas have been proposed and all are flawed in some way or another. This is largely because every decision to curtail an area of spending within the NHS automatically entails disadvantaging at least one group of people. The debate, therefore, cannot be conducted in a truly objective manner – everybody has a vested interest, and they will argue that they are the victims of injustice if their interests are sacrificed.

This chapter begins with a look at how the courts have approached the issue of resource allocation, and then moves on to a discussion of some of the ethical issues. Inevitably, however, these two overlap, and any attempt to separate them is certain to be artificial. Thus, there will be the occasional digression when a legal case throws up an interesting moral dilemma.

2 LEGAL ASPECTS OF RESOURCE ALLOCATION

A WHAT THE COURTS CAN DO

Imagine a hospital Trust that makes a decision to close its Accident and Emergency department, meaning that the local inhabitants will have to travel another 30 miles if they wish to receive emergency treatment. The means by which the public can challenge this decision in the courts is known as *judicial review* – the people who make this challenge are not seeking compensation (as they would if this was a negligence case), but are simply asking the court to order the Trust to reverse its decision.

The purpose of judicial review, therefore, is to control the exercise of administrative discretion by public authorities. In other words, it serves as a check and counterbalance to the arbitrary and mendacious abuse of power that might be exercised by those in public office. This includes, not only hospital Trusts, but also local authorities and Government ministers. The primary function of those who hold public office is to serve the public, and judicial review is the means by which they can be pulled back to the straight and narrow path should they be tempted to wander.

At least, this is the theory. In practice, the courts have tended to show extreme reluctance to interfere with the decisions of public bodies or Ministers of State, rendering the judicial review process a tortuous path for those who feel aggrieved by those decisions. Part of the problem lies with what is known as the policy/operational distinction – the courts do not feel equipped to challenge *policy* decisions of public bodies, and these are therefore considered non-justiciable; but the *operation* of that policy may be flawed, and the courts may feel more confident in ruling upon these matters. However, it has been noted by a number of commentators (Bailey and Bowman, 1986; Newdick, 2005) that this distinction is rarely clear; and, where there is doubt, the court's default position is to rule in favour of the public body.

Notwithstanding this, there are a number of things that the courts can rule upon:

a   The court can declare that a public body or public official is acting *ultra vires*. The literal translation of this term is 'beyond the powers', and it means that the body or official is making decisions for which they have not been given the authority. An example is the following:

Box 6.1   *R v Secretary of State for the Home Department, ex parte Fire Brigades Union and others [1995]*

The Home Secretary of the day (Michael Howard) sought to abolish the Criminal Injuries Compensation Scheme, which had been set up to provide compensation for victims of violent crime. The Fire Brigades Union felt that its members were often likely to be such victims, and therefore, this decision was going to impact upon them adversely. They argued that the Home Secretary had abused his powers and was thereby acting unlawfully.

The Court of Appeal agreed with the Fire Brigades Union, holding that the Home Secretary had acted *ultra vires*, and therefore unlawfully. His position as Home Secretary gave him a large number of discretionary powers, but this was a step too far. In consequence, if he wanted to abolish the Criminal Injuries Compensation Scheme, he must lay it before Parliament, wherein it would be debated and voted upon. All of this would take time, of course, and the Opposition might be able to delay its passage until the next election, which is precisely the situation that the Home Secretary wished to avoid. He could, in theory, have decided to ignore the ruling, for the court has no means by which to enforce its decision; but this would effectively be stating that he considered himself to be above the law, and this could prove fatal to his chances of being elected at the next general election.

b   The court can declare that a public body or official has acted *irrationally*. The definition of what it means to be irrational in this context comes from an old case (*Associated Provincial Picture Houses v Wednesbury Corporation [1947]*), and which received further clarification in *Council of Civil Service Unions v Minister for the Civil Service [1984]*:

It applies to a decision that is so outrageous in its defiance of logic or of accepted moral standards that no sensible person who had applied his mind to the question to be decided could have arrived at it (per Lord Diplock at 951).

Therefore, anybody who makes such a decision is said to be *Wednesbury unreasonable*. The wording of Lord Diplock's statement, however, makes it clear that it is only likely to apply to those who have taken leave of their senses. If, for example, some money had been earmarked for the upgrading of a paediatric ward, but the Chief Executive instead decided to use this money to re-decorate his office, then the charge might stick. Such circumstances are going to be rare though; and while the *allegations* of irrationality may be common, the findings of guilt are considerably less so.

c   Finally, the court can rule that a public body or official failed to satisfy a *legitimate expectation* of the public. This, perhaps, is what brings the majority of healthcare-related cases before the courts for judicial review, and it stems in large part from the wording of the NHS Act 1977 (subsequently replaced by the NHS Act 2006, although the obligations of the Health Secretary remain the same). In particular, section 1 is the most-frequently quoted passage:

It is the Secretary of State's duty to promote a comprehensive health service designed to secure improvements:

a In the physical and mental health of the people, and

b In the prevention, diagnosis and treatment of illness.

What is meant by the phrase 'a comprehensive health service'? To some, it means anything and everything: it means, for example, that cosmetic surgery, infertility treatment and gender re-assignment should all be freely available in the NHS, because all of these can be said to secure improvements in the physical and mental health of those concerned. Section 3, however, provides the Secretary of State with a wide measure of discretion when it says that it is his/her 'duty to provide [health care services] to such extent as he considers necessary to meet all reasonable requirements'. In other words, the Secretary of State is empowered to decide what is 'reasonable', and s/he is therefore empowered to restrict the allocation of resources for some procedures.

Given this wide measure of discretion available to the Secretary of State and the reluctance of the courts to become involved in policy decisions, it is not surprising that successful actions in judicial review are uncommon. And yet, despite the low chances of success, the number of these cases coming before the courts has increased in recent years. Why should this be? The answer seems to be that the cases are virtually guaranteed to attract maximum publicity, which will inevitably prove embarrassing for the public bodies. If a Healthcare Trust decides that it will not fund a certain type of treatment, the general public are likely to sympathise with those who have been denied it; and the conflict played out in court is often portrayed by the media as a contest between good and evil. A good example of this can be seen in the following case:

Box 6.2   *R v Sheffield Health Authority, ex parte Seale [1994]*

Mrs Seale was 37 years old and sought infertility treatment. However, the health authority had a policy which refused treatment to anybody above the age of 35. Their argument was that the chances of success of this treatment inevitably decline as one ages, and that there should therefore be a cut-off point. In contrast, Mrs Seale acknowledged that age was a factor to be taken into consideration, but she could not accept that a 37-year-old person's chances were significantly less than those of a 35-year-old.

Almost inevitably, Mrs Seale lost the case. Not only was the court unwilling to chal-lenge a policy decision of the health authority, but also it could not accept that it had acted in a *Wednesbury unreasonable* manner. Its decision was not arbitrary, but rather was based upon clinical grounds. Despite this, however, there were two unforeseen consequences of the case. First, the publicity generated by it prompted an anonymous benefactor to fund the fertility treatment, and Mrs Seale subse-quently gave birth to a baby boy (Pattinson, 2009). Second, a circular went round to all fertility clinics shortly afterwards, stating that each case should be decided on its own merits, and that a blanket policy which refused treatment to women over the age of 35 was discriminatory. Thus, Mrs Seale may have lost the case, but she won the argument, and the policy has subsequently been amended to benefit those who come after her.

Having examined the role of the courts in judicial review, we now need to look at a few cases that have come before them. In so doing, we may be able to identify key features that determine the likelihood of success or failure.

B CASES THAT HAVE BEEN LOST

There are many cases that could have been selected for this section, but three are most commonly cited. The first is as follows:

Box 6.3   *R v Secretary of State for Social Services, ex parte Hincks [1980]*

A previous Government had promised to build an extension to a hospital so that ortho-paedic services could be improved in the area. However, the costs became prohibitive, and the new Government decided to shelve these plans. Four people sought judicial review of this decision, arguing that it was the Secretary of State's duty to provide a comprehensive orthopaedic service.

Not surprisingly, the court held that this was a policy decision of the Government, and therefore non-justiciable. The Secretary of State is constrained by the resources avail-able to him and by current Government economic policy. In consequence, he cannot be expected to meet every demand for healthcare services, but should meet only those 'he considers necessary' (NHS Act 2006, section 3). In effect, the court is saying here: 'It is not for judges to determine the policy of Government, for this is the function of the elected representatives of the people. If anybody dislikes the decisions made by Government, s/he will know what to do at the next General Election.'

Clearly, governmental decisions are unlikely to meet with a successful challenge in the courts unless it can be shown that a Minister of State is acting *ultra vires*.

Logically, therefore, an aggrieved party might have better fortune when challenging the decision of an individual health authority. Consider the following case:

Box 6.4   *R v Central Birmingham Health Authority, ex parte Walker [1987]*

Mrs Walker's baby had been born prematurely, and required an operation to repair a hole in the heart. However, a shortage of neonatal intensive care nurses meant that the operation had to be cancelled several times. Mrs Walker sought judicial review of this decision and asked the court to order that the operation take place.

Such cases are, of course, incredibly emotive, and they will quickly find their way onto the front page of most newspapers. Once again, however, the court felt unable to intervene, for the health authority managers were much better-placed to make these decisions. As Sir John Donaldson M.R. said (at 35):

> It is not for this court, or indeed any court, to substitute its own judgement for the judgement of those who are responsible for the allocation of resources.

The court could only intervene, therefore, if the health authority could be shown to have acted completely unreasonably when allocating its resources, but this was not the case here. The court was satisfied that the baby's condition was not life-threatening, and so, delays to the operation were more inconvenient than dangerous. Indeed, if the health authority had decided to operate and the child came to harm, Mrs Walker might have had a case in negligence, for her baby would have been exposed to an unnecessary risk because of the staff shortages.

Hot on the heels of this case came a similar scenario (*R v Central Birmingham Health Authority, ex parte Collier [1988]*), in which a four-year-old boy required open heart surgery. The case received short shrift from the court: the issues had been extensively discussed in *Walker*, and the claimants were (by implication) wasting the court's time. However, this case was *not* exactly the same, for the boy's condition was much more critical than that of the child in *Walker*. Newdick (2005) suggests that the court had an opportunity here to subject the health authority's policy to careful scrutiny, for an exposé of their failings would have forced them to develop a better system of administration. That the court did not do this, though, is illustrative of the fact that it prefers to take a passive approach to such matters. One can accept that its natural inclination is to be protective of public bodies, for they often have to make difficult decisions and they are the people who are best equipped to make them. But equally, the public have a right to expect that the court will demand a level of transparency from such bodies, and should insist that they are able to account for their policy.

If *Walker* stirred the emotions, the next case boiled them into a ferment:

Box 6.5: *R v Cambridge Health Authority, ex parte B [1995]*

A 10-year-old girl required treatment for leukaemia, but the health authority declined to offer this. They argued that the low chances of success of the treatment did not justify its expense.

Almost inevitably, the media picked up on this case and portrayed it as a situation where a child's life was being sacrificed so that the health authority could save money. In fairness, counsel for the health authority contributed to this perception, probably because they were trying to use every conceivable argument to win their case (Ham, 1999); but what this meant was that all other arguments tended to be ignored. Certainly the judge in the High Court became convinced that this was the central argument of the health authority:

> Where the question is whether the life of a 10-year old child might be saved by however slim a chance, the responsible Authority must do more than toll the bell of tight resources; they must explain the priorities that have led them to decline to fund the treatment (per Laws, J. at 17).

His finding for B was challenged by the health authority in the Court of Appeal, by which time it had taken greater care to ensure that the issues were presented more clearly. This was never an issue of funding, for the health authority frequently offered treatment costing this much to those who needed it. The real issue was that it was unlikely to succeed: the side-effects of the treatment were extremely unpleasant and it was not in B's interests to experience them with such a low chance of success. It would, instead, be much kinder to allow her to die in as much comfort as possible so that her last days would be pain-free. Note that resources never completely disappear from the picture, and one might argue that it is unethical to spend money on futile treatment when it could be used more productively in other patients. Nevertheless, the important point to make is that the health authority's decision was a *clinical* one, rather than one determined by the allocation of resources.

In finding for the health authority, Sir Thomas Bingham M.R. stated (at 137):

> Difficult and agonising judgements have to be made as to how a limited budget is best allocated to the maximum advantage of the maximum number of patients. That is not a judgement which the court can make.

The problem with cases of this kind is that the outcome of any decision made is impossible to predict with accuracy. There is evidence that at least one of the paediatricians involved in B's care agonised over the decision to withhold treatment (Ham, 1999); and these misgivings would undoubtedly have increased when an anonymous benefactor came forward to fund it in the private sector, resulting in an apparent remission. The child survived for another year, dying in May 1996 after complications arising from the treatment. It is not known how the father (who had apparently campaigned on his daughter's behalf with a kind of missionary zeal) felt about this: did he think that an extra year of life was better than a few months, or did he feel guilt at insisting upon his daughter receiving this unpleasant treatment? Nor, for that matter, can we be certain how the child herself felt, although there is some evidence that towards the end of her life she had begun to acknowledge that the health authority's original decision had been correct (*Nursing Times*, 1996).

What is clear, however, is that the court case forced the health authority to be more open about its reasons for declining treatment. It was a lack of transparency and an apparent lack of willingness to engage in debate that drove B's father onwards. Whether greater transparency would have avoided a court case is doubtful, but it may not have gone beyond the High Court and there would have been a better chance that the media would have represented the issues more accurately.

C CASES THAT HAVE BEEN WON

As mentioned earlier, the cases that have been won are comparatively rare and, as such, attract maximum publicity. There is a common theme that runs through many of them, though, and a good illustration of this can be seen in the following case:

Box 6.6   *R v North Derbyshire Health Authority,*
ex parte Fisher [1997]

A patient was suffering from multiple sclerosis, but was told that his health authority would not fund the drug beta interferon. His argument was that the Department of Health had issued guidelines on the use of beta interferon, and that it should be given to those who fall into certain categories of the illness. The health authority countered that its effectiveness was still largely unknown, and did not therefore merit the cost outlay.

The court held that the health authority did not have to follow Department of Health guidelines, for these do not have legal authority. However, if they are going to depart from them, they should be able to give clear and rational reasons for doing so. In this case, the health authority was unable to give such reasons, and its policy was therefore declared unlawful. The court will generally make the assumption that health authorities are acting in good faith (i.e. in the best interests of the patients in their locality), but here this assumption was overturned; the health authority's obfuscation and manipulation of the truth made it clear that they had no intention of funding the drug, regardless of the chances of its success.

'Blanket bans' on certain types of treatment, therefore, are unlikely to be considered rational, unless the health authority can provide sound clinical evidence that the treatment does not work. The same principle can be found in *R v West Sussex Primary Care Trust, ex parte Ross [2008]*, where a patient with multiple myeloma was refused the drug Lenalomide, despite the recommendation of his consultant. The PCT's guidelines on the use of this drug were so confused that they effectively meant that *nobody* would ever receive this drug.

The next case involved another blanket ban, but this time it was on a type of surgical procedure rather than on a particular drug.

Box 6.7   *North West Lancashire Health Authority v A, D and G [1999]*

Three transsexuals were refused gender re-assignment surgery by the health authority. The health authority's argument was that this treatment was clinically ineffective in terms of health gain, and that other medical conditions assumed a higher priority when allocating the limited healthcare resources. A, D and G, however, argued that there was sufficient evidence to show that the treatment could be effective in a number of cases.

The court accepted that a health authority has to make difficult decisions when allocating its limited resources, and it is not for the court to tell them how to make those decisions. Equally, it could not be considered unreasonable to place gender re-assignment down the list of its priorities. However:

> Where a strong and respectable body of medical opinion considers gender reassignment procedures as effective in suitable and properly selected cases, ... it is not open to a rational health authority simply to determine that a procedure has no proven clinical benefit while giving no indication of why it considers that that is so (per Buxton, L. J. at 170).

In other words, the health authority had decided to ignore the medical evidence, treating transsexualism as a state of mind, rather than an illness; and their policy effectively amounted to a blanket ban on this procedure, which was both irrational and illegal. Note that the court is not saying specifically that A, D and G all fitted into that special category of people who would benefit from this surgery, and they were certainly not ordering that the surgery should take place. They were simply saying that the health authority's policy made no rational sense, and that a greater degree of transparency was required when making these decisions.

The case is of particular interest in that it raises an ethical issue. Should the resources of the NHS be spent on gender re-assignment procedures, or should they be conserved for use in more life-threatening conditions? Parliament could decide, for example, that all such treatments should be funded privately, in which case North West Lancashire Health Authority's policy would not have been declared illegal. Moreover, many will have difficulty in empathising with those who wish to change their gender, and will consider such treatment as an expensive waste of resources.

Would it make a difference, though, if we became aware that there was a *physical* reason for transsexualism, rather than it being merely a psychological disorder? The question came into sharp focus in the tragic case of David Reimer, the broad facts of which are set out below:

Box 6.8

Two identical twin boys were born in Canada in 1965, and the parents decided to have them circumcised. Unfortunately, the procedure went horribly wrong on one of the boys, and his penis was destroyed. The parents were therefore faced with a terrible choice: either allow the child to remain as a boy but to grow up without a penis, or to castrate him and bring him up as a girl. The latter was the favoured option of a celebrated psychologist, Dr John Money, who saw this as the ultimate nature–nurture experiment. His belief (shared, incidentally, by many psychologists of the day) was that gender identity is essentially a social construct and is determined by how others react to us, especially in the formative years. Thus, if a child is clothed in pink dresses and given dolls to play with, that child will grow up thinking that s/he is a girl. Similarly, a child could be made to believe that s/he is a boy if given the appropriate clothing and toys.

Dr Money's arguments were enough to convince the parents, and the child was duly castrated at the age of 22 months, with the additional formation of a rudimentary vagina. In the years that followed, Dr Money wrote many papers in leading journals, testifying to the success of this experiment, claiming that the child was a happy little girl and was very well adjusted. As it turned out, however, the truth was very different: she had a miserable childhood, in which she would refuse to wear dresses, had no female friends but was unable to be accepted by her brother's friends, and refused to play with dolls. As she entered her teenage years, her behaviour, gait and looks became increasingly more masculine (despite the use of oestrogens), isolating her still further.

At age 14, the parents eventually revealed the truth to their child, who immediately began a series of operations to convert back to the male gender (bilateral mastectomy, phalloplasty, etc.). Unfortunately, however, the psychological damage was irreversible, and he eventually committed suicide in 2004, aged 38. In fairness, there were a number of other factors which contributed to his suicide (Colapinto, 2004), but it would be unwise to assume that the experiment with his gender had nothing to do with it.

Admittedly, this sad tale represents a digression from our exposition of judicial review and its relationship to healthcare resources. But it is the clearest example we have that suggests that gender identity has a physical basis and cannot be manipulated by psychological means (Kruijver et al., 2000). If this is true, it should ensure that transsexuals are treated with more compassion, and it also suggests that a blanket ban on gender re-assignment procedures will condemn a number of people to a lifetime of unnecessary suffering.

The following two cases do not raise significantly different issues to those already discussed, but they represent an interesting contrast. The first is as follows:

Box 6.9 *R v Secretary of State for Health, ex parte Pfizer [2002]*

The Secretary of State for Health had restricted the circumstances in which certain drugs (including Viagra) could be prescribed on the NHS for treatment of erectile dysfunction. The drug company argued that the Secretary of State had failed to conduct an analysis as to whether treatment for erectile dysfunction should be regarded as constituting a lower priority than the treatment of other non-life-threatening conditions (e.g. hormone replacement therapy, skin care products, etc.). The Secretary of State countered that this expense could not be justified in view of the competing priorities for NHS resources. Moreover, he argued that this was an essentially political judgement that was not within the province of a reviewing court.

Before we discuss the judgement of the court and its reasoning, consider the second case:

Box 6.10 *R v Swindon NHS Primary Care Trust and another, ex parte Rogers [2006]*

Mrs Rogers tested positive for HER2, a type of breast cancer, and her Consultant asked the PCT if it would be prepared to pay for Herceptin. The Trust refused, arguing that the drug was still largely experimental with no proven efficacy: it had not received a licence from the European Medicines Agency, and it had not been given approval from NICE. Mrs. Rogers maintained that this policy was arbitrary and irrational (and therefore unlawful), and that it was inconsistent with the policy of other Trusts.

It will probably come as no surprise to learn that *Pfizer* lost and *Rogers* won (although she originally lost her case in the High Court), but the reasoning behind these decisions is not entirely easy to understand. In *Pfizer*, the court appears to have taken a very passive approach (in keeping with many of its earlier decisions on such matters), holding that the Secretary of State was not required to conduct a detailed analysis of competing priorities. Therefore, his aim to improve the economics of the state health system was sufficient justification for him to impose the restriction. By contrast, in *Rogers*, the Court of Appeal held that the PCT *did* have to give reasons for withholding Herceptin, and these reasons should stand up to logical scrutiny. Thus, their policy of withholding this treatment 'save in exceptional circumstances' would be rational only if the PCT could outline what those circumstances were. In the absence of such a definition, this amounted to a complete refusal of funding, which was irrational.

How, then, is it possible to reconcile these two judgements, where a PCT is expected to be fully accountable for its resource decisions, whereas the Secretary of State can seemingly do much as s/he pleases without having to justify him/herself? There are probably several answers to this question, but three appear to stand out from the rest:

1 Mrs Rogers had a life-threatening condition, whereas the same could not be said for those suffering from erectile dysfunction. This does not explain why the NHS should be prepared to fund treatment for *other* non-life-threatening conditions, but the contrast between these two will be very clear to many. However, it is equally clear that minimal thought is being given to the social and psychological consequences of erectile dysfunction. It could, for example, lead to marriage breakdowns, depression, and possibly even suicide. Does this mean, therefore, that *physical* conditions have a higher priority than *psychological* ones? And, if so, does this explain why psychiatric medicine is continually starved of resources by comparison with its physical counterpart?

2 Mrs Rogers had a *voice*: in other words, she was prepared to stand before the TV cameras and speak to the press, and she was able to stir up an enormous wave of public sympathy, which inevitably impacted upon the decision of the court. By contrast, it is inconceivable that an army of impotent men would march on Whitehall to demand access to Viagra; and it is worth noting that the case was brought by the drug company, rather than any individual sufferer of the condition. Inevitably, Viagra is not going to excite the same level of public sympathy as treatment for breast cancer, but the implications of this observation are more far-reaching. It suggests, in effect, that decisions on resource allocation are heavily influenced by those who shout the loudest and who can mobilise the most support. 'The squeaky wheel gets the oil', as they say, and this means that those who have no voice are destined to be disadvantaged. One thinks, therefore, of the mentally ill, those with learning disabilities, and the elderly, all of whom are fated to be part of a 'Cinderella service'.

3 Finally, *Pfizer* was a decision made by the Secretary of State, whereas *Rogers* was a decision made by the PCT. As mentioned earlier, the courts are very reluctant to challenge decisions made by Government, and the public will have an opportunity to voice their disaffection with policy at the next general election. They do not have the same power to remove members of a Trust Board, and the courts will therefore expect a higher level of transparency from them.

D SUMMARY

We have seen that judicial review cases coming before the courts are on the increase, and that there is growing evidence that the chances of success are improving (Pattinson, 2009). Certainly, the courts are more demanding of Trusts (although not necessarily of

Governments) that the reasons for their decisions are open, transparent and logical; and any departure from this runs the risk of having their policies declared unlawful. Moreover, there has been one decision of the court that is guaranteed to raise the hopes of many who feel that they are being disadvantaged by the system.

Box 6.11   *R v Bedford Primary Care Trust, ex parte Watts [2004]*

Mrs Watts was 74 years old and needed a bilateral hip replacement, but was told by her PCT that she would need to wait a year for this operation. She applied to have the operation in France, but the PCT refused to fund this and reduced her wait to four months instead. However, Mrs Watts went ahead with the operation in France and asked the PCT to reimburse her expenses. When it refused once more, she sought judicial review of this decision.

This case eventually went to the European Court of Justice, where it was acknowledged that the NHS must refund the costs of treatment abroad if patients experience undue delays in treatment at home. There are, however, two conditions that must also apply: first, the patient must seek authorisation from the NHS before going abroad to access treatment; and second, the NHS is entitled to delay treatment to patients if that delay is not unreasonable. It would not, for example, be acceptable to use long waiting lists as an excuse for delay, because each patient must be assessed on his/her own individual *clinical* merits. In *Watts*, it was held that a 4-month delay was not unreasonable in the circumstances, and therefore the case did not benefit this patient directly. But, will it open the floodgates to a host of similar claims? Pattinson (2009) and Brazier and Cave (2007) suggest that it might, although Newdick (2005) argues that only the strong and articulate are likely to benefit. If this is true, it would be hard to disagree with his contention that 'A system which skews health care rights in this way has little to recommend it'. Thus, if Government, the courts and the Trusts themselves all perpetuate and accentuate an inequitable system (albeit unwittingly in most cases), it is clear that answers to these problems should be sought elsewhere. In consequence, we need to turn our attention to a discussion of the ethics of resource allocation.

3 ETHICAL ASPECTS OF RESOURCE ALLOCATION

This chapter began with an assumption that resources are finite, and, in consequence, there has to be some limit placed upon the costs of healthcare. This does not mean, however, that resources cannot be increased. For example, taxation could be increased to provide more revenue for the NHS, although this would be deeply unpopular politically and might have an adverse effect upon the economy. Similarly, a greater proportion of the Gross Domestic Product could be allocated to health – currently 8.4 per cent (Office for National Statistics, 2008). This would have the advantage of leaving the levels of taxation as they are, but inevitably it means that other areas of Government spending would have to decrease. From where would these extra resources be drawn? From education, social security benefits, defence? All of us will have our own views of how the Government should spend our taxes, but every decision made has its consequences, and these consequences may have severe effects on individual groups of people, and possibly the community at large.

For the sake of argument, let us assume that resources will remain the same, neither increasing nor decreasing. Our problem now is to decide how to use those resources to their maximum efficiency. Let us begin, therefore, by examining the following hypothetical scenario:

Box 6.12

A 23-year-old man was walking across a street one night when he was struck by a passing car. The driver of the car was returning home from the pub, and tests revealed that he was well in excess of the legal blood alcohol limit. After hitting the pedestrian, he lost control of the car and ran into a lamp-post. Both men are critically ill and need intensive care. However, there is only one bed available in the ITU at the local hospital. All ITUs in neighbouring hospitals are full, and transfer to the nearest available bed is considered too risky. Which patient should get the ITU bed?

A certain element of 'willing disbelief' is required for this scenario, since the likelihood is that arrangements could be made to ensure that both patients receive some form of treatment, even if does not necessarily match the ideal. Moreover, most healthcare professionals would probably argue that, where there is a straight choice between two critically ill patients, the one who is most likely to survive should be treated in preference to the other. This would be the professional and non-judgemental position to hold, for healthcare practitioners should be making *clinical* decisions rather than moral judgements. It is not absolutely certain, however, that this is always the case, and is something to which we will need to return shortly. The scenario does, though, raise a number of issues which could have wider implications for the allocation of resources.

A IS IT SIGNIFICANT THAT THE DRIVER OF THE CAR WAS INTOXICATED?

Leaving aside the possibility that the driver's drinks had been spiked in the pub by some mischievous and malevolent individual, the clear implication is that he has been responsible for his own injuries and for those of the pedestrian. Should he survive, the likelihood is that he will be criminally liable for this incident, and it is probably fair to say that most people would consider him to be *morally culpable*.

Viewed in this light, it would seem that his interests should be sacrificed in favour of the pedestrian, for the latter is the innocent victim of another person's carelessness. But does this mean, therefore, that all people who have brought their illness upon themselves should be denied treatment unless they are prepared to pay for it? One thinks of smokers who develop heart and lung disease, the obese who suffer from hypertension and gastro-oesophageal reflux, and the alcohol abusers who sustain liver disease. Perhaps we could take this further and deny free care to those who are injured playing sports: this behaviour carries a known risk, and those who are prepared to run it should not expect the public to finance their treatment.

As we head down this 'slippery slope', we begin to realise that 'most patients have contributed to some extent to their health problems' (Hope et al., 2008: 208), and any pretence that we may have to be morally superior starts to fade. In truth, smokers have been denied vascular surgery by an increasing number of surgeons, but this is essentially a clinical decision. In other words, the surgeon is not making a moral judgement about smoking, but is citing conclusive research-based evidence to show that the *outcome* of the surgery will be compromised if the patient continues to smoke (Underwood and Bailey, 1993). Others will argue, though, that surgical outcomes can be adversely affected by a number of other factors (gender, age, weight, etc.), and to single out smoking in this way seems rather unfair (Shiu, 1993). Moreover, there may be a variety of issues that have contributed to a lifestyle behaviour that are beyond the control of the individual – e.g. genetics, upbringing – (Hope et al., 2008); and we can acknowledge that poverty will often prevent people from being able to eat healthily.

Others might argue that smokers and drinkers contribute extensively to the economy already, because tobacco and alcohol are heavily taxed, and denial of treatment would therefore be very unfair. This begs the question of whether the NHS would be better or worse off if nobody smoked or drank alcohol to excess. Logically, we must assume that the wards would not be as full of people with cardio-vascular, respiratory and liver disease; but they would still be full, for people will find different things to die of!

Notwithstanding the debate about moral culpability, the General Medical Council (2006) has stated clearly that doctors should not be making these kinds of judgements, and that each patient should be assessed on his/her individual clinical merits (para. 7). The Nursing and Midwifery Council (2008) makes similar demands on its registrants ('You must not discriminate in any way against those in your care'), as does the Health and Care Professions Council (2008). Therefore, the fact that the driver in our scenario was intoxicated should not, of itself, be a determining factor when deciding which of the two patients should receive treatment.

B WOULD IT MAKE A DIFFERENCE IF THE PEDESTRIAN WAS SUICIDAL AND HAD DELIBERATELY WALKED INTO THE PATH OF THE CARE?

If this were true, we would still be left with the uncomfortable fact that the driver was intoxicated and therefore not in full control of his faculties. In other words, a completely sober driver might have been able to avoid the pedestrian and thereby prevent the collision. Let us imagine, though, that the pedestrian planned his suicide so carefully that even the reflexes of a Formula 1 driver would not have been sufficient to avoid him. This leaves us with a dilemma: should healthcare be reserved for those who *want* to be treated, and therefore denied to those who seek to end their own lives?

An argument against this would be that the suicidal patient is not a fully autonomous agent, for his psychosis or depression is such that he is unable to make a competent decision. Of course, it would usually be impossible for the healthcare professionals to know the full circumstances of the incident, and they would not be in a position to make this kind of judgement. Even if they were in full possession of the facts, they might be able to argue that depression is a treatable illness, and saving the pedestrian's life would not therefore be a waste of effort. It is by no means certain, however, that a suicidal patient is not acting autonomously. Suicides are not always the result of depression or psychosis, and they can be the product of a fully rational mind. In such circumstances, it could be argued that frustration of the pedestrian's wish to kill himself represents 'a fundamental contempt for the wishes of the agent' (Harris, 1985: 204).

In the heat of the moment, none of these considerations are likely to enter the minds of the healthcare professionals: their responsibilities are going to lie in stabilising the physical condition of their patients, and the psycho-social issues can be debated later. Imagine, though, that the pedestrian is given the best care available, entailing an enormous expenditure of physical and material resources. He survives the experience, is discharged from the hospital, and then jumps off a cliff. Would we be entitled to say that this had been a waste of resources, and that those resources would have been better utilised on those who retain an appreciation of life?

C WOULD IT MAKE A DIFFERENCE IF THE DRIVER WAS AN EMINENT SCIENTIST AND/OR THE PEDESTRIAN WAS MENTALLY DISABLED?

What is being asked here is whether some lives are worth saving more than others. The most common response (and the legal one, for that matter) is that everybody is equal and is deserving of equal treatment in terms of healthcare; but, it may not necessarily be the most ethical response. Should a person's value be measured by his/her contribution to society? The Utilitarian would probably argue that it should, for there is greater potential for human happiness to be maximised by preserving the life of the scientist over that of the person with Down's syndrome. Imagine, for example, that the scientist is on the verge of a major breakthrough, which could provide a cure for one of mankind's most deadly diseases. Would we be prepared to sacrifice this possibility on the cross of equality? Imagine also, though, that the scientist's 'breakthrough' was going to be the development of a new weapon of mass destruction. Does his life now become *less* valuable than that of our Down's syndrome patient?

Perhaps the issue of resources and the mentally disabled is brought most clearly into focus when considering transplantation. Savulescu (2001) notes that a shortage of available hearts means that a number of children on the waiting list will inevitably die before transplantation. Therefore, if a child with Down's syndrome is given a heart transplant, this must mean that a child without Down's syndrome has been sacrificed. In consequence, he argues that we must take quality of life into account when allocating resources. This is not the same as saying that the person with Down's syndrome has *no* quality of life, but is simply contending that it is likely to be less than that of somebody without the syndrome. It is not possible to know how many people with learning disabilities have been the *recipients* of organ transplants, but it would not be stretching the imagination too far to suspect that the figure is a low one (and certainly much smaller than the number of people with learning disabilities who have been *donors*).

The final point to make on this question is whether or not it would make a difference if it was known that one of the patients was a convicted criminal. Of course, there are degrees of criminality and a large variety of offences that could be classified as criminal behaviour; but imagine that one of these patients is the worst kind that we could think of (say, for example, a serial killer, a rapist, or a paedophile). As mentioned earlier, the NMC Code of Conduct makes it clear that considerations of this kind should not affect the care given to patients, for each individual is entitled to the same treatment. If we were to pick and choose which patients should be looked after, we may soon be basing our resource decisions on a patient's race, colour, religion, gender or sexual orientation. Clearly, this should not be allowed to happen, and the healthcare practitioner should endeavour to maintain a professional approach at all times and with all patients. In practice, however, one suspects that the relationship with the criminal patient is going to be different than it would be with other patients. It is one thing to be professional, but it is quite another thing to develop a rapport with that person.

D WOULD IT MAKE A DIFFERENCE IF THE PEDESTRIAN WAS 85 YEARS OLD?

Or, to put it another way, should treatment be given to the young in preference to the old? Beauchamp and Childress (2001) note that the question may be decided on clinical grounds. Thus, in our scenario, and with all things being equal, it would be reasonable to assume that the 23-year-old has a greater probability of survival. Leaving this to one side, though, many of us will intuitively feel that, in a straight choice, the younger person should take priority over the older patient. If, for example, you come across two people drowning – one a 90-year-old, and the other a 10-year-old child – and you only had time to save one, which would you choose?

This position has come to be known as the 'fair innings' argument (Lockwood, 1988), its main contention being that older people have had their chance of life, whereas younger people have not yet been given this chance. If it is a tragedy to grow old, it is an even bigger tragedy *not* to grow old (Harris, 1985), because the latter have been denied the opportunity to live a normal life span.

Despite our intuitive leanings towards this position, however, there are a number of difficulties with it. For one thing, it is inherently agist in that it discriminates against a certain section of the population. Pattinson (2009) also notes that ageism is tantamount to sexism, for a majority of the elderly will be female. Moreover, an establishment of priorities based upon age will inevitably be arbitrary and may become quite meaningless. It is one thing to say that a 23-year-old should take priority over an 85-year-old, but does this also imply that he should receive preferential treatment if the pedestrian was 27 years old? Finally, one might argue that the 85-year-old has spent a lifetime contributing to the NHS, whereas the 23-year-old has only just begun to do so. It might seem inherently unfair, therefore, that he should be denied treatment at the point where he needs it most.

Because of these flaws, Harris (1985) argues that the 'fair innings' argument has little to commend it, and suggests that the value of a person's life can only be determined by the individual him/herself:

> [The anti-ageist argument] locates the wrongness of ending an individual's life in the evil of thwarting that person's desire to go on living and argues that it is profoundly unjust to frustrate that desire merely because some of those who have exactly the same desire, held no more strongly, also have a longer life expectancy than the others (p. 90).

The logical conclusion to be drawn from this argument is that preference should be given to those who value their lives the most strongly, regardless of their age and regardless of what we would consider to be the quality of that life. Harris acknowledges that not everybody will agree with this position, but it neatly side-steps the possibility that certain groups of people will be discriminated against because of a characteristic that they exhibit. It is somewhat ironic that we are exhorted to live healthy lives so that we live longer, but should then be denied treatment because we have reached old age. Moreover, the signs are that the anti-agist argument will increase in vigour as time goes by: the population in the UK is ageing considerably (Office for National Statistics, 2010), and this group is likely to form a powerful political lobby in the future.

E WOULD IT MAKE A DIFFERENCE IF THE PEDESTRIAN WAS SINGLE, AND THE DRIVER HAD THREE YOUNG CHILDREN?

We are assuming here that the driver is a model of fatherhood and that his death could have severe psychological and financial repercussions on his wife and three children. The opposite might be true; but, even allowing for this possibility, should the fact that he has dependents be a relevant consideration when allocating resources? The primary argument in favour of this position is that his death will have an adverse effect upon *others*, whereas this is less likely to be the case with the single person. This is not to say that the single person's death will go unmourned, but simply to state that the loss of the driver will have more tangible and far-reaching consequences for the lives of others.

Some support for this argument comes from the courts themselves. In *R v Swindon PCT, ex parte Rogers [2006]*, it was suggested that funding of expensive treatment (in this case, Herceptin) could be better justified if the woman had a disabled child, for the latter had a heavy reliance upon her. Newdick (2007), however, contends that this is inequitable, and that resource decisions should be determined on clinical grounds alone. In other words, which patient will derive the most therapeutic benefit? We might also argue that discrimination on the basis of the number of dependents could establish a dangerous precedent. For example, it may suggest to people that their best chances of receiving healthcare lie in having a family. Of all the possible reasons for having children, this must rank fairly low in the scale of morality.

F WOULD IT MAKE A DIFFERENCE IF THE PEDESTRIAN WAS AN ILLEGAL IMMIGRANT?

The obvious point to this question is that the illegal immigrant has not contributed to the resources of the nation, and should not therefore be a recipient of its care. We could make the same argument about children, although there is at least a potential that they will be major contributors in the future. There would be no such potential if the pedestrian had severe learning disabilities, yet many would consider that he took priority over the immigrants. Is this because the resources of the NHS should be reserved solely for citizens of the UK?

This is not a new argument, and nor is it confined to the UK. Prottas (1986) cites the case of Luiza Magardician, a 20-year-old Romanian citizen who came to New York in the hope of obtaining a kidney transplant. The poverty of the health system in her own country meant that her chances of securing a transplant there were non-existent, and she believed that America (the 'land of plenty') would be able to help her. However, official policy dictated that, where there was a shortage of donors, American citizens would head the queue, and thereby take priority over non-US citizens.

Prottas argues that membership in the community that supplies the organs is a legitimate criterion to employ when allocating these resources, and he feels that the official policy is justified. He goes on to suggest that the organs have been supplied *by* Americans in a spirit of generosity; and the clear implication (although not expressly stated) is that they were donated *for* Americans (and nobody else).

A similar line of reasoning can be found when the Leader of the Opposition in the UK announced a proposed policy to screen all immigrants for tuberculosis and HIV and return them to their country of origin if they were found to be positive (Triggle, 2005). His contention was that infected people would endanger the health of the native population, and the cost of treating them would be prohibitive (i.e. the resources expended on this treatment would be better-utilised in the care of resident UK citizens). Notwithstanding the fact that screening itself is very expensive and notoriously inefficient (Bakhshi, 2006), it is clear that such a policy was guaranteed to feed into the prejudices of many sectors of the population against foreigners in

general and immigrants in particular. But do wealthy countries have a moral obligation to help the people from developing nations? Consider the following hypothetical scenario, developed by Baggini (2006) from an idea by O'Neill (1997):

Box 6.13

A ship has capsized and 12 people have managed to get onto a lifeboat. The lifeboat
itself can hold 20, so there is plenty of space for the survivors. Moreover, there are sufficient rations to ensure that they will remain adequately nourished until they are
rescued. One of those in the boat notices that there are still people in the water who
are in danger of drowning and who are screaming for help. He suggests that the boat
should pick them up because there is space available, but he is outvoted by the remainder of the crew. Their argument is that their resources would inevitably be diluted and
that life would certainly be much less comfortable. Moreover, it was not their fault that
the people are in danger, and therefore, there is no duty to rescue them.

If the actions of the crew seem cruel, heartless and deeply immoral, we should remember
what this scenario represents. The lifeboat is the developed world, whereas the drowning people are those from the poorer nations. Perhaps there are some flaws with this
analogy, but it is difficult to escape the conclusion that, if affluent nations have the
means to help others, they also have a moral obligation to do so. As Baggini (2006) says:

> The lifeboat analogy suggests that it is not so much that we would be good people if we
> did [help], but that we are terribly wrong not to (p. 66).

There is also, perhaps, a more compelling reason for the UK to assist those from countries of the former Empire. Schama (2003) notes that there were devastating famines
in India throughout the years of the British Raj, nearly all of which were created by
removal of the local people's sources of income (so that British manufacturing goods
did not have to compete with those from India). We might argue that we cannot be
called to account for the sins of our forefathers, but the inconvenient truth is that we
owe much of our present standard of living to those people. Therefore, we are inextricably bound up in the collective guilt of a nation that created the conditions for mass
starvation. This is not to say that the Empire was always a force for evil, since there
are many positive features that one could point to; it is simply that there is a moral debt
to be paid here, and we should be prepared to acknowledge it. Nor, for that matter,
should we forget that the NHS has recruited extensively from poorer nations, thereby
depriving those countries of another national resource (Pattinson, 2009).

Our scenario, therefore, appears no closer to resolution. Perhaps the most simple
answer would be to treat the first patient that comes through the door. This would
mean that the allocation of resources is determined by *lottery*, which has the advantage of treating every person equally, but which could produce outcomes that are

intuitively wrong. Moreover, it would mean handing the decision over to the para-medics, for they will be the people who will choose which patient to bring in first.

Admittedly, our scenario may not be a daily feature of hospital life, but the issues discussed will exercise the minds of those working in transplant units on a regular basis. Imagine, for example, that there are 100 people on the waiting list for a liver transplant. When a liver becomes available, the first priority of the clinical staff is to ascertain which of the potential recipients is a histo-compatible match. Let us imag-ine further that this reduces the number to six. The clinicians will be faced with the same moral dilemmas posed by our scenario – who should receive the liver, and by what criteria should this decision be made? There have been a number of suggestions for a resolution of the problems posed by issues of resource allocation, and it is to these that we now turn.

4 POSSIBLE SOLUTIONS TO PROBLEMS OF RESOURCE ALLOCATION

A QUALITY-ADJUSTED LIFE YEARS

Quality-adjusted life years (QALYs) represents an attempt to produce a formula to determine the value of a treatment for a particular individual relative to its cost. Thus, if a treatment will bring one additional year of healthy life, it will have a QALY of +1. If the additional year of life was less than healthy, it will have a QALY of −1. If death results from the treatment or the disease, the QALY will be rated as 0. Therefore, according to the QALY principle, death is preferable to a year of unhealthy life. The real value of QALYs, however, is that they enable us to quantify the value of a treatment, thereby providing compelling reasons for either adopting or rejecting it as an item of expenditure. The following hypothetical scenario illustrates how the calculation is made:

Box 6.14

A patient currently has a quality of life score of 0.6 and a life expectancy of 10 years. Treatment for his illness is expected to improve his quality of life by 0.2 and his life expectancy by a further 5 years.

   Thus, the calculation is: $(0.8 \times 15) - (0.6 \times 10) = 12 - 6 = 6$.

   If the treatment costs £10,000, the cost per QALY = $10,000 \div 6 = £1,667$.

It follows, therefore, that any treatment with a lower cost per QALY score should be considered more cost-effective and should, in consequence, be the preferred option. Not surprisingly, however, there are a number of criticisms of this approach (Harris, 1985; Campbell et al., 2005; Pattinson, 2009). For one thing, it suggests that the interests of minority groups should be sacrificed: a heart transplant, for example, will almost inevitably produce a low QALY score, but it means the difference between life and death for the unfortunate patient. For similar reasons, QALYs are seen as being inherently agist (Joiner, 1999), for the lower life expectancy among the elderly will reduce the QALY score; and they also discriminate against the disabled (for it will be assumed that they have a lower quality of life). Perhaps most damaging to the concept of QALYs is its unquestioning faith in the ability of doctors to estimate a patient's life expectancy with any accuracy, and its belief that a value can be attributed to a patient's quality of life.

Despite these criticisms, though, QALYs represent a good effort to produce a formula for calculating the value of healthcare treatments. They are essentially Utilitarian, for their purpose is to produce the maximum amount of good within the resources available. As such, they are entirely equitable, and better alternative formulae have not been forthcoming. The pseudo-scientific nature of QALYs, however, makes it difficult to apply the formula with any great confidence, although Pattinson (2009) notes that NICE prefers to use it when the costs of a particular treatment are significantly high.

B RE-STRUCTURE THE NHS OR HAVE A DIFFERENT HEALTHCARE SYSTEM ALTOGETHER

If this argument is to have any strength, it must rest on the premise that the NHS is inefficient and wastes many of the resources that are allocated to it. Certainly, there are many examples that testify to this claim, and successive Governments have made repeated attempts to re-organise the NHS. It has to be said, though, that a number of these re-organisations have created confusion rather than stability, and have thereby become counter-productive. Notwithstanding this, it is also possible to argue that the NHS is actually quite efficient, for it delivers much comparative to the resources expended upon it. Moreover, productivity has increased considerably in recent years, particularly after the delegation of many doctors' tasks to nurses (DH, 1999).

This is not to say that the efficiency of the NHS cannot be improved from its present state, although there are some who will argue that it is fundamentally unsalvageable and that we should look to the examples of healthcare systems in other countries. It is difficult to envisage moving to a system similar to that in the USA, where the quality of healthcare appears to be directly related to one's ability to pay. By contrast, the German system seems to be popular with the people (Green et al., 2005) and delivers a high quality service, but it demands a heavy burden of taxation (currently about 14 per cent of one's income).

There are elements of privatisation within the UK healthcare system already, for certain treatments (e.g. some cosmetic procedures, infertility treatment, etc.) are only available if the recipient is willing to pay for them. Some will argue that this is the thin end of the wedge, and that there are indicators of increasing privatisation throughout the NHS. In the midst of this debate, we can probably discern two facts: first, politicians are coming increasingly to acknowledge that the UK economy cannot sustain a high quality NHS in its present form; second, despite the frequent criticism of its performance and the horror stories that appear in the newspapers on a regular basis, the NHS remains a national institution and one towards which the public feel protective. Any assault upon its fundamental principles, therefore, will lose votes, and every political party is fully aware of this. In consequence, any move towards privatisation would have to be done by stealth, rather than by a radical overhaul. One cannot help feeling, though, that a more open and honest debate would be more likely to produce a positive result.

C THE NHS SHOULD FOCUS ON PREVENTIVE CARE RATHER THAN CURATIVE TREATMENTS

The NHS has been likened to a policeman who keeps rescuing drowning people from a river, whereas he would be better employed by walking upstream to find out who has been throwing them in. In other words, the NHS is a *sickness* service, focusing the majority of its resources on treating the effects of unhealthy behaviour, rather than on preventing those behaviours in the first place.

Recognition of the importance of preventive medicine was acknowledged within the Oregon healthcare experiment in 1987, when resources were diverted away from an organ transplant programme and towards basic healthcare provision for low-income children and pregnant women (Oberlander et al., 2001). Whereas 34 people were adversely affected by this decision over a period of two years, 1,500 people stood to benefit. A clearer example of Utilitarianism in action could not be found, but the policy had a more far-reaching motive. If children were given better health-care, they would be less likely to develop illnesses in the future, and would therefore produce less of a drain on resources.

This argument clearly has a certain logical appeal, but it presupposes that health-care is the primary determinant of an individual's health status. In fact, the evidence suggests that it has only minimal impact, and that greater significance should be placed on housing, education and employment (in terms of both physical and mental health) (Beauchamp and Childress, 2001). If this is true, it suggests that we should be taking resources *away* from healthcare altogether so that they are utilised in other spheres. The evidence is intangible enough to prevent it from having a strong influence on official policy, but it cannot be completely ignored.

Equally, though, we should not ignore the contention that individuals themselves have a responsibility to try and lead a healthy lifestyle as much as possible (Lord McColl, 1995; Mason and Laurie, 2011).

D THE STATE SHOULD FUND A BASIC MINIMUM OF HEALTHCARE, AND NO MORE THAN THIS

This argument contends that there is a level of healthcare to which all people should be entitled in a civilised society, and the State should therefore be prepared to resource this. But, if individuals require more than this basic minimum, they should have to pay for it themselves. Campbell et al. (2005), however, note that defining what is meant by 'minimum entitlement' is essentially an insuperable obstacle. They point to the example of New Zealand, where agreement failed to be reached even after 10 years of debate on the subject.

They also acknowledge that any agreement upon a limit will be determined by how much the State is prepared (or able) to pay. Inevitably, this comes down to how much the general public are prepared to pay from their taxes. Should, therefore, the public be involved in making these decisions? An effort to do so was made in Oregon, where a number of meetings were arranged to canvass the views of local citizens upon how healthcare resources should be utilised. Newdick (2005), however, reports that the majority of attendees at these meetings were employees of the healthcare system, and cannot therefore be said to be representative of the population. Moreover, even if a representative sample could be canvassed, one has to doubt that the people could be truly objective or knowledgeable enough to make these kinds of judgements (Herring, 2008). Certainly these initiatives lend themselves to all the frailties of group dynamics, for it is inevitable that the most articulate and the most forceful will hold centre stage: the weak, elderly and disabled, by contrast, will either have no voice or will be drowned out. Perhaps one of the most damning criticisms of these ventures is that it can be seen as a form of cowardice – any decisions made are guaranteed to have an adverse effect on some people, but, as the public criticism grows, the health service managers will be able to say: 'This was *your* decision, not ours; and you must therefore accept the responsibility for it'.

Despite these criticisms, though, there is something to be said for encouraging public involvement in resource decisions, even though their opinions may not be determinative of the outcome. The argument that the public lack the necessary knowledge only really works after attempts have been made to increase that knowledge. And, as Pattinson (2009) says:

> Leaving rationing and other morally-loaded decisions largely in the hands of doctors encourages the view that medical ethics is something for doctors alone (p. 54).

CONCLUSION

It is to be hoped that the foregoing has highlighted some of the issues surrounding resource allocation, but equally, it is acknowledged that it has not provided any conclusive answers. In part, this is because the debate is rarely conducted in an impartial and objective manner. As Frankel et al. (2000) state:

> The rationing debate is profoundly unscientific. The problem it seeks to address is assumed rather than expressed in any refutable form, and the literature is dominated by assertion, political analysis and ethical debate (p. 40).

Thus, the issues tend to be either too sensitive for politicians to engage in open debate for fear of losing votes, or the discussion is dominated by people with a particular 'axe to grind'. Clearly, those efforts that have been made to develop a system of rationing have frequently been controversial, divisive and deeply flawed. Experience dictates, therefore, that a 'one rule fits all' philosophy is destined to fail, for it is not going to be adequate to cover all eventualities; and, in consequence, it is necessary to adopt a flexibility of approach (Mason and Laurie, 2011).

The paradox for healthcare practitioners is that they are faced with two conflicting paradigms. Their professional training and socialisation is heavily influenced by deontological principles, which can be found throughout the various Codes of Conduct. However, the reality of practice compels them to be Utilitarians. It is no longer possible, therefore, to treat one patient without consideration of the impact this will have for the supply of resources for other patients. It means, in consequence, that hard choices have to be made, and the high quality of care towards which healthcare professionals strive may have to be sacrificed in certain areas.

It is impossible to predict with any certainty what the future holds, but at least one thing is certain: the issues associated with resource allocation will not disappear, and all the signs are that they will intensify with the passage of time. It is incumbent upon us all, therefore, to address our minds to the problem so that the debate is conducted by as many informed, balanced and objective people as possible.

REFERENCES

TEXTS

Baggini, J. (2006) *The Pig That Wants to be Eaten*, 2nd edn. London: Granta Books.

Bailey, S.H. and Bowman, M.J. (1986) 'The policy/operational dichotomy – a cuckoo in the nest', *Cambridge Law Journal*, 45 (3), November: 430–56.

Bakhshi, S. (2006) *Tuberculosis in the United Kingdom: A Tale of Two Nations*. Leicester: Troubadour Publishing Ltd.

Beauchamp, T.L. and Childress, J.F. (2001) *Principles of Biomedical Ethics*, 5th edn. Oxford: Oxford University Press.

Brazier, M. and Cave, E. (2007) *Medicine, Patients and the Law*, 4th edn. London: Penguin Books.

Campbell, A., Gillett, G. and Jones, G. (2005) *Medical Ethics*, 4th edn. Oxford: Oxford University Press.

Colapinto, J. (2004) 'Gender gap: what were the real reasons behind David Reimer's suicide?' *Slate Magazine*. Available from: www.slate.com/id/2101678/. Accessed: 16/3/10.

Department of Health (1999) *Making a Difference. Strengthening the Nursing, Midwifery and Health Visiting Contribution to Health and Healthcare*. London: Department of Health.

Frankel, S., Ebrahim, S. and Davey Smith, G. (2000) 'The limits to demand for health care', *British Medical Journal*, 321, 1 July, 40–4.

General Medical Council (2006) *Maintaining Boundaries*. London: GMC.

Green, D.G., Irvine, B. and Cackett, B. (2005) Health care in Germany. Available from: www.civitas.org.uk/pubs/bb3Germany.php. Accessed: 4/8/10.

Ham, C. (1999) 'The role of doctors, patients and managers in priority setting decisions: lessons from the "Child B" case', *Health Expectations*, 2: 61–8.

Harris, J. (1985) *The Value of Life*. London: Routledge.

Health and Care Professions Council (2008) *Standards of Conduct, Performance and Ethics*. London: HCPC (July).

Herring, J. (2008) *Medical Law and Ethics*, 2nd edn. Oxford: Oxford University Press.

Hope, T., Savulescu, J. and Hendrick, J. (2008) *Medical Ethics and Law: the Core Curriculum*, 2nd edn. London: Churchill Livingstone Elsevier.

Joiner, A. (1999) 'Quality adjusted life years and the allocation of health to the elderly: ethical considerations', *Journal of Orthopaedic Nursing*, 3: 81–4.

Kruijver, F.P.M., Zhou, J-N., Pool, C.W., Hofman, M.A., Gearen, L.J.G. and Swaab, D.F. (2000) 'Male-to-female transsexuals have female neuron numbers in a limbic nucleus', *The Journal of Clinical Endocrinology and Metabolism*, 85 (5): 2034–41.

Lockwood, M. (1988) 'Quality of life and resource allocation', in J.M. Bell and S. Mendes (eds), *Philosophy and Medical Welfare*. Cambridge: Cambridge University Press.

Lord McColl of Dunhill (1995) 'Ethical issues in healthcare prioritisation: a political viewpoint', *British Journal of Urology*, 76, Suppl. 2: 55–7.

Mason, J.K. and Laurie, G.T. (2011) *Mason and McCall Smith's Law and Medical Ethics*, 8th edn. Oxford: Oxford University Press.

Newdick, C. (2005) *Who Should We Treat? Rights, Rationing and Resources in the NHS*, 2nd edn. Oxford: Oxford University Press.

Newdick, C. (2007) 'Judicial review: low-priority treatment and exceptional case review', *Medical Law Review*, 15 (2): 236–44.

Nursing and Midwifery Council (2008) *The Code: Standards of Conduct, Performance and Ethics for Nurses and Midwives*. London: NMC (May).

Nursing Times (1996) 'Did the NHS fail child B?', *Nursing Times*, 92 (36): 33–6, (September 4).

Oberlander, J., Marmor, T. and Jacobs, L. (2001) 'Rationing medical care: rhetoric and reality in the Oregon health plan', *Canadian Medical Association Journal*, 164 (11), (May 29): 1583–7.

Office for National Statistics (2008) *Expenditure on Health Care in the UK*. London (April).

Office for National Statistics (2010) Available from: www.statistics.gov.uk/cci/nugget.asp?id=949. Accessed: 4/8/10.

O'Neill, O. (1977) 'Lifeboat Earth', in W. Aitken and H. La Follette (eds), *World Hunger and Moral Obligation,* London: Prentice-Hall.

Pattinson, S.D. (2009) *Medical Law and Ethics*, 2nd edn. London: Sweet & Maxwell.

Prottas, J.M. (1986) 'In organ transplants, Americans first?' Hastings Center Report, October.

Savulescu, J. (2001) 'Resources, Down's syndrome, and cardiac surgery', *British Medical Journal*, 322 (7291): 875–6.

Schama, S. (2003) *A History of Britain* (Vol. 3). London: BBC Worldwide Ltd.

Shiu, M. (1993) 'Refusing to treat smokers is unethical and a dangerous precedent', *British Medical Journal*, 306: 1048–9.

The Beveridge Report (1942) *Report on Social Insurance and Allied Services*. HMSO (Cmnd. 6404).

Triggle, N. (2005) Will health checks have an impact? Available from: http://news.bbc.co.uk/1/hi/health/4267575.stm. Accessed: 4/8/10.

Underwood, M.J. and Bailey, J.S. (1993) 'Should smokers be offered coronary bypass surgery?', *British Medical Journal*, 306: 1047–8.

CASES

Associated Provincial Picture Houses v Wednesbury Corporation [1947] 2 All ER 680.
Council of Civil Service Unions v Minister for the Civil Service [1984] 3 All ER 935.
North West Lancashire Health Authority v A, D and G [1999] 53 BMLR 148.
R v Bedford Primary Care Trust, ex parte Watts [2004] EWCA Civ 166.
R v Cambridge Health Authority, ex parte B [1995] 25 BMLR 5 (HC); 2 AllER 129 (CA).
R v Central Birmingham Health Authority, ex parte Collier [1988], unreported.
R v Central Birmingham Health Authority, ex parte Walker [1987] 3 BMLR 32.
R v North Derbyshire Health Authority, ex parte Fisher [1997] 8 Med LR 327.
R v Secretary of State for the Home Department, ex parte Fire Brigades Union and others
    [1995] 2 AC 513.
R v Secretary of State for Social Services, ex parte Hincks [1980] 1 BMLR 93 (CA).
R v Secretary of State for Health, ex parte Pfizer [2002] EWCA 1566.
R v Sheffield Health Authority, ex parte Seale [1994] 25 BMLR 1.
R v Swindon NHS Primary Care Trust and another, ex parte Rogers [2006] EWCA Civ 392.
R v West Sussex Primary Care Trust, ex parte Ross [2008] EWHC 2252.

LEGISLATION

NHS Act 1977
NHS Act 2006

Scenario (discussion at end of book)

A heart has become available, and the following patients have all been found to be compatible recipients:

1 Joseph: 50 years old and married for 26 years. He has two children (24 and 22), both of whom have left home. He is the editor of a local newspaper, and participates in numerous charity events. He was diagnosed with heart failure two years ago, following a massive myocardial infarction. His physical health is deteriorating quite quickly and his psychological status has been assessed as unstable. Part of the reason for his heart attack was that he has always been a highly stressed individual. He was also a chain smoker (40 cigarettes per day), although he has managed to reduce this to three per day.

2 Anna: 22 years old, single and still living with her parents. She was diagnosed with myocarditis five years ago following a viral infection, since which time her heart function has steadily declined. She is currently unemployed and left school with no qualifications. She is very angry about her illness, but refuses to allow the symptoms to control her life. Thus, despite the unpleasant consequences for her health, she insists upon going out on a regular basis with her friends, during which she drinks alcohol to excess.

3   Jennifer: 14 years old and living with her parents. She was born with congenital heart defects and has had a couple of operations, but she is now in severe heart failure. At school, she is considered academically very bright and a possible candidate to study at Oxford or Cambridge. However, her illness has resulted in numerous breaks in her education, and she would not be ready to take her GCSEs. Her illness and prognosis depress her, but she is adamant that she does not want a heart transplant. In her words, 'I would rather die than walk around with another person's heart inside me.'

4   James: 65 years old and living with his gay partner. He has had a series of heart attacks over the last five years and is now in severe heart failure. Numerous lifestyle behaviours have contributed to this situation (he is overweight and he has been a lifelong smoker), but there is also a strong hereditary link. He is a pharmaceutical researcher and is currently working on a new treatment for breast cancer. Although he has no family, his partner is clearly very attached to him, and he himself has expressed a strong desire to go on living.

On the assumption that there are no differences in histo-compatibility between these patients, which of them should receive the heart, and why?

7

MENTAL HEALTH

Learning Objectives

At the end of this chapter, the reader will:

1   Have an understanding of the Mental Health Act 1983 (as amended by the Mental Health Act 2007), and of its key provisions.

2   Acknowledge the distinction between formal and informal admission.

3   Be familiar with the guiding principles of the Mental Health Act Code of Practice.

4   Consider the legal and ethical implications of force-feeding, ECT, and behavioural modification.

5   Understand the concept of Deprivation of Liberty Safeguards.

1 INTRODUCTION

'They called me mad, and I called them mad,

and damn them, they outvoted me.'

The seventeenth-century playwright Nathaniel Lee recalls his enforced committal to Bethlem psychiatric hospital (quoted in Porter (2002)), and thereby encapsulates the central questions that have resonated through the ages. What does it mean to be 'mentally ill', who makes these diagnoses (and how), and when can we say that somebody is 'cured'?

The official definition of mental illness can be found in the Mental Health Act 1983 (s1 [2]), amended by the Mental Health Act 2007 (s1 [2]), in which it is described as 'any disorder or disability of the mind'. As Mason and Laurie (2011) state, this definition is *so broad as to be almost beyond restrictive interpretation* (p. 428), and certainly does not take us much further. Perhaps its breadth was calculated to ensure that none in need of psychiatric treatment 'slipped through the net'; but equally, it creates an opening for abuse of the power invested in those with the authority to detain people against their wishes.

Moreover, as Herring (2010) notes, the popular image of mental illness has undergone changes through the ages. At one time, we have accepted that a degree of mental disturbance is necessary for the creation of great works of art, music and literature (the 'tortured genius'); at others, we have feared the mentally ill as being violent, unpredictable and potentially homicidal (the 'dangerous lunatic'). The Mental Deficiency Act 1913 authorised the incarceration of unmarried women who gave birth while on poor relief, justifying this decision by stating that such individuals demonstrated clear evidence of moral depravity and mental defectiveness (Jackson, 2010). Similarly, it was not until 1993 that homosexuality disappeared from the official classification of mental disorders (Bartlett and Sandland, 2007).

For Szasz (1970) and other members of the anti-psychiatry movement, this 'fluidity' of interpretation is unacceptable and needs review. Thus, it is argued that what we call a psychiatric disorder is often nothing more than a description of a behaviour that people are not prepared to tolerate. Whereas, in the past, society was shocked by single mothers and homosexuals, modern society is largely much more tolerant of these things. By contrast, however, we are probably less likely to tolerate the 'eccentric' individual within society than were our forefathers.

Clearly, there is some force behind these arguments and we would be unwise to dismiss them completely. Indeed, the suggestion that nearly one in four people have at least one diagnosable psychiatric disorder (NHS Information Centre, 2009) may say more about the medicalisation of mental health and of societal/personal expectations than it does about the nature of mental disturbance. Nevertheless, it is equally clear that an unquestioning acceptance of this position would possibly deny treatment to those who are very ill. The MHA Code of Practice (DH, 2008) is rather more helpful in outlining those conditions which could be categorised as mental disorder:

Box 7.1 Categories of mental disorder

1 Affective disorders, such as depression and bipolar disorder.
2 Schizophrenia and delusional disorders.
3 Neurotic disorders, such as anxiety, phobias, obsessive-compulsive disorders, post-traumatic stress disorder, and hypochondriacism.
4 Organic disorders, such as dementia.
5 Personality disorders, which may (or may not) be caused by brain injury.

(Continued)

(Continued)

6　Mental and behavioural disorders caused by psycho-active substance use.
7　Eating disorders, non-organic sleep disorders, and non-organic sexual disorders.
8　Autistic spectrum disorders.
9　Behavioural and emotional disorders of children and adolescents (e.g. attention deficit hyperactivity disorder).

The Code of Practice is keen to emphasise that this is not an exhaustive list, suggesting that others can be added from time to time. But the Mental Health Act 2007 also *removed* two categories: learning disability and drug/alcohol misuse. Having said this, it is acknowledged that both may be accompanied by abnormally aggressive or seriously irresponsible conduct and/or associated with other mental disorders, in which case they will fall within the ambit of the Mental Health Act.

Hope et al. (2008) argue that legislation for the mentally ill is preferable to relying upon the common law, for the latter is better at dealing with short-term problems (whereas mental disorder generally requires long-term treatment). They also contend that legislation is more likely to prevent abuse of power than is the common law, although the potential clearly remains. The Mental Health Act permits enforced detention of individuals for indefinite periods and even if those individuals are assessed as competent to make their own decisions. More than this, they can be incarcerated if they are *perceived* to be a risk to others, even though they may not actually have committed a crime. As Jackson (2010) notes, this contravenes fundamental principles of criminal justice, and Harris (1985) casts considerable doubt upon its morality: if 'dangerousness' is a criterion of enforced detention of the mentally ill, such people 'must at the very least have made some attempt to damage others or have taken palpable steps towards such an attempt' (p. 218).

The perceived risk to the public from mentally disordered individuals has acquired increasing prominence in recent years (more of which later), even though the *actual* risk is very small (Herring, 2010). But this is only the first of a number of paradoxes pertaining to care of the mentally ill. For example, Campbell et al. (2005) ask us to consider the paranoid schizophrenic who is convinced that authority figures are preparing to take him to a strange place against his will and compel him to take mind-bending drugs. What is likely to happen to this person? Inevitably, his worst fears will become realised, and what began as a delusion will soon become a reality. The difficulties of establishing a therapeutic relationship with this individual are all too apparent.

Jackson (2010), on the other hand, identifies the inherent conflict of duties for members of the mental health team. The General Medical Council (2006) make it clear that the care of the patient should be a doctor's 'first concern'; and yet, detention of the mentally ill often seems to be more about protection of the public. If society expects mental health professionals to be jailers, it is doubtful that many of them would have signed up on this understanding.

The courts have frequently been very deferential to the psychiatric profession, arguing that doctors are in a unique position to provide 'objective medical expertise' (*Winterwerp v The Netherlands [1979]*). In consequence, few medical decisions are declared unlawful, even though it is known that psychiatry is an inexact science and that doctors are unlikely ever to be certain that their judgements are correct (*R (on the application of JB) v Haddock [2006]*). In fairness, psychiatrists are better placed to make clinical decisions than a judge, but an unquestioning faith in their abilities protects them from close scrutiny and serves to reduce patients' rights correspondingly (Bartlett, 2007). The decision in the following case serves as a good example of this:

Box 7.2   *R (on the application of G, N and B) v Nottinghamshire Healthcare NHS Trust [2008]*

Three detained patients at Rampton Hospital (a high security unit) challenged a decision to prevent them from smoking. Although the Health Act 2006 had established a smoking ban in public places, it had allowed designated smoking areas in mental health units. However, this exemption was removed in July 2008, and the nature of the unit meant that smoking outside was not a viable option.

The patients argued that, to all intents and purposes, Rampton was their *home*, and therefore they should be allowed the same rights as private citizens. The court, however, upheld the contention of the Trust that the hospital was an *institution*, and consequently not exempt from the regulations. This decision is defensible, but it could easily have gone the other way (Coggon, 2009). It becomes less defensible when one considers that the State has created an exemption for prisoners: if a prison is not an institution, it becomes difficult to know what is. This defiance of logic suggests that a diagnosis of mental illness requiring detention automatically entails a suspension of fundamental human rights. It would, of course, be grossly unfair to assume that this is the case; but equally, continued vigilance is imperative if this situation is to be avoided.

Having thus outlined some of the legal and ethical difficulties associated with caring for the mentally ill, we now need to see how the system works. Before doing this, however, it may be helpful to offer a few definitions of key concepts:

Box 7.3   Definitions

1 **Approved Clinician (AC):** in charge of the treatment of an informal patient, and has the power to prevent self-discharge from care. May be a doctor, psychiatric nurse, psychologist, occupational therapist or social worker.

(Continued)

(Continued)

2 **Responsible Clinician (RC)**: takes the clinical lead for a patient detained under the Mental Health Act, and may grant a leave of absence, make a Community Treatment Order (and revoke it), and discharge patients from detention. Formerly known as Responsible Medical Officers (RMOs), a term which ended in November 2008.

3 **Approved Mental Health Professional (AMHP)**: assists in the assessment process and makes determination of the grounds for detention (in conjunction with a doctor). Formerly known as Approved Social Workers (ASWs) – the role is essentially the same, but can now be performed by psychiatric nurses, occupational therapists, and psychologists.

4 **Second Opinion Appointed Doctor (SOAD)**: an independent Consultant Psychiatrist, appointed by the CQC, and whose role is to decide whether treatment for the detained patient is justifiable.

5 **Mental Health Review Tribunal (MHRT)**: an independent body, which has the responsibility for hearing applications and reviewing the cases of those detained under the Mental Health Act. It has the power to discharge detained patients if the relevant criteria are met.

6 **Care Quality Commission (CQC)**: created by the Health and Social Care Act 2008, and integrates services formerly carried out by the Healthcare Commission, Commission for Social Care Inspection, and the Mental Health Act Commission. Specifically in relation to mental health, it monitors the operation of the Mental Health Act and oversees the treatment of patients subject to detention.

7 **Nearest relative**: a hierarchy of kinship is recognised by the Mental Health Act 2007 (s26), and the person with greatest claim has the power to request discharge of the detained patient. The nearest relative should normally be consulted in all matters pertaining to the patient's care, but may be displaced by a County Court if acting unreasonably.

8 **Independent Mental Health Advocate (IMHA)**: helps detained patients to understand and exercise their legal rights. Also helps informal patients who are being considered for psycho-surgery or surgical implantation of hormones (s57), or ECT (s58A).

9 **Independent Mental Capacity Advocate (IMCA)**: established by the Mental Capacity Act 2005, this person's role is to help incapacitated people who face important decisions about serious medical treatment and/or change of residence.

The major legislation pertaining to mental disorder is the Mental Health Act 1983. The Mental Health Act 2007 did not replace this Act, as was hoped by a number of people, but instead made several amendments. The result is that the process is now much more confusing than it already was, and has disappointed many (Bowen, 2007). Nevertheless, it may be possible to clarify the situation by considering the following fictional scenario:

Box 7.4   A suitable case for treatment

Jim is a 47-year-old male, who has a long history of mental health problems, having been diagnosed with paranoid schizophrenia at the age of 28. He has required hospitalisation on a couple of occasions, but was last discharged into the community seven months ago. Since that time, he has resided in a flat and has managed reasonably well under the supervision of a community psychiatric nurse (CPN). However, the CPN has had some suspicions that Jim has not been taking his medication. One evening, he is found in the street in his pyjamas, and it is clear that he is hallucinating. He is very noisy and abusive, and is haranguing other pedestrians. His neighbours call the police.

As we explore this patient's journey, there will be opportunities to digress from time to time and discuss a variety of concepts pertaining to mental health.

2 POLICE POWERS

If a person appears to be suffering from a mental disorder in a public place, the police are empowered (by virtue of s136) to remove that person to 'a place of safety'. The police officer would need to be able to justify that removal served the individual's best interests and/or was necessary for the protection of others, but it is not necessary for a definitive diagnosis of mental illness to have been made at this stage. If Jim had been acting strangely within his own home, the police would still have powers to enter his premises and remove him, but they would require a warrant from a Justice of the Peace (s135). Moreover, only an Approved Mental Health Professional (AMHP) can apply for such a warrant.

Both ss135 and 136 enable detention for up to 72 hours, and their purpose is to enable examination by an AMHP and for arrangements to be made regarding treatment and care. The 'place of safety' is defined in s135 (6) as a hospital, care home, police station or 'any other suitable place the occupier of which is willing temporarily to receive the patient'. In the past, removal under s136 has almost inevitably been to a police station (Bartlett and Sandland, 2007). However, a report by the Royal College of Psychiatrists (2008) acknowledged that it is an unsuitable environment for such patients, and their recommendation that s136 rooms should be available in acute psychiatric hospitals has been accepted. These facilities are expected to open at any time of the day and night and should be staffed separately from the rest of the institution.

Reasonable force is also permitted if the individual resists removal, although this is not specifically stated within the Mental Health Act. The authority for this comes from the Police and Criminal Evidence Act 1984 (PACE): s117 empowers the police to use force when executing a warrant (i.e. s135), and s24 empowers them to arrest someone who:

a   represents a danger to him/herself and/or others; and/or
b   is offending public decency; and/or
c   is causing an obstruction of the highway.

3 INFORMAL ADMISSION

The patient in our scenario clearly falls within the ambit of s136, and we now find him in a psychiatric hospital being interviewed by an AMHP. It is the responsibility of the AMHP to assess the patient's competence to make decisions on his own behalf, and the test outlined in s3 of the Mental Capacity Act 2005 should be used for this purpose (see Chapter 4). The AMHP will also assess the severity of the patient's symptoms, and make a determination of whether or not he requires hospitalisation. If the patient is both competent and requires treatment, he could be admitted as an informal patient with his consent (s131). Moreover, a 16- or 17-year-old can consent to admission, providing that s/he has capacity to do so, and this consent cannot be over-ridden by a parent.

The vast majority (90 per cent) of those receiving in-patient psychiatric treatment are informal admissions (Dimond, 2011), and there are clear advantages to this. From a service perspective, it eliminates much of the bureaucratic process associated with sectioning patients; from the patient's perspective, it avoids the stigma of enforced detention; and from a therapeutic perspective, it fosters an atmosphere of mutual trust and cooperation which should ensure compliance with treatment before and after release. Evidence suggests, however, that the element of freedom that informal admission is supposed to bring is something of an illusion (Bartlett and Sandland, 2007; Jones, 2009). In other words, the patient is faced with a Hobson's choice: either consent to informal admission *or* face enforced detention under section (Chadwick and Todd, 1992). Moreover, an informal patient who is receiving treatment for mental disorder but who decides to leave the hospital can be forcibly detained by a nurse for up to six hours if it is felt that his/her mental disorder is such that it is necessary for his/her health or safety or for the protection of others (s5 [4]). Within this period, an Approved Clinician should attend the patient, at which point the holding powers of the nurse automatically cease.

4 ASSESSMENT

Our scenario suggests that Jim is not competent to make a decision and that he requires hospitalisation. He therefore needs to be sectioned under the Mental Health Act, which has enormous significance for any individual, and which epitomises the ultimate in paternalism. Beauchamp and Childress (2001) define paternalism thus:

> the intentional over-riding of one person's known preferences or actions by another person, where the person who over-rides justifies the action by the goal of benefiting or avoiding harm to the person whose preferences or actions are over-ridden (p. 178).

Clearly, paternalism involves the withdrawal of power from one individual (whether by means of coercion or simply by withholding information) and its subsequent acquisition by those in authority. Equally, for all its beneficent intentions, it is open to abuse. The Mental Health Act Code of Practice (DH, 2008) seeks to restrain the abuse of power by offering the following guiding principles for healthcare practitioners:

Box 7.5   Guiding Principles

1   The purpose of decisions taken under the Act must be to minimise the undesirable effects of mental disorder, promote recovery, and protect others (1.2).
2   Restrictions on liberty must be the minimum necessary (1.3).
3   Each patient should be treated with respect and consideration (1.4).
4   Patients (and their carers) should be involved in decision-making as much as possible (1.5).
5   Resources should be used efficiently (1.6).

In order to detain a patient under the Mental Health Act, s2 is initially invoked, which authorises admission for assessment. Admission must be founded on the written recommendations of two registered medical practitioners (s2 [3]), although only one is required in an emergency (s4). The latter expires after 72 hours, whereas admission under s2 can last for up to 28 days. This section is non-renewable and can only apply to assessment: in consequence, if treatment is required and/or the period of detention is to last for more than 28 days, s3 needs to be invoked.

An application for admission of a patient for assessment (and treatment) can be made by that person's nearest relative (s11). The 'nearest relative' is defined in very broad terms in s26, but has actually been widened under the 2007 Act to include civil partners. In addition to making an application for admission, the nearest relative has the right to be fully consulted on all matters pertaining to the patient, to apply to a Mental Health Review Tribunal for review of the case, and to discharge the patient after giving 72 hours' notice. Inevitably, these powers can be curtailed by a court, and they can be revoked entirely if the nearest relative is acting unreasonably and/or against the interests of the patient (s29: and applied in *R (on the application of MH) v Secretary of State for Health [2009]*, where the mother of a severely mentally disabled woman refused permission for her daughter to be placed in long-term residential accommodation). Moreover, the patient is not generally in a position to choose who this person will be, as the following case illustrates:

Box 7.6   *Dewen v Barnet Healthcare Trust and Barnet London Borough Council [2000]*

A man had been detained for treatment, and there was conflict over who should qualify as his nearest relative. The patient felt that it should be his son, for he was the eldest, and he would be more likely to press for the father's release. The court, however, stated that the daughter took precedence, because she was the patient's primary carer at home.

5 TREATMENT

A GENERAL CONSIDERATIONS

Our patient has now been admitted to hospital under s2, and in-depth assessment reveals that he is in desperate need of treatment. For this purpose, s3 of the Mental Health Act must be invoked, which allows for detention of up to six months. This can be renewed indefinitely for periods of one year, although the case must be referred to a Mental Health Review Tribunal after six months (s68), and thereafter every three years. As with s2, an application for admission under s3 can only be made by two registered medical practitioners (s3 [3]).

In *Winterwerp v The Netherlands [1979]*, the European Court set out the minimum criteria for detention:

  i The patient must be declared by a suitable doctor to be of 'unsound mind'.

  ii The disorder must be of a nature to justify detention.

  iii The disorder must persist throughout the period of detention.

The Mental Health Act 1983 had been more specific than this when defining mental disorder, stating that the patient must fit into at least one of four categories: mental illness, severe mental impairment, psychopathic disorder or mental impairment. All of these, however, were removed by the 2007 Act, thereby echoing the *Winterwerp* criteria more closely. Nevertheless, the 2007 amendments did add one extra criterion: namely, that 'appropriate medical treatment' should be available to the patient (s3 [2] [d]). 'Medical treatment' is defined in s145 (1), and includes nursing and rehabilitation, although there is no necessity for it to guarantee success. Its purpose 'is to alleviate, or prevent a worsening of, the disorder or one or more of its symptoms or manifestations' (s145 [4]).

This broad definition gives considerable leeway to mental health practitioners. It can be used to justify detention, even though any improvements in the patient's condition may take a long time to occur (*R v Cannon's Park Mental Health Review Tribunal, ex parte A [1994]*). It authorises treatment for *other* mental disorders, even if they were not the original reasons for detention (*R v Ashworth Hospital, ex parte B [2005]*). And, more significantly, it provides an excuse to remove certain individuals from society (*Hutchinson Reid v United Kingdom [2003]*): it is a comparatively simple matter to argue that release of such individuals will lead to deterioration of their mental condition.

Herring (2010) suggests that this reduces mental health to a warehousing of incurables (i.e. those whom society is not prepared to tolerate); and Jones (2009) acknowledges those who have perceived a potential conflict with the European Convention on Human Rights. Certainly, it can be difficult in some cases to distinguish whether detention is for the benefit of the patient or of the general public, and Pattinson (2009) notes the fundamental differences in the way the law treats the mentally ill. For example, a Jehovah's Witness is able to refuse a blood transfusion, even though such refusal may result in his/her death. A competent person sectioned under the Mental Health Act, however, does not have the right to refuse psychiatric treatment. This difference must exist, therefore, to protect the interests of others, rather than the patient him/herself.

But what if the risk of danger to the public could be eliminated? Consider, for example, the case of Peter Sutcliffe ('The Yorkshire Ripper'), a man who brutally murdered a number of women. The court acknowledged that these crimes were committed because of a serious mental illness, and imprisonment would therefore be inappropriate. In consequence, he currently resides in a high security psychiatric institution, and is likely to remain there for the remainder of his life. Let us imagine, though, that a 'magic pill' comes onto the market, which immediately removes all semblance of mental disorder from Sutcliffe's mind. He can now be said to have been cured, and no longer represents a danger; but what should be done with him? Transfer to a prison seems illogical, given that he was not in control of his actions when the crimes were committed. But, equally, continued detention in a psychiatric hospital no longer serves any useful purpose. The only logical solution, therefore, is to release him into the community, but this would undoubtedly be very unpopular. Would we continue to insist upon retribution for these dreadful acts, even though the factors causing them are no longer in existence?

Perhaps thankfully, this is not a dilemma with which we are likely to be faced in the near (or distant) future. However, consideration of such matters may help us to examine how we feel about the mentally ill. Do we believe that they should have the same rights as those who are physically ill, or should they be removed from the public gaze? If the mental causes of criminal behaviour could be cured, would we still insist upon retribution?

B NATURE OF THE TREATMENT

Whether a patient is competent or not, treatment can be given without his/her consent under s63 of the Mental Health Act. There are, however, three conditions applied to this power granted to mental health professionals:

i   The treatment must be for the mental disorder, and not any other physical disorder from which the patient may be suffering. It would not, for example, be possible to invoke the Mental Health Act to compel a patient to undergo a hernia repair. In such cases, the competent patient will either consent to the treatment, or his refusal must be respected. If incompetent, treatment could be given providing that it can be justified to be in his 'best interests' (Mental Capacity Act 2005, s4). As we shall soon see, though, the courts have extended the range of what constitutes treatment for mental disorder.
ii The treatment must be given by or under the direction of the approved clinician in charge of the patient's care.
iii S63 does not apply to forms of treatment to which sections 57, 58 or 58A have application. Some explanation of these sections is required here.

Section 57 relates to 'any surgical operation for destroying brain tissue or for destroying the functioning of brain tissue' (s57 [1] [a]). This operation was much more commonly performed in the past, frequently leading to disastrous results. It is now much less common, and only two centres offer this treatment in the UK (one in Scotland and one in Wales). In the ten years between 1997 and 2007, 53 patients were referred to the Mental Health Act Commission for surgery, and the operation was authorised in 43 of these cases (MHAC, 2008, para. 6.87). In the following two years, two patients were referred and both were authorised (MHAC, 2009, para. 3.62).

Before it can be undertaken, not only must the patient consent to it, but also a registered medical practitioner (not connected with the case) and two others (one of whom must be a nurse, and the other neither a doctor nor a nurse) must certify in writing that the patient is fully competent to make this decision and is aware of its implications. Moreover, the doctor must be satisfied (and be prepared to justify) that psycho-surgery is an appropriate treatment for the patient's condition. Interestingly, in Scotland, consent of the patient is not imperative, but such decisions must be made in each case by the Court of Session (Mental Health (Care and Treatment) (Scotland) Act 2003, ss234–6).

Clearly, the rules need to be rigorous before authorisation is given for treatment that is irreversible and carries a variety of risks. Section 57 (1) (b), however, empowers 'other forms of treatment as may be specified … by regulations made by the Secretary of State'. The only other treatment that has been so specified under this section is 'the surgical implantation of hormones for the purpose of reducing male sexual drive' (The Mental Health Regulations 2008, reg. 27 [1]). Acknowledgement that hormone implants were covered by s57 had, in fact, been made much earlier than 2008, although the following case adds a slight complication:

Box 7.7   R v Mental Health Act Commission, ex parte X [1988]

A 27-year-old compulsive paedophile (X) had served three prison sentences for acts of indecency upon young boys. Upon his release, he contacted a psychiatrist, who prescribed Goserelin (a drug normally used in the treatment of prostate cancer, which reduces testosterone levels). After administering two of the monthly injections, the doctor then contacted the Mental Health Act Commission to check whether this amounted to treatment under s57. The MHAC stated that it did, and instructed that the patient must be certified as competent to consent to the treatment by a panel of three members nominated by them. When this panel eventually met, it decided that the patient was not competent and that the treatment should not be given. X applied for judicial review of this decision.

The court held that the decision to withhold the medication had been irrational, for the patient was clearly competent and there was significant evidence that the Goserelin had effectively reduced his sex drive. However, an 'injection' cannot be classified as 'surgical implantation', and therefore, it is not covered by s57. Thus, s58 is a more appropriate mechanism for securing approval for the administration of Goserelin as a treatment for mental disorder (Jones, 2009).

Section 58 is invoked when treatment for the mental disorder goes beyond three months. Until that time, s63 authorises an Approved Clinician (AC) to prescribe and order the administration of treatment without the patient's consent and without seeking special permissions. Beyond three months, however, the AC must secure the agreement of a Second Opinion Appointing Doctor (SOAD) for treatment to continue. The SOAD is a doctor appointed by the Care Quality Commission (CQC), who visits the hospital to give a second opinion regarding the approval of certain forms of treatment. The SOAD's involvement is not necessary if the patient consents to the treatment and the AC has certified that s/he is capable of giving consent; but, in the absence of this capacity, the SOAD must consult with two other persons, one of whom will be a nurse, and the other will be neither a nurse nor a doctor. Both of these two individuals must be 'professionally concerned with the patient's medical treatment' (s58 [4]).

The role of the SOAD enables the continued provision of treatment without a patient's consent, while at the same time offering safeguards against the possible abuse of medical power. It is also, however, a very bureaucratic and resource-intensive process, and doubts have been cast upon the willingness of SOADs to challenge decisions of the AC. As Bartlett and Sandland (2007) state: 'the SOAD system has done little to protect patients from overenthusiastic treatment regimes or abuses of their legal rights' (p. 332). Despite this, the law demands that the SOAD must give the reasons for his/her opinion in writing, and these reasons must be able to stand up to logical scrutiny (see *R (on the application of John Wooder) v Dr. Graham Fegetter and the Mental Health Act Commission [2002]*). Equally, however, the burden falls to the patient to show that the SOAD has been remiss in some significant part of his/her duty before a clinical decision is overturned (see *R (on the application of Wilkinson) v Broadmoor Special Hospital RMO and others [2001]*).

C WHAT CONSTITUTES TREATMENT?

We have already seen that 'treatment' includes not merely the administration of medication, but also 'nursing, psychological intervention and specialist mental health habilitation, rehabilitation and care' (s145 [1]). However, the treatment must be directed towards alleviating, or preventing a worsening of, the *mental disorder* (s145 [4]). From time to time, cases have arisen which fall somewhere between physical and mental disorders, and the courts have been asked to interpret the meaning of the Act. One such case was the following:

Box 7.8   *Re KB [1994]*

KB was 18 years old and had suffered from anorexia nervosa since the age of 14. She had been sectioned under the Mental Health Act, and the hospital had invoked s58 to compel her to receive naso-gastric feeding. Both KB and the Mental Health Act

(Continued)

> *(Continued)*
>
> Commission, however, contended that the feeding was for *physical* symptoms, not mental disorder, and the Mental Health Act did not therefore apply. The Health Authority countered that naso-gastric feeding was an appropriate medical treatment for this particular mental disorder.

The court found for the Health Authority, and its rationale is best expressed in the following extract from the speech of Ewbank, J. (at 146):

> If the symptoms [of the mental disorder] are exacerbated by the patient's refusal to eat and drink, the mental disorder becomes progressively more and more difficult to treat, and so the treatment by naso-gastric tube is an integral part of the treatment of the mental disorder itself.

Since this case, there have been others that have stretched the meaning of 'treatment' under the Mental Health Act. *B v Croydon Health Authority [1995]*, for example, involved a patient who had a borderline personality disorder and who refused to eat as a means of self-harm. The court authorised force-feeding, because psychological therapies had no chance of success unless she was physically well. *Tameside & Glossop Acute Services Trust v CH [1996]* went one step further by authorising a Caesarean section on a pregnant schizophrenic woman, arguing that failure to carry this out would cause the death of the foetus, which in turn would cause a deterioration of the woman's mental health.

Taken together, therefore, these three cases demonstrate that non-psychiatric care can be given under the Mental Health Act in a variety of circumstances. Not surprisingly, though, this approach has attracted a range of criticisms. For example, in *Tameside*, the judge appears rather too willing to accept the psychiatrist's suggestion that psychological interventions would be unlikely to succeed if the woman lost her baby (Montgomery, 2003); but it is difficult to see how this conclusion could be reached with any certainty, and it seems just as likely that enforced submission to an invasive procedure will have had a deleterious effect upon her mental health. Moreover, if both the court and the psychiatrists are arguing that mental and physical conditions are inextricably linked (i.e. that one impacts upon the other), it becomes difficult to reconcile the decision in *Re C [1994]* (Bartlett and Sandland, 2007). In this case, a paranoid schizophrenic refused the amputation of a gangrenous leg, and the court held that he had the right to do so: although sectioned, he was competent to make this decision, and the treatment did not fall within the scope of the Mental Health Act (see Chapter 4).

Another criticism, relating specifically to the anorexia cases, is that force-feeding is a short-term solution, which does nothing to address the *causes* of the mental disorder, and which may in fact render the long-term prospects of recovery much more difficult to achieve. Lewis (1999) cites a variety of experts on the subject of

anorexia nervosa, who all maintain that the disorder is a manifestation of the sufferer's need to exercise control over her life. It is, of course, misdirected; and can
only be corrected if the individual is helped to develop a sense of personal autonomy.
For this to be achieved, a therapeutic relationship of trust must be created between
patient and carer, but this becomes much more difficult whenever the latter inserts
a naso-gastric tube against the patient's will. In consequence, there are real concerns
that force-feeding will entrench attitudes, and that the patient will become a chronic
sufferer. The obvious counter-argument to this is that, if psychological interventions
are more difficult after force-feeding, they are impossible if the patient has died as a
result of malnutrition. But clearly, the decision to impose naso-gastric feeding is not
one that should be taken lightly, and Lewis (1999) suggests a few key questions that
should be asked beforehand:

Box 7.9   Questions to ask before deciding to force-feed

1 Is the patient's life in serious and/or imminent danger? And, does force-feeding represent the only viable treatment option?
2 If force-feeding is employed, when will it be stopped? Will it be discontinued when
   the patient is out of danger, or when she has returned to her optimum weight? It is
   argued that the latter may seem the preferable option, but is more likely to have a
   damaging psychological effect.
3 Has force-feeding been used before on this patient? The more it has been employed,
   the less likely it is to be effective. Its purpose becomes simply to keep somebody
   alive in a state of perpetual misery.

The final criticism relates to the way in which the judicial approach can be corrupted
to justify the withholding of fundamental human rights. As Bartlett and Sandland
(2007) state:

> There is little doubt that the current definition of 'medical treatment' is sufficiently
> broad to enable measures to control and manage patients who, by medical criteria, are
> untreatable. This makes it difficult to understand the language of 'medical treatment'
> other than as a metaphor for the social control of the putatively dangerous (p. 333).

D ELECTRO-CONVULSIVE THERAPY (ECT)

ECT is one of those treatments that was designed specifically for the management
of mental disorder, but which is no less controversial than force-feeding. Part of the
reason for the controversy is that its original use was based upon an assumption that
has since been discredited: namely, that epilepsy and schizophrenia were mutually

and biologically antagonistic (Sabbatio, 1998). Another reason is that it was certainly over-used in the past, so that its efficacy was often highly questionable and it produced long-term neurological damage in a number of patients (Campbell et al., 2005). Despite this, there is little doubt that ECT has been beneficial in a number of cases, and has particular application in the management of severe depressive disorders and affective psychoses (and also, in the treatment of schizophrenia which has been unresponsive to more standard forms of therapy (Fear, 2005)).

Whereas ECT used to be given under s58 to a competent refusing patient if a SOAD agreed to it, acknowledgement of the objections to this form of treatment has led to amendments in the 2007 Act. Therefore, ECT now has its own special provisions in s58A, which can be summarised thus:

i The patient must consent to the treatment if competent, and the Approved Clinician or SOAD must certify that the patient has full understanding of it. ECT can no longer be given to a competent patient who refuses it.

ii ECT can be given without consent if the patient is incompetent, but the doctor must be able to justify that this is so, and must consult with two other persons who are professionally concerned with the patient's treatment (one of whom will be a nurse, and the other will be neither a nurse nor a doctor).

iii Even if the patient is incompetent, ECT should not be given if it conflicts with an Advance Decision of the patient (made when competent), or if it is in conflict with decisions made by somebody with Lasting Power of Attorney, a deputy, or the Court of Protection. Needless to say, each of these decisions can be challenged in court, but only a judicial pronouncement can authorise ECT in these circumstances.

iv The refusal of a competent patient and the terms of a valid Advance Decision could both be over-ridden if the ECT (and any other forms of treatment) was *immediately necessary* to save his/her life, *or* to prevent a serious deterioration of the mental disorder, *or* alleviate suffering, *or* to prevent the patient from behaving violently or being a danger to himself or others (s62). Note that the emphasis has been placed on the term 'immediately necessary': the emergency nature of the treatment automatically implies that there is not time to go through the more common routes; and it also implies that it would be inappropriate to invoke it for treatment under s57 (neurosurgery/hormonal implants) or to use it repeatedly.

These safeguards represent a considerable concession to those who have argued that ECT is used both inappropriately and indiscriminately, but there will always remain those who contend that it should be abolished completely. Would a mental health nurse have the right to refuse participation in the procedure if s/he had a conscientious objection to it? The following case answered this question:

Box 7.10 *Owen v Coventry Health Authority [1986]*

Mr Owen was a Registered Mental Nurse who was asked to participate in the administration of ECT, but he refused. Disciplinary proceedings were conducted and he was given a written warning. When, a few months later, he again refused to participate, he was dismissed. An Industrial Tribunal found for the Health Authority, as did the court on appeal. The latter held that 'it was an implied term of his contract that he as an employee would comply with lawful and reasonable instructions given in the course of his employment' (per Bingham, L.J.). He might have had grounds for objection to its use in specific patients, but he had a duty to raise these concerns with the appropriate personnel. Even then, if the clinician responsible for the patient is satisfied that ECT is an appropriate therapy, the nurse is obliged to provide the assistance that is required of him/her.

E BEHAVIOUR MODIFICATION

Let us imagine that the patient in our original scenario, having been admitted to hospital, demonstrates increasing evidence of violence, aggression, and general anti-social behaviour. He will almost certainly have received medication (under s63), and he may be given ECT (under s58A). On the assumption that neither of these have worked to any significant degree, it seems reasonable to suggest that behaviour modification techniques may offer some chance of success. Which methods in the list below would you consider to be acceptable methods of achieving this objective?

Box 7.11   Behaviour modification techniques

1   Withholding a patient's access to his/her bank account.
2   Immersing the patient in a cold bath whenever s/he demonstrates aggression.
3   Physical restraint when the patient shows signs of violence (which may include the use of a strait jacket or handcuffs).
4   Physical violence (e.g. slaps whenever the patient is verbally or physically abusive).
5   Electric shocks.
6   High decibel noise.
7   Unpleasant tasting food.
8   Segregation from the rest of the patients and seclusion in solitary confinement.

The truth is that all of these measures have been adopted at one time or another. Suspension of access to a patient's bank account is known as a Ulysses bargain (Campbell et al., 2005), its rationale being that an individual cannot be trusted to manage his/her financial affairs until fully competent. A mental health team managed to convince the European Court that handcuffing a patient to a bed was 'a therapeutic necessity' (*Herczegfalvy v Austria [1992]*); and s139 of the Mental Health Act gives protection from prosecution for those staff who physically restrain patients, providing that the use of this force is both reasonable and necessary. An illustration of this principle can be seen in the following case:

Box 7.12   *Pountney v Griffiths [1975]*

A patient at Broadmoor alleged that a male nurse punched him and used unnecessary force in ushering him back to his ward. The nurse was initially convicted (although given a conditional discharge), but the House of Lords held that the nurse had appropriately discharged his function pertaining to the control of patients in his charge.

Bartlett and Sandland (2007) note that this decision would not excite controversy if the nurse's account of the events was true. There must, however, have been serious doubts about this, given that the court of first instance felt that assault had been proven. Nevertheless, the case demonstrates the ease with which the courts will interpret such interventions as 'treatment', and how they will offer protection to staff unless there is incontrovertible evidence of abuse. The difficulty for patients and practitioners, though, is that what begins as a genuine attempt to rehabilitate a patient can soon degenerate into a form of control, where punishment of inappropriate behaviour is performed to the exclusion of the reinforcement of desired behaviour. This shift is usually insidious, and is much more likely where the institution is isolated from the public gaze. As Bowden (1981) says, when reviewing the Boynton Report (DHSS, 1980) – an investigation into allegations of abuse at Rampton hospital:

> The type of patient admitted to Rampton hospital occupies a lowly position in the hierarchy of priorities within psychiatry, and any second class group gets second class services (p. 16).

It falls, therefore, to the professional bodies to issue guidance on what constitutes acceptable practice. The Code of Practice (DH, 2008) states that forms of restraint 'must never be used as punishment or in a punitive manner' (para. 15.8); and that they should 'be reasonable, justifiable and proportionate [and] be used only for as long as is absolutely necessary' (para. 15.22). Similarly, the Royal College of Nursing (2008) contends that the use of restraint should always be a last resort, and that good quality care can often avoid its necessity:

> In essence, a combination of well-considered environmental features and a workforce that has developed person-centred care reduces the need for inappropriate restraint (p. 4).

If the use of restraint is controversial, the practice of secluding patients is even more so. The Code of Practice (DH, 2008) defines seclusion as: 'the supervised confinement of a patient in a room, which may be locked. Its sole aim is to contain severely disturbed behaviour which is likely to cause harm to others' (para. 15.43). The Code emphasises that its use can only be justified when all other measures have failed (para. 15.45), and it lays down clear guidance on the procedure to be followed. Thus, there should be a documented report every 15 minutes, and the patient should be reviewed by two nurses every two hours (and by a doctor every four hours) (para. 15.51). Nurses have the power to order seclusion, but it is expected that the doctor would attend as soon as possible (para. 15.49). However, the question of how much authority the Code has in the prescription of policy was decided in the following case:

Box 7.13 *R (on the application of Munjaz) v Mersey Care NHS Trust [2005]*

A mentally ill patient became increasingly psychotic, aggressive and violent, and was eventually transferred to a high security unit (Ashworth hospital). Here, he was secluded on a number of occasions and for long periods of time. He contended that the hospital was acting unlawfully, because it did not adhere to the Code's guidelines for medical review. He also argued that the hospital was in breach of Article 3 of the Human Rights Act, for prolonged seclusion amounted to 'inhuman and degrading treatment'.

Having won his case in the Court of Appeal, the House of Lords overturned this decision (by a majority of three to two), holding that the Code constituted *guidance*, rather than a set of legal principles. In consequence, practitioners are entitled to depart from it, although they should have good reasons for doing so. It should be mentioned that Lord Steyn (dissenting), while accepting that departure from the principles in the Code was permissible, did not accept that the hospital had provided good enough reasons. However, this was a minority view, and the majority accepted that the Trust was dealing with a very difficult individual, and that their response was appropriate.

Clearly, though, seclusion is not a decision to be taken lightly, particularly in view of the fact that its consequences can be disastrous. In *Keenan v United Kingdom [1995]*, for example, a prisoner with a history of mental health problems hanged himself within 24 hours of being placed in solitary confinement. The court accepted that Article 2 of the European Convention on Human Rights (the 'right to life') had not been breached, because the authorities had acted reasonably. However, there had been a breach of Article 3 (the 'right to freedom from inhuman and degrading treatment'), for the punishment had failed to take account of its likely impact upon a seriously disturbed individual.

Within a psychiatric institution, the staff have a special duty to sectioned patients (i.e. to monitor them closely and to protect them from harm). Authority for this position comes from *Savage v South Essex Partnership Trust [2008]*, where a detained patient absconded from the hospital and threw herself in front of a train. Although the court held that the hospital had acted reasonably (and was therefore not in breach of Article 2), the result might have been different if 'the conditions in the … hospital wing had been markedly inferior to those in an ordinary hospital and had contributed to the patient's death' (per Lord Scott, at para. 10). Moreover, the hospital did not escape a charge of negligence, which the House of Lords stated should be decided at another trial. The special duty does not extend to voluntary patients (see *Rabone and another v Pennine Care NHS Trust [2010]*), although here too an action in negligence is possible if a known risk of suicide has been disregarded.

6 DISCHARGE

The patient in our original scenario has made a good response to treatment, and thoughts now turn to considerations of discharge from care. There are three main possibilities here, each of which will be reviewed.

A ABSOLUTE DISCHARGE

Section 23 empowers health authorities to give an absolute discharge to patients, and this can be invoked at any time during the patient's admission, even though s/he cannot personally apply for review of the detention for at least six months. The hospital managers have a duty to inform detained patients of their right to apply to a Mental Health Review Tribunal 'as soon as is practicable after the commencement of the patient's detention' (s132 [1] [b]). If the patient is incapacitated, and therefore unable to make this application, there appears to be no compulsion upon the hospital to make it on his/her behalf (*MH v SSDH [2005]*); although it is argued that a European Court would expect the health authority to take all reasonable steps to safeguard the interests of such vulnerable patients (Bartlett and Sandland, 2007).

Similarly, the Responsible Clinician has an ongoing duty to review the reasons for the patient's detention and consider whether or not they continue to be satisfied (*Winterwerp v The Netherlands [1979]*). To comply with Article 5 of the Human Rights Act 1998, the authorities must be able to justify that continued detention is necessary (i.e. it is not the patient's responsibility to demonstrate that detention is unnecessary). Nevertheless, this remains a considerable obstacle for patients, as the following case illustrates:

Box 7.14   *R v Mental Health Review Tribunal for the South Thames Region, ex parte Smith [1998]*

A schizophrenic patient was detained in hospital and his condition had stabilised following the administration of medication. He was essentially fit for discharge, but his doctor argued that he would quickly relapse if released into the community, because he would refuse to take his medication.

Section 72 empowers discharge of a patient, provided that s/he is not suffering from a mental disorder 'of a nature or degree which makes it appropriate for him to be liable to be detained' (s72 [1] [b] [i]). In *Smith*, it was successfully argued before the court that, while the *degree* of his illness no longer justified detention, its *nature* did. Therefore, although the two concepts are usually indistinguishable, the court was forced to treat them separately in this case. It might be argued that the court manipulated the language of the Act to ensure that a clinical decision received judicial favour. The case may also suggest that a *diagnosis* of mental illness is sufficient to warrant continued detention. This probably overstates the position, but Bartlett and Sandland (2007) see *Smith* as 'another example of protectionism overriding patients' rights and interests' (p. 403).

The following case illustrates yet another difficulty for patients:

Box 7.15   *R (on the application of Tagoe-Thompson) v Central and North West London Mental Health NHS Trust [2003]*

A paranoid schizophrenic patient applied to a Mental Health Review Tribunal in the hope of securing release from detention. Of the three people who sat on the panel, two favoured discharge, but the third opposed release.

Section 23 (4) states that the power to discharge may be exercised 'by any three or more members' of the hospital authority who have given such authorisation. The court's interpretation of this phrase was that *at least three* should be in agreement before a patient is discharged. By extension, therefore, a majority decision would be acceptable if the committee contained five or seven members, but it must be unanimous if only three hear the case. This rather restrictive interpretation of the Act ensured that the clinician's objections to discharge were heard, but the result could easily have gone the other way. The legal position is therefore uncertain until a higher court either confirms or rejects the decision in *Tagoe-Thompson*.

Although these difficulties for patients will suggest that power is unequally distributed, we should not forget the burden of responsibility falling to hospital authorities and clinicians. In *Holgate v Lancashire Mental Hospitals Board [1937]*, the granting of leave to a detained patient resulted in him entering a woman's home and savagely assaulting her. The hospital and its clinicians were all held liable in negligence. Montgomery (2003) suggests that the decision in this case has been effectively overruled by *Palmer v Tees Health Authority [1999]*, where the court refused to hold a hospital responsible for injuries sustained by a victim who could not be identified in advance (see Chapter 5). However, the circumstances of *Holgate* suggest that procedures and protocols had been remarkably lax, and the court would certainly expect a health authority to act reasonably and professionally.

For those patients who have a history of violence and who represent a risk to the public, orders for discharge can only be made with the consent of the Secretary of State for Justice (s41). A patient placed under such a restriction order must accept that his/her detention is indefinite, and that the order does not require regular renewal. Moreover, the court has made it clear for whom such orders are designed to benefit:

> No longer is the offender regarded simply as a patient whose interests are paramount ...
> Instead the interests of public safety are regarded (per Butler, J. in *R v Birch [1989]* at 211).

Discharge is not impossible in these circumstances, but it will undoubtedly come with a number of conditions to maximise the safety of the public. These may require the patient to live at a particular location, to attend for treatment, and to consent to the supervision of a social worker or probation officer. The patient can be recalled to hospital at any time (s42 [3]), but a European court has held that clinically objective and reasonable reasons should be given for doing so (*K v United Kingdom [1998]*, reversing an earlier decision by the Court of Appeal that reasons were not required: *R v Secretary of State for the Home Department, ex parte K [1990]*).

The absolute discharge of any detained patient presupposes a level of confidence that s/he no longer represents a threat to him/herself or others. As has been stated earlier, though, such confidence is likely to be rare, given the inexact nature of mental health as a science. In consequence, a staged approach may offer an opportunity to meet the needs of the patient while retaining a level of control. This brings us to the second of our possibilities.

B LEAVE OF ABSENCE

Section 17 empowers the Responsible Clinician to grant a detained patient 'leave to be absent from the hospital subject to such conditions (if any) as that clinician considers necessary' (s17 [1]). This period of absence could be for a specified period or it could be indefinite (s17 [2]); but equally it can be revoked at any time (s17 [4]).

It has been argued that s17 presents ethical problems, for the 'conditions' that can be imposed upon the patient are not defined, and are therefore placed within the unchecked power of the clinician (Bowen, 2007). Moreover, the power to recall a patient from leave appears to require little more than a hunch on the part of the Responsible Clinician. This does not, of course, automatically imply that patients' rights are being systematically abused: it simply suggests that the vagueness of the law creates the possibility of huge variations in practice across the country.

In fairness, though, the 2007 Act amended s17 by insisting that the Responsible Clinician must consider Supervised Community Treatment (SCT) if the period of leave is for more than seven days (s17 [2A]). SCT provides greater safeguards against abuse, and the amendment to s17 should ensure that it ultimately ceases to be a mechanism for long-term community treatment (Bowen, 2007).

C SUPERVISED COMMUNITY TREATMENT (SCT)

The introduction of Community Treatment Orders (CTOs) (ss17A-G) is arguably the most important change in the 2007 Act, and has been the most controversial. The genesis of CTOs can be traced back to the case of Christopher Clunis, who was a paranoid schizophrenic but who had stopped taking his medication. In 1992, he brutally killed a completely random stranger (Jonathan Zito), and the resultant outrage convinced the Government that public safety needed greater protection.

In reality, there is no evidence to suggest that CTOs either increase or decrease the rate of homicides by mentally disordered individuals (Churchill et al., 2007), and their introduction could be seen as little more than a knee-jerk reaction. Nevertheless, they provide for a more formalised method of granting leave of absence than is covered by s17 alone, while at the same time helping to reassure the public. Section 17A empowers a Responsible Clinician to discharge a patient into the community 'subject to his being liable to recall in accordance with section 17E' (s17A [1]). The clinician must be satisfied that the patient's mental disorder is such that it requires continued treatment, but also that it would be possible to provide this in the community (s17A [5]). Moreover, an Approved Mental Health Professional must agree with this decision and confirm this in writing (s17A [4]). Considerable leeway is given to the Responsible Clinician to impose conditions on the CTO (s17B [4]), but one condition is mandatory: namely, that the patient must make himself available for examination (s17B [3]). Failure to do so will breach the terms of the CTO and will almost certainly result in compulsory recall of the patient to hospital (s17E [2]).

The duration of the CTO is initially for six months, but it can be extended for a further six months, and thereafter for periods of one year (s20A [1 and 3]). The Responsible Clinician, however, must examine the patient within the two months preceding the expiry date of the CTO (s20A [4]).

Jackson (2010) cites criticisms that the wording of these amendments to the Act remains open to interpretation, and that the significant power to recall patients invested in clinicians may lead to arbitrary (and ultimately unethical) practice. There have also been suggestions that certain groups may be inappropriately subjected to CTOs (e.g. young black men) (Mental Health Act Commission, 2009: 2.81). Notwithstanding these criticisms, however, the amendments probably represent an acceptable compromise between those who champion the cause of patient rights and those who have concerns for public safety. As with most compromises, neither side will be completely satisfied, but more time is needed before passing judgement on the effectiveness of the changes.

D AFTERCARE SERVICES

If enforced detention under the Mental Health Act represents a loss of freedom and of other fundamental rights that most of us take for granted, it does have at least one advantage over informal admission. The sectioned patient who is discharged into the community (whether this is by means of an absolute discharge, a leave of absence, or a Community Treatment Order) is entitled to the provision of aftercare services (s117), which can include accommodation, medical and nursing supervision, and training services. Moreover, these services must be provided free of charge (see *R v Manchester City Council, ex parte Stennett [2002]*). Informal patients requiring residential accommodation, by contrast, must apply to the National Assistance Act 1948, wherein means-tested charges are payable (s22). The apparent injustice of this situation, where two identical patients can be treated very differently depending upon whether or not they have been detained, has not escaped the attention of a number of commentators (Jones, 2009), and efforts by the authorities and the courts to justify this position seem somewhat hollow.

Once the decision has been made to discharge the patient (either absolutely or conditionally), the authorities have a responsibility to end the detention as soon as possible. In *Johnson v United Kingdom [1997]*, it was acknowledged that the authorities need time to ensure that appropriate aftercare services are put in place before discharge can be considered safe, but unreasonable delays to this process amount to a breach of Article 5 (1) of the European Convention on Human Rights (i.e. the right to liberty). The success of *Johnson*'s appeal to the European court, however, can be contrasted with the following case:

Box 7.16   *R v Secretary of State for the Home Department and another, ex parte IH [2003]*

A patient had been detained at Rampton hospital following the mutilation of his three-year-old son, and a court finding of not guilty by reason of insanity. Eight years later, he was considered suitable for a conditional discharge. However, the primary condition of discharge was that he should be under the supervision of a forensic psychiatrist, but one could not be found. IH contended that he was being unreasonably detained and that his rights under Article 5 were therefore being breached. The court held that the conditions of supervision had to be met in this instance if discharge was to be safe. If they could not be met, the alternative was not discharge, but rather continued detention.

Despite the services available to discharged patients, we should not forget that *high quality* community care comes at a price (Jackson, 2010), and no Government has hitherto been prepared to invest heavily in this area (Maude, 2007). As Bartlett and Sandland (2007) state: 'We can only have the care – and the control – that we are prepared to pay for' (p. 449). The demands on the public purse are, of course, extensive, and the likelihood of raising funds in this area is destined to be slim when one considers that its patients have a limited voice and even less influence. Bartlett and Sandland's comment, though, raises a key point: it is not discharge of detained patients into the community that represents a risk to the public, but how we treat them once they are there. Sub-standard accommodation, lack of employment, and shortage of income are all likely to contribute to a worsening of the patient's mental condition.

Box 7.17   Summary of key sections of the Mental Health Act 2007

Mental Disorder

Police powers

Formal admission

s135
Remove individual from his/her *home* to a place of safety, but only after a warrant issued by JP.

s136
Remove individual from *public place* to a place of safety

Detention for up to 72 hours

Informal admission (s131)

Short-term holding powers (if patient unsafe to discharge him/herself (**s5**)

Assessment

s2
Requires recommendation of 2 doctors, and lasts for up to 28 days.

s4
In an emergency, only 1 doctor's recommendation needed, but this expires after 72 hours.

Doctor (up to 72 hours)

Nurse (up to 6 hours)

Treatment (s3)
Requires recommendation of 2 doctors. Enables detention for up to 6 months, renewable for a further 6 months, and yearly thereafter.

s63
(Enables treatment for psychiatric condition to be given without patient consent.)

s57
(Psycho-surgery and surgical implantation of hormones – patient must consent and be certified as competent to do so.)

s58
(For treatment given under s63 lasting more than 3 months – requires approval of SOAD.)

s58A
(ECT – consent required by competent person. If incompetent, doctor and 2 others agree that treatment is justified.)

s62
Treatment given to competent patient without consent if *immediately necessary* to save life or prevent serious deterioration of condition.

Discharge

Absolute discharge (s23)
– granted by 3 or more members of hospital authority who have such authorisation.

Leave of absence (s17)
– conditions of leave set by doctor, and patient can be recalled to hospital at any time.

Community Treatment Order (ss17A-G)
– discharge into community, but most comply with treatment, and can be recalled to hospital.

Aftercare Services (s117)
– accommodation, medical and nursing supervision, and training services, provided free of charge.

7 DEPRIVATION OF LIBERTY SAFEGUARDS

Before concluding our discussion of mental health law, it is necessary to consider an aspect that is not covered by our scenario, but which has major implications for practitioners. The issue was thrown sharply into focus by the following case:

Box 7.18   *R v Bournewood Community Mental Health NHS Trust, ex parte L [1998]*

L was a 48-year-old autistic patient, who was profoundly retarded: he was unable to speak, he was frequently agitated, he had a history of self-harming behaviour, and his level of understanding was severely limited. For more than 30 years of his life, he was a resident in a psychiatric hospital, but was eventually discharged on a trial basis into the community and went to live with paid carers. He attended a Day Centre, but, on one occasion, he became very disturbed. His carers could not be contacted, so he was given a sedative, taken to Casualty, and then assessed by a psychiatrist, who considered that he needed in-patient treatment. He was not sectioned under the Mental Health Act 'because he appeared to be fully compliant and did not resist admission'. However, he was frequently sedated to ensure that he remained tractable, and the psychiatrist vetoed visits by his carers to ensure that he did not try to leave with them. His carers argued that the hospital had no right to detain him, and they sought damages for false imprisonment and assault.

This landmark case sought answers to two fundamental questions. First, was L detained, or was he free to leave at any time he chose? The High Court judge was content that this was an informal admission, and only sectioning the patient could compel him to stay in hospital. The Court of Appeal, however, took a different view:

> We do not consider that the judge was correct to conclude that L was 'free to leave'. We think that it is plain that, had he attempted to leave the hospital, those in charge of him would not have permitted him to do so' (per Lord Woolf M.R., at 639).

The House of Lords ultimately agreed with the High Court on this point, although only by a majority of three to two. Lord Steyn summarised the dissenting position thus (at 305): 'The suggestion that L was free to go is a fairy tale'.

Having dealt with this issue, the courts then moved on to a more abstract question: does informal admission require active consent, or merely the absence of dissent? The High Court contended that the common law principle of necessity applied here (from *Re F [1989]*): in other words, L was an incompetent patient (and therefore unable to consent on his own behalf), so treatment could be given without consent, provided that it was in his 'best interests'. The Court of Appeal rejected this approach, arguing that the Mental Health Act created a complete regime, and took precedence over the common law. Either a patient was sectioned under the Mental Health Act (in which case detention was lawful), *or* he was an informal admission (in which case any attempt to prevent him from leaving the hospital would amount to false imprisonment).

The Court of Appeal's decision sent shock waves through the mental health profession, for reasons we shall come to shortly. The House of Lords, however, ultimately overturned this ruling, and it justified its decision by reference to the Percy Commission (1957), whose report led to the Mental Health Act 1959. Within this report and the Parliamentary debates that preceded the legislation, it was clear that the intention was to ensure that patients should receive treatment quickly without incurring the bureaucratic problems associated with sectioning.

The 'problems', however, tend to be faced more by the organisation than the individual patient. The House of Lords, considering the implications of the Court of Appeal's decision, identified that it would mean that 22,000 patients would need to be sectioned immediately, and a further 48,000 admissions would need to be sectioned per year. Most nursing homes are not registered to receive detained patients, so they would either have to go through the detailed process of registration, or they would have to discharge all of their incapacitated patients. Moreover, it is evident that the number of extra Mental Health Review Tribunals that would be required would put an immense strain upon the service.

For the patient, it might be argued that being sectioned is stigmatising and remains on his medical record for the rest of his life, but this would not have been a concern to L. Instead, he would have been denied all of the benefits of being sectioned: i.e. regular reviews of his detention by a Mental Health Review Tribunal, and an entitlement to the range of aftercare services provided by Health Authorities and local authorities. Lord Steyn acknowledged this anomaly when he stated (at 308):

> Given that such patients are diagnostically indistinguishable from compulsory patients, there is no reason to withhold the specific and effective protections of the Act of 1983 from a large class of vulnerable mentally incapacitated individuals. Their moral right to be treated with dignity requires nothing less.

Lord Steyn took some comfort from the fact that reform of the Mental Health Act was under consideration, but this was beaten to the post by an appeal to the European Court of Human Rights (*HL v United Kingdom [2005]*). Here, the court held that the Mental Health Act was in conflict with the European Convention, and that L's right to liberty and security (Article 5) had been violated. Note that the court was *not* stating that all incapacitated patients should be sectioned, but simply that appropriate safeguards should be put in place to ensure that their interests and rights should be protected.

In consequence, Deprivation of Liberty Safeguards have now been introduced, which Mason and Laurie (2011) describe as an 'interesting compromise' (p. 412). These regulations were inserted into the Mental Capacity Act 2005 (Schedule A1) by means of the Mental Health Act 2007 (Schedule 7), and were implemented in April

2009. The key document explaining the rationale for their implementation and the procedure that must be followed is the DOL Code of Practice (Ministry of Justice, 2008). This Code acknowledges that the distinction between restraint and deprivation of liberty is a fine one and is open to interpretation. Nevertheless, where restraint or restrictions are 'frequent, cumulative and ongoing' (s2.12), care providers should consider seeking authorisation from the relevant bodies to ensure that they remain within the law. Thus, not everybody who is mentally incapacitated and who has a mental disorder will need DOL authorisation: if such patients require no long-term restrictions to ensure their safety (or the safety of others), they will remain in much the same position as they always were. The people for whom DOLS apply must:

a   Be suffering from a mental disorder;
b   Be 18 years of age or older;
c   Lack the capacity to consent on their own behalf;
d   Be informal admissions: DOLS do not apply to those patients sectioned under the Mental Health Act; and
e   Need to be given care in circumstances that amount to a deprivation of liberty.

In addition to these requirements, deprivation of liberty will only be lawful if it can be justified to be in the patients' best interests (i.e. to protect them from harm), that it is a proportionate response, and that there is no less restrictive alternative (s1.13). The procedure for obtaining DOL authorisation can be summarised thus:

Box 7.19   Procedure for obtaining DOL authorisation

1   When a 'managing authority' (i.e. a hospital or care home) considers that one of its patients qualifies, or is likely to qualify, for DOL, authorisation must be sought from a 'supervisory body' (i.e. Primary Care Trust or local authority).
2   The 'managing authority' will subsequently submit an application for a standard authorisation, which must be processed by the supervisory body within the next 28 days. It should be obvious, therefore, that a good deal of foresight and forward planning is necessary to ensure that DOL authorisation is in place at the time that it is going to be needed. In circumstances where this is not possible, the managing authority can make an urgent authorisation on its own behalf, but this must not exceed seven days, and an application for a standard authorisation must be made to the supervisory body within this time.
3   The managing authority must inform the patient's family, friends and carers that this process is taking place, unless it is impossible or impractical to do so. If nobody has been notified, the supervisory body must instruct an Independent Mental Capacity Advocate (IMCA) to represent the patient. This person's role is to support the patient through the process, endeavour to enhance his/her understanding, and be prepared to challenge any aspect that is not procedurally or morally correct (Cowley and Lee, 2011).

4   The supervisory body then selects assessors to undertake a range of assessments to determine whether or not DOL is appropriate. At least two assessors will be required per case, and none should be a relative of the patient. The assessments performed are:

   i   An age assessment – the patient must be at least 18 for DOL to be applicable.

   ii A no refusals assessment – there must be no conflict with a valid Advance Decision made by the patient when competent, or with a valid decision made by somebody with Lasting Power of Attorney.

   iii A mental capacity assessment – the patient must lack the necessary competence to make decisions on his/her own behalf. The test of mental capacity is outlined in the Mental Capacity Act 2005 (s3), and has been discussed in Chapter 4.

   iv An eligibility assessment – the patient must not be sectioned under the Mental Health Act, or likely to require detention under this Act in the near future.

   v   A mental health assessment – the patient must be suffering from a mental disorder (as defined by the Mental Health Act 2007 [s1]), and this assessment must be carried out by a doctor (either a psychiatrist or a GP with a special interest in mental health).

   vi A best interests assessment – because this is usually the longest and most complex of the assessments, it is recommended that it should be performed last (because it will be unnecessary if the patient has not met the criteria of any one of the previous assessments). It can be undertaken by an Approved Mental Health Professional who has been suitably trained for this purpose, but must also be a different person to the individual who carried out the mental health assessment, and s/he must not be involved in the care or treatment of the patient. The best interests assessor must be satisfied that DOL is necessary and proportionate, and should seek the views of the patient, carers, and family where appropriate.

5   The best interests assessor will then file a report to the supervisory body and will make recommendations. The supervisory body is entitled to determine which of the recommendations should apply, but it cannot exceed the period of authorisation suggested by the best interests assessor (the maximum of which is 12 months). The standard authorisation is subsequently made (in writing) and the managing authority is constrained to comply with any conditions specified within the document. Note that the DOL authorisation does not, in itself, give an authority to treat a patient – it simply empowers a hospital or care home to impose the necessary (and least restrictive possible) restrictions upon a person's liberty.

6   A DOL authorisation can be reviewed at any time, and the managing authority has a duty to request one if the patient's circumstances change. Moreover, the lawfulness of the authorisation can be challenged in the Court of Protection; and the Care Quality Commission (CQC) has an ongoing duty to monitor the operation of DOLS.

Whether or not these safeguards represent a significant advance in the rights of mentally disordered and incapacitated patients is open to debate. It might be argued that the introduction of DOLS was motivated more by a desire to reduce bureaucracy than by a genuine concern to uphold and protect patients' dignity. Bowen (2007) notes that there is no mechanism to enforce referral of a case to the Court of

Protection, and it is therefore left entirely to the patient and his/her representative. In consequence, a patient may be deprived of his/her liberty for years without a legal challenge. Moreover, evidence suggests that applications for DOL authorisation are not as many as one might expect, and there are large regional variations (NHS Information Centre, 2010). A more charitable view, however, would be that this is a comparatively recent innovation, and time is needed before carers and authorities feel comfortable with its practical application. If this is true, though, the role of the CQC assumes even greater importance during this transition period.

CONCLUSION

This chapter has endeavoured to give a brief overview of the Mental Health Act 2007 and has covered a range of issues pertaining to mental illness. The over-riding impression, however, is that a diagnosis of mental disorder (particularly psychotic disturbances) exposes an individual to restrictions and enforced treatment that would not be tolerated in any other context. The justification for this suspension of fundamental human rights has always been that it serves the long-term interests of the patient, but Herring (2010) detects a level of hypocrisy in this when he states:

> It is notable how the law has been far more ready to protect the 'general public' from the mentally ill than it has been to protect the mentally ill from the 'general public' (p. 571).

The law cannot, therefore, be relied upon to protect such patients' rights. If the mentally ill are to be afforded appropriate protection, continued and ongoing vigilance must be maintained by their champions. Such vigilance will include education of the public, and it must include pressurising Governments to increase the range of resources available for care of the mentally ill.

REFERENCES

TEXTS

Bartlett, P. (2007) 'A matter of necessity? Enforced treatment under the Mental Health Act', *Medical Law Review*, 15, Spring: 86–98.

Bartlett, P. and Sandland, R. (2007) *Mental Health Law: Policy and Practice*, 3rd edn. Oxford: Oxford University Press.

Beauchamp, T.L. and Childress, J.F. (2001) *Principles of Biomedical Ethics*, 5th edn. Oxford: Oxford University Press.

Bowden, P. (1981) 'Reviews', *Psychiatric Bulletin*, 5: 15–16. Available at: http://pb.repsych.org/.

Bowen, P. (2007) *Blackstone's Guide to the Mental Health Act 2007*. Oxford: Oxford University Press.

Campbell, A., Gillett, G. and Jones, G. (2005) *Medical Ethics*, 4th edn. Oxford: Oxford University Press.

Chadwick, R. and Todd, W. (1992) *Ethics and Nursing Practice: A Case Study Approach*. London: The MacMillan Press.

Churchill, R., Owen, G., Singh, S. and Hotopf, M. (2007) *International Experiences of Using Community Treatment Orders*. London: Department of Health (March 7).

Coggon, J. (2009) 'Public health, responsibility and English law: are there such things as no smoke without ire or needless clean needles?', *Medical Law Review*, 17, Spring: 127–39.

Cowley, J. and Lee, S. (2011) 'Safeguarding people's rights under the Mental Capacity Act', *Nursing Older People*, 23 (1), February: 19–23.

Department of Health (2008) *Code of Practice: Mental Health Act 1983*. London: Department of Health (7 May 2008).

Department of Health and Social Security (1980) *Report of the Committee of Inquiry into Rampton Hospital (Boynton Report)*. London: HMSO (Cmnd. 8073).

Dimond, B. (2011) *Legal Aspects of Nursing*, 6th edn. Harlow: Pearson Education.

Fear, C.F. (2005) 'The use of ECT in the treatment of schizophrenia and catatonia', in A. Scott (ed.), *The ECT Handbook: the Third Report of the Royal College of Psychiatrists' Special Committee on ECT*. London: The Royal College of Psychiatrists.

General Medical Council (2006) *Good Medical Practice*. London: GMC (November).

Harris, J. (1985) *The Value of Life*. Abingdon: Routledge & Kegan Paul.

Herring, J. (2010) *Medical Law and Ethics*, 3rd edn. Oxford: Oxford University Press.

Hope, T., Savulescu, J. and Hendrick, J. (2008) *Medical Ethics and Law: The Core Curriculum*, 2nd edn. London: Churchill Livingstone Elsevier.

Jackson, E. (2010) *Medical Law: Text, Cases and Materials*. Oxford: Oxford University Press.

Jones, R. (2009) *Mental Health Act Manual*, 12th edn. London: Sweet & Maxwell.

Lewis, P. (1999) 'Feeding anorexic patients who refuse food', *Medical Law Review*, 7, Spring: 21–37.

Mason, J.K. and Laurie, G.T. (2011) *Mason and McCall Smith's Law and Medical Ethics*, 8th edn. Oxford: Oxford University Press.

Maude, P. (2007) 'Ethical problems occurring in mental health and psychiatric care', in G. Hawley (ed.), *Ethics in Clinical Practice: An Interprofessional Approach*. Harlow: Pearson Education.

Mental Health Act Commission (2008) *Twelfth Biennial Report 2005–2007*. London: The Stationery Office.

Mental Health Act Commission (2009) *Thirteenth Biennial Report 2007–2009*. London: The Stationery Office.

Ministry of Justice (2008) *Mental Capacity Act 2005 Deprivation of Liberty Safeguards: Code of Practice*. London: The Stationery Office.

Montgomery, J. (2003) *Health Care Law*, 2nd edn. Oxford: Oxford University Press.

NHS Information Centre (2009) *Adult Psychiatric Morbidity in England, 2007: Results of a Household Survey*. London (January 27).

NHS Information Centre (2010) *Mental Capacity Act 2005, Deprivation of Liberty Safeguards Assessments (England)–First Report on Annual Data, 2009/10*. London (September). Available at: www.ic.nhs.uk.

Pattinson, S.D. (2009) *Medical Law and Ethics*, 2nd edn. London: Sweet & Maxwell.

Percy Commission (1957) *Report of the Royal Commission on the Law Relating to Mental Illness and Mental Deficiency (1954–1957)*. London: HMSO (Cmnd. 169).

Porter, R. (2002) *Madness: A Brief History*. Oxford: Oxford University Press.

Royal College of Nursing (2008) *'Let's Talk About Restraint': Rights, Risks and Responsibility*. London: RCN (March).

Royal College of Psychiatrists (2008) *Standards on the Use of Section 136 of the Mental Health Act 1983 (2007): Report of the Multi-agency Group Led by the Royal College of Psychiatrists*. London. RCP. September.

Sabbatio, R.M.E. (1998) 'The history of shock therapy in psychiatry', *Brain & Mind*, December 1997/February 1998. Available at: www.cerebromente.org.br/n04/historia/shock_i_htm.

Szasz, T. (1970) *Ideology and Insanity: Essays on the Psychiatric Dehumanisation of Man*. Garden City, NY: Doubleday.

CASES

B v Croydon Health Authority [1995] 1 All ER 683.
C, Re [1994] 1 All ER 819.
Dewen v Barnet Healthcare Trust and Barnet London Borough Council [2000] 2 FLR 848 (CA).
F, Re [1989] 2 All ER 545 (HL).
HL v United Kingdom [2005] ECHR 720 (Application 45508/99).
Herczegfalvy v Austria [1992] 15 EHRR 437.
Holgate v Lancashire Mental Hospitals Board [1937] 4 All ER 19.
Hutchison Reid v United Kingdom [2003] 37 EHRR 9.
Johnson v United Kingdom [1997] 40 BMLR 1; 27 EHRR 296.
K v United Kingdom [1998] 40 BMLR 20.
KB, Re [1994] 19 BMLR 144.
Keenan v United Kingdom [1995] 10 BHRC 319.
MH v SSDH [2005] UKHL 60.
Owen v Coventry Health Authority [1986], unreported.
Palmer v Tees Health Authority [1999] Lloyd's Rep. Med. 351.
Pountney v Griffiths [1975] 2 All ER 881.
R (on the application of G, N and B) v Nottinghamshire Healthcare NHS Trust [2008] EWHC 1096 (Admin.).
R (on the application of JB) v Haddock [2006] EWCA Civ. 961.
R (on the application of MH) v Secretary of State for Health [2009] UKHL 60.
R (on the application of Munjaz) v Mersey Care NHS Trust [2005] UKHL 58.
R (on the application of Tagoe-Thompson) v Central and North West London Mental Health NHS Trust [2003] The Times, 18th April.
R (on the application of Wilkinson) v Broadmoor Special Hospital RMO and others [2001] EWCA Civ. 1545.
R (on the application of John Wooder) v Dr. Graham Fegetter and the Mental Health Act Commission [2002] EWCA Civ. 554.
R v Ashworth Hospital, ex parte B [2005] UKHL 20.
R v Birch [1989] 11 Cr. App. R. (S) 202.
R v Bournewood Community Mental Health NHS Trust, ex parte L [1998] 1 All ER 634 (CA); 3 All ER 289 (HL).
R v Cannon's Park Mental Health Review Tribunal, ex parte A [1994] 2 All ER 659.
R v Manchester City Council, ex parte Stennett [2002] UKHL 34.
R v Mental Health Act Commission, ex parte X [1988] 9 BMLR 77.
R v Mental Health Review Tribunal for the South Thames Region, ex parte Smith [1998] 47 BMLR 104 (QBD).
R v Secretary of State for the Home Department and another, ex parte IH [2003] UKHL 59.
R v Secretary of State for the Home Department, ex parte K [1990] 3 All ER 562.
Rabone and another v Pennine Care NHS Trust [2010] The Times, 14th October.
Savage v South Essex Partnership Trust [2008] UKHL 74.
Tameside & Glossop Acute Services Trust v CH [1996] 1 FLR 762.
Winterwerp v The Netherlands [1979] 2 EHHR 387.

LEGISLATION

Health Act 2006
Health and Social Care Act 2008
Human Rights Act 1998

Mental Capacity Act 2005
Mental Deficiency Act 1913
Mental Health Act 1959
Mental Health Act 1983
Mental Health Act 2007
Mental Health (Care and Treatment) (Scotland) Act 2003
National Assistance Act 1948
Police and Criminal Evidence Act 1984
The Mental Health (Hospital, Guardianship and Treatment) (England) Regulations 2008, SI 2008/1184.

Scenarios (answers at back of book)

1   Bill is a 52-year-old man, who has paranoid schizophrenia and has had many admissions to hospital over the last 30 years. He has a history of non-concordance with medication, and the Community Mental Health Team (CMHT) visit him twice a week at his home. He has now been diagnosed with terminal lung cancer, and there has been a rapid deterioration of his mental and physical health in recent weeks. He initially accepted Macmillan Nurse support and Meals-on-Wheels, but he is now refusing all help. He is not ill enough to warrant admission to the Hospice, and the Macmillan Nurses are reluctant to engage in his care because of his mental illness. However, the CMHT are not equipped to provide physical care. Eventually, he refuses all care, and the CMHT are unable to gain access to his home.

Analyse the legal and ethical issues posed by this scenario, and consider the most appropriate response to the dilemma that it raises.
[**For some assistance with this question,** *look at* **GJ** v Foundation Trust, PCT and the Secretary of State for Health [2010] **1 FLR 1251.**]

2.   Joanne is 15 years old, and she has had frequent psychotic episodes in recent years. There is evidence that she has been experiencing visual and auditory hallucinations, and has expressed suicidal thoughts. In addition, she has been violent and aggressive towards her parents, to the extent that she is eventually admitted to a psychiatric ward. Following the administration of anti-psychotic medication, her mental state improves significantly, and she presses for discharge. Her social worker is convinced that she is lucid and rational; but her doctor is convinced that she would not take her medication in the community and would thereby quickly revert to a psychotic state.

Consider the legal and ethical issues arising from this scenario, and suggest the most appropriate response.
[**For some assistance with this question,** *look at* Re R (a minor) (wardship: medical treatment) [1992] **1 FLR 190.**]

8

CHILDREN

Learning Objectives

At the end of this chapter, the reader will:

1 Have an understanding of the law of consent pertaining to children.

2 Be aware of the key legislation designed to protect the interests of children.

3 Acknowledge the prevalence and nature of child abuse, and be aware of the measures currently in place that seek to prevent it.

4 Have an understanding of the legal and ethical issues when considering end of life decisions in children.

1 INTRODUCTION

In years gone by, the position of children in society can best be illustrated by the following extract from a law of the early eighteenth century:

> If a parent be provoked to a degree of passion by some miscarriage of the child or servant, and the parent shall proceed to correct the child with a moderate weapon, and shall by chance give him an unlucky stroke so as to kill him, that is but a misadventure.

In other words, children were considered part of the property of their parents, who had complete control over them (including, in some cases, the power of life and death). Women fared little better in this system, which acknowledged only their right to 'reverence and respect' (Blackstone, 1765) from their children. Divorce, while both rare and expensive, inevitably meant that the mother abandoned all contact with her children, even if they were left in the custody of a mercilessly abusive father.

Thus, it is possible to see that the slow and evolutionary emancipation of women is shadowed by changing attitudes towards children. The latter has inevitably progressed more slowly, but the two are inextricably linked. In 1839, the Custody of Infants Act empowered the Chancellor to award the custody of children under the age of seven to the mother rather than the father (Brandes, 2000), provided that she was of 'unblemished character'. She would not, for example, be awarded custody if she had been found guilty of adultery. The Matrimonial Causes Act 1857 moved divorce proceedings out of the Ecclesiastical Courts and into the common law courts: this effectively made divorce a more realistic prospect and thereby served to protect an increasing number of women and children. Finally, the Infant Custody Act 1873 enabled mothers to obtain custody until the child was 16, and indicated that custody should be determined by the needs of the *child* rather than the rights of either parent. This Act represented the first indication that the child's welfare was of paramount importance, and this principle has increased in intensity over the years so that it has now acquired the status of a sacred mantra.

More of this later, but suffice it to say at this stage that children are now perceived as autonomous young people whose opinions and wishes should be taken into account. This does not automatically imply that those wishes should determine the outcome, but we can see that it represents a significant shift from the position of the early eighteenth century. This chapter seeks to address four main outcomes: consent; some of the key legislation; child abuse; and end of life issues pertaining specifically to children. Inevitably, these sub-divisions will be seen as artificial, for there is often a high degree of overlap between them. However, while acknowledging this weakness, it may still be possible to clarify a number of issues related to child law.

2 CONSENT

A THE CHILD AGED 16–18

We begin with a category of children who present as something of an anomaly within the law. While an individual does not officially become an adult until the age of 18, the Family Law Reform Act 1969 empowers children between the ages of 16 and 18 to consent on their own behalf for medical, surgical and dental treatment (section 8), and the Mental Capacity Act 2005 makes an assumption that they are competent unless proven otherwise (section 1 [2]). It is doubtful that s/he would be able to consent for organ donation or research without parental approval; and it remains the case that *refusal* of treatment can be over-ridden by a parent or a court, even if the child is competent to make this decision. If the child is *incompetent*, there are two mechanisms by which consent to treatment can be effected: the parents can consent on the child's behalf; and the Mental Capacity Act 2005 authorises treatment without consent to persons over the age of 16 (section 2 [5]), provided that the treatment is in the individual's best interests.

B THE INCOMPETENT CHILD UNDER THE AGE OF 16

The presumption in law is that a child below the age of 16 is incompetent to make a decision, and that someone with parental responsibility must therefore consent on that child's behalf. As we shall see later, this is a rebuttable presumption, although the onus will fall upon the healthcare professional to justify why it has been overturned. Of more importance at this stage is the concept of parental responsibility. The Children and Young Persons Act 1933 had already acknowledged that parents have a legal duty to care for their children (s1 [1]); but the Children Act 1989 finally put paid to the notion of parental rights, replacing them instead with parental *responsibilities* (section 3 [1]). In other words, parents have a duty to act in the best interests of their children; and, if they fail to do this, a higher authority (namely, a court of law) will step in and take over from them.

There are many cases illustrating this principle, but two stand out as representing an interesting contrast while upholding the same tenet of law.

Box 8.1 *Re D [1976]*

An 11-year-old girl suffered from Soto's syndrome, which is a rare genetic disorder, characterised by a number of physical abnormalities, mild mental retardation and general clumsiness (National Institute of Neurological Disorders and Stroke, 2008). Her mother considered that the risk of her becoming pregnant was very real, but that she would never be able to look after any children. To prevent this situation from occurring, she discussed the possibility of sterilisation for her daughter, and a consultant gynaecologist agreed to perform the procedure. However, an educational psychologist felt that this was the wrong course to take, and applied for the girl to be made a ward of court.

Despite the fact that the mother consented to the procedure and that the surgeon was in agreement with her, both failed to convince the court that this operation was in the child's best interests and permission for it to proceed was refused. This case almost stands alone as an instance of where the court has refused to allow the sterilisation of a mentally disabled female, and Brazier and Cave (2007) note that the case would never have come to court had it not been for the persistence of the educational psychologist. Having said that, *Re B [1987]* has since stated that all cases involving sterilisation of minors should now come before the courts.

Box 8.2 *Re B [1981]*

A baby girl was born with Down's syndrome and an intestinal obstruction. It was acknowledged that surgery to correct the obstruction could have prolonged her life by at least 20 to 30 years, but the parents felt that it would be kinder to allow her to die. The medical staff refused to operate in the absence of parental consent, but the local authority sought a court order authorising the operation to be performed by other named surgeons.

In a celebrated and often quoted judgment, the court ruled that the operation must go ahead even in the face of parental refusal. It has been celebrated largely because it represents a change of perspective: from a presumption that a disabled life is not worth living (and therefore not worth saving), to a recognition that a diagnosis of Down's syndrome is insufficient justification for ending a life (Read and Clements, 2004). For our purposes, though, it illustrates that the parental right to refuse consent for treatment upon their children can be over-ridden if that refusal is in conflict with the child's best interests.

Thus, we have two cases – one where the parent has consented, and one where the parents have refused consent – and both of these decisions have been overturned by a higher authority. In both of these cases, the parents and doctors were broadly in agreement, and only the intervention of interested third parties meant that the issues were played out in court. In many other situations, parents and doctors will be in disagreement (for example, *Re A [2000]*; *Re Wyatt [2004]*; *NHS Trust v A [2008]*; etc.): such cases almost always relate to end of life decisions, and will be discussed in more detail later on. Suffice it to say at this stage that the courts usually prefer medical testimony when it is in conflict with parental wishes; but there was one case which bucked this trend:

Box 8.3   *Re T [1997]*

A child was born with a life-threatening liver defect (biliary atresia), and three consultant paediatricians argued that a liver transplant was not only imperative, but also that it had a good chance of success. The mother, however, refused to give her consent to the operation, largely because an earlier operation had been unsuccessful and had caused her child considerable pain and distress.

Despite the court's presumption in favour of life, and despite the strong medical evidence that the operation carried the likelihood of a successful outcome, the decision went in favour of the mother. This decision has been heavily criticised and has been described as 'a rogue judgement' (Birchley, 2010). Certainly, it is difficult to reconcile it with earlier and later cases, where the views of parents are always described as 'important', but which rarely affect the outcome. Perhaps the fact that both parents were healthcare professionals (intensive care nurses) gave their testimony a credibility in court that is frequently denied to others. Perhaps, also, the fact that they had fled the country with their child prompted the court to take a pragmatic approach and recognise the difficulties of enforcing treatment. It must be said, though, that neither of these factors formed the basis for the court decision. Rather, great emphasis was placed upon the added burden to the mother of looking after a child who would require 'many years of special care' (per Butler-Sloss, L.J. at 252). Why this should be perceived as a burden when the mother was repeatedly described as 'caring' by the judges and when her training as a healthcare professional should have made it easier for her than for others, is difficult to explain (Fox and McHale, 1997).

Nevertheless, the case serves as an interesting illustration of the fact that parental opinions can still sometimes influence judicial decisions. It would, however, be a mistake to think that this was the norm, and the parents of T ran a real risk of prosecution for manslaughter, as can be seen in the following case:

Box 8.4   R v Harris and Harris [1993]

A 9-year-old girl was diagnosed with diabetes, and her parents were told that she needed insulin. They did not, however, return to the hospital, and could not be contacted. A few weeks later, the child was admitted in a diabetic coma and subsequently died. Her father was convicted of manslaughter and imprisoned for two and a half years, while her mother was given a suspended sentence.

The fact that both parents were Rastafarians had some bearing on this case. First, there were suggestions that social services and the healthcare professionals did not pursue the parents with as much vigour as they might have done because they were concerned about the possibility of confrontation and subsequent allegations of racism (Boggan, 1993). Second, there was a generally held assumption that the religion of the parents prevented them from accessing orthodox healthcare, and that their daughter was therefore the victim of this dogma (Brahams, 1993). Certainly, as Rastafarians, they were vegetarians, and expressed some concern that their daughter was going to receive porcine insulin. Nevertheless, their religion does not prevent them from seeking and receiving orthodox medical treatment when there is a necessity to do so. There seems little doubt, therefore, that the daughter was the tragic victim of a terrible misunderstanding and a failure of communication.

Having said this, it is equally clear that a deeply held religious conviction will not serve as a defence to neglect and/or manslaughter if a child is harmed or dies as a result. A better example of this principle can be found in the old case of *R v Senior [1899]*, where the defendant had strong religious objections to the use of any medicine. This prevented him from seeking treatment for his sick child who then died, and he was subsequently convicted of manslaughter. As Rutledge, J. has said, in an American case (*Prince v Massachussets [1944]*):

Parents may be free to become martyrs themselves. But it does not follow that they are free in identical circumstances to make martyrs of their children (at 170).

To summarise the foregoing, it is possible to identify a few key principles:

1 Parents have a duty to act in the best interests of their children.
2 Their rights to consent/refuse on behalf of their children can be over-ridden by a court of law, even if the healthcare professionals are prepared to respect their decisions.
3 Where parents and healthcare professionals are in disagreement, a court will normally find for the latter, although they must be able to provide a strong argument that treatment/non-treatment is in the best interests of the child.

A further complication arises, however, if the parents are in disagreement with each other. Generally speaking, the consent of one parent is sufficient to authorise treatment, and even the consent of a competent child would serve as a defence. This is what Lord Donaldson called a legal 'flak jacket' (*Re W [1993]*), which serves as a protective mechanism for healthcare professionals against possible allegations of battery. The difficulty becomes more acute, though, when the healthcare professional is made fully aware that both parents are in disagreement with each other, and perhaps even more so when the refusing parent is the primary caregiver. Consider the following scenario:

Box 8.5   *Re B [2003]*

A father wanted his child to have the full range of immunisations (including the MMR vaccine), but the mother was vehemently opposed to this. The child was living with the mother, who was neither married to, nor living with, the father. The father, however, had parental responsibility and was in frequent contact with the child.

This case was heard in conjunction with a similar case (*Re C [2003]*), and the outcome in both was identical. First, although the views of the primary caregiver will often hold sway, the principle of the child's welfare dictated that immunisation should be given, for the State has an obligation to provide preventive health care under article 6.2 of the UN Convention on the Rights of the Child 1989. Second, it was held that immunisation was one of those areas where *both* parents must agree, and that the consent/refusal of one parent was insufficient if the other made his/her objections known. If agreement cannot be reached, responsibility for the decision will fall to the court. Quite obviously, the onus falls upon the objecting parent to make his/her opinions known to the healthcare professionals, and the latter would be protected if this was not the case. It is interesting to speculate upon what would happen if both parents refused the immunisations: it is doubtful that a health authority would feel that this was serious enough to challenge in court; and, even if it did, there are no guarantees that a court would insist upon the vaccinations.

The other areas where consent is required by both parents are changing the child's surname and male circumcision for non-therapeutic reasons. An example of the last of these can be seen in the following case:

Box 8.6   Re J [2000]

A child had a Christian mother and a Muslim father, although neither was committed to either faith. The child, however, was born a Muslim; and, following separation of the parents, the father sought a court order authorising circumcision. The mother opposed this application, and the court held that both parents must be in agreement before the procedure could be carried out (citing section 2 [7] of the Children Act 1989). The operation was not clinically indicated, its effects were irreversible, and it carried a number of risks.

It follows, therefore, that non-therapeutic circumcision of male children *is* lawful if both parents are in agreement. Whether it is ethically correct or not is another matter, and both the General Medical Council (2008) and the British Medical Association (2007) have remained non-committal on the issue, preferring to leave this to the conscience of individual surgeons. Female circumcision, incidentally, is prohibited by the Female Genital Mutilation Act 2003 (section 1).

Moreover, there are some procedures on children which require court approval even in the presence of two consenting parents: sterilisation (see *Re B [1987]*), donation of non-regenerative tissue (e.g. kidney), possibly cosmetic surgery, and abortion (although the latter could be performed if a competent child gave her consent). The golden rule running through these instances is that, where there is doubt, court approval should be sought (Herring, 2010).

Perhaps the area where disagreement between adults is most likely is that concerning paternity tests on children. Consider the following scenario:

Box 8.7   Re F [1993]

W was having sexual relationships with both her husband (H) and another man (B). The relationship with B subsequently ended, but a few months later, W gave birth to a child (C). Upon discovering the existence of C, B asked for blood tests to be taken on the child to determine her paternity. W refused, and the case came before the court.

The court held that the application for a blood test would be refused, for the child was already in a stable family and thought of her mother's husband as her father. Therefore, discovery that B was the father would almost certainly destabilise this family unit and would thereby be detrimental to C.

It is, of course, possible to imagine variations on this scenario (where, for example, B may have a congenital or hereditary disorder), and the outcome might be different in each case. In *Re H [1996]*, a similar situation to *Re F* resulted in the blood test being ordered: here, the husband had left the home, and the stability of the family unit was not therefore an issue. In consequence, it is not possible to predict the outcome of these cases with any certainty, for each will turn upon the facts. The key question for any court is this: 'Is it in the child's best interests (or, at the very least, *not against* the child's interests) for the blood test to be taken?' If the answer to this question is in the affirmative, the blood test will be ordered. Thus, in *Re F*, the interests of W, B and H had no influence on the outcome, however strongly those interests were advanced – it was only the interests of C that mattered to the court. The Family Law Reform Act 1969 has since been amended (by the Mental Capacity Act 2005) to reflect this principle (sections 3 and 4).

Before concluding this section on the incompetent child, one further question arises. Who gives consent for treatment of a child if the parents are themselves below the age of 16? The issue does not appear to have been addressed by the courts, although it seems that consent of a parent would be valid if s/he was assessed as being competent to make this decision. If the parents are incompetent, Dimond (2008) suggests that the grandparents could be asked to accept this responsibility. However, although this represents a sensible approach (by ensuring that everybody is involved in the decision-making process), it is doubtful that it represents good law, for the grandparents do not have parental responsibility. The most that they can do, therefore, is *assent* to the procedure; and the healthcare professionals would be justified in proceeding with treatment if they could argue that it was necessary and in the best interests of the child. Once again, though, any conflict between the stakeholders is best resolved by the courts.

C THE COMPETENT CHILD UNDER THE AGE OF 16

The previous section indicated that the presumption of incompetence in a child below the age of 16 is rebuttable, and the case which established this principle is the following:

Box 8.8   *Gillick v West Norfolk and Wisbech Health Authority [1985]*

A circular was distributed by the Health Authority (following guidance from the Department of Health) to all GPs in the area informing them that it would be permissible to prescribe contraception to teenage girls without informing their parents. Mrs Gillick challenged this in the courts, arguing that teenage girls were incapable of consenting to medical treatment on their own behalf, and that the GPs were therefore legally bound to inform the parents. In the absence of such disclosure, she maintained that the GPs would be committing a battery.

This case enjoyed a stormy passage through all three English courts. Mrs Gillick lost in the High Court, won in the Court of Appeal, and eventually lost in the House of Lords (but only by a majority of three to two). In fairness, one of the dissenting Law Lords (Lord Templeman) had no issues with children consenting to treatment per se (and it is arguable that Mrs Gillick did not see this as a problem either (Brazier and Cave, 2007)) – he simply perceived difficulties with the specific circumstances of this case: 'There are many things which a girl under 16 needs to practise, but sex is not one of them' (at 433).

However, his attempt to separate consent to contraception from other areas of consent was destined to fail, for it is not possible to have one without the other: either s/he is competent to consent or s/he is not. The better position was summarised by Lord Scarman in the following extract:

> the parental right to determine whether or not their minor child below the age of 16 will have medical treatment terminates if and when the child achieves a sufficient understanding and intelligence to enable him or her to understand fully what is proposed (at 423).

In other words, a person's right to consent on his/her own behalf can begin long before the sixteenth birthday, provided that s/he can demonstrate an ability to comprehend the full ramifications of the decision. This principle has been given statutory authority in Scotland by means of The Age of Legal Capacity (Scotland) Act 1991, but it remains a tenet of the common law in England and Wales. It authorises healthcare professionals to administer treatment to children below the age of 16 without informing the parents, and thereby gives them a legal defence to charges of battery. It should be clear, though, that the defence only holds good if the child has been assessed as competent. How is this to be done?

Some guidance came from the *Gillick* case itself, although this related specifically to the administration of contraceptive treatment to teenage girls. It has come to be known as the Fraser guidelines (arising, as it did, from the speech by Lord Fraser), and can be summarised thus:

Box 8.9 The Fraser Guidelines

Before administering contraceptive treatment to a girl under the age of 16 years, the healthcare professional must be satisfied that:

1   She understands the advice given to her.
2   She cannot be persuaded to tell her parents (or allow the healthcare professional to tell them).
3   It is likely that she will have sexual intercourse whether or not she receives contraception.
4   Her physical and/or mental health might suffer if she is refused contraception.
5   It is in her best interests to receive contraceptive treatment and advice, and this should be given without informing her parents.

Mrs Gillick had argued that the provision of contraception by a GP amounted to encouragement of illegal sexual intercourse (Sexual Offences Act 1956), but this contention was dismissed by the House of Lords. Their reasoning was that the doctor would be acting in the child's best interests, and s/he should not be punished for fulfilling his/her duty. One might also argue that the simple provision of contraception does not automatically imply that the girl will engage in intercourse – in other words, the doctor cannot be certain that a crime is about to be committed. The fact that neither of these arguments is entirely convincing will have prompted a change in the law, so that the Sexual Offences Act 2003 now gives statutory protection to healthcare professionals:

A person is not guilty of aiding, abetting or counselling the commission against a child of an offence ... if he acts for the purpose of –

a protecting the child from sexually transmitted infection,

b protecting the physical safety of the child,

c preventing the child from becoming pregnant, or

d promoting the child's emotional well-being by the giving of advice (Section 73 [1]).

The House of Lords in *Gillick* also suggested that it would be permissible to perform an abortion on a teenage girl without informing her parents, and this issue came before the court in the following case:

Box 8.10   *R (on the application of Axon) v Secretary of State for Health and another [2006]*

Mrs Axon challenged guidance from the Department of Health, which stated that parental consent was not necessary for contraception, treatment of sexually transmitted disease, or abortion if such treatment was in the child's best interests and the child was competent to consent to it. The court rejected this claim, stating that the principles in *Gillick* held firm and were applicable to all sexual health services.

In contrast to Mrs Gillick, Mrs Axon was not asking for a right to consent on behalf of her children, but merely to be *informed* about the treatment that they were undergoing (Bridgeman, 2006). On the face of it, this does not seem an unreasonable request, but the court was quick to perceive the flaw in this argument. Young people often seek advice and treatment for sexual matters on the express understanding that their parents will not be informed. If this position was reversed, they would be less likely to access healthcare services, with potentially disastrous consequences.

The *Gillick* case, of course, specifically related to issues of contraception, but the Law Lords clearly intended that the principle of enabling consent in children should apply across a range of other health matters. Unfortunately, no method of measuring competence to consent was proposed (Bijsterveld, 2000), and one could argue that the threshold was set so high that many children would be destined to fail it. For example, Lord Scarman said that, to be considered competent, a child must understand 'moral and family' questions and their emotional implications (at 424); but this is a higher test than the Mental Capacity Act 2005 requires for an adult (Pattinson, 2009).

Successive cases have sought to add some meat to the bones erected by *Gillick* and have considered some of the factors that need to be taken into account:

1   Age: It seems reasonable to assume that competence to consent is a developmental process, and is therefore more likely in an older child than a younger child. Or, as Lord Donaldson put it in *Re W [1993]*:

'as experience of life is acquired and intelligence and understanding grow, so will the scope of the decision making which should be left to the minor' (at 81).

In *R v D [1984]*, Lord Brandon had suggested that competence was unlikely to be found in a child under the age of 14; but he was expressing a personal opinion, rather than stating a principle of law. When, in one study (Alderson, 1993), healthcare professionals were asked the age at which they thought that children could consent for themselves, the average response was 10.3 years (although the children themselves thought that it should be 14 years). In reality, of course, each child will be different, and any attempt to establish a minimum age of consent fails to reflect this observation.

2   Gravity of the decision: As we shall see later, even a competent child cannot refuse life-saving treatment; but it is equally clear that a higher level of understanding is required if the procedure is complex and carries significant risks (General Medical Council, 2007). Thus, it seems extremely unlikely that a child would ever be considered competent to consent to organ donation or gender reassignment (*Re W [1993]*).

3   Fluctuating competency: In *Re R [1992]*, a 15-year-old girl was a patient in an adolescent psychiatric unit and had been prescribed anti-psychotic medication. She argued that she should be discharged, for she was no longer mentally ill, and a social worker supported her claim. Her doctor, however, was convinced that she would refuse the medication upon discharge, and would quickly revert to a psychotic state. The court accepted the medical position: although the evidence suggested that R was competent, it was clear that this was a temporary state. In such circumstances, her decisions could carry no weight; or, as Lord Donaldson stated:

'"Gillick competence" is a developmental concept and will not be lost or acquired on a day to day or week to week basis' (at 26).

4   Pressure on the child from a third party: If a child is subjected to the undue influence of another (usually a parent), the courts will generally conclude that s/he lacks sufficient maturity to make a decision. The most common application of this principle is when a

child refuses life-saving treatment, and there are a number of cases serving as illustrations (to be discussed later). It could also apply, though, if a child agreed to provide an organ for a sibling, following pressure from the parents.

While the above factors and the Fraser guidelines are of some assistance when making determinations of competence, they are not quite as helpful as one might wish. For example, much of the guidance focuses on the information that must be conveyed to the child, but does not explain how the healthcare professional can be confident that the child has understood it. Admittedly, it is impossible to give highly specific guidance when each case is different; but equally, it is clear that simply giving information to a child and relying upon a hunch that s/he has understood it is not enough. Therefore, some form of two-way communication is of importance, where the child is encouraged to participate fully in the conversation. Thus, the child should be asked to describe what s/he understands about his/her condition and about the proposed treatment; s/he should be encouraged to express any concerns that s/he might have; and s/he should be given an open invitation to ask questions (Kemp et al., 2008).

This does not, of course, represent a fail-safe system, but it goes a long way to determining the competence of a child to consent. It is important to remember that the burden of rebutting the presumption of incompetence falls upon the healthcare professional, who must be able to give clear reasons for making this judgement. If, therefore, the child fails to engage in conversation and/or fails to demonstrate understanding, the healthcare professional will be entirely justified in refusing to proceed with treatment without parental consent. Indeed, the healthcare professional would be taking a considerable risk with his/her career if such factors were ignored.

The foregoing has suggested that a competent child has the power to consent to treatment on his/her own behalf, even in the face of parental refusal. But, does a competent child have the right to *refuse* treatment? Logically, there is no reason to suppose otherwise, and this appears to have been the lesson emerging from *Gillick*. However, two cases soon dispelled this illusion: the first (*Re R [1992]*) has already been discussed, and the facts of the second are as follows:

Box 8.11   *Re W [1993]*

A 16-year-old girl suffered from anorexia nervosa, but she refused to be transferred to a specialist unit for treatment. A number of signs pointed to the conclusion that she was competent to make a decision, but it was held that her refusal could be over-ridden by her parents and the court.

The decisions in both *Re R* and *Re W* have been criticised by a number of commentators and on a number of grounds. For one thing, it could be argued that neither girl was truly competent, and that it might have been better to section them under the Mental Health Act 1983 (Alderson, 2000). The fact that the courts did not do this implies that that they were concerned about the possible stigmatisation the girls might experience if this appeared on their medical records (Brazier and Bridge, 1996). Regardless of the motive, though, these two cases have served to confuse the principle outlined in *Gillick*. In *Re W* especially, the court acknowledged that children should be *involved* in decisions affecting their healthcare, but this fell a long way short of giving them the power to control their own destiny (Jackson, 2010).

The apparent victory for children's rights won in *Gillick* was therefore short-lived, for a judgement of competence appears to be predicated on its agreement with medical opinion. A number of subsequent cases have confirmed the power of the courts in such matters, and one of the most well-known was the following:

Box 8.12   *Re E [1993]*

A boy aged 15 years and 9 months was suffering from leukaemia, and needed a life-saving blood transfusion. As a practising and committed Jehovah's Witness, he felt compelled to refuse the blood transfusion, as did his parents. The court, however, stated that it would not allow a young boy to martyr himself for the sake of his religion, and ruled that the transfusion must be administered.

There can be little doubt that *E* was competent: he knew exactly what he was doing and he fully understood the consequences of his refusal. The judge sought to cast doubt upon this level of understanding by suggesting that the boy could not have contemplated 'the pain he has yet to suffer' (per Ward, J. at 391); but this has something of a hollow ring to it. It is much more likely that the judge was operating from a public policy perspective – in other words, society has an interest in preserving the lives of its children, even if they have no wish to be saved. In itself, this is not an ignoble position to hold, but it would be much less confusing if this was openly expressed, rather than endeavouring to undermine the concept of *Gillick* competence (Grubb, 1999). If the judge felt that E's religious beliefs were the product of an immature mind or heavily influenced by his parents, he was soon to be disabused of this opinion. When E reached 18, he needed another blood transfusion: once more, he refused, and this time nobody could do anything, for nobody can overturn the refusal of a competent adult.

The same factors can be seen at work in *Re L [1998]*, in which a 14-year-old girl had extensive burns and needed surgical treatment. The likelihood was that she would need a blood transfusion, but her Jehovah's Witness faith prevented her from giving her consent to this. It was held that she was incompetent, largely because she lacked full understanding of the consequences of her refusal. However, the doctor had refused to give her this information and had thereby induced her incompetence. Moreover, the court was heavily swayed by the evidence of a psychiatrist, who asserted that the girl had been exposed to the undue influence of her parents; but he had never actually seen her before making this assessment (Montgomery, 2003). Clearly, the concept of Gillick competence has little real value when it can be so easily overturned.

The case of *Re S (1994)* has a number of similarities with the previous two. Here, a 15-year-old girl had thalassaemia and required monthly blood transfusions; but she subsequently converted to the Jehovah's Witness faith and began to refuse the transfusions. Once more, the influence of her mother was considered sufficient justification for over-ruling her refusal; but Brazier and Bridge (1996) argue that this was not the only factor. The painful daily injections that formed the mainstay of her treatment, and the fact that her condition had stunted her growth must have made her feel that she had suffered enough. The court, however, was not prepared to give credibility to these opinions.

Religious objections were over-ruled again in *Re P [2003]*, even though the patient was almost 17 years old (and thereby presumed to be competent under the Family Law Reform Act 1969). Religion did not play a part in *Re M [1999]*, where a 15-year-old with heart failure refused a heart transplant. Her objections were largely psychological in that she did not relish the prospect of having another person's heart inside her, and nor did she approach the prospect of having to take medication for the rest of her life with any enthusiasm. As expected, the court effectively ignored these objections, although Mason and Laurie (2011) argue that 'this decision must surely represent the outermost reaches of acceptable paternalistic practices' (p. 74).

Re M is in contrast to the case of Hannah Jones, a 13-year-old girl who had been diagnosed with leukaemia when aged five. Chemotherapy had left her with a hole in the heart and she needed a heart transplant, but she refused (de Bruxelles, 2008). Astonishingly, she persuaded the health authority to drop the case: but why? In an echo of *Re T [1997]*, Hannah's mother was an intensive care nurse, and her support of her daughter's refusal might have had some influence. A more likely reason, however, is that the transplant carried a number of risks: not only were the chances of success rated as slim, but also there was a possibility that the anti-rejection drugs might induce a relapse of the leukaemia. The decision to accept Hannah's refusal was therefore made on clinical grounds, rather than being an acknowledgement of children's rights to determine their own destiny. Had the health authority pursued this case to court, it is reasonable to assume that the decision would have followed the same pattern as that of *Re M*. As it transpired, Hannah's condition subsequently showed signs of improvement and she withdrew her objections to the heart trans-plant (Weaver, 2009).

There has been one situation where a 15-year-old Jehovah's Witness has been allowed to refuse a blood transfusion. Joshua McAuley sustained multiple injuries when he was pinned against a wall by a car, but the hospital accepted his right to decline a transfusion (Roberts, 2010). It is conceivable (although not reported) that the injuries were so severe that a blood transfusion would not have made the differ-ence between life and death. If this were so, Joshua's situation would not represent the change in philosophy that is apparent at face value.

These cases clearly show that the concept of Gillick competence is a one-way street; or, as Herring (2010) states: 'It is almost as if the law is saying to children, "we will respect your right to autonomy but only if you give the right answer!"' (p. 207). Perhaps we can accept that a child's welfare is more important than his/her decision-making authority (Pattinson, 2009); and perhaps we can argue that someone is in a much better position to exercise autonomy when adulthood has been reached (Herring, 2010). It is doubtful, however, that an 18-year-old is signifi-cantly more mature than a 17-year-old, and this dividing line takes no account of individual abilities. Indeed, Brook (2000) argues that a child with a chronic illness or disability may actually be in a stronger position to make a decision, because s/he will often have an insight which is advanced for their chronological age.

The above cases deal with situations where treatment was considered necessary to save the lives of children; but it is less clear whether referral would be over-ridden if the treatment related to non-life-threatening conditions. Lord Balcombe (in *Re W [1993]*) seemed to suggest that the court would have 'a strong predilection to give effect to the child's wishes' (at 88); but he confined such observations to 16- or 17-year-old children. Another case of the same year (*South Glamorgan County Council v W and B [1993]*) saw the court over-rule a child's refusal to submit to medical and psychiatric assessment, even though the Children Act 1989 expressly states that this decision should be respected if the child is competent (sections 38 [6], 43 [8], and 44 [7]).

Many, no doubt, will see the courts' approach to children as the simple expres-sion of common sense. If, as adults, we have a *duty* to do the best for our children, this must encompass an insistence that they accept life-preserving and life-enhancing treatment. Others will perceive that this paternalistic approach is a relic of the past, taking little account of the cultural and philosophical changes within our society. Bijsterveld (2000), for example, argues that we should reverse the presumption that a child is incompetent. In other words, a healthcare professional would no longer have to justify why s/he has accepted a child's consent or refusal, but instead must be able to show why it has been overturned. This may not, of itself, make any dif-ference to the outcome, but it would at least give greater credence to the concept of children's rights.

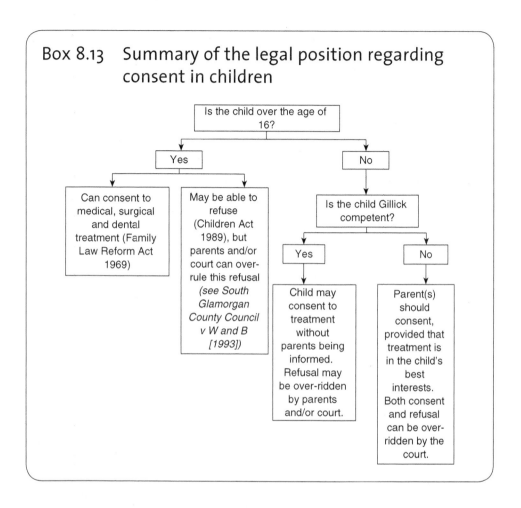

Box 8.13   Summary of the legal position regarding consent in children

3 LEGISLATION

PARENTAL RESPONSIBILITY

There is a presumption enshrined in law that a child's interests are best served by remaining within the family and being raised by his/her parents (Children Act 1989, section 17 [1b]). As with all presumptions, of course, this is rebuttable, and we will shortly move on to discuss those situations where the principle is over-ruled. At this stage, however, it is necessary to examine the concept of parental responsibility, and try to ascertain its meaning. The Children Act 1989 (s3 [1]) offers the following definition: 'all the rights, duties, powers, responsibilities and authority which by law a parent of a child has in relation to the child and his property'.

But, to whom does this section apply? Inevitably, it will apply to the *mother*, unless she forfeits these rights or is proven to be incapable of exercising them. It also applies to the *father*, as long as he is married to the mother at the time of insemination or birth (Children Act 1989, section 2 [1]). If the father is *not* married to the mother, however, the position becomes more complicated. He can acquire parental responsibility by marrying the mother (Family Law Reform Act 1987, section 1); or, providing the child's birth was registered after 1 December 2003, he acquires it if he registers as the child's father on the birth certificate (Adoption and Children Act 2002, amending section 4 of the Children Act 1989). Perhaps the legal position of the unmarried father is best summed up in the following diagram (adapted from Children's Legal Centre, 2006a).

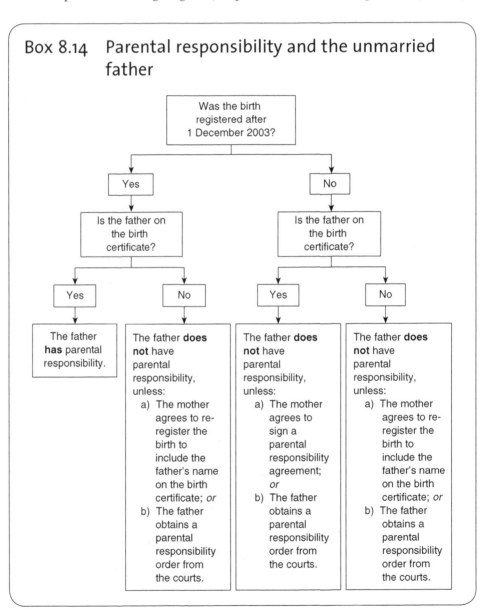

Box 8.14   Parental responsibility and the unmarried father

Was the birth registered after 1 December 2003?

Yes

No

Is the father on the birth certificate?

Is the father on the birth certificate?

Yes

No

Yes

No

The father **has** parental responsibility.

The father **does not** have parental responsibility, unless:
a) The mother agrees to re-register the birth to include the father's name on the birth certificate; *or*
b) The father obtains a parental responsibility order from the courts.

The father **does not** have parental responsibility, unless:
a) The mother agrees to sign a parental responsibility agreement; *or*
b) The father obtains a parental responsibility order from the courts.

The father **does not** have parental responsibility, unless:
a) The mother agrees to re-register the birth to include the father's name on the birth certificate; *or*
b) The father obtains a parental responsibility order from the courts.

In addition to these principles, the unmarried father may acquire parental responsibility if he is appointed as the child's guardian following the mother's death (Children Act 1989, section 5). In short, *all* fathers exercising parental responsibility will have some form of documentary evidence to confirm these rights (Montgomery, 2003). It may be a marriage certificate, a parental responsibility agreement with the mother, a birth certificate denoting registration of the father's name, or a parental responsibility order from the courts. Once acquired, parental responsibility will remain even if the parents divorce (Children Act 1989, section 2 [b]): should either or both of the parents re-marry, the step-parent(s) may be able to make a parental responsibility agreement provided that all parties are willing to accept the situation (Children Act 1989, section 4A [1]), but this will not remove parental responsibility from those who already have it. The only way that parental responsibility can be ended is if the child is given up for adoption, and it will remain even if the child is cared for by a grandparent or a care order is in place. This can, however, create difficulties, as the following case illustrates:

Box 8.15   *B v B [1992]*

A mother delegated the care of her daughter to the child's grandmother. However, the girl's school would not accept the consent of the grandmother for school outings, and nor would the GP accept it for routine immunisations.

Clearly, both the school and the GP were acting within the law, but the law served only to disadvantage the child. The solution was to obtain a Residence Order from the court, which gave the grandmother parental responsibility (and thereby the power to consent on behalf of the child) (Children Act 1989, section 12 [2]).

The courts are not generally loath to refuse parental responsibility orders, provided that the interests of the child are best served by such agreements. Where they are not, applications will be refused, as can be seen in the following case:

Box 8.16   *GB v RJB and GLB [2009]*

H was a 3-year-old child, who had lived all his life with his grandmother (GB), for his parents had separated before his birth. A residence order had been granted to the grandmother, but the child's father (RJB) also applied for such an order (supported by the child's mother (GLB)). Both the High Court and the Court of Appeal granted the application, but the Supreme Court overturned these decisions, arguing that the welfare of the child was of paramount importance and that this would be adversely affected if the continuity of his living arrangements was disrupted.

There are, of course, many examples of where parental responsibility orders have been refused by the courts, and they commonly involve some defect in the character of the father (e.g. *Re H [1998]*, where the father had demonstrated violent behaviour towards children; and *Re P [1998]*, where the father had possession of indecent photographs of children). This, however, is not always the case, as the following illustrates:

Box 8.17   *Re W [1992]*

A woman was pregnant by a man, and agreed that the child should live with the father following her birth. Two days after the birth, a Residence Order was duly granted to the father, but the mother then changed her mind and applied to the court for the return of the child. Although the court could find no obvious problem with the father, it acknowledged that the interests of a child who was less than one month old were better served by being with the mother (unless it could be shown that the mother was unfit). The Residence Order was therefore revoked.

The above would seem to suggest that the law is heavily weighted in favour of the biological mother, and there is some truth in this. In *Re G [2006]*, for example, two daughters had been born to a woman (G) by means of artificial insemination at a clinic abroad. When her lesbian relationship with her partner (W) broke down, the latter applied for a Residence Order in respect of the girls. This was initially granted, largely because G had broken an agreement to reside in the same area as W, but also because the court could not distinguish between one woman and another on the grounds of a biological relationship. On appeal, however, the House of Lords held that this biological relationship 'was an important and significant factor' (per Baroness Hale at para. 44), and reversed the decision of the Court of Appeal. As a matter of interest, even if a shared residence Order had been granted, it seems unlikely that W would have been held liable for child support payments. This situation arose in *T v B [2011]*, the court held that liability for such payments only applied to *legal* parents (as defined by the Children Act 1989, Schedule 1). The definition of legal parents could only be extended by Parliament and was not therefore a matter for the courts.

At all times, though, the court will be most heavily influenced by the welfare of the child, and this means that the presumption in favour of the mother is rebuttable. This is something to which we will return shortly, for it is a key element of the Children Act 1989. Before doing this, however, it is worth considering the additional problems that can be created by advances in technology. The following two cases both involve fertility treatment and relate to issues pertaining to fatherhood.

Box 8.18   *Re R [2005]*

An unmarried couple sought IVF treatment because the male partner had become infertile following treatment for testicular cancer. When IVF was unsuccessful, the couple separated, but the woman continued to undergo further treatment (without informing the clinic of the separation from her partner). She eventually had a child, and her former partner applied for parental responsibility. The application was refused, because the man was not married to the mother, he was not the genetic father of the child, and his relationship with the woman had ended before the successful treatment had been given. Under the terms of the Human Fertilisation and Embryology Act 1990 (section 28 [3]), he could not therefore be called the father.

Grubb (2003) notes that the woman's deceit has gone unpunished here, although the IVF clinic could have avoided this situation by seeking the consent of *both* partners before each treatment cycle. Nevertheless, the outcome of this case is that the child was declared fatherless: whether this is a good or a bad thing (or, indeed, if it matters at all) is a matter for debate. At least the man would have been spared the burden of child maintenance payments, but his court action suggests that this was not uppermost in his mind.

Box 8.19   *The Leeds Teaching Hospitals NHS Trust v Mr. A, Mrs. A and others [2003]*

Two couples (Mr and Mrs A, and Mr and Mrs B) underwent fertility treatment. However, the sperm of Mr B was mistakenly used to fertilise Mrs A's eggs, and she subsequently gave birth to twins. This error might not have come to light had it not been for the fact that Mr B was black and Mrs A was white. Both Mr A and Mr B argued that they were the father of these children.

The court held that Mr A had not consented to the use of Mr B's sperm, and therefore he was not the legal father (Human Fertilisation and Embryology Act 1990, section 28 [2]). Thus, Mr B was the legal father, although Mr A would be able to apply for adoption or parental responsibility orders. We might assume that the couples here would be entitled to compensation, but a similar case heard in Northern Ireland suggest otherwise. In *A and B (by C, their mother and next friend), A (Health and Social Services Trust) [2011]*, the black twins born to a white mother as the result of a mistake at the fertility clinic brought a negligence claim against the Trust, arguing that they had been subjected to abusive comments by other children as a result of their colour. The court (citing *McFarland v Tayside Health Board [2000]*) held that a normal baby cannot be considered a harm, and that (by extension) all the elements of negligence had not been satisfied.

In most cases, of course, the question of who is the father of the child will be easily answered, but the above two cases demonstrate the complexities that modern developments can create. Nevertheless, having explored the issue of parental responsibility, we now need to examine, in some depth, the primary piece of legislation pertaining to children.

4 THE CHILDREN ACT 1989

A THE WELFARE PRINCIPLE

There are many Children Acts, but the one of 1989 is the major piece of legislation pertaining to children in this country, and it sets out the fundamental premises that the welfare of the child is paramount and that children have a right to be listened to. Prior to its enactment, there were two main influences that impacted upon its key principles. The first was the UN Convention on the Rights of the Child 1989: although it was eventually ratified by all countries except for two (Somalia and the USA) *after* the Children Act (September 1990), there can be little doubt that the prevailing philosophy that formed the basis of discussion leading up to ratification would have entered the consciousness of the UK legislators. In other words, the concept of children's rights was already in the forefront of people's minds, and the Children Act 1989 gave added expression to these.

The second influence was that of the Cleveland child abuse scandal, which occurred two years earlier. Two paediatricians at a Middlesbrough hospital (Dr Marietta Higgs and Dr Geoffrey Wyatt) diagnosed 121 cases of suspected child abuse, using a reflex anal dilatation test. Dilatation of a child's anus suggested that sexual abuse had taken place, but the same result could be achieved if the child was constipated. Nevertheless, the two paediatricians were convinced of the scientific rigour of this test, resulting in the break-up of families where no abuse had taken place (Deer, 1988). No doubt, a number of the 121 cases were genuine instances of abuse, and this was sufficient to prevent either doctor from showing any evidence of contrition. But the psychological trauma of those children who were torn away from their parents is difficult to imagine; and it was with this in mind that the Children Act 1989 endeavoured to ensure that the unity of the family should be safeguarded in all but the most extreme of cases. In essence, this is a recognition that *all* parents (regardless of social class, level of education, race, etc.) are potentially capable of violence towards their children, particularly when highly stressed. This does not mean that they are necessarily bad parents, but that they need extra support at certain times. Therefore, a spirit of cooperation, negotiation and partnership is more likely to serve the interests of children than tearing them away from their parents.

We have earlier mentioned the paramountcy of the child's welfare, and this is a recurring theme throughout the Children Act 1989. Given its importance, it is not surprising to discover that the whole of section 1 is devoted to this principle, and it outlines a checklist of how it is to be determined. Thus, a court will consider:

  i   The wishes and feelings of the child (1 [3a]).
  ii The child's physical, emotional and educational needs (1 [3b]).
 iii The likely effect on the child of a change in circumstances (1 [3c]).
 iv The age, sex and background of the child (1 [3d]).
  v Any harm the child has suffered or is at risk of suffering (1 [3e]).
 vi The capability of the parents and others to meet the child's needs (1 [3f]).

The welfare principle sounds obvious in theory, but the difficulty is that many cases have made it unclear what is in a child's best interests (Birchley, 2010). This means, in effect, that the court is likely to be swayed by the most eloquent lawyers, rather than working to a clearly defined guideline. Nowhere is this better illustrated than in the last of the above considerations. Imagine, for example, a child born to a couple who are educationally subnormal: they will need some help with the practical aspects of caring for a child, but they remain as capable as anybody else of demonstrating love for their offspring. Are the child's best interests served by remaining with his/her parents and thereby guaranteed to be raised in a loving environment? Or would they be best served by foster parents, who could ensure that the child's intellectual development is stimulated? Would it make a difference if the child also had learning disabilities? These are not easy questions to answer: we may have strong views on such matters (born either through experience or intuition), but each opinion can be undermined by strong opposing arguments.

Where the child has severe mental and physical disabilities (and will therefore never be in a position to exercise his/her personal autonomy), Birchley (2010) argues that his/her interests are inextricably bound up with those of the parents. Consider the following situation that occurred in the USA a few years ago (The 'Ashley Treatment' [2007]):

Box 8.20   The 'Ashley Treatment'

Ashley was a 9-year-old girl, whose body was growing normally, but whose mental and physical abilities failed to develop. The cause was never determined, but it quickly became clear that there was no prospect of improvement and that she would remain completely dependent on others for the rest of her life. Her parents called her a 'pillow angel', because she remained exactly where she lay, unable to move her position. In recognition of the fact that Ashley would continue to grow, and thereby be more difficult to care for, her parents agreed to the following three procedures: high-dose oestrogen therapy to prevent further physical growth; a hysterectomy to prevent the onset of menstruation; and breast-bud removal to prevent the development of breasts.

This drastic treatment was always certain to polarise opinion. Was this treatment designed to help Ashley, or was it designed to make life easier for her parents? In reality, it is probably impossible to distinguish between the two, for one is dependent upon the other. If, for example, she was allowed to develop physically, the time would soon come when the parents were unable to give her the care she needed and she would therefore need to be placed in a nursing home. By ensuring that she remained small, she could continue to be easily transported so that she could be fully included in the activities of family life.

The *Ashley* case in the USA provided support for the mother of Katie Thorpe in the UK – a 15-year-old girl with cerebral palsy and the mental capacity of an 18-month-old child. The mother sought to have a hysterectomy performed on her daughter, so that the latter did not experience the onset of menstruation. Once again, the interests of the mother were a feature of the central arguments: was the proposed surgery intended to make her life easier, or was it being done in Katie's interests? There are those who will contend that, even if the mother's interests are the main driving force, Katie's interests are still being served, because she would be easier to care for. There are others, however, who see such measures as a movement towards the forced sterilisation of people with learning disabilities (Gibb, 2007). As it transpired, the mother was initially unable to persuade a gynaecologist to perform the procedure, but he later relented and Katie underwent a hysterectomy (Huahima, 2009).

B COURT ORDERS

The following table is designed to give a broad overview of the measures available to courts when assessing the needs of children. Needless to say, none of them are taken lightly, and the last-named (Wardship) must always be seen as a last resort. Nevertheless, when used appropriately, they represent considerable power to protect the interests of children. There are many examples of the application of each of these orders, but only one is named so that a flavour is given. Equally, each of these cases is inevitably more complicated than can be presented here, and the order depicted is usually only one aspect of the judicial decision. Most of these orders are dispensed by a magistrates' court, and are therefore unreported: those that find their way to the High Court and above generally have complex grounds of appeal.

Box 8.21   Court Orders

Order	Relevant section of the Children Act 1989	Meaning	Application
Prohibited Steps and Specific Issue orders	s8 (1)	Orders to *either* forbid a particular course of treatment, *or* to resolve a dispute by ordering that consent to it be given.	*Re C [2000]* An HIV-positive mother had views about the causes and treatment of the disease, which conflicted with medical thinking. She, therefore, refused to allow her child to be tested for HIV, but the court held that the test was clearly in the child's best interests.
Care order	s31	The local authority shares parental responsibility with the parents. The child may be removed from the care of the parents, although the latter can still usually consent	*Lancashire County Council and another v A (a child) [2000]* A, a baby girl, was cared for by a child-minder while her parents were at work. The child subsequently sustained serious non-accidental injuries,

Order	Relevant section of the Children Act 1989	Meaning	Application
		to treatment. Such orders are only made if the child 'is suffering, or likely to suffer, significant harm', and this harm must be attributable to the parents.	and a care order was put in place. The parents contended that such an order only applied if *they* were responsible for the harm; but the court held that the parents' delegation of child-care to another did not absolve them of their responsibilities.
Supervision order	s35	The local authority undertakes a duty to 'advise, assist and befriend the supervised child'; and is empowered to take reasonable steps to ensure that the order is complied with.	*Re O [2001]* A woman with severe mental health problems had 5 children, the first 4 of which had been taken into care. The local authority applied for a care order when the fifth child was born, but the court allowed a supervision order only. The court's reasoning was that the mother's mental health had improved to a large extent, the risk of harm to the child was low, and both parents had been cooperative with the authorities.
Emergency Protection order	s44	The child is taken into care, but only for 8 days (although this can be renewed once for up to 7 days). Before making this order, the court must be satisfied that the child is likely to suffer significant harm if not removed, and that the parents are frustrating access to the child.	*Re O [1993]* A child born prematurely suffered from respiratory distress syndrome and would inevitably need a blood transfusion. The parents, however, were both Jehovah's Witnesses and refused their consent. The magistrates made an Emergency Protection Order, and this decision was upheld by the High Court.

(Continued)

(Continued)

Order	Relevant section of the Children Act 1989	Meaning	Application
Child Assessment order	s43	This order is made when there are suspicions that the child is suffering physical and/or mental harm. It does not remove the child from the home, but empowers the local authority to conduct a detailed examination of the child's circumstances.	*South Glamorgan County Council v W and B [1993]* Three children were in the custody of their father following his divorce from the mother. All 3, however, had psychiatric problems, living as virtual recluses within the home. The youngest (a 15-year-old girl) showed particular problems, refusing to attend school and being verbally abusive. The court, following the advice of a psychiatrist, made a Child Assessment Order, compelling her to be admitted to an adolescent unit for psychiatric examination.
Wardship	s100	The child is placed in the care, or under the supervision, of a local authority, and no important step in the child's life may be taken without the court's permission (e.g. major treatment decisions). This provision was originally in the Family Law Reform Act 1969 (s7), but s100 of the Children Act 1989 places severe restrictions on its use.	*Re L [1990]* A child sustained non-accidental injuries when she was 1 month old, and was taken into care. The local authority decided that the child should not go back to the parents, but the grandparents sought leave to be considered as the long-term carers of the child. The court refused the grandparents' claim, holding that the child's interests were best served by a complete break from this family.

5 AGE-BASED LEGISLATION

The table below owes much to the work of Rogalski (2010) and her predecessors, but has been presented in a slightly different format. It is intended to illustrate how legal responsibility is a developmental concept, rather than an all-or-nothing situation. The age of 18 is clearly a major watershed in the life of an individual, for s/he thereby becomes an adult with all the rights and responsibilities that this entails. However, as can be seen below, legal rights and responsibilities begin at a very early age, and are steadily accumulated throughout childhood.

Box 8.22   At what age can a person...:

Legal right / responsibility	Age	Relevant legislation
1 Enter a bar?	• At any age in the company of a person over the age of 18. Note that the publican reserves the right to exclude those who may cause a disturbance to other customers. • At age 16, can enter a bar alone, but may only buy non-alcoholic drinks.	Licensing Act 2003 (s145)
2 Drink alcohol?	• At age 5 in private. • At age 16, beer, cider or wine may be drunk with a meal, if accompanied by an adult. • At age 18, can buy and drink alcohol; and can apply for a licence to sell alcohol.	Children and Young Persons Act 1933 (s5) Licensing Act 2003 (s149) Licensing Act 2003 (ss146 and 111).
3 Smoke?	At any age; but not allowed to buy them until 18. If caught smoking in a public place when under 16, a police officer is entitled to seize tobacco and cigarette papers (but not pipes or tobacco pouches).	Children and Young Persons Act 1933(s7 [1]), as amended by Children and Young Persons (Sale of Tobacco etc.) Order 2007.
4 Babysit?	At any age, but 16 is frequently recommended as the minimum age.	—

(Continued)

(Continued)

Legal right / responsibility	Age	Relevant legislation
5 Have body piercing?	At any age, although parental consent is usually required.	—
6 Have tattooing?	At age 18.	Tattooing of Minors Act 1969 (s1)
7 Take employment?	• At age 14, part-time 'light work' may be undertaken, providing: a No more than 2 hours are worked on a school day or a Sunday. b No work is done before 7a.m. or after 7p.m.. c No more than 5 hours a day (or 25 hours a week) is worked during the school holidays. • At age 16, can work full-time if left school (as long as it is not in a betting shop or bar). • Above the age of 16, employer must pay the national minimum wage. There are different rates for 16–17-year-olds, 18–20-year-olds, and those aged 21 and over.	Children and Young Persons Act 1933 (s18) Education Act 1996 (s558)
8 Give blood	At age 17, without parental consent, provided that the individual is assessed as competent to make this decision.	Blood Safety and Quality Regulations 2005 (Part 3)
9 Open a bank account?	• At age 7, can open a National Savings Account or TSB account. • At age 10, most banks will permit the opening of an account, although this remains at the discretion of the manager. Note that a person is not liable for his/her debts until 18, and so, it is unlikely that a loan or overdraft will be given. • At age 16, can buy Premium Bonds; and can open an Individual Savings Account (ISA).	National Savings Bank Regulation 1972 (Reg. 6) Minors' Contracts Act 1987 (s1 [6]) Premium Savings Bonds Regulations 1972 (s4) Individual Savings Account Regulations 1998 (s12)

Legal right / responsibility	Age	Relevant legislation
10 Be convicted of a criminal offence?	• At age 10, full criminal responsibility must be accepted. A child cannot be convicted of a crime before this age, but may be placed under the supervision of a social worker or member of the youth offending team.	Crime and Disorder Act 1998 (ss11 and 34)
	• At age 12, a detention and training order may be imposed (for up to 24 months) for offences that would have incurred imprisonment if an adult.	Powers of Criminal Courts (Sentencing) Act 2000 (s100)
	• At age 17, can be sent to a remand centre or prison.	Children and Young Persons Act 1969 (s23)
	• At age 18, criminal charges are dealt with in the adult courts.	Children and Young Persons Act 1933 (s46 [1])
11 Make a will?	At age 18; But can make a will earlier than this if a seaman or serving in the armed forces.	Wills Act 1837 (s7) Wills (Soldiers and Sailors) Act 1918 (s1)
12 Join the armed forces?	At age 16, with parental consent.	–
13 Enter or live in a brothel?	Under the age of 4, above age 16.	Children and Young Persons Act 1933 (s3)
14 Marry?	• At age 16, with parental consent. • A civil partnership may also be registered at 16.	Marriage Act 1949 (s3 [1]) Civil Partnership Act 2004 (s4)
	• Parental consent is no longer required when both parties are 18.	Family Law Reform Act 1969 (s1)
15 Have sexual intercourse?	• At age 16, all sexual activity (heterosexual and homosexual) is permitted, provided that it is mutually consensual and that both partners are 16 or over.	Sexual Offences Act 2003 (ss9 and 13)
	• A teacher or supervisor commits an offence if s/he engages in sexual activity with a pupil or charge before the latter is 18.	

(Continued)

(Continued)

Legal right / responsibility	Age	Relevant legislation
16 Drive?	• At age 16, can hold a licence to drive an invalid carriage or moped. • At age 17, can hold a licence to drive a car, motorcycle, and light van. • At age 18, can apply for an HGV licence, provided a member of the Young Driver's Scheme. Otherwise, minimum age is 21.	Road Traffic Act 1988 (s101)

6 CHILD ABUSE

It is impossible to obtain accurate figures of the prevalence and incidence of child abuse and neglect, because much of this remains hidden and unreported. We know that there are approximately 32,000 children on the child protection register in the UK (NSPCC, 2007), and that in 2007/08, 55 children were killed at the hands of their parents or by someone known to the child (Laming, 2009). These figures compare reasonably well with other developed nations, but they cannot tell the whole story and are therefore lacking in reliability.

The picture becomes even more complicated when attempting to assess the incidence of each particular type of abuse, for children often suffer more than one at a time (Children's Legal Centre, 2006b). Similarly, the concept of 'significant harm', necessitating intervention by the authorities, comes in different forms: for example, it may be a single event (such as a violent assault), or it could be slow and insidious (such as neglect and emotional abuse) (DH, 2010: s1.28). The following table illustrates the categories of abuse and gives a definition of each. There is, of course, no shortage of examples to illustrate these categories, but one is given for each.

Box 8.23 Categories of child abuse

Type of abuse	Definition	Example
1 Physical	This involves the 'hitting, shaking, throwing, poisoning, burning or scalding, drowning,	*R v BS [2010]* A man subjected his children and step-children to numerous

Type of abuse	Definition	Example
	suffocating, or otherwise causing physical harm to a child' (DH, 2010: s1.33).	and savage beatings over a prolonged period of time. On one occasion, he stubbed out a cigarette on a child's arm, and others came close to strangulation. He was sentenced to 9 years' imprisonment.
2 Emotional	This is 'the persistent emotional maltreatment of a child such as to cause severe and persistent adverse effects on the child's emotional development' (DH, 2010: s1.34). It may involve bullying, teasing, or convincing the child that s/he has no value and is unloved; but interestingly, it also applies when parents are over-protective, thereby preventing their children from normal interaction with others.	*Re B (Children) [2008]* A combination of physical and verbal violence towards the children, plus the antagonism between members of the household and with others (i.e. neighbours) effectively meant that the children were constantly in a stressful environment, and were therefore unable to develop emotional stability and maturity. An interim care order was made so that the children could be removed from the home.
3 Sexual	This involves 'forcing or enticing a child or young person to take part in sexual activities, not necessarily involving a high level of violence, whether or not the child is aware of what is happening' (DH, 2010: s1.35). Obviously, this will include rape and oral sex, but will also include kissing and inappropriate touching. In addition, encouraging or forcing children to look at pornography or sexual activities will constitute an abuse.	*R v Townsend-Oldfield [2010]* A woman was convicted of inciting children to engage in sexual activity with her common-law husband; and the man was convicted of indecent assault and unlawful sexual intercourse with a girl under the age of 13. Each was sentenced to 4 years' imprisonment.

(Continued)

(Continued)

Type of abuse	Definition	Example
4 Neglect	This is 'the persistent failure to meet a child's basic physical and/or psychological needs, likely to result in the serious impairment of the child's health or development' (DH, 2010: s1.36). It can include a failure to provide adequate food, clothing or accommodation; and it can involve a failure to seek medical care when needed by the child.	*R v Sutherland [2010]* A 13-month-old boy was found dead in his home. He was covered in faeces, in a state of decomposition, and his skin showed signs of ulceration, inflammation and scabs (including a severe nappy rash). His death was probably as a result of septicaemia; his mother was sentenced to 27 months' imprisonment.

The last of these categories covers a broad range of situations, and some would argue that obesity in children is a form of neglect (Jeffreys, 2007). Clearly, it is not as damaging as starving the child, but the provision of *too much* food exposes him/her to the risks of emotional abuse (feelings of inadequacy and bullying by other children), plus the risks of physical complications in later life (heart disease, hypertension, diabetes, etc.). Education of the parents offers a better alternative to punitive measures, but should children be removed from those homes where the parents are resistant to advice? Opinion is inevitably divided, some taking a much harder line than others. The issue illustrates that there will be occasions when the best interests of the child are not entirely clear-cut, and either position could result in further damage. Moreover, hard-line approaches have a tendency to become progressively more radical with the passage of time, so that the potential remains for asthmatic children to be separated from parents who smoke. Viner et al. (2010) suggest that child protection services should only become involved if parents persistently reject advice, refuse to engage with weight management initiatives, or actively seek to sabotage such initiatives. They also argue that obesity may be symptomatic of deeper underlying problems, such as emotional or even sexual abuse, and that healthcare professionals should be mindful of this.

We have seen that the Children Act 1989 has provisions in place to protect children from abuse; but, as with all such measures, they are only as effective as the people who implement them. The case of Victoria Climbié was a tragic illustration of what can happen when the appropriate services fail to function efficiently.

Box 8.24 Victoria Climbié

Victoria was born in the Ivory Coast. When she was nearly seven, her aunt visited the family and offered to take her back to France so that she could receive a good education. The French authorities soon became concerned about Victoria's absenteeism from school; but, before they could act upon this, the aunt moved Victoria to London. Evidence of verbal and emotional abuse was manifested at this time; but Victoria's problems really began when she and her aunt moved in with the latter's lover. This man clearly resented the presence of Victoria, and his physical abuse of her became ever more apparent. She was admitted to hospital a couple of times, but a doctor failed to recognise the symptoms, and a social worker and police officer both concluded that it was safe for her to be discharged home.

In the remaining seven months of Victoria's life, she was forced to sleep in a bath; she was tied up inside a plastic bag; her hands were tied with masking tape so that she had to eat food like a dog; she was regularly beaten, and her blood was found splattered around the walls of the flat. Upon her final admission to hospital, she was found to be hypothermic (caused by malnutrition, a damp environment and restricted movement) and she had multi-organ failure. When she died, 128 injuries were found on the body by the pathologist at the post-mortem. Both the aunt and her lover were convicted of murder and are currently serving life sentences.

We can be appalled at the mentality of individuals who are prepared to inflict this level of pain and misery upon small children; but the truth is that such people have existed in every generation throughout history. However, an efficient child protection service should have been able to halt the process of abuse long before Victoria's death. Lord Laming's inquiry into this case (DH and Home Office, 2003) noted that there were failures of the system at every level; and that there were at least 12 opportunities to intervene, but not one of them was taken up. The paediatric service in the hospital came in for special criticism, and a recommendation was made to strengthen organisational processes throughout the country.

It was as a result of Lord Laming's inquiry that the Children Act 2004 came into being, and its primary function was to improve and integrate children's services so that all the appropriate agencies and professionals would work together to safeguard children. The key provisions of the Act can be summarised thus:

a   The appointment of a **Children's Commissioner** (sections 1–9), who is required to ensure that children meet the outcomes of the UN Convention on the Rights of the Child 1989 (i.e. protection from harm and neglect; education and training; social and economic well-being; and physical, mental and emotional well-being). He has powers to investigate individual cases, and he produces an annual report to Parliament.

b   Each children's services authority must appoint a **Director of Children's Services** (sections 18–19), who is responsible for local authority education, health and social services provided to children.

c   Children's services authorities must establish **Local Safeguarding Children's Boards** (LSCBs) (sections 13–16), which will coordinate the activities of all agencies involved in child protection.

d   The establishment of a **national database** with information about children (section 12). This should help to ensure that abusive parents do not escape attention of the local authority by moving to another part of the country.

These and other provisions are designed to facilitate a more cohesive partnership between agencies involved in the care of children so that information is shared and communication is enhanced. It is acknowledged that the investigation of suspected child abuse is difficult (Laming, 2009) and that it invites acrimony. Moreover, although Victoria Climbié was a child who should certainly have been taken into care, there are going to be many more cases that are less clear-cut. The Children Act 2004 outlaws punishment of a child that causes bodily harm (section 58), but it stops short of imposing criminal sanctions on parents who smack their children. The UK is one of only five countries within the European Union that have not banned slapping and has been criticised on numerous occasions (Brooks, 2010), but it continues to stand firm on this issue.

Thus, if slapping is allowed, and if the local authority should endeavour to maintain the family unit as much as possible, the work of children's services can be seen as a delicate balancing act. Almost inevitably, there will be occasions when the professionals get it wrong, and the provisions of the Children Act 2004 did nothing to protect 'Baby P'.

Box 8.25   'Baby P'

'Baby P' (subsequently identified as Peter Connolly) lived with his mother, who had separated from the child's father when he was three months old, following affairs with two men. The second of these moved into the house and subsequently engaged in the systematic beating of the child. This abuse was also carried out by the man's brother, who moved into the house for a period of five weeks. When Peter died at the age of 17 months, his body was covered in bruises and scabs, his hair had been shaved to the scalp, and he was discovered to have had eight broken ribs and a broken back.

The full details of this child's abuse are much more distressing than can be recorded here; but, once again, the case illustrated a catalogue of failure by all who came into contact with Peter: the paediatrician who failed to diagnose that he had broken bones; the social worker who accepted the mother's excuses for the child's injuries because she was fully cooperative; and the health visitor who only saw the child four times in six months because the mother kept cancelling appointments (Fresco, 2008). There were others who were implicated, of course, including the team manager, the Director of Children's Services, and Peter's GP. All of them received a variety of sanctions, largely, one suspects, because of the public outrage that followed revelation of the details of the case. It is difficult to sympathise with them, but it is equally difficult to see how these punitive measures will prevent similar cases in the future.

It was with this in mind that Lord Laming sought a more proactive approach (Laming, 2009), and he made six key recommendations. In essence, he argued that 'explicit strategic priorities' should be established for the protection of children; there should be sufficient resources to enable childcare services to function efficiently; there should be enhanced training for all who are in the front line of child protection (most notably, social workers and health visitors); and the time for child protection cases to be heard by the courts should be shortened (from the current average of 45 weeks). In addition, he suggested the establishment of a short-term National Safeguarding Delivery Unit, which would drive these measures forward.

In a time of economic stringencies, demands for increased resources frequently fall upon deaf ears; but Lord Laming's recommendations make it clear that ultimate responsibility for child protection lies with the Government. In other words, in the absence of appropriate resources, it will be more difficult to shift the blame onto the traditional scapegoats when the next 'Baby P' case hits the headlines.

So, as a healthcare professional, what should one do if child abuse is suspected? As a private citizen, there is actually no legal duty to report abuse (Children's Legal Centre, 2006b), although one could argue that there is a moral duty. However, by virtue of one's employment in a health service organisation, there is a legal and contractual obligation to safeguard children. Thus, suspected abuse should be reported to the police, social services or the NSPCC, whereupon an investigation will be conducted. If there is evidence of harm (or the risk of harm), a case conference is arranged. The child will subsequently be put on the 'at risk' register and a child protection plan will be drawn up (which is reviewed every six months until the child becomes 18).

The parents are generally fully involved in this process and are kept informed of the allegations and investigation, unless the suspicion is of sexual abuse (Hope et al., 2008). However, on a paediatric ward, it is seen as good practice to ensure that the child is never left unattended with the parents (Dimond, 2008).

The duties of the healthcare professional are fairly clear, but perhaps the safeguarding of children should be seen as the responsibility of everybody. The NSPCC (2011) cites evidence in support of the contention that child abuse is often linked with cruelty to animals. Veterinary surgeons would be in a position to notice this, even if they did not see the child; and neighbours too could report it. It is not difficult to understand why people should be reluctant to get involved in cases of suspected child abuse, for there are never any winners in these situations. But the cases of Victoria Climbié and Peter Connolly are graphic illustrations of the horrors that can occur when nobody does anything.

7 END OF LIFE DECISIONS PERTAINING TO CHILDREN

End of life decisions will be covered in more detail in Chapter 10, but those pertaining to children have particularly emotive connotations and are probably best dealt with separately here. Most judicial decisions tend to defer to medical opinion even if this is in direct conflict with the views of the parents (or even other healthcare professionals). This is not altogether surprising, but it can lead to controversy, and this controversy is often acrimonious.

An illustration of this comes from one of the earlier cases:

Box 8.26   *R v Arthur [1981]*

A baby was born with Down's syndrome, and his parents considered that it would be better to allow him to die. When he eventually died three days later, his doctor (Dr Arthur) was charged with murder. The prosecution, initiated by the pressure group *Life*, alleged that he ordered that the baby should not be fed or hydrated, and that he even prescribed a drug (DF118) to suppress the child's appetite. It was further alleged, therefore, that the cause of death was starvation, as a direct result of the doctor's orders.

This case ultimately failed on an issue of causation, for it was discovered that the baby had multiple problems, any one of which could have caused his demise. However, there is no evidence that Dr Arthur was aware of these problems when he made the decision to withhold nutrition and hydration (Read and Clements, 2004); and some have suggested that the judge was unable to acknowledge that doctors make errors (Brazier and Cave, 2007). Certainly, the judge sought support for his direction to the jury to acquit Dr Arthur by emphasising that the child had been 'rejected by its parents' (per Farquarson, J.), although he acknowledged that the child must also be 'irreversibly disabled'.

Parental rejection, as a factor in allowing a child to die, was expressly rejected in a case of the same year (*Re B [1981]*). This case has been discussed earlier (Box 8.2), but its importance is that the court made its position on such cases much more clear: disability is not a valid reason for allowing a child to die; parental rejection of the child will not in any way determine the outcome; and the fall-back position of the court is to make judgements to preserve life wherever possible.

This does not mean, of course, that *all* lives should be saved, and the court added some gloss to its position in the following case:

Box 8.27   *Re J [1990]*

A baby was born 13 weeks prematurely, and sustained severe brain damage. His prognosis was that paralysis, blindness and deafness were likely to develop, although he

---

was also expected to live to his teenage years. The hospital (and the child's parents) sought a declaration that it would be lawful to withhold resuscitative measures if the child developed an infection or respiratory problems, and thereby allow him to die.

The court acceded to the hospital's request. Although there was recognition that disability in itself is not sufficient justification for withholding treatment, and that the court's presumption is in favour of life-preserving measures, the best interests of the child must remain paramount. Thus, 'there will be cases in which ... it is not in the interests of the child to subject it to treatment which will cause increased suffering and produce no commensurate benefit' (per Lord Donaldson at 938).

Inevitably, the concept of what constitutes a child's best interests is enormously subjective, and is not often a decision with which the courts are comfortable. In consequence, they must rely upon the testimony of experts, but which ones should they listen to? Consider the following case:

Box 8.28 *An NHS Trust v D [2005]*

D was born with mitochondrial cytopathy – a genetic neurological condition, which caused her to have continuous epileptic seizures. Although her condition stabilised, her doctors believed that she was in a vegetative state and had no prospect of recovery. They asked that they should be allowed to refrain from resuscitative measures if the child developed breathing difficulties, but this action was opposed by the parents.

The court was impressed with the evidence of the two medical experts, both of whom contended that the child had minimal awareness. The child should therefore be allowed to die peacefully, rather than suffer the indignity of futile and invasive resuscitation methods. A range of other healthcare workers (including a nurse, paediatric therapist, speech and language therapist and occupational therapist) all had a different story to tell, however. They had much closer contact with the child than had the doctors, and they all felt that the child was becoming more alert and responsive. All of this evidence was dismissed rather cursorily by the judge, suggesting that the court 'may defer to a particular type of scientific/medical expertise and may discount other, more intuitive or relationship-based evidence' (Morris, 2009: 366).

A similar situation can be found in the case of Charlotte Wyatt:

Box 8.29 *Re Wyatt [2004]*

Charlotte had been born prematurely and had irreparable respiratory and brain damage. She was both blind and deaf, and her doctors considered that her life expectancy was unlikely to be more than a few months. They therefore asked the court for permission to refrain from ventilation if Charlotte stopped breathing, but the parents disagreed.

It will not be a surprise to learn that the court agreed with the doctors; but Charlotte confounded their prognosis by remaining alive. In 2005, therefore, the parents were back in court (*Re Wyatt [2005]*), arguing that her condition had improved some-what: she required less oxygen supplementation and there was evidence that she was able to see and hear (albeit at a rudimentary level). Once again, the court accepted medical evidence that the improvement in her condition was minimal, and so, upheld the original order. This decision was also affirmed by the Court of Appeal later that year (*Portsmouth NHS Trust v Wyatt [2005]*). That the court should pre-fer the testimony of doctors to that of the parents is not difficult to understand; but it seems equally reluctant to hear the views of other healthcare professionals. In the case of Charlotte Wyatt, the people who spent most time with her, and who were in the best position to comment upon her progress, were the nurses; but Brazier (2005) notes that their voices 'are barely heard in the courtroom drama' (p. 416). More than eight years after her birth, Charlotte remains alive and continues to make progress (albeit slowly).

Despite the foregoing, there have been instances when the courts have rejected medical requests to withhold treatment. One such case was *An NHS Trust v B [2006]*, where a child was diagnosed with spinal muscular atrophy. By the time the case came before the court, the child had only minimal movement, he was being fed via a gastrostomy tube, and he required artificial ventilation. He did not, however, appear to have lost cognitive function and he was able to register pleasure. This was sufficient for the court to hold that it was in his best interests to continue with ven-tilation, even though all his doctors favoured withdrawal.

Moreover, the concept of untrammelled medical authority to decide the fate of a sick child had already been dealt a death blow by the European Court of Human Rights in the following case:

Box 8.30   *Glass v United Kingdom [2004]*

A child, aged 12, had been born with cerebral palsy, hydrocephalus and epilepsy. Following a tonsillectomy, he developed post-operative infections and his doctors thought that he was dying. They therefore commenced a Diamorphine infusion, con-trary to the wishes of the parents. After some violent exchanges between the medical team and the family, the child was removed from the hospital, and the parents sought judicial review of the Trust's decision not to treat their child.

This action was rejected by both the High Court and the Court of Appeal, but the European Court held that the doctors were under an obligation to seek parental con-sent for treatment or withdrawal of treatment. Failure to do this would put them in breach of Article 8 of the European Convention on the Protection of Human Rights and Fundamental Freedoms 1950 (respect for private life). Note that the court is not saying that parental views should determine the outcome, but simply that they should be taken into consideration. Where there is disagreement between doctors and parents, the court should be the final arbiter (unless treatment is urgent). The fact that the child was still alive several years after the incident suggests that parental opinion can sometimes be of more value than medical judgement (Pattinson, 2009).

Parental disagreement with medical opinion was a key feature of the final case to be considered in this section:

Box 8.31   *Re A [2000]*

Conjoined twin girls (Jodie and Mary) were born of Maltese parents, who travelled to England to receive specialist treatment. It quickly became clear that, if the twins were separated, Mary would inevitably die, because she was dependent upon Jodie for a blood supply. If they were *not* separated, however, both children would die within a comparatively short time period. The parents opposed the surgery on religious grounds (both being devout Roman Catholics), but the hospital initiated court proceedings. The High Court and the Court of Appeal both found for the Trust: the operation was performed and Mary died.

Not surprisingly, this case excited (and continues to excite) enormous controversy. Was the death of Mary a homicide, or was it an unfortunate (although foreseen) side-effect of the surgery (Uniacke, 2001)? Did Jodie's interests outweigh those of her sister, and, if so, why? The judgment in the Court of Appeal is lengthy and detailed, and this tells us two things. First, the court acknowledged that this was a terribly difficult decision to make, but that the responsibility lay with them to make it. Second, they endeavoured to explore all possible avenues before arriving at a considered judgment. Both of these factors are to be applauded, but it does not automatically imply that they arrived at the right decision.

The three judges in the Court of Appeal arrived at their decision by different means, each one of which has been criticised. Brooke, L.J., for example, invoked the principle of necessity, i.e. it was necessary to terminate one life in order to save another. Ward, L.J. went one step further, arguing that Jodie had a right to defend herself, even if this meant the death of her sister. Finally, Walker, L.J. contended that Mary's death resulted from her own inability to sustain life independently of Jodie.

We can adopt a Utilitarian position and argue that the saving of one life is preferable to the death of two. Alternatively, we might prefer a Deontological position, which would hold that the intentional termination of a life (however well-meaning) is intrinsically wrong. At no point, however, were parental wishes allowed to influence the outcome, and this has come in for criticism (Hewson, 2001). We have seen that medical opinion commonly prevails in end of life decisions, but this case was different from the rest. The issues were so finely balanced, incorporating both legal and ethical considerations in equal measure, that this case moved away from a discussion of purely clinical matters. In such circumstances, there is no reason to suppose that medical opinion should carry any more weight than anybody else's. Hewson (2001), rather unhelpfully, suggests that the Court of Appeal should have refused to hear the case, because it was more of an ethical debate than a legal one. Clearly, though, somebody had to make the decision, and the courts remain the best option that we have. Nevertheless, in making this judgment, it could be argued that the court has confused the law regarding murder, thereby stirring up problems for the future (McEwan, 2001).

REFERENCES

TEXTS

Alderson, P. (1993) *Children's Consent to Surgery*. Buckingham: Open University Press.

Alderson, P. (2000) 'The rise and fall of children's consent to surgery', *Paediatric Nursing*, 12 (2), March: 6–8.

Bijsterveld, P. (2000) 'Competent to refuse?' *Paediatric Nursing*, 12 (6), July: 33–5.

Birchley, G. (2010) 'What limits, if any, should be placed on a parent's right to consent and/ or refuse to consent to medical treatment for their child?' *Nursing Philosophy*, 11 (4), October: 280–5.

Blackstone, W. (1765) *Commentaries on the Laws of England*. Oxford: Clarendon Press.

Boggan, S. (1993) 'The girl that nobody saved', *The Independent*, Monday 6 December. Available from: nobody-saved-1465753.html.

Brahams, D. (1993) 'Religious objection versus parental duty', *Lancet*, 342 (8881): 1189.

Brandes, J.R. (2000) 'Child custody: history, definitions, New York law', *New York Law Journal* (November 28). Available from: www.brandeslaw.com/child_custody/child_custody_art.htm.

Brazier, M. (2005) 'An intractable dispute: when parents and professionals disagree', *Medical Law Review*, 13, Autumn: Commentary, 412–18.

Brazier, M. and Bridge, C. (1996) 'Coercion or caring: analysing adolescent autonomy', *Legal Studies*, 16: 84–109.

Brazier, M. and Cave, E. (2007) *Medicine, Patients and the Law*. London: Penguin Books.

Bridgeman, J. (2006) 'Young people and sexual health: Whose rights? Whose responsibilities?', *Medical Law Review*, 14, Autumn: 418–24.

British Medical Association (2007) *The Law and Ethics of Male Circumcision – Guidance for Doctors*. London: BMA, November..

Brook, G. (2000) 'Children's competency to consent', *Paediatric Nursing*, 12, No. 5, June: 31–5.

Brooks, L. (2010) 'Smacking is an assault on children', *The Guardian*, April 30.

Children's Legal Centre (2006a) *Parental responsibility*. Available from: www.childrenslegal centre.com/.

Children's Legal Centre (2006b) *Child protection*. Available from: www.childrenslegalcentre.com/.

De Bruxelles, S. (2008) 'Dying girl Hannah Jones wins fight to turn down transplant', *The Times*, November 11. Available from: www.timesonline.co.uk/tol/life_and_style/health/article5127163.ece.

Deer, B. (1988) 'Why we must now start listening to the children', *The Sunday Times*, July 10. Available from: http: //briandeer.com/social/cleveland-child.htm.

Department of Health (2010) *Working Together to Safeguard Children: A Guide to Inter-agency Working to Safeguard and Promote the Welfare of Children*. London: Department of Health (March).

Department of Health and the Home Office (2003) *The Victoria Climbié Inquiry: Report of an Inquiry by Lord Laming*. London: HMSO (Cmnd. 5730), January.

Dimond, B. (2011) *Legal Aspects of Nursing*, 6th edn. Harlow: Pearson Education..

Fox, M. and McHale, J. (1997) 'In whose best interests?', *Modern Law Review*, 60, 5, September: 700–9.

Fresco, A. (2008) 'After 17 months of unimaginable cruelty, Baby P finally succumbed', *The Times*, November 12.

General Medical Council (2007) *0-18 Years: Guidance For All Doctors*. London: General Medical Council.

General Medical Council (2008) *Personal Beliefs and Medical Practice*. London: General Medical Council.

Gibb, F. (2007) Should the Court of Appeal allow Katie Thorpe's womb to be removed? *Times Online*, October 18. Available from: http://business.timesonline.co.uk/tol/business/law/columnists/article2685 361.ece.

Grubb, A. (1999) 'Refusal of treatment (child): competence', *Medical Law Review*, 7, Spring: Commentary, 58–61.

Grubb, A. (2003) 'Assisted conception: parentage and treatment "together"', *Medical Law Review*, 11 (1): Spring, Commentary, 128–31.

Herring, J. (2010) *Medical Law and Ethics*, 3rd edn. Oxford: Oxford University Press.

Hewson, B. (2001) 'Killing off Mary: was the Court of Appeal right?', *Medical Law Review*, 9, Autumn: 281–98.

Hope, T., Savulescu, J. and Hendrick, J. (2008) *Medical Ethics and Law: The Core Curriculum*, 2nd edn. London: Churchill Livingstone Elsevier.

Huahima (2009) Mysteries and questions surrounding the Katie Thorpe case. Available from: http://huahima.wordpress.com/2009/04/20/mysteries-and-questions-surrounding-the-katie-thorpe-case/.

Jackson, E. (2010) *Medical law: Text, Cases, and Materials*, 2nd edn. Oxford: Oxford University Press.

Jeffreys, B. (2007) Child obesity 'a form of neglect'. Available from: http://news.bbc.co.uk/1/hi/health/6749037.stm.

Kemp, E.C., Floyd, M.R., McCord-Duncan, E. and Lang, F. (2008) 'Patients prefer the method of "Tell back-collaborative inquiry" to assess understanding of medical information', *Journal of the American Board of Family Medicine*, 21 (1), Jan.–Feb., 24–30.

Laming, Lord (2009) *The Protection of Children in England: A Progress Report*. London: HMSO (12 March).

Mason, J.K. and Laurie, G.T. (2011) *Mason and McCall Smith's Law and Medical Ethics*, 8th edn. Oxford: Oxford University Press.

McEwan, J. (2001) 'Murder by design: the "feel-good factor" and the criminal law', *Medical Law Review*, 9, Autumn: 246–58.

Montgomery, J. (2003) *Health Care Law,* 2nd edn. Oxford: Oxford University Press.

Morris, A. (2009) 'Selective treatment of irreversibly impaired infants: decision-making at the threshold', *Medical Law Review*, 17, Autumn: 347–76.

National Institute of Neurological Disorders and Stroke (2008) *NINDS Sotos syndrome information page*. Available from: www.ninds.nih.gov/disorders/sotos/sotos.htm.

National Society for the Prevention of Cruelty to Children (2007) *Prevalence and Incidence of Child Abuse and Neglect*. Available from: www.nspcc.org.uk/.

National Society for the Prevention of Cruelty to Children (2011) *Understanding the Links: Child Abuse, Animal Abuse and Domestic Violence* (16 January). Available from: www.nspcc.org/inform/research/findings/understandingthelinks_wda48278.html.

Pattinson, S.D. (2009) *Medical Law and Ethics*, 2nd edn. London: Sweet Maxwell.

Read, J. and Clements, L. (2004) 'Demonstrably awful: the right to life and the selective non-treatment of disabled babies and young children', *Journal of Law and Society*, 31 (4), December: 482–509.

Roberts, L. (2010) 'Teenage Jehovah's Witness refuses blood transfusion and dies', *Daily Telegraph*, 18 May. Available from: www.telegraph.co.uk/health/healthnews/7734480/Teenage-Jehovas-Witness-refuses-blood-transfusion-and-dies.html.

Rogalski, H. (2010) *At What Age Can I...?: A Guide to Age-based Legislation*. Colchester: Children's Legal Centre.

The 'Ashley Treatment': towards a better quality of life for 'pillow angels' (2007). Available from: http:ashleytreatment.spaces.live.com/Blog/cns!E25811FDOAF7C!1837.entry.

Uniacke, S. (2001) 'Was Mary's death murder?', *Medical Law Review*, 9, Autumn: 208–20.

Viner, R.M., Roche, E., Maguire, S.A. and Nicholls, D.E. (2010) 'Childhood protection and obesity: framework for practice', *British Medical Journal*, 341, c3074.

Weaver, M. (2009) 'Right-to-die teenager Hannah Jones changes mind about heart transplant', *The Guardian*, 21 July. Available from: www.guardian.co.uk/uk/2009/jul/21/hannah-jones-heart-transplant.

CASES

A (children) (conjoined twins), Re [2000] 4 All ER 961.

B (a minor) (wardship: medical treatment), Re [1981] 1 WLR 1421 (CA).

B (a minor) (wardship: sterilisation), Re [1987] 2 All ER 206 (HL).

B (a child) (immunisation), Re [2003] EWCA Civ. 1148

B (children), Re [2008] UKHL 35.

B v B (a minor) (Residence Order) [1992] 2FLR 327.

C (a child) (HIV Test), Re [2000] Fam. 48.

C (welfare of child: immunisation), Re [2003] EWCA Civ. 1148.

D (a minor) (wardship: sterilisation), Re [1976] 1 All ER 326.

E (a minor: wardship: medical treatment), Re [1993] 1 FLR 386.

F (a minor) (blood tests: parental rights), Re [1993] 3 All ER 596.

G (children) (residence: same sex partner), Re [2006] UKHL 43.

GB v RJB and GLB (In Re B (a child)) [2009] UKSC 5.

Gillick v West Norfolk and Wisbech Area Health Authority [1985] 3 All ER 402 (HL).

Glass v United Kingdom [2004] 1 FLR 1019, ECtHR.

H (a minor) (blood tests: parental rights), Re [1996] 4 All ER 28.

H (parental responsibility), Re [1998] 1 FLR 855.

J (a minor) (wardship: medical treatment), Re [1990] 3 All ER 930 (CA).

J (child's religious upbringing and circumcision), Re [2000] 1 FCR 307.

L (a minor) (wardship: jurisdiction), Re [1990] 1 FCR 509.

L (medical treatment: Gillick competence), Re [1998] 2 FLR 810.

Lancashire County Council and another v A (a child) [2000] 2 All ER 97.

M (child: refusal of medical treatment), Re [1999] 2 FLR 1097.

NHS Trust v A (a child) and others [2008] 1 FLR 70.

NHS Trust v B and others [2006] EWHC 507 (Fam.).

NHS Trust v D and others [2005] EWHC 2439 (Fam.).

O (a minor) (medical treatment), Re [1993] 2 FLR 149.

O (a child) (supervision order: future harm), Re [2001] 1 FCR 289.

P (parental responsibility), Re [1998] 2 FLR 96.

P (medical treatment: best interests), Re [2003] EWHC 2327 (Fam.).

Portsmouth NHS Trust v Wyatt [2005] 1 WLR 3995.

Prince v Massachussets [1944] 321 US 158.

R (a minor) (wardship: consent to treatment), Re [1992] Fam. 11 CA.

R (a child) (IVF: paternity of a child), Re [2005] 2 AC 621 (HL).
R (on the application of Axon) v Secretary of State for Health and another [2006] EWHC 37.
R v Arthur [1981] 12 BMLR 1.
R v BS [2010] EWCA Crim. 2691.
R v D [1984] AC 778.
R v Harris and Harris [1993] Times News Report, 29 October.
R v Senior [1899] 1 QB 283.
R v Sutherland [2010] EWCA Crim. 1855.
R v Townsend-Oldfield [2010] EWCA Crim. 2451.
S (a minor) (consent to medical treatment), Re [1994] 2 FLR 1065.
South Glamorgan County Council v W and B [1993] 1 FLR 574.
T (a minor) (wardship: medical treatment), Re [1997] 1 All ER 906 (CA).
W (a minor) (Residence Order), Re [1992] The Times, 22 May.
W (a minor) (medical treatment), Re [1993] Fam. 64.
Wyatt (a child) (medical treatment: parent's consent), Re [2004] EWHC 2247.
Wyatt (a child) (medical treatment: continuation of order), Re [2005] EWHC 693 (Fam.).
The Leeds Teaching Hospitals NHS Trust v Mr. A, Mrs. A and others [2003] EWHC 259 (QB).

LEGISLATION

Adoption and Children Act 2002
Blood Safety and Quality Regulations 2005
Children Act 1989
Children Act 2004
Children and Young Persons Act 1933
Children and Young Persons Act 1969
Children and Young Persons (Sale of Tobacco etc.) Order 2007
Civil Partnership Act 2004
Crime and Disorder Act 1998
Custody of Infants Act 1839
Education Act 1996
European Convention on the Protection of Human Rights and Fundamental Freedoms 1950
Family Law Reform Act 1969
Family Law Reform Act 1987
Female Genital Mutilation Act 2003
Human Fertilisation and Embryology Act 1990
Individual Savings Account Regulations 1998
Infant Custody Act 1873
Licensing Act 2003
Marriage Act 1949
Matrimonial Causes Act 1857
Mental Capacity Act 2005
Mental Health Act 1983
Minors' Contracts Act 1987
National Savings Bank Regulation 1972
Powers of Criminal Courts (Sentencing) Act 2000
Premium Savings Bonds Regulations 1972
Road Traffic Act 1988
Sexual Offences Act 1956

Sexual Offences Act 2003
Tattooing of Minors Act 1969
The Age of Legal Capacity (Scotland) Act 1991
United Nations Convention on the Rights of the Child 1989
Wills Act 1837
Wills (Soldiers and Sailors) Act 1918

Scenarios (answers at back of book)

1 James is a 10-year-old boy, who was born with cerebral palsy and who is profoundly disabled. His limbs are severely contracted and he is unable to change position by himself. In addition, he is unable to swallow without choking, and so, is currently being fed via a percutaneous endoscopic gastrostomy (PEG) tube. His parents love him dearly and have never considered putting him into care, but they are finding it increasingly difficult to move James as he begins to grow bigger. They have there-fore reduced the volume of the feeds so that James remains at a weight that enables him to be moved easily. They maintain that this also ensures that he can be lifted into a car and taken on trips with the rest of the family.

Consider the legal and ethical implications of this situation.

2 A young married couple have a 13-month-old son. Both parents, however, are of low intelligence, and neither of them are employed. They live in deprived conditions and have very little money, but have demonstrated love for their child. The child subse-quently becomes ill and refuses to take food, but the parents believe that this is sim-ply a minor and temporary disturbance which will eventually cure itself. Moreover, they are reluctant to call the doctor, because Social Services have intimated that they might take the child into care if they are concerned for his safety. Two weeks later, the child is found dead in his cot, and malnutrition is diagnosed as the primary cause.

Consider the legal liability of the parents, and the responsibilities of the support services in this scenario.
[For some assistance with this question, look at R v Sheppard [1980] 3 All ER 899 (HL) and R v Lowe [1973] 1 All ER 805 (CA).]

3 Julie is a 14-year-old girl who attends the GP surgery requesting the contraceptive pill. She is seen by a Nurse Practitioner who specialises in sexual health, but is accompa-nied by a man who states that he is her stepfather. She claims that she is not sexually active, but suffers from painful dysmenorrhoea and believes that the pill will help. The nurse asks the stepfather to leave the room so that she can talk to Julie alone, but he insists on staying because he wants to be able to report accurate information back to the girl's mother. Moreover, Julie herself makes it clear that she wants him to stay, and appears to be somewhat in awe of him. She is reluctant to speak, and appears content for the stepfather to answer most of the questions.

What are the legal and ethical implications of this scenario, and how should it be handled?

9

PROFESSIONAL CONDUCT

Learning Objectives

At the end of this chapter, the reader will:

1 Have an understanding of professional Codes of Conduct, and of the expectations demanded of healthcare practitioners.

2 Be aware of the process of investigation following allegations of professional misconduct, and of the sanctions available to the professional bodies.

3 Acknowledge the key areas of misconduct that come before the Professional Conduct Committees, and how the Committees deal with them.

4 Be able to identify some of the underlying reasons for errors within healthcare, and consider ways in which they can be minimised.

5 Have an understanding of the concept of Whistleblowing, and of the Public Interest Disclosure Act 1998.

1 INTRODUCTION

Oscar Wilde once defined Experience as 'the name men give to their mistakes'. While this has a strong ring of truth to it, it is also possible to learn from the mistakes of others, and this is one of the main purposes of this chapter. It begins with a broad exposition of the conduct that the professional bodies *expect* of their practitioners, and moves on to examine how they deal with allegations of misconduct. Having outlined a few key statistics, the discussion will then analyse a variety of scenarios to illustrate salient learning points. The chapter concludes by discussing the nature of errors and misconduct (i.e. how do they occur, and what can be done to prevent them?), and the concept of whistleblowing.

2 THE PROFESSIONAL CODES

For *nursing*, the Code of Conduct (NMC, 2008) represents an extended statement of the accountability of registered practitioners, and its key provisions can be summarised thus:

Box 9.1   NMC Code of Conduct

As a registered nurse, midwife or health visitor, you must:

- Respect the patient or client as an individual.
- Obtain consent before you give any treatment or care.
- Cooperate with others in the team.
- Protect confidential information.
- Maintain your professional knowledge and competence.
- Be trustworthy.
- Act to identify and minimise the risk to patients and clients.

Note the use of the word 'must' in the opening line. A simple substitution of this word with 'should' would have created a basis for negotiation and compromise, which the NMC was determined to avoid. Thus, it follows that any registered nurse who fails to uphold any one or more of these principles will be in breach of the Code of Conduct and will subsequently be subject to disciplinary action by the professional body.

Within *medicine*, guidance on appropriate conduct is contained in the booklet *Good Medical Practice* (GMC, 2006). As one might expect, it covers much the same ground as outlined above, although it is more detailed in some areas and endeavours to be specific to medicine where possible. Indeed, all the healthcare professions (pharmacy, dentistry, physiotherapy, etc.) will embrace these principles, which are at the heart of ethical practice; and there is an argument for producing a standard Code to cover all practitioners. That this has not happened may be a feature of the tribalism that exists between professions; but it is of importance to note that each of these Codes imposes a higher standard upon practitioners than the law actually demands (Montgomery, 2003). This is particularly true of Consent, where the GMC acknowledged the necessity for involvement of the patient in decision-making and the provision of full and accurate information several years before the courts arrived at this conclusion (see *Chester v Afshar [2004]*, discussed in Chapter 4).

Despite this, the Codes have not been without their critics. Pattison and Wainwright (2010), for example, see the NMC Code more as a weapon with which to beat nurses, 'rather than as a means of valuing or nurturing ethical development in practitioners' (p. 16). They cite the fact that *individual* accountability is emphasised, even though modern wisdom states that errors and misconduct generally occur because of *systems* failures (Reason, 1990; Merry and McCall Smith, 2001). Moreover, a truly ethical Code would demand more of its practitioners than merely 'reporting concerns' to a higher authority when unsafe practice is identified. Certainly, the example of Graham Pink (see later) would suggest that the NMC is reluctant to support those who press these concerns when they have not been acted upon.

Notwithstanding these criticisms, though, the Codes represent best available guidance for practitioners upon what is expected of them as a bare minimum. Moreover, it is important to note that they are not cast in stone: the NMC Code, for example, has undergone numerous revisions since its introduction in 1983, and will no doubt be altered again in years to come. None of the Codes have any legal authority, but they have strongly persuasive powers in a court. In other words, when a judge is called upon to determine whether or not a healthcare professional has been guilty of malpractice, s/he will look at the appropriate Code to identify what constitutes acceptable conduct. With this in mind, it becomes clear that the Codes are more than statements of principles; they are also a force for change, development and improvement of care.

3 THE INVESTIGATIVE PROCESS

Each of the professional bodies has its own structure and process for investigating allegations of misconduct, and these can be seen on the following websites:

Box 9.2 Websites of the professional bodies

- Medicine: www.gmc-uk.org/
- Nursing: www.nmc-uk.org/
- Dentistry: www.gdc-uk.org/
- Health and Care Professions Council (which includes physiotherapists, occupational therapists, paramedics, and 12 other allied health professions): www.hpc-uk.org/
- Pharmacy: www.pharmacyregulation.org/

There are minor differences in each, but there is also considerable overlap. With this in mind, what follows is a composite structure and process, which embraces the key features of each.

A AREAS OF REVIEW

Fundamentally, there are four main areas that the professional bodies will review:

1   Misconduct: this is loosely defined as behaviour which falls short of what can reasonably be expected of a healthcare professional. As mentioned above, the 'reasonable expectation' is that the practitioner will conform to the principles outlined in the Codes or professional guidance; but this does not mean that all instances of misconduct will find themselves being referred to the professional bodies. These bodies will expect employers to deal with minor offences, and are therefore only concerned with those cases where public safety is at risk (Griffith and Tengnah, 2010). The misconduct that subsequently finds its way to the Professional Conduct Committees is either a single very serious offence, or (more likely) is a series of misdemeanours which call into question the practitioner's ability to ensure a safe environment for patients.

2   Lack of competence: this relates to those areas where a practitioner is considered unfit to practise by virtue of a lack of knowledge, skill or judgement. Almost inevitably, this vague description is capable of a variety of interpretations, and the Fifth Report of the Shipman Inquiry (2004) criticised the apparent arbitrariness of this provision. Equally, however, those accused of incompetence can often point to failings within the system: i.e. lack of suitable educational opportunities, lack of ongoing support and supervision, etc. Where a practitioner's competence is called into question, the professional bodies would (at the very least) expect the employer to take corrective action in the first instance (i.e. re-training and/or conditions imposed upon practice). The concern of the professional bodies, therefore, tends to be reserved for those who continue to make mistakes after extensive support and who lack insight into their failings. Every generation of professionals will undoubtedly come across a 'rogue practitioner': an individual who lacks any semblance of self-awareness, and who has no understanding of his/her limitations (despite mounting evidence that they exist). Such individuals are dangerous and must be stopped if patient care is not to be endangered.

3   Character issues: these cases concern aspects of the practitioner's character, which call into question his/her suitability to be a healthcare professional. Cases of this nature coming before the Professional Conduct Committees almost inevitably involve some form of criminal behaviour, but it is important to note that it does not have to be directly related to one's employment. In other words, the healthcare professional is expected to behave like a model citizen both inside and outside of work. There are a few cases discussed later which illustrate this principle; but suffice it to say at this stage that the police will automatically report *all* criminal offences to the practitioner's respective professional body.

4   Serious ill health: this relates to long-term, untreated or unacknowledged physical or mental health conditions. Although the professional bodies tend to deal with such matters in a more sympathetic manner, their primary concern will always be the safety of the patients. In other words, if a practitioner's health is having an adverse impact upon his/her ability to function safely, restrictions will need to be placed upon his/her practice.

B STRUCTURE

The diagram below is a very simplified depiction of the structure of the professional bodies:

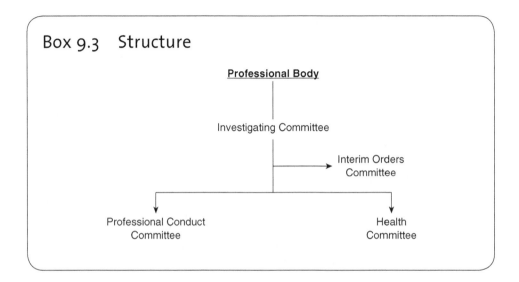

Box 9.3   Structure

As mentioned earlier, there are a number of differences between the professional bodies. For example, a Professional Performance Committee is to be found in the General Medical Council and General Dental Council, but *not* in the Nursing and Midwifery Council or Health and Care Professions Council. Moreover, the NMC has a separate Midwifery Committee, while the GMC adds one or two other layers to this structure. Nevertheless, for all practical purposes, the diagram in Box 9.3 identifies the key committees tasked with the investigation and judgement of allegations of professional misconduct.

When an allegation of misconduct is made to the professional body, the case is first considered by two *screeners*, one of whom will be a registrant of the respective body, and the other a lay person. The fundamental purpose of this stage is to determine whether or not there is a case to answer, and it thereby serves as a filter mechanism. In practice, a significant number of cases will not proceed beyond this point, either because there is no evidence of guilt or because the offence is considered too trivial to go any further.

Those cases considered worthy of further attention are passed on to the *Investigating Committee* (known, in the General Medical Council, as the Preliminary Proceedings Committee). If the purpose of the screener is to establish whether or not there is a case to answer, the Investigating Committee is there to decide whether or not the case is serious enough to be referred to the Professional Conduct Committee (or Health Committee). This distinction is admittedly a subtle one, and de Prez (2002) contends that the purpose of the system is to give the practitioner 'two chances to escape the full hearing' (p. 40). This may, however, be more for the benefit of the system than for the individual practitioner, since it has difficulty in coping with the current workload. Therefore, the fewer cases that reach the third stage, the more likely they are to be dealt with in a timely fashion. Thus, of the 4,211 cases reported to the Nursing and Midwifery Council in 2010–11 (NMC, 2011), only 647 found their way to the Professional Conduct Committee and 38 to the Health Committee. Similarly, of the 5,773 cases reported to the General Medical Council in 2009 (GMC, 2010), only 270 were heard by the Professional Conduct Committee. If the case is serious enough, it will be referred to the Interim Orders Committee, which has the power to suspend the practitioner immediately until the case is heard by the Professional Conduct Committee.

The final stage, of course, is the *Professional Conduct Committee* (or Health Committee). The hearing proceeds in much the same way as a court case, where evidence for both the prosecution and defence are heard by a panel of registrants and lay people. The defendant (but not the complainant) has the right to legal representation, and the sanctions available to the panel are considered below. In determining whether or not misconduct has been established, the professional bodies are now constrained to employ the *civil* standard of proof (i.e. the practitioner must be guilty 'on the balance of probabilities'). Formerly, the *criminal* standard had been used (i.e. guilt 'beyond reasonable doubt'), but the Ritchie Inquiry (DH, 2000a) into the case of Dr Rodney Ledward had recommended that this should be altered. Briefly, Dr Ledward was a gynaecologist who was allowed to continue practising for several years, despite the fact that he caused untold damage to numerous women. The Inquiry identified several failings of the system, some of which will be covered later. Its recommendation to alter the standard of proof, though, was not adopted by the Nursing and Midwifery Council, who concluded that the criminal standard should be retained. Ultimately, however, the matter was taken out of their hands by the Health and Social Care Act 2008 (s112, adding s60A to the Health Act 1999), which enforced all professional bodies within the NHS to adopt the civil standard. The effect of this change is that it has now become much easier to establish guilt of the accused.

C SANCTIONS

There are a range of options available to the Professional Conduct Committee, one of which is to exonerate the accused completely. In practice, however, this is comparatively uncommon, largely because the filtering process tends to prevent such cases coming before the panel. The sanctions can therefore be summarised in ascending order of severity.

1   Caution: essentially, this is a reprimand following a finding of guilt, and a warning that the behaviour cannot be tolerated. Future incidents of misconduct are therefore likely to be dealt with much more severely. The caution does not affect the healthcare professional's practice, but it remains against his/her name on the register for anything from one to five years.

2 Conditions of Practice Order: this enables the healthcare professional to continue to practise, but with the imposition of limitations to that work. Thus, examples might include
the suspension of prescribing rights for doctors or an order preventing a nurse from
administering drugs. Such orders can remain for anything up to three years, during which
time the registrant would be expected to engage in further training to ensure that s/he
can resume full duties safely.

3 Interim Suspension Order: we have already mentioned that this order is imposed if a
registrant has been accused of a serious offence, and s/he poses a threat to patient
safety. In itself, it is not a finding of guilt, for only the Professional Conduct Committee
can make this judgement after a full hearing, but it ensures that the registrant is removed
from practice while the case is being investigated. Such orders are also employed when a
registrant has been accused of a serious criminal offence and is awaiting trial. The
Professional Conduct Committee will not consider the offence until after the court hearing, and this may take some time. An Interim Suspension Order should not, though, be in
place for longer than 18 months.

4 Suspension: as above, this has the effect of removing a healthcare professional temporarily from the register, and can remain in place for up to one year. However, while the registrant remains on full pay following an Interim Suspension Order, a suspension imposed
by the Professional Conduct Committee carries no such luxury, and thereby represents a
loss of livelihood to the practitioner. When reviewing the suspension at the end of its
term, the panel will need to be convinced that the registrant has sought to address the
failings which brought him/her to them in the first place. Failure to provide evidence of
this may result in the ultimate sanction.

5 Removal from the register: variously known as 'striking off' or 'erasure', this sanction
ensures that the accused is no longer able to practise as a healthcare professional. It
does not, of itself, prevent the individual from obtaining employment as a Healthcare
Assistant (or any other health-related occupation that is not tied to a professional body),
and the anomaly that this produces has not gone unnoticed (Griffiths and Robinson,
2010; Nursing Times.net, 2011). Moreover, it is not necessarily a permanent sanction, for
an individual may apply for restoration to the register after a period of five years. As
before, the panel will need to be assured that restoration does not pose a risk to patient
safety, and they can specify a variety of conditions that must be met (e.g. further training, counselling, etc.).

The Health Committee has much the same powers, although removal from the
register may be considered unreasonable and inappropriate in most circumstances
(Pattinson, 2009). It remains an option if the healthcare professional refuses help
and/or patient safety continues to be at risk; but a more likely scenario is that s/he
will be suspended indefinitely, and the practitioner can apply to have this reviewed
every two years.

Despite the powers that Professional Conduct Committees wield, they do not necessarily represent the final arbiter in cases of misconduct, for the registrant can appeal
against the decision to the High Court. It should be noted, however, that the chances
of success are limited, for the courts are very reluctant to interfere with the decisions
of the professional bodies. As Buckley, J. stated (in *R v The Professional Conduct
Committee of the UKCC, ex parte Wood and Thompson [1993]*): 'the members of

such tribunals will be chosen for their knowledge and experience ... Thus, their decisions are not to be taken lightly'.

Notwithstanding this, there are examples of Professional Conduct Committee decisions being overturned, particularly if there have been procedural irregularities or the sanction is perceived as being especially harsh. An instance from nursing can be seen in the following scenario:

Box 9.4   *Hefferon v UKCC [1998]*

A school nurse mistakenly gave a vaccination to a child who was not due for it. She did not inform her manager, but reported the incident to the doctor. The child was examined by the doctor, and it was clear that no harm had been done. Upon discovering this error, the nurse's manager reported her to the professional body, who determined that this was serious professional misconduct, and she was struck off the register. On appeal, however, the High Court quashed the decision of the Professional Conduct Committee, holding that the disciplinary process had been unjust. For example, she had not been allowed to present her case or challenge the evidence against her. Moreover, although she failed to report the error to her line manager, there was no stated written procedure requiring her to do so.

Similarly, in *Dad v General Dental Council [2000]*, the Professional Conduct Committee's decision to suspend a dentist for 12 months for driving whilst disqualified was held to be 'wrong and unjustified' (per Lord Hope). The fact that this same dentist was later removed from the register having been convicted of fraud and dishonesty (*Dad v General Dental Council [2010]*) might suggest that the panels are better judges of character than they have been given credit for: certainly, the court was not prepared to uphold the second appeal.

There are examples from medicine too, and some of these will be discussed later. Generally, though, the courts will endorse decisions of the Professional Conduct Committees, even when these seem unnecessarily severe to the casual observer. A good illustration of this can be seen in the following case:

Box 9.5   *Finegan v General Medical Council [1987]*

A GP prescribed large quantities of Controlled Drugs to his wife when she turned to him for help following the loss of a child, and the breakdown of trust in her relationship with her own doctor. The Professional Conduct Committee imposed a Conditions of Practice Order upon him, forbidding him from prescribing *any* drug to *any* patient. The High Court subsequently rejected the doctor's appeal against this decision.

For a GP, the withdrawal of prescribing rights represents an intolerable (and largely impractical) restriction of practice. Technically, he was not breaking the law by prescribing for his own wife, although it is considered poor practice by the profession (GMC, 2008: para. 4): it is, for example, open to abuse and the practitioner will find it difficult to maintain a professional and objective perspective. Nevertheless, the penalty seems wildly disproportionate to the offence: he represented a danger to only one person (his wife), and preventing him from prescribing for her would automatically have removed this risk.

Cases such as *Finegan* suggest that there is more at play than protection of the public. De Prez (2002) argues that sanctions imposed by the professional bodies are becoming tougher in order to appease critics and thereby stave off the threat of deregulation. Certainly, there was evidence to support this idea in *Roylance v General Medical Council (No. 2) [2000]*, where the Chief Executive of Bristol Royal Infirmary was removed from the register, following the inquiry into the paediatric heart surgery scandal. Although Dr Roylance was not directly involved in the surgery itself, the General Medical Council held that he should have reported his medical colleagues when death rates were significantly higher than in comparable units. However, the GMC's own rules at the time appeared to discourage such reporting, for doctors were forbidden to engage in 'disparagement' of fellow professionals (GMC, 1998).

Similarly, Williams (2010) contends that the decision to erase Professor Roy Meadows from the register appears to have been prompted by the adverse publicity, rather than a clear analysis of the facts. Professor Meadows was an expert witness at a trial where a woman was accused of causing the death of her child. His testimony secured a conviction, which was subsequently overturned on appeal, and the GMC later found him guilty of serious professional misconduct. His appeal to the court, however, met with a positive response (*Meadows v General Medical Council [2006]*), for the GMC was found to have overstepped the mark this time: his testimony had not been dishonest or deliberately misleading, and the only reason that it had secured a conviction was that the defence counsel had failed to ask the right questions.

Another possible reason for sanctions becoming tougher is that the professional bodies are seeking to preserve the status and dignity of their respective professions. They would undoubtedly argue that professional dignity and patient safety are mutually compatible, for patients are likely to have more faith and trust in those professions who enthusiastically rid themselves of their 'rotten apples'. Such a sentiment was expressed by Lord Rodger in *Gupta v General Medical Council [2001]* at para. 21: 'the reputation of the profession is more important than the fortunes of any individual member'.

Equally, however, the increasing numbers of erasures that such a policy entails could have the opposite effect. De Prez (2002), for example, suggests that the GMC in particular has produced unrealistic expectations of its practitioners, and that a higher number of failures are an inevitable consequence:

> the arm of self-regulation in medicine can be seen to be attempting to convince those concerned that registration represents more than competence and professional probity but a conscience beyond reproach; a superhuman paragon of virtue (p. 48).

There is one more factor to consider, which impacts upon the deliberations of Professional Conduct Committees. Their decisions are continually monitored by the Council for Healthcare Regulatory Excellence (CHRE): a body formerly known as the Council for the Regulation of Health Care Professionals and established by the NHS Reform and Health Care Professionals Act 2002 (s25) in response to the Kennedy Report (Bristol Royal Infirmary Inquiry, 2001). It covers nine regulatory bodies and is at liberty to refer a case to the High Court if it believes that a Professional Conduct Committee decision is too lenient (s29). An illustration of this mechanism at work can be seen in the following case:

Box 9.6   *Council for the Regulation of Health Care Professionals v General Dental Council and another (Fleischmann) [2005]*

The General Dental Council suspended a dentist for one year after he had been convicted of downloading sexual images of children onto his computer. The Council appealed against this decision to the High Court, who agreed that erasure was the only suitable penalty for this offence.

Although rare, there are examples from medicine and nursing (e.g. *Council for the Regulation of Health Care Professionals v General Medical Council and another (Ruscillo); Same v Nursing and Midwifery Council and another, GMC intervening (Truscott) [2004]*). On the one hand, it is possible to derive some comfort from the fact that patient safety is being assured in this way; on the other, though, the healthcare professional is placed in a position of double jeopardy (Brazier and Cave, 2007). It is conceivable that this breaches Article 6 of the Human Rights Act 1998 (the right to a fair trial), although this has not been challenged to date and there is nothing in the Article that expressly forbids being tried for the same offence twice. Moreover, a Professional Conduct Committee is not, strictly speaking, a court of law. Nevertheless, there is something a little morally suspect about a system that exposes individuals to further proceedings simply because the CHRE did not like the original decision. In addition, in their efforts to avoid the inevitable humiliation and embarrassment that such court cases will entail, Professional Conduct Committees are much more likely to err on the side of draconian sanctions.

D STATISTICS

Nursing The first disciplinary cases in nursing were heard in the 1920s, and Pyne (1982) has analysed the first hearings. Of these, the majority (19) involved theft of some nature: 12 nurses were caught stealing from shops (mainly ladies' hats), three from patients, three from employers or colleagues, and one from family and friends. All but one of these was struck off the register, including one nurse who took food from the ward that would otherwise have gone to waste. The solitary nurse who escaped this censure was a deputy matron, who received powerful support from senior authorities in both medicine and nursing.

Other cases concerned personal conduct *outside* of the workplace (seven) – e.g. bearing illegitimate children, living in adultery, being drunk and disorderly in a public place; conduct *inside* the workplace (three) – being drunk on duty, sleeping while on night duty, forging a character reference; and the remaining one involved the unlawful possession and taking of morphine. All but three of these were removed from the register.

My purpose in outlining these cases is not only to demonstrate the draconian nature of nursing's professional body in its early stages, but also to illustrate how it was responding to (and reflecting) the prevailing cultural philosophy of the day. You will observe, for example, that there were no patient abuse cases at this time, even though it was known that physical mistreatment of patients was not uncommon. Moreover, Pyne (1982) notes that, even in these early days, nurses were being removed from the register 'to maintain the purity of the profession'.

Thankfully, the menace of hat theft appears to be largely behind us now, but it is interesting to make comparisons with the latest statistics (NMC 2011).

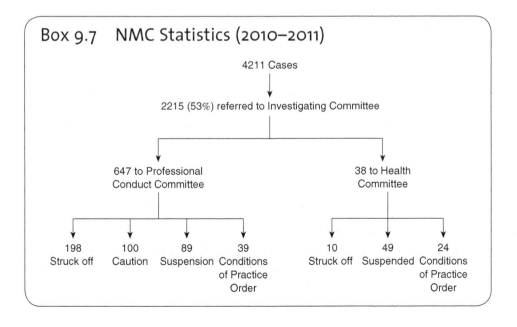

Box 9.7   NMC Statistics (2010–2011)

4211 Cases

2215 (53%) referred to Investigating Committee

647 to Professional Conduct Committee

38 to Health Committee

198 Struck off

100 Caution

89 Suspension

39 Conditions of Practice Order

10 Struck off

49 Suspended

24 Conditions of Practice Order

These figures represent the bulk of the decisions, although more specific details can be found within the Report. The figures for the Health Committee include a number of cases that had been held over from the previous year. The major allegations heard by the Professional Conduct committee can be summarised thus:

a   Dishonesty (including theft)   25%
b   Lack of Competence (including neglect)   24%
c   Abuse (including inappropriate relationships with patients)   22%
d   Unsafe practice   7%
e   Convictions   5%
f   Poor record keeping   4%

Figures for the Health Committee, by contrast, can be illustrated thus:

a   Substance abuse   27%
b   Mental or physical health   39%
c   Other (e.g. conduct and competency)   34%

There are a number of observations to make when analysing these figures. First, although the number of complaints to the Nursing and Midwifery Council has demonstrated a gradual incline over the years, the figure of 4,211 represents approximately 0.6 per cent of the nursing population, and it is important to keep this in perspective. Second, many of the cases appearing before the Professional Conduct Committee involve more than one allegation. It would, for example, be difficult to locate an instance where poor record keeping is the sole reason for erasure; but it is widely recognised that such practice is generally an indicator of failings in other areas of the healthcare professional's practice (NMC, 2009). Third, the figures suggest that the filtering process is very effective in limiting the number of cases that come before the Professional Conduct Committee. Once there, however, the likelihood of erasure from the register is quite high, and this statistic will undoubtedly increase when the adjourned cases have all been heard.

The final observation to make is that almost 40 per cent of those struck off (n=76) were male nurses, even though they constitute only 11 per cent of the nursing population. Indeed, in earlier years, the figure has approached 50 per cent, and it is interesting to speculate why this should be. Some might argue that it vindicates those who contend that nursing is not a suitable occupation for men, for it requires qualities that are generally considered to be feminine; but even these people would be hard-pressed to argue that women have the monopoly over compassion. It is conceivable that, because they represent a minority, their misdeeds tend to be more noticeable than those of their female colleagues, and are therefore more likely to be reported. This argument has a certain appeal, but is not entirely convincing. Perhaps a more credible explanation is that male nurses are frequently called upon to deal with those patients who present with the most challenging behaviour. Thus, if a patient is confused (for whatever reason) and is aggressive, s/he will generally be nursed in a side-room, and one nurse (usually a male) will be asked to monitor that patient closely. Continued exposure to this behaviour over several days will inevitably be very wearing, and it does not stretch the imagination too far to envisage a point at which the nurse's patience and tolerance evaporate.

There may be some truth in this suggestion, but it is impossible to generalise, each case having its own individual characteristics. It must be concerning, though, that the number of men appearing before the Professional Conduct Committee is disproportionate to their numbers on the register, and is something that merits further investigation.

Medicine   At the time of writing, the latest statistics are from 2009 (GMC, 2010), and can be summarised thus:

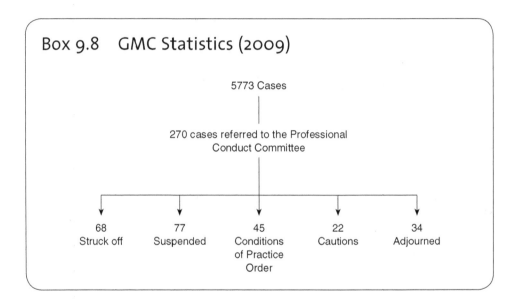

Box 9.8   GMC Statistics (2009)

5773 Cases

270 cases referred to the Professional Conduct Committee

| 68 Struck off | 77 Suspended | 45 Conditions of Practice Order | 22 Cautions | 34 Adjourned |

Once again, the efficient nature of the filtering process is noticeable: the number of cases referred to the General Medical Council is actually higher than that of nursing, but the number appearing before the Professional Conduct Committee is significantly lower. Similarly, erasure from the register is a distinct possibility for anybody whose case gets this far, the most common reason for which is improper relationships with patients (n=15). Other reasons include:

a	Sub-standard treatment	9
b	Failure to inform other employer regarding suspension/restriction	9
c	Failure to respect a patient's dignity	7

d   Indecent behaviour   7
e   Inappropriate prescribing   5
                                                              (GMC, 2009)

Dentistry   As with medicine, the most recent statistics relate to 2009 (GDC, 2010), and can be summarised as follows:

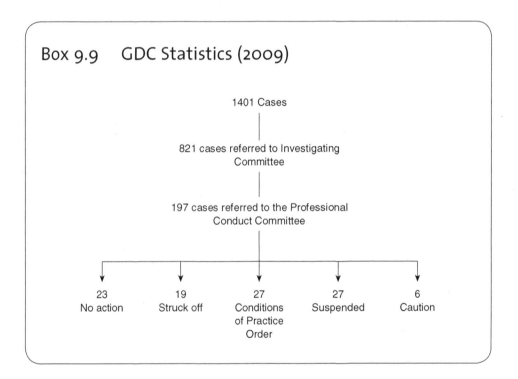

Box 9.9   GDC Statistics (2009)

1401 Cases

821 cases referred to Investigating Committee

197 cases referred to the Professional Conduct Committee

| 23 No action | 19 Struck off | 27 Conditions of Practice Order | 27 Suspended | 6 Caution |

The remaining cases were either adjourned or closed. Clearly, one would expect dentists to form the majority of these cases, given that the nature of their work exposes them to the most likely source of patient complaint. However, registrants with the General Dental Council also include other dental care professionals (dental hygienists, dental nurses and dental technicians), and several of these cases involved such people. Of particular note, though, is the smaller percentage of erasures when compared with nursing and medicine. This may reflect a less severe philosophy than can be found in other professional bodies, but it may also be an acknowledgement that dentists and their co-workers rarely endanger patients' lives.

The list of issues considered by the Professional Conduct Committee is rather long, but the main ones can be outlined thus:

Box 9.10   Issues considered by the Professional Conduct Committee of the General Dental Council

Poor treatment	42
Personal behaviour (and inappropriate behaviour)	21
Poor practice management	17
Fraud	17
Failure to obtain consent	17
No professional indemnity insurance	13
Conviction	12

Health and Care Professions Council   As mentioned earlier, the Health and Care Professions Council is the over-arching professional body for 15 allied health professions, and the statistics can be summarised thus (HCPC, 2011):

Box 9.11   HCPC Statistics (2011)

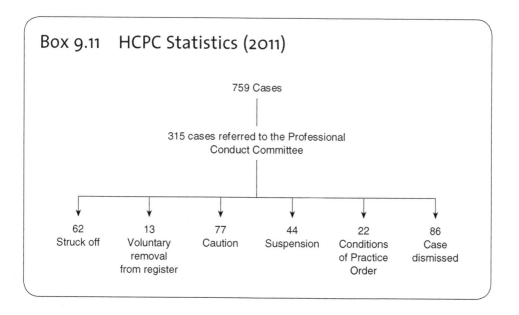

759 Cases

315 cases referred to the Professional Conduct Committee

62	13	77	44	22	86
Struck off	Voluntary removal from register	Caution	Suspension	Conditions of Practice Order	Case dismissed

---

Similar to nursing, the figure of 759 represents 0.35 per cent of the total registrants, but there are significant differences between each of the allied health professions:

Box 9.12   Cases reported to the HCPC by profession

Paramedics	188
Practitioner psychologists	118
Physiotherapists	104
Chiropodists / podiatrists	78
Occupational therapists	62

---

4 CASES

The variety of cases that we could discuss is immense, and each one is unique in its own way. The people coming before the Professional Conduct Committees range from the unfortunate to the misguided and to the deliberately malevolent. The purpose of this section, however, is not to focus on the extreme examples, but to try and extricate a few guiding principles for practitioners.

A CASES INVOLVING INAPPROPRIATE RELATIONSHIPS WITH PATIENTS

Box 9.13   *Case 1 (Evans v General Medical Council [1984])*

A doctor had a six-year adulterous relationship with one of his patients, although she had not consulted him for several years prior to their relationship. The doctor was struck off the register, and he appealed to the High Court.

In this instance, the High Court upheld the decision of the Professional Conduct Committee and Dr Evans's erasure was confirmed. This case has echoes of an earlier case (*De Gregory v General Medical Council [1961]*), although the patient in this example had long ceased to be registered with the doctor's practice. For Lord Denning, this had no relevance:

> He [i.e. the doctor] gained his access to the home in the first place by virtue of his professional position ... It is an abuse of his professional relationship with the husband and

father for him to enter upon an improper association with the wife and mother of the family. It was infamous conduct in a professional respect, even though she herself has ceased to be his patient (at 966).

Whether *De Gregory* would have been decided in the same way today is open to doubt. In *Nwabueze v General Medical Council [2000]*, a GP was struck off for having a sexual relationship with a former patient, although she had ceased to be registered at the surgery a year earlier. However, his appeal to the High Court was successful on this occasion; and this helps us to identify a key issue. Where a patient seeks medical treatment from a healthcare professional, there is almost inevitably an imbalance of power in favour of the latter. Equally, where there is imbalance of power, there is potential for abuse. This potential becomes even more likely when the patient is mentally and emotionally disturbed, as the following case illustrates:

Box 9.14   Case 2

A mental health nurse was employed as a substance misuse worker, and formed an attachment with one of his female clients. He sent her a number of text messages; telephoned her outside office hours; attempted to kiss her on one occasion; and asked if she would like to go out for a drink.

It will come as little surprise to learn that this nurse was struck off the register, and there would have been no value in appealing against this decision. His defence that the patient initiated and desired the relationship cut no ice with the Professional Conduct Committee: she was a vulnerable individual, and the nurse should have maintained a professional relationship with her at all times. Had the relationship become sexual, it is likely that the nurse would also have been charged with a criminal offence (Sexual Offences Act 2003, s38), and may well have been imprisoned for up to 14 years. Her mental state might have suggested that she was not competent to give a valid consent, and that the nurse had thereby abused his privileged position. Moreover, he would lay himself open to blackmail so that the patient would be able to continue to finance her drug habit.

  Gallop (1998) notes that many healthcare professionals who find themselves in this situation manage to deceive themselves into believing that they can handle things without causing damage to their client. However, 'Sexual contact is never seen as in the client's best interest. It is usually considered a manifestation of a troubled therapist' (p. 43). It is not difficult to see how such relationships can develop when the bond between mental health nurse and patient needs to be close if it is to be therapeutic. The responsibility for ensuring that it does not go beyond a professional relationship, however, lies not with the patient but with the healthcare worker. Gallop (1998) suggests, therefore, that staff should be educated upon how to recognise when matters are getting out of control and how to handle these

situations sensitively. Equally importantly, each member of staff should acknowledge and accept a responsibility to each other: early recognition of an inappropriate relationship between healthcare worker and patient will help to ensure that the
former does not find him/herself before a Professional Conduct Committee, and
the latter will be spared additional emotional distress.

Having outlined the dangers of forming inappropriate relationships with patients
for doctors and nurses, it is interesting to make a comparison with dentistry:

Box 9.15   Case 3

A female dentist conducted a sexual relationship with a male patient for about two
years. She then telephoned the patient's wife to inform her of the relationship, and the
wife made a complaint to the General Dental Council.

In this case, the Professional Conduct Committee conceded that the dentist's behaviour had little to commend it, and was thereby likely to bring the profession into
disrepute. The fact that she initially denied the charge also exposed her as being
dishonest. However, the patient could not be considered to be vulnerable in this
instance (in contrast to those patients who are physically and/or mentally ill), and
this affair was unlikely to have affected her clinical judgement. She therefore
escaped with a caution and a reprimand.

A similar situation arises when a relationship develops between colleagues. The
Professional Conduct Committees do not normally concern themselves with the
actions of two competent and consenting adults unless they bring the reputation of
the profession into disrepute and/or patient care is affected detrimentally. One such
example can be seen in the following case:

Box 9.16   Case 4

A dental nurse had an ongoing sexual relationship with the dentist for whom she
worked, frequently engaging in intercourse before the morning list started, during the
lunch break, and after the afternoon list had finished. She was sacked by the Primary
Care Trust, but took her case to an Employment Tribunal. Details of the affair automatically became public at this juncture, and she found herself being besieged by press
reporters. She subsequently agreed to be interviewed by *Closer* magazine in the belief
that she would no longer be pestered by the press.

The fact that this particular magazine was frequently available in dental surgeries
would have done nothing to enhance the reputation of the profession; but the

Professional Conduct Committee felt that she had been punished enough and issued her with a suspension for two months.

B CASES INVOLVING CONDUCT OUTSIDE OF WORK

These cases tend to fall into one of two categories: those that can be said to have an indirect impact upon a healthcare professional's ability to do his/her job, and those which bring the reputation of the profession into disrepute. An example of the former can be seen in the following:

Box 9.17   Case 5 (*Marten v Royal College of Veterinary Surgeons' Disciplinary Committee [1966]*)

A vet kept some animals on a farm, which were allowed to die from neglect. He was struck off the register, but appealed to the High Court, arguing that this was a *private* matter and did not therefore affect his work as a vet. The High Court rejected this appeal, holding that his peers would consider his conduct disgraceful, and that a person who could treat animals so cruelly had no place being a vet.

There have been instances where a nurse working on an adult ward and a dentist have both been convicted in a Crown Court for making indecent photographs of children. Both were erased from the register following these convictions, the central argument being that such individuals are simply unsuitable to be healthcare professionals. It is not entirely clear, however, that the same reasoning was being applied in the following case:

Box 9.18   Case 6 (*Crabbie v General Medical Council [2002]*)

A doctor was convicted of causing death by dangerous driving and with excess alcohol in her body. She was sentenced to five years' imprisonment, and was subsequently struck off the medical register. She appealed against the latter, arguing that this was a health-related problem, rather than an issue of professional conduct. She had shown signs of alcohol dependency, and she contended that her case should have been heard by the Health Committee.

The court rejected this argument, holding that the doctor's offences were so serious that erasure from the medical register was entirely justified. Certainly, the fact that the doctor had caused the death of somebody would have weighed heavily in the deliberations of both the Professional Conduct Committee and the court. But it is difficult to see how public protection was automatically enhanced by her erasure: she only represented a danger to the public when she was driving, and it could be argued that this danger was increased following the removal of her occupation. The logical conclusion to be drawn, therefore, is that the Professional Conduct Committee felt that she had brought the reputation of the profession into disrepute, and this was the reason for her erasure.

Nevertheless, not all cases of this nature will result in such draconian sanctions, and an example from the General Dental Council serves to illustrate this:

Box 9.19   Case 7

A dental hygienist was convicted on a charge of drink-driving and failing to provide a specimen of breath for analysis. She was fined £60, disqualified from driving for three years, and committed to prison for four months (suspended for 18 months). She appeared before the Professional Conduct Committee because it was felt that her fitness to practise was impaired by reason of her conviction.

A key difference between this case and the one immediately preceding it is that the latter resulted in the death of an innocent person. Nevertheless, the reputation of the profession has still been damaged, particularly as all such instances are likely to be reported in the press. However, the Professional Conduct Committee acknowledged that none of her patients were endangered in the course of her work, and they issued her with a reprimand. A significant factor influencing this decision was that the dental hygienist had undertaken and completed a rehabilitation course, and she showed some insight into her problems. This, then, is a key lesson to be learned for all those unfortunate enough to find themselves before a disciplinary hearing: the Professional Conduct Committee is much more likely to look kindly upon the practitioner who shows genuine remorse for his/her actions, and who has taken measures (of his/her own volition) to correct deficiencies. Of course, each case will be assessed according to its merits, but the practitioner who shows no insight and no contrition is destined to repeat his/her misdemeanours, and this will impact upon the final judgment.

C CASES INVOLVING CONDUCT INSIDE WORK

These cases relate either to incompetent practice or cruel and immoral practice, although there are situations when the distinction becomes blurred. For a long time, it was thought that only the second of these justified erasure, but the following case helped to clarify matters:

> ## Box 9.20   Case 8 (McCandless v General Medical Council [1996])
>
> A doctor failed to refer three patients to hospital, two of whom subsequently died while the third was admitted in a serious condition. Upon being struck off from the register, he appealed to the court, arguing that a finding of serious professional misconduct could only stand if his practice had been *morally* blameworthy.

The court rejected this appeal, holding that seriously *negligent* treatment equates to serious professional misconduct. As Lord Hoffman said (at 55): 'the governing bodies are under a duty to protect the public against the genially incompetent as well as the deliberate wrongdoers'. It is generally the case, however, that incompetent practice is manifested long before it reaches a crisis point, and the employing authority should acknowledge its failure to recognise and act upon such practice at an earlier stage. This was certainly the finding of the judge in a case where a surgeon pleaded guilty to the manslaughter of a patient during a liver operation, in which the latter lost several pints of blood (*The Times*, 2004). Although sentenced to 21 months' imprisonment, the sentence was suspended for two years. This was largely because there had been a history of negligence with this doctor over a period of three years, but the Trust had done nothing to address it. Had they acted 'with the rigour that the public is entitled to expect' (per Sir Stephen Mitchell), the doctor would probably have been spared the trauma of a court appearance and it is conceivable that the patient's life would not have been endangered.

The responsibility of employers for minimising incompetent practice is something to which we shall return later, but it can be seen in the background to many of these cases. It can certainly be observed in the case of Richard Neale, a gynaecologist who had been struck off the register in Canada, but who somehow managed to retain a licence to practise in the UK. The report into his conduct (DH, 2004) outlined a 12-year period in which Neale botched countless operations, leaving many women maimed. As the complaints mounted, he was eventually forced to move elsewhere, but was able to do so easily because the hospital gave him a good reference.

The combination of arrogance and incompetence exhibited by Neale is a dangerous mixture, but the mechanism for checking its excesses appeared to be largely absent. Unquestionably, the dominance of the consultant in a hospital setting inhibits staff from raising concerns (as identified by the report), but the hospital's best response was to offload the problem onto another. This policy may be interpreted as a manifestation of isolationism, laziness, or simply cowardice. Whatever the truth of the matter, it is clear that the hospital took a long time to address the problem, and then acknowledged no responsibility to the patients of other areas of the country.

In fairness, it is not always possible for employers to identify potential problems with staff. For example, Amanda Jenkinson was an intensive care nurse who was jailed for tampering with equipment. Although she had a history of mental illness (depression and suicidal tendencies), she had not reported this to the hospital when she was employed; and, as Kenny (1996) notes: 'The Catch 22 is that the best means employers have of detecting a personality disorder relies on the honesty of the person being scrutinised' (p. 19). The case of Beverley Allitt (discussed in Chapter 5) is another instance in a similar vein, although the Clothier Report (1994) identified some measures that employers could adopt. Equally, though, it has been acknowledged that none of the recommendations of the Shipman Inquiry would have prevented Harold Shipman from murdering his patients (Case, 2011).

The deranged practitioner is mercifully rare, but a much more significant factor impinging upon quality of patient care is that of resources. At times, low staffing levels will often compel practitioners to take short cuts, and it might lead to them working outside their own limitations. Such practices almost always begin as a genuine desire to meet the demands of patient care within the constraints imposed by the employer. Ultimately, however, a low level of investment in the staff will lead to low morale, and the suspension of educational opportunities in order to save money will lead to increased levels of stress. In such circumstances, it is not difficult to see how levels of care begin to decline, and there are many illustrations of this.

Payne (2000) cites the example of a nursing home for the elderly in Melbourne, where an investigation uncovered a catalogue of abuse. For instance, scabies-infected patients were given kerosene baths, and one patient's broken arm went undetected for a week. The underlying reason for this decline in care was not difficult to find: in 1998, nursing homes in Australia were allowed to determine staffing levels based upon an assessment of patients' needs. In consequence, the numbers of qualified staff were drastically reduced so that the proprietors of the homes could maximise their profits.

Closer to home, the examples of Maidstone and Tunbridge Wells, where at least 90 patients died following two outbreaks of *Clostridium difficile* infection (Healthcare Commission, 2007), and Mid-Staffordshire NHS Foundation Trust (Francis Report, 2010) both identify a loss of patient dignity, a lack of fundamental care, and a breakdown in communication with patients. Both inquiries also highlighted a preoccupation with finances by senior management, and a culture that discouraged questioning or initiative by junior staff. In the case of Mid-Staffordshire, this policy achieved exactly what it had set out to do: the books were balanced and the Trust was granted Foundation status. However, the damage that was done in the process is incalculable.

In other situations, the mistreatment can occur when the client base poses particularly challenging problems, and when the care setting is isolated from public view. Such was the case in Rampton hospital (Boynton, 1980) and on two separate occasions in Ashworth hospital (Blom-Cooper et al., 1992; Fallon et al., 1999). Both of these hospitals are high-security institutions in which severely mentally ill patients are housed. It is inconceivable that staff will go to work one day and suddenly decide that they will be unpleasant to their patients: the decline of standards is much more insidious than this. So insidious, in fact, that its perpetrators are unaware of it, and it takes an outsider to notice that things are not as they should be.

Finally, there are those circumstances where the practitioner takes advantage of his/her privileged access to patients for his/her own nefarious purposes. There are a number of examples of this, including a physiotherapist who was struck off the register after sexually assaulting a vulnerable female patient on three occasions (National Health Executive, 2011a). One case which was appealed in the High Court is as follows:

Box 9.21   Case 9 (*Muscat v Health and Care Professions Council [2008]*)

A radiographer took an X-ray and MRI on two female patients and exposed them without necessity. He was struck off the register, but appealed his case, arguing that sedation given to the two patients would have clouded their memory of events. The court dismissed this defence as mere conjecture and therefore rejected his appeal.

D CASES INVOLVING FALSE REPRESENTATION AND FRAUD

False representation as a nurse (i.e. without an appropriate qualification) constitutes an offence under Article 44 of the Nursing and Midwifery Order 2001, and is punishable with a fine of up to £5,000. Similar penalties exist for the impersonation of other healthcare professionals. Even with such a qualification, though, practitioners can still be called to account if they are dishonest with their employers and/or patients, as the following case illustrates:

Box 9.22   Case 10

A nurse applied for a job as a Sister, and claimed to have undertaken a variety of post-registration courses. It transpired that all of these claims were false, and some of the courses that she claimed to have undertaken never actually existed. Her name was subsequently removed from the register (NMC News, 2001a).

It is also incumbent upon healthcare professionals to disclose any criminal convictions to prospective and/or current employers, for none are exempt from the provisions of the Rehabilitation of Offenders Act 1974 (Exceptions Order 1975). Failure to do so has resulted in removal from the register, as has failure to inform an employer of being sacked from a previous post for gross misconduct.

Fraud comes in many forms, but a depressingly familiar scenario is exhibited by the following case:

Box 9.23   Case 11

A critical care nurse was on paid NHS sick leave, but worked hundreds of shifts for a private agency. Over a period of almost three years, it is estimated that he defrauded the NHS of well over £40,000. He was sentenced to imprisonment for nine months, and his case was referred to the Nursing and Midwifery Council (National Health Executive, 2011b). At the time of writing, his case has not been heard, but it is a reasonable assumption that erasure is the most likely outcome.

In summary, honesty is a virtue expected of healthcare practitioners by patients, employers and professional bodies: protection of the public and preservation of the reputation of the profession are both heavily dependent upon it. This brings us to the final category to be discussed.

E CASES INVOLVING GIFTS AND LOANS

Each of the professional bodies has a policy statement pertaining to gifts and loans from patients. The NMC Code of Conduct (2008), for example, states:

> You must refuse any gifts, favours or hospitality ... [and] ... you must not ask for or accept loans from anyone in your care or anyone close to them (sections 18 and 19).

Similarly, the General Medical Council (2006) advises that:

> You must not encourage patients to give, lend or bequeath money or gifts that will directly or indirectly benefit you (section 2c).

Finally, the Health and Care Professions Council's Code of Corporate Governance echoes the same sentiments, although it allows the receipt of gifts 'of a token nature' (i.e. flowers, pens, diaries, calendars, and bottles of wine). There are a number of reasons for this policy, the most obvious being that patients may use gifts as a means of obtaining preferential treatment (NMC, 2008: section 18). If this strategy is successful, other patients will feel pressurised to offer gifts as well, and the situation would quickly get out of control. Another reason is that, by their nature, patients are generally vulnerable: their physical and/or mental condition may affect their cognitive processes, and the potential for exploitation of this vulnerability is very real (GMC, 2006: section 2b). It is not difficult to see how the acceptance of a small gift quickly comes to be seen as a 'perk' of the job, leading eventually to total corruption of the practitioner. The final reason is that each healthcare professional, however important, is but a single cog within a large machine, and each patient's care and rehabilitation is dependent upon scores of personnel. Thus, the patient may be particularly grateful for the attention lavished upon him/her by one individual, but recovery would not have been possible without the efforts of countless others (cooks, cleaners, maintenance engineers, etc.), whose work goes largely unseen. In consequence, the singling out of one member of staff for the bestowal of a gift or favour seems unjust.

One suspects that the taking of gifts from patients is more prevalent than is reported, for it can be very difficult to refuse an insistent patient. Quite apart from the temptation thrown in one's path, there is a possibility that the patient may be offended by a rejection of his/her generosity. Before considering ways in which such situations should be handled, however, we should perhaps look at a few scenarios that illustrate the potential pitfalls.

Box 9.24   Case 12

An overseas nurse formed a close attachment with a hospital patient, and gave him a distressed story about missing her children. When she broke down into tears, the patient responded by giving her £1,000 (£600 as a gift, and £400 as a loan). None of this money was repaid to the patient, and the nurse was struck off the register (NMC News, 2009).

Whatever the truth of her story, it was unprofessional to burden the patient with it. Moreover, this is a clear illustration of the exploitation of a person's vulnerability. It is conceivable that repayment of the money of her own volition might have saved her registration, but it would not have altered the fact that this was serious professional misconduct.

Box 9.25   Case 13

A doctor was treating a psychiatric patient, who gave him monetary gifts totalling £150,000. He was also made a beneficiary in her will, and inherited £1.2million when she died. The Professional Conduct Committee found that he had made no effort to dissuade the patient from making these gifts, he had not sought advice from his professional colleagues, and he had never considered withdrawing from her care. With these things taken together, his assertion that the doctor–patient relationship was unaffected was easily rejected by the panel, and he was struck off the register.

Not all such scenarios will result in erasure, although the accused must furnish credible extenuating circumstances. An illustration of this can be found in the following:

Box 9.26   Case 14

An overseas nurse was working in a nursing home, and accepted a gift of £500 from the wife of one of the residents. Her subsequent denial that she had taken the money did nothing to endear her to the Professional Conduct Committee, but it was acknowledged that cultural issues may have affected how she responded to the offer of a gift. In consequence, she was issued with a suspension order for nine months, so that she would have an opportunity to reflect upon her behaviour and address deficiencies.

Some might see this as rather a generous judgement in the light of what has gone before. That the gift was given by the wife of a resident suggests that it was an inducement to provide preferential care, the nurse accepted the money without question, and she then sought to disguise her actions. Nevertheless, the recognition that cultural diversity played a part in this scenario is an important lesson to learn for all practitioners, since it identifies that education in such matters must be included in the orientation packages for overseas nurses.

So, how should the practitioner react when offered a gift by a patient or relative? There are, perhaps, no easy answers, but the experience of the cases above should point us in the right direction. The first and most obvious piece of advice is that no gift should be accepted from patients or their relatives while those patients are still receiving care, for this will be interpreted as an inducement to provide preferential care. This becomes less of an issue once the patient has been discharged, but it remains good practice to refuse politely the offer of gifts. The reasons for this should be explained clearly to the patient, while acknowledging his/her generosity. If the patient remains insistent, s/he should be advised to donate the gift to the ward or Trust, rather than to an individual. In this way, no single individual is a beneficiary, and the donation of money can be invested in the improvement of care for future patients.

Above all else, practitioners should be open, honest and completely transparent about such matters. Thus, if a healthcare professional is made the beneficiary in a patient's will, there is a duty to report this immediately to the line manager and to seek appropriate advice. However tempting it may be to keep quiet about it, the problems that it is likely to cause will not seem worth the effort in the long run. Moreover, healthcare professionals should acknowledge that there is no such thing as a 'perk of the job'. They already receive payment for the service that they provide, and they have no right to expect or accept additional 'bonuses'.

5 ERRORS WITHIN HEALTHCARE

If we accept that humans are fallible, then we must accept that errors will occur within healthcare. This is stating the obvious, but it should not deter us from seeking to minimise the sources of error. The traditional response has been that of the 'blame culture', where the focus is on the individual practitioner who committed the mistake. It is assumed that punitive measures taken against this person will serve as redress for the unfortunate patient who was the victim of the error, and will send out a clear signal to all other healthcare professionals 'to be more careful in the future'.

In recent years, however, numerous commentators have identified the inherent flaws within this philosophy. For one thing, it is desperately unfair: quite apart from the fact that different professions within the NHS are often treated very differently when a mistake occurs, the person making the error is usually as much a victim as the patient. Both Reason (1990) and Merry and McCall Smith (2001) have illustrated how errors are generally the culmination of a series of shortfalls within the system. Thus, to blame the individual does nothing to correct these failings, and makes it almost certain that the same mistake will occur in the future.

Perhaps the most graphic example of this can be seen in the case of *R v Prentice (1993)*, discussed in Chapter 3. Here, a doctor was required to give two cytotoxic drugs to a young patient with leukaemia: Methotrexate (to be given intrathecally) and Vincristine (to be given intravenously). Both were given intrathecally and the patient died. The doctor was convicted of gross negligence manslaughter (although this was subsequently overturned on appeal). If this had been the only time that this mistake occurred, the punishment meted out to the doctor would have been seen to have served its purpose. But it was *not* the only time, and has in fact occurred several times since (the death or permanent disability of the patient being the inevitable result on each occasion) (DH, 2008). Thus, rather than focus attention on the practitioner, the human tragedies that followed might have been avoided if thought had been given to designing a system that made it impossible to connect a syringe of Vincristine to the intrathecal catheter. Any practitioner who subsequently managed to overcome this obstacle would have had to do so *deliberately*.

Errors are much more likely when leadership and communication are poor, and when the service has been starved of adequate resources (Bristol Royal Infirmary Inquiry, 2001). For this, one might look towards management as being the foundation stone for all errors within the NHS, but they too are under pressure from the Government to increase throughput for less expense. In turn, the Government is under pressure from the public to deliver a high quality service without raising taxation. Perhaps, then, we should all accept a measure of responsibility for healthcare errors!

Nevertheless, there are other factors at play here. It has been acknowledged, for example, that the law of negligence reinforces a blame culture within the NHS, and thereby discourages the reporting of errors while encouraging defensive attitudes (Newdick, 2002). Where the penalties are so severe, both in terms of monetary losses and professional reputations, it is inevitable that a culture of secrecy will emerge, making it impossible to learn from mistakes (House of Commons Health Committee, 2009).

The professions themselves contribute to this situation. Quick (2006), for example, notes that medicine in particular likes to encourage a notion of infallibility. This has largely arisen because of the need to secure patient trust, but has to be seen as 'intellectually dishonest, hypocritical and ... [preventive of] ... lessons being learned' (p. 28). The Bristol Royal Infirmary Inquiry (2001) identified that the tribalism between professions in the NHS undermines their ability to communicate properly with each other and to agree upon a core set of values.

With all of this in mind, it is hardly surprising that errors occur, and we might instead wonder why they are not more prevalent than is currently the case. The Government's response was to publish a paper entitled *An Organisation with a Memory* (DH, 2000b), which encouraged a systems-based approach to the investigation of errors, rather than the punitive approach. In other words, if errors occur because of faults within the system of working, it is the *system* that should be corrected if the same mistakes are not to recur. To this end, the National Patient Safety Agency (NPSA) was established, its fundamental remit being to encourage the growth of a systems-based approach (and the subsequent decline of the blame culture), and to require healthcare institutions to report all adverse incidents and near-misses. The hope is that each organisation can learn from the mistakes of each other, rather than simply from their own errors.

The work of the NPSA can be viewed on its website (www.npsa.nhs.uk), but its success is open to question. Healthcare organisations have now learnt the rhetoric of a systems-based philosophy, but Quick (2006) notes that the reality is often very different, for the focus remains on identifying individual errors. Part of the reason for this, of course, is that the blame culture is deeply ingrained within the NHS; it has existed for many years, and one cannot expect it to be swept away so easily. Certainly, in the short term, it is more convenient, less expensive and less time-consuming to blame an individual than it is to correct deficiencies in the system. Moreover, there are concerns (not altogether unfounded) that a systems-based approach will serve to protect the incompetent practitioner. This idea, however, is a misunderstanding of how the investigative process should work, and the ultimate goal should always be the enhancement of patient safety. As Merry and McCall Smith (2001) observe, the idea that punitive measures will deter unsafe practice has no meaning when one considers that the vast majority of errors are unintentional. Therefore, if organisations really want to retain the deterrence principle, it should be directed at those who are able to affect change within the system.

6 WHISTLEBLOWING

Whistleblowing is a term used to describe the reporting of concerns to a higher authority about another's practice or the system of work, especially where such concerns pose a danger to patients and/or other staff. The term itself has certain derogatory connotations, and the exercise of its function is fraught with danger. As Yamey (2000) has said: 'Whistleblowers have been likened to bees: a whistleblowing employee has only one sting to use, and using it may well lead to career suicide'. There have been a number of high profile whistleblowers, who have found themselves subject to victimisation, abuse and economic deprivation as a result of their activities. Burrows (2001) cites the medical examples of doctors Dawson and Edwards, both of whom raised concerns about senior colleagues, and both of whom suffered 'dire consequences'. In nursing, Graham Pink raised concerns about the staffing levels on his elderly care ward, and was ultimately removed from his job. Finally, Dr Bolsin blew the whistle on the surgeons at Bristol Royal Infirmary, and he eventually felt compelled to emigrate to Australia as a result of his treatment from other medical colleagues.

These are but a small handful of cases to illustrate the problems associated with blowing the whistle. The double jeopardy, however, is that *not* reporting concerns when they come to light can be equally damaging, for the individual who does nothing automatically becomes an accomplice to the wrongdoer. To stand by and observe the abuse of patients or to ignore the incompetence of colleagues is to deny one's obligation to enhance patient safety and ensures that malpractice will continue. When Dr Dunn (a consultant anaesthetist) failed to investigate complaints about a locum colleague who was incompetent and dangerous, he was found guilty of misconduct by the Professional Conduct Committee (Dyer, 1994).

What the whistleblower will always find difficult to escape is the notion that informing on one's colleagues is somehow underhand. It is resonant of the classroom 'tell-tale' or the police informer who 'grasses' on his friends. Moreover, the motive of the whistleblower will frequently be called into question: for example, if a GP reports a colleague, would s/he have something to gain by that person's removal from the practice? Certainly, the act of blowing the whistle is destined to create conflict where once there might have been harmony, and this can be a very uncomfortable situation for everybody.

Henriksen and Dayton (2006) outline a variety of factors inhibiting whistleblowing. Some of these include the fear of retaliation and deference to authority, but there are also a number of sociological reasons. For example, conformity with the group enables individuals to become accepted and integrated, whereas 'rocking the boat' can quickly lead to social isolation. Similarly, groups working under stress generally feel the need to reach consensus, even if this means making bad decisions (a concept known as 'groupthink'). The individual who questions accepted practice simply adds to the stress, not only of him/herself, but also that of others.

The recognition that whistleblowing was so difficult, and that patient safety would inevitably be compromised as a result, led to the introduction of the Public Interest Disclosure Act 1998. Its fundamental purpose is to give protection to those who disclose information in the public interest and who find themselves victimised as a result (NHS Executive, 1999). Thus, they would be able to bring a claim to an employment tribunal and could receive substantial compensation. In addition, confidentiality clauses within NHS contracts (the so-called 'gagging' clauses) are void if they are in conflict with the central aims of the Act.

Burrows (2001) raises a few doubts about the likely effectiveness of this Act. For example, it would appear that the burden of proof rests with the whistleblower, for his/her concerns must be 'substantially true' (s43F). Moreover, there should be no doubt that the whistleblower is acting in anything but 'good faith' (s43C). Both of these can be called into question, and the whistleblower remains in a highly vulnerable position. Indeed, her own research suggested that there remains a deep mistrust of management among healthcare practitioners, and a firm belief that whistleblowing is unlikely to make a difference.

What the Act does achieve, however, is to prompt (although it does not require) organisations to set up a whistleblowing policy. In doing so, it forces the issue into the open, and makes some inroads into the prevailing culture. That this has not been happening quickly enough for the Government is evident from a Heath Select Committee report (House of Commons Health Committee, 2009), which found the NHS 'largely unsupportive of whistleblowing'. Clearly, problems remain, and plans exist to amend the NHS Constitution so that staff would be *expected* to raise concerns at the earliest opportunity (National Health Executive, 2011c). It should be evident, though, that such measures will only work if there is clear evidence that whistleblowers are being protected. As Yamey (2000: 70) observes:

> If whistleblowing requires *courage,* there is something wrong with the system. A system that has mechanisms for early recognition and open management of problems would render the necessity for whistleblowers obsolete.

REFERENCES

TEXTS

Blom-Cooper, L., Brown, M., Dolan, R. and Murphy, E. (1992) *Report of the Committee of Inquiry Into Complaints About Ashworth Hospital.* London: HMSO (Cmnd. 2028).

Boynton, J. (1980) *Report of the Review of Rampton Hospital.* London: HMSO (Cmnd. 8073).

Brazier, M. and Cave, E. (2007) *Medicine, Patients and the Law*, 4th edn. London: Penguin Books.

Bristol Royal Infirmary Inquiry (Kennedy Report) (2001) *Learning from Bristol: The Report of the Public Inquiry Into Children's Heart Surgery at the Bristol Royal Infirmary 1984–1995.* London: HMSO (Cmnd. 5207), July.

Burrows, J. (2001) 'Telling tales and saving lives: whistleblowing – the role of professional colleagues in protecting patients from dangerous doctors', *Medical Law Review*, 9, Summer: 110–29.

Case, P. (2011) 'Putting public confidence first: doctors, precautionary suspension, and the General Medical Council', *Medical Law Review*, 19, Summer: 339–71.

Clothier Report (1994) *The Allitt Inquiry: An Independent Inquiry Relating to Deaths and Injuries on the Children's Ward at Grantham and Kesteven Hospital During the Period February to April 1991.* London: HMSO.

De Prez, P. (2002) 'Self-regulation and paragons of virtue: the case of "fitness to practise"', *Medical Law Review*, 10, Spring: 28–56.

Department of Health (2000a) *Inquiry into Quality and Practice within the NHS Arising From the Actions of Rodney Ledward (Chair: Jean Ritchie)*. London: The Stationery Office/ Department of Health.

Department of Health (2000b) *An Organisation With a Memory*. London: The Stationery Office/Department of Health.

Department of Health (2004) *Committee of Inquiry to Investigate How the NHS Handled Allegations About the Performance and Conduct of Richard Neale (Chair: HH Judge Matthews)*. London: HMSO (Cm. 6315), September.

Department of Health (2008) *Updated National Guidance on the Safe Administration of Intrathecal Chemotherapy*. London: Department of Health (HSC 2008/001).

Dyer, C. (1994) 'Consultant found guilty of failing to act on colleague', *British Medical Journal*, 308, 809.

Fallon, P., Bluglass, R., Edwards, B. and Daniels, G. (1999) *Ashworth Special Hospital: Report of the Committee of Inquiry*. London: HMSO (Cmnd. 4194).

Francis Report (2010) *Independent Inquiry Into Care Provided by Mid-Staffordshire NHS Foundation Trust: January 2005–March 2009*. London: The Stationery Office, March.

Gallop, R. (1998) 'Abuse of power in the nurse-client relationship', *Nursing Standard*, 12, 37: 43–7.

General Dental Council (2010) *Annual Report and Accounts 2010*. London: The Stationery Office.

General Medical Council (1998) *Good Medical Practice*. London: General Medical Council.

General Medical Council (2006) *Good Medical Practice*. London: General Medical Council, November.

General Medical Council (2008) *Good Practice in Prescribing Medicines – Guidance for Doctors*. London: General Medical Council, September.

General Medical Council (2009) *FTP Fact Sheet 2009: Allegations*. Available from: http:// gmc-uk.org/Allegations. pdf_33097341.pdf.

General Medical Council (2010) *2009 Annual Statistics: Fitness to Practise*. London: General Medical Council.

Griffith, R. and Tengnah, C. (2010) *Law and Professional Issues in Nursing*, 2nd edn. Exeter: Learning Matters Ltd.

Griffiths, P. and Robinson, S. (2010) *Moving Forward with Healthcare Support Workforce Regulation*. London: National Nursing Research Unit, July.

Healthcare Commission (2007) *Investigation Into Outbreaks of Clostridium Difficile at Maidstone and Tunbridge Wells NHS Trust*. London: Commission for Healthcare Audit and Inspection, October.

Health and Care Professions Council: *Code of Corporate Governance*. Available from: www. hpc-uk.org/aboutus/council/codeofcorporategovernance/index.asp.

Health and Care Professions Council (2011) *Fitness to Practise Annual Report 2011*. London: HCPC.

Henriksen, K. and Dayton, E. (2006) 'Organisational silence and hidden threats to patient safety', *Health Services Research*, 41 (42); 1539, August.

House of Commons Health Committee (2009) *Patient Safety: Sixth Report of Session 2008–09*. London: The Stationery Office (HC151-I), 3 July.

Kenny, C. (1996) 'Mind games', *Nursing Times*, 92 (46): November 13, 18–19.

Merry, A. and McCall Smith, A. (2001) *Errors, Medicine and the Law*. Cambridge: Cambridge University Press.

Montgomery, J. (2003) *Health Care Law*, 2nd edn. Oxford: Oxford University Press.

NHS Executive (1999) *The Public Interest Disclosure Act 1998: Whistleblowing in the NHS*. Health Service Circular (HSC 1999/198), August.

2011a) Sex assault physiotherapist struck off. Available from: http://
:xecutive.com. 2 February.

2011b) Nurse jailed for sick pay con. Available from: http://national
:.com. 28 April.

!011c) Protection for NHS whistleblowers. Available from: http://national
:.com.

Newdick, C. (2002) 'NHS governance after Bristol: holding on or letting go?', *Medical Law Review*, 10, Summer: 111–31.

Nursing and Midwifery Council (2008) *Code of Professional Conduct: Standards for Performance, Conduct and Ethics*. London: NMC.

Nursing and Midwifery Council (2009) *Record Keeping: Guidance for Nurses and Midwives*. London: NMC, July.

Nursing and Midwifery Council (2011) *Annual Fitness to Practise Report 2010-2011*. London: The Stationery Office, July.

NMC News (2001a) *Nurses Who Doctor the Facts* (November).

NMC News (2009) *Nurse Struck Off for Taking Money* (November 10).

Nursing Times.net (2011) *Struck off nurses 'still on wards' says Weir-Hughes* (27 September). Available from: www.nursingtimesnet/nursing-practice/clinical-specialisms/management/.

Pattinson, S.D. (2009) *Medical Law and Ethics*, 2nd edn. London: Sweet & Maxwell.

Pattison, S. and Wainwright, P. (2010) 'Is the 2008 NMC Code ethical?', *Nursing Ethics*, 17 (1): 9–18.

Payne, D. (2000) 'The bitter fruits of staff cuts', *Nursing Times*, 96 (13), March 30: 14–15.

Pyne, R.H. (1982) *Professional Discipline in Nursing, Midwifery and Health Visiting*, 2nd edn. London: Blackwell Scientific Publications.

Quick, O. (2006) 'Outing medical errors: questions of trust and responsibility', *Medical Law Review*, 14, Spring: 22–43.

Reason, J. (1990) *Human Error*. New York: Cambridge University Press.

The Shipman Inquiry Fifth Report (2004) *Safeguarding Patients: Lessons From the Past – Proposals For the Future*. London: The Stationery Office (Cmnd. Paper Cm 6394), December.

The Times (2004) 'Hospital failures help save killer surgeon from jail', June 24.

Williams, C. (2010) 'The trouble with paediatricians', *Medical Law Review*, 18, Autumn: 389–416.

Yamey, G. (2000) 'Protecting whistleblowers', *British Medical Journal*, 320: 70.

CASES

Chester v Afshar [2004] UKHL 41.

Council for the Regulation of Health Care Professionals v General Dental Council and another (Fleischmann) [2005] The Times, 8 February.

Council for the Regulation of Health Care Professionals v General Medical Council and another (Ruscillo); Same v Nursing and Midwifery Council and another, GMC intervening (Truscott) [2004] The Times, 27 October.

Crabbie v General Medical Council [2002] UKPC 45.

Dad v General Dental Council [2000] 1 WLR 1538 (PC).

Dad v General Dental Council [2010] CSIH 75.

De Gregory v General Medical Council [1961] AC 957.

Evans v General Medical Council [1984], unreported.

Finegan v General Medical Council [1987] 1 WLR 121.

Gupta v General Medical Council [2001] 64 BMLR 56.

Hefferon v UKCC [1998] Current Law, May 1998, 221.

Marten v Royal College of Veterinary Surgeons' Disciplinary Committee [1966] 1 QB 1.

McCandless v General Medical Council [1996] 30 BMLR 55.

Meadows v General Medical Council [2006] EWCA Civ. 1390.

Muscat v Health and Care Professions Council [2008] EWHC 2798 (Admin.).

Nwabueze v General Medical Council [2000] 1 WLR 1760.

R v Prentice [1993] 4 All ER 935.

R v The Professional Conduct Committee of the UKCC, ex parte Wood and Thompson [1993], unreported.

Roylance v General Medical Council (No. 2) [2000] 1 AC 311 (PC).

LEGISLATION

Health Act 1999

Health and Social Care Act 2008

Human Rights Act 1998

NHS Reform and Health Care Professions Act 2002

Nursing and Midwifery Order 2001

Public Interest Disclosure Act 1998

Rehabilitation of Offenders Act 1974 (Exceptions Order 1975)

Sexual Offences Act 2003

Scenarios (answers at back of book)

1 Jackie is a Staff Nurse working in a nursing home, which accommodates registered mentally ill persons. It is a 50-bedded unit, and the residents frequently exhibit challenging behaviour. Moreover, it is generally short-staffed, but this situation has been exacerbated over the last six weeks because of staff holidays and a high sickness rate. Jackie is working the current shift with three Healthcare Assistants, all of whom are keen, but who are very inexperienced. The pressure is clearly beginning to tell on her as she screams at residents who behave inappropriately. In addition, when one resident becomes physically aggressive in response to these verbal attacks, she pins him to the ground, cracking one of his ribs. The Healthcare Assistants are shocked by what they witness, and report Jackie to their employer. Following a hearing, she is dismissed from her post, and the employer reports her to the Professional Conduct Committee.

Which element(s) of the Code of Conduct are invoked in this scenario, and how should the Professional Conduct Committee deal with it?

(Continued)

(Continued)

2 A paramedic has recently been divorced from his wife, and has moved out of the family home. He is currently living in a bedsit and is paying large alimony sums to his ex-wife for the maintenance of their three children. He becomes increasingly depressed by his living conditions, the fact that he is continuously short of money, and because he has little contact with his children. A friend offers him some LSD and ecstasy tablets to help his mental state, and they seem to have the desired effect, albeit temporary. He realises, too, that he can supplement his income by selling these tablets on the street, and forms a partnership with his friend. However, he is caught in an undercover police operation, and he is convicted at the Crown Court. He is sentenced to six months' imprisonment, suspended for one year.

His case inevitably comes before the Professional Conduct Committee, but how should it be handled?

3 A dental hygienist has been working in a practice for three months, but she is now experiencing sexual harassment from one of the dentists. He frequently makes inappropriate comments about her appearance, gives her neck and shoulder massages in the rest room if he finds her there alone, and constantly asks her to go out on a date with him. When she complains that this is making her uncomfortable, he tells her that he can make or break her future, and that she should think very carefully before rejecting his advances. In addition, he frequently smells of alcohol when he arrives for work in the mornings. At times, he appears unsteady, but his dental nurse has been with him for a number of years and is very supportive, helping to ensure that each session runs as smoothly as possible.

How should the dental hygienist handle this situation?

10

END OF LIFE DECISIONS

Learning Objectives

At the end of this chapter, the reader will:

1 Have an understanding of a range of concepts pertaining to end of life decisions, and be able to distinguish between active and passive euthanasia.

2 Be aware of the primary arguments for and against withdrawal of artificial nutrition and hydration for patients in a permanent vegetative state.

3 Acknowledge the primary arguments for and against physician-assisted suicide and voluntary active euthanasia.

4 Be aware of the Dutch law on euthanasia, and consider the validity of current safeguards to prevent abuse.

1 INTRODUCTION

Niels Bohr, the Danish physicist and founder of modern quantum theory, was once quoted as saying: 'those who are not shocked when they first come across [it] cannot possibly have understood it' (Kumar, 2009). Regretfully, however, euthanasia is one of those areas that can excite shock and horror without necessarily a full appraisal of the issues. It is one of the most controversial areas of healthcare, and it is capable of polarising public opinion. Indeed, Jackson (2010) argues that interest in the subject is increasing, because people are living longer these days and are therefore more likely to have chronic, debilitating and painful illnesses. Add to this the recognition that people are now more aware of their personal rights of autonomy, and that religion has less influence on our society than in the past, and it becomes easy to see that the concept of euthanasia will remain in the forefront of public debate.

There is already a vast amount of literature on the subject, and those who seek to add to it run the risk of confusing the issues, rather than clarifying them. Nevertheless, the purpose of this chapter is to examine the law as it relates to end of life decisions in the United Kingdom, explain a few of the concepts that inform the debate, and then to consider the legal position in other jurisdictions (to see if the lessons learned there can be translated to our own society). Unlike in some earlier chapters, no attempt is made to separate law and ethics, for it is impossible to talk about one without mentioning the other. Nor does this chapter look specifically at end of life decisions pertaining to *children*, unless a case raises a particularly relevant point. Such issues have already been covered in Chapter 8, most notably the case of *Re A [2001]*.

A common and convenient starting point in any discussion of euthanasia is to offer up a few definitions, and the concept is usually separated into an active and a passive form. Active euthanasia implies that a person's life has been brought deliberately to a premature end by means of an intervention by a healthcare professional (e.g. a lethal injection); and it can be sub-divided further into the following three categories:

a   voluntary (i.e. at the patient's request).
b   non-voluntary (i.e. where the patient is unable to make a decision).
c   involuntary (i.e. where the patient, although competent, has not consented to euthanasia).

As Brazier and Cave (2007) note, all three of these constitute the crime of murder in the United Kingdom as the law currently stands. Passive euthanasia can also be sub-divided into the above three categories, and usually implies the withholding or withdrawing of life-sustaining treatment, so that nature is allowed to take its course. The term is also applied to the administration of life-shortening drugs (e.g. powerful painkillers), as long as the primary purpose of those drugs is to alleviate the patient's symptoms. This is a point to which we shall return in some detail later on, but suffice it to say at this point that passive euthanasia carries a legal defence in certain situations, and is seen by most as both morally acceptable and good healthcare practice in those situations.

There are, however, at least a couple of problems with these definitions. For one thing, it is not always possible to determine with any certainty whether the actions or inactions of healthcare professionals constitute active or passive euthanasia, and the leading case in this area is a good illustration of this confusion. Moreover, Montgomery (2003) notes that passive euthanasia can carry the same legal sanctions as its active counterpart if the healthcare professional had a duty to take measures to preserve the life of a patient. Imagine, for example, the following scenario:

Box 10.1

A young patient is brought into hospital with a chest infection. The doctors decide to withhold antibiotics and the patient subsequently dies. Their argument is that it was the *disease* that caused the death, and therefore, the withholding of antibiotics has simply allowed nature to take its course.

There may be extraneous factors that provide an acceptable justification for the doctors' decision (for example, the patient may already have a terminal illness); but, in the absence of these, we would have to say that they have failed in their duty and are thereby legally, morally and professionally culpable.

The Royal College of Physicians and British Society of Gastroenterology (2010) advocate that the term 'euthanasia' should be reserved for its active form, for 'passive euthanasia' causes confusion. For the reasons stated above, however, a complete disregard for the latter could potentially create more problems. The RCP have in mind those situations where the clinical issues are clear and where the healthcare professionals are acting in good faith. Unfortunately, however, there will be cases where either or both of these factors are absent. The distinction between active and passive euthanasia pervades the case law and the literature, and cannot therefore be ignored. Perhaps the concept of euthanasia is usefully considered as a distinction between the incompetent patient and the competent patient. Although there is a strong measure of overlap between the two, there are enough significant differences to enable the distinction to bring a little clarity to the discussion.

2 THE INCOMPETENT PATIENT

The leading case in this field is that of *Airedale NHS Trust v Bland [1993]*, the broad facts of which can be stated thus:

Box 10.2 *Airedale NHS Trust v Bland [1993]*

Tony Bland was 17 years old when he attended an FA Cup semi-final at Hillsborough football ground on 15 April 1989. In the disaster that followed, Tony was one of those who sustained severe crush injuries. He had been in cardio-respiratory arrest for about eight minutes before the paramedic services got to him, whereupon (incredibly) he was resuscitated. However a later brain scan demonstrated that the prolonged duration of anoxia had caused his cerebral cortex to 'resolve into a watery mass' (per Lord Keith at 856). He was therefore in what is now known as a permanent vegetative state (PVS): he was completely unaware of his surroundings and totally insensate. The fact that his brain stem remained intact, though, meant that his heart and lungs continued to function without assistance. His parents and the hospital asked for the court's permission to withdraw the artificial nutrition and hydration (ANH), so that he could be allowed to die.

This case was heard before the High Court, the Court of Appeal and the House of Lords. In total, nine judges made speeches outlining the reasons for their decision, and the pages of text ran into three figures. These facts alone tell us three things: first, the courts were fully aware that this was a case of huge significance; second, that they took their responsibilities very seriously and were prepared to explore every possible aspect;

and third, that they recognised that only they were going to be in a position to make this judgement. In consequence, their courage and diligence cannot be faulted, but this does not automatically imply that they arrived at the correct decision.

All nine judges came to the same conclusion (albeit by different routes), all accepting that ANH could be withdrawn from Tony Bland. It is important to note the true cause of his death, though: it was *not* the injuries he sustained at Hillsborough, nor was it the fact that he was in PVS. He could, at least in theory, have survived for many years in this condition, and Campbell et al. (2006) record that the longest reported survival is 37 years. Thus, the only logical conclusion to be drawn is that Tony Bland died of dehydration as a direct result of being denied his only means of fluid replacement. In recognition of this, the hospital caring for him asked the court if withdrawal of ANH would constitute the crime of murder, for which there is only one sentence: life imprisonment.

Not surprisingly, this case raised many issues, and they are perhaps best seen as a series of conflicts between diametrically opposed perspectives.

A WHICH IS OF GREATER IMPORTANCE: THE SANCTITY OF LIFE OR THE QUALITY OF LIFE?

The sanctity of life principle states that life is a gift from God, and only God can take it away. Clearly, this position emanates from, and is heavily influenced by, religious teachings, and we should not forget that the law in this country owes its origins to Christian principles. One does not necessarily have to be particularly religious to hold this view, though, for it is also supported by those who believe in the equal value of all human life (Herring, 2008). Certainly, it is the default position of the courts, and is best expressed by Taylor, L.J. (at 52) in *Re J [1991]*:

> the court's high respect for the sanctity of human life imposes a strong presumption in favour of taking all steps capable of preserving it, save in exceptional circumstances.

The last phrase in this quotation is significant, because it implies that the courts fall short of adopting the Vitalist position, which holds that life should be preserved *at all costs* (Pattinson, 2009). The courts acknowledge that there are some situations where the continued sustenance of a patient demeans life, rather than enhances it; and Brazier and Cave (2007) note that 'unlimited access to technology may sometimes be as cruel as the illness itself' (p. 486). At what point a person's life becomes so intolerable or lacking in value (so that it is no longer worth living) is a key feature of this debate. Consider the following American case:

Box 10.3   In the matter of Claire Conroy [1985]

Ms Conroy was an elderly lady who had end-stage Alzheimer's Disease and who required all nursing care. Among the long list of her problems, she was confined to bed and contracted into a semi-foetal position. She had heart disease, hypertension and diabetes; her left leg was gangrenous to the knee; she had several bed sores; she was incontinent of faeces; she was unable to speak, and her ability to swallow was very limited.

On a more positive note, however, she was able to interact with her environment in some limited ways. For example, she had some movement in her head, neck, hands and arms, and her eyes sometimes followed individuals in the room. In addition, she moaned occasionally when moved, and she sometimes smiled when her hair was combed or she was given a comforting rub.

The court heard arguments from the hospital that this lady's life no longer had any meaning and that keeping her alive by means of ANH compromised her dignity. As things transpired, she died before this case came before the court, thereby rendering any judicial decision somewhat moot. Nevertheless, the case received a full hearing, because it was recognised that this was not a unique situation, and healthcare professionals were keen to have guidance on what to do in these matters. At the first trial court, permission was granted to withdraw ANH, but this decision was reversed in the appeal court. However, the Supreme Court of New Jersey found in favour of the first judge's decision, arguing that ANH was equivalent to ventilation and that: 'the net burdens of the patient's life with treatment should clearly and markedly outweigh the benefits that the patient derives from life'.

Many will take issue with the decision in this case, and it does pose a few problems (Mason and Laurie, 2011). For example, there appeared to be a presumption that the patient was in severe and intractable pain, but this is by no means certain. A gangrenous leg would normally be agonising, but Ms Conroy's diabetes had probably induced a peripheral neuropathy (http://www.medicinenet.com/diabetic_neuropathy/article.htm). Moreover, there are clear dangers in making subjective judgements about the quality of a patient's life. Ms Conroy was perhaps an extreme case, but there will be other cases where the disabilities are not as severe. It is one thing to say 'If *I* were in that person's position, I would not want to carry on living'; but it does not automatically imply that the individual patient feels the same way, nor can it be assumed that I would not change my mind if I were ever to find myself in this situation.

If this case had been heard in the United Kingdom, it seems likely that the result would have been different; and support for this assertion comes from the following case:

Box 10.4   *W Healthcare NHS Trust and another v H and another [2004]*

The patient, aged 59, had suffered from multiple sclerosis for almost 30 years, and she now required all nursing care. Although she was conscious, she was completely disorientated and no longer recognised her own family. She had been fed by means of a

(Continued)

(Continued)

percutaneous gastrostomy tube (PEG) for the last five years, but this fell out and the family asked the hospital not to re-insert it. They further claimed that she had expressed a wish, when competent, that she should not be kept alive if she could no longer recognise her daughters. The hospital, however, believed that the tube should be reinstated.

The court found in favour of the hospital, for there was no evidence that the patient had made an Advance Decision to refuse treatment, and nor could she have considered the full implications of the withdrawal of ANH. In other words, she would suffer if feeding was withdrawn (unlike Tony Bland, who was completely insensate).

In terms of their facts, the differences between this case and that of *Claire Conroy* are not significant, but the findings of the respective courts clearly are. In an English court, the presumption in favour of life can only be overturned if continued treatment imposes a truly intolerable burden upon the patient. This 'intolerability test' – which saw its genesis in *Re B [1981]* and which secured endorsement in *Re J [1991]* and *W Healthcare NHS Trust v H [2004]* – has been apparently disapproved by the Court of Appeal in *Wyatt v Portsmouth Hospitals NHS Trust [2005]*. However, even though the court has stated that the 'best interests' test is the one to use, it also acknowledges that intolerability is a valuable guide in the search for those interests. Thus, Foster's (2005) contention that the judges in *Wyatt* have confused the law by dismantling the intolerability test seems a little pessimistic.

But where does this leave us in our discussion of the *Bland* case? It is comparatively easy to argue that Tony Bland no longer had a reasonable quality of life – in fact, he had *none* of the features that we would consider make a life meaningful. And yet, continued survival was not *intolerable* to him. How could it be, when he had no consciousness and no sensations? Therefore, arguments citing quality of life as justification for the withdrawal of ANH appear to fall short when applied to patients in PVS. If we are to find a valid reason, we must look elsewhere.

B IS WITHDRAWAL OF ANH AN ACT OR AN OMISSION?

If a terminally ill patient is admitted to hospital with a chest infection and the doctors decide to withhold antibiotics, we would call this an Omission. The antibiotics might have prolonged the life of that patient, but they would also thereby have prolonged his suffering, for the disease was destined to kill him. Thus, not only would the withholding of life-prolonging treatment be legally acceptable in this instance, most would also see it as being morally justifiable. If, on the other hand, the doctor administers a lethal injection to put an end to the man's suffering, this would be an Act (or a Commission, if you prefer). Not only would this incur the disapproval of the public and professional bodies, it would be a criminal offence, regardless of the doctor's motives.

Put in this way, the distinction between Acts and Omissions seems straightforward; and both the law and morality can accept that the latter is permissible, whereas the former is not. However, situations in practice are frequently more complicated than this, and perhaps the best-known example illustrating confusion between the two concepts comes from Rachels (1975):

Box 10.5

Smith stands to gain a large inheritance if his six-year-old nephew dies. He therefore creeps up behind him while he is having a bath and drowns him.

Jones also stands to gain a large inheritance from the death of his nephew and has precisely the same intentions as Smith. However, before he can commit the deed, the nephew slips in the bath, hits his head, becomes unconscious, and sinks beneath the water. Jones does nothing to rescue him.

In this scenario, Smith has committed an Act, whereas Jones is guilty of an Omission; but is there a moral difference between the two? Rachels believes not, arguing that both uncles are equally reprehensible and culpable. In doing so, he argues that the moral distinction between Acts and Omissions must, of necessity, be bogus. Not everyone would put it this strongly, though. For example, Campbell et al. (2006) contend that the 'facts' of this scenario are so shocking that they distort our perceptions. If we were to accept Rachels's position without question, there would be no moral difference between failing to send aid to a village whose inhabitants were starving and driving through the village with a machine-gun, shooting people indiscriminately.

For all this, attempts to justify a course of action by appealing to the Acts/Omission distinction frequently run into difficulties of semantics and logic. In speaking of the discontinuation of artificial ventilation, Kennedy (1991) says: 'To describe turning off the machine as an omission does some considerable violence to the ordinary English usage' (p. 351). Mason and Laurie (2011) concur: not switching the ventilator on in the first place would be an omission, but one has to *act* to turn it off. The same difficulties face us when we turn our attention back to *Bland*. The Official Solicitor (who represented Tony Bland in court) argued that the removal of the naso-gastric tube was an Act, and this would inevitably hasten death. The Law Lords, however, disagreed:

In my judgement, essentially what is being done is to omit to feed or ventilate; the removal of the naso-gastric tube or the switching off a ventilator are merely incidents of that omission (per Lord Browne-Wilkinson at 881).

Thus, the court managed to achieve its desired objective by holding on to the Acts/ Omission distinction. Whether one accepts their reasoning is largely a matter of personal choice, but it is difficult to avoid the conclusion that this escape route was a little too convenient. We must therefore look for alternative justifications for withdrawing ANH.

C WAS WITHDRAWAL OF ANH IN TONY BLAND'S 'BEST INTERESTS'?

It was the considered belief of Tony Bland's parents that, if in a position to voice an opinion, he would not want to live in the state that he was now in. They had no firm evidence to support this assertion, though, because he had expressed no opinions on the subject before his injuries were sustained. Nevertheless, they felt confident in assuming that this is exactly what he would have said, and that it was therefore in his best interests to die. These arguments are often supported by reference to our treatment of sick animals: in other words, if an animal was suffering and/or its life no longer had any meaning for it, we would put the poor creature out of its misery.

There are two problems with this argument. First, there are many things that we do to animals that we would not dream of doing to humans. Second, we have already established that Tony Bland was not suffering. Therefore, to say that death was in his best interests stretches the bounds of logic, as Lord Mustill came to recognise:

> By ending his life the doctors will not relieve him of a burden become intolerable, for others carry the burden and he has none ... The distressing truth which must not be shirked, is that the proposed conduct is not in the best interests of Anthony Bland, for he has no best interests of any kind (at 894).

Others have suggested that someone in PVS can still have interests. Pattinson (2009), for example, argues that a being with 'no interests' would have no status, and therefore would be owed no moral duties. Clearly, nobody would have suggested that this was true of Tony Bland. Similarly, Jackson (2010) contends that it would not be unreasonable to assume that he had an ongoing interest in ending the distress of his family. Whatever the truth, we unquestionably run into difficulties when we say that a person would be 'better off dead', because none of us have any proof of what being dead is like. We may have an idea, particularly if we hold strong religious views, but the only time that we will ever know for certain is when we ourselves die (and perhaps not even then, if death is equivalent to oblivion).

Once again, therefore, our search for a justification for withdrawing ANH from Tony Bland runs into an obstacle. Perhaps the next issue discussed in the case offers new hope.

D DOES ANH CONSTITUTE TREATMENT OR IS IT A NECESSITY OF LIFE?

The point of this question is that medical treatment can be withdrawn lawfully if it can be seen to serve no useful purpose. A basic necessity of life, however, cannot be withdrawn without incurring a charge of criminal neglect. The fact that Tony Bland was completely dependent upon the healthcare staff for his nutritional needs has no relevance to this question, for the same situation exists with a baby who relies totally on his/her mother to provide him/her with sustenance. Nor (if we accept that ANH constitutes a necessity) could Tony Bland have pre-empted this situation with an Advance Decision, for the Mental Capacity Act Code of Practice (2007) states that refusals cannot apply to 'basic or essential care' (s 9.28). The Code of Practice goes on to define such care as warmth, shelter, hygiene, and oral nutrition/hydration; and the last of these suggests that feeding by means of a tube would fall outside this category.

Certainly, the provision of such feeding involves the use of medical devices, and it requires the skills of a range of qualified healthcare professionals. Such considerations were sufficient to convince the court:

> [In answer to] the argument that feeding by means of the nasogastric tube was not medical treatment at all, but simply feeding indistinguishable from feeding by normal means, ... I am of opinion that regard should be had to the whole regime, including the artificial feeding, which at present keeps Anthony Bland alive. That regime amounts to medical treatment and care, and it is incorrect to direct attention exclusively to the fact that nourishment is being provided (per Lord Keith at 861).

Some will see this as a simple expression of common sense, while others will feel that it has skirted over the issues rather too easily. It would, for example, have been possible to feed Tony Bland with a spoon, for most PVS patients will retain primitive gag, cough, suck and swallow reflexes (Campbell et al., 2005). No doubt this would have been a slow and tortuous process, and there would always be the risk of aspiration. It would, in consequence, carry greater risks than ANH; but equally it would remove it from the sphere of 'medical treatment' and put it firmly within the orbit of 'basic care'.

Considerations such as this may have added to the confusion surrounding this case, but ultimately they were never destined to alter its outcome. The reason for this is that the question posed at the beginning of this section is essentially a 'red herring'. The Official Solicitor (representing Tony Bland) had argued that 'feeding in order to sustain life is *necessarily* for the benefit of the patient' (per Lord Lowry at 876); but the court unanimously held that he derived no benefits from it at all. In other words, it served no useful purpose whatsoever, and was therefore futile. By logical extension, treatment or care that is futile can be withdrawn. Such arguments could never hope to satisfy proponents of the sanctity of life doctrine, but they were sufficient to be accepted as a legal principle, which has been applied in a variety of later cases.

E SHOULD TONY BLAND HAVE BEEN ALLOWED TO DIE OF DEHYDRATION, OR SHOULD HE HAVE BEEN KILLED QUICKLY BY MEANS OF LETHAL INJECTION?

Following withdrawal of ANH, it took Tony Bland ten days to die; if he had been given a lethal injection, it would have taken only a few minutes. There is something rather unsettling about all of this, for it is difficult to avoid the conclusion that there has been an element of moral hypocrisy at play here. The *purpose* of the court's decision was that Tony Bland should die: that was the inevitable consequence of withdrawing ANH, and they were in no doubt about this. So, why did they not grasp the nettle with both hands and sanction the lethal injection?

The answer provided by Lord Goff (at 867–8) was that it represented the difference between an Act and an Omission. Killing by means of lethal injection was an Act, and therefore unlawful; withdrawal of ANH was an Omission, and therefore acceptable. This is not entirely convincing, and we have already discussed the difficulties in drawing a moral distinction between the two. A more cogent reason, perhaps, is that expressed by Lord Goff a little earlier: 'once euthanasia is recognised as lawful in these circumstances, it is difficult to see any logical basis for excluding it in others' (at 867). In other words, he was concerned about the possibility of a 'slippery slope', where active killing of patients would be extended to a much broader range of cases. This is a concept to which we shall return shortly, but suffice it to say at this stage that the court felt that the lethal injection was a step too far. In consequence, Tony Bland was allowed to linger for ten days until his final passing. This seems somehow less humane than its alternative and a lot less dignified, despite the strenuous efforts of the court to display its caring credentials.

It would be fair to say that Tony Bland did not suffer during these ten days, for the extent of his brain damage rendered him incapable of experiencing such feelings. But it would not have been pleasant for the staff or the relatives to watch him slowly slip away. In the American case of *Schindler v Schiavo [2003]* a young woman was in PVS and her husband sought the court's permission to withdraw ANH. Consent was eventually obtained, but not without the forceful objections of the woman's parents, who let the world know how she died:

> Watching someone being starved and dehydrated to death, let alone your own daughter, is something so cruel that it can never be forgotten. Terri's dying face was skeletal. Her skin was blotchy, parched and peeling. Terri's lips and tongue were cracked and dry. Witnessing her life ebbing away as she desperately struggled for a breath of air is beyond the realm of human comprehension. Yet, [those who were responsible for this] had the audacity to say she died a peaceful death with dignity (www.slobokan.com).

If we were to accept the legal and moral validity of the lethal injection, we would then be faced with the question of whose responsibility it would be to administer it. There might be an argument for a peripatetic squadron of people, who would have no special interest in each case and who could therefore dispense their services dispassionately. More likely, however, the onus would fall upon those healthcare professionals who were closely involved in the care of the patient. This would normally, although not necessarily, be a doctor, and practice would undoubtedly acknowledge the rights of the practitioner to exercise a conscientious objection. Many would raise such an objection; but equally, a number would be prepared to do it. Kinnell (2000) notes that the medical profession 'attracts some people with a pathological interest in the power of life and death' (p. 1594); but this does not detract from the fact that most would be acting from a genuine sense of caring.

F DID BLAND REPRESENT AN EXTREME CASE, OR WAS THIS THE BEGINNING OF A SLIPPERY SLOPE?

The House of Lords was very keen to establish that *Bland* did not establish a precedent, and that all future cases must come before the court if withdrawal of ANH is to be legally sanctioned. It was acknowledged that a body of case law might be built up over time to render recourse to the courts unnecessary, but this would probably take several years. In the meantime, Lord Goff (drawing upon advice from the British Medical Association's Medical Ethics Committee) sought to lay down some guidelines for future judges (at 871). Thus, before considering withdrawal of ANH from patients in PVS, the court must be satisfied of four things:

1 Every effort had been made to rehabilitate the patient for at least six months after the injury.
2 That the diagnosis of irreversible PVS had not been made until at least 12 months after the injury.
3 That the diagnosis of irreversible PVS had been made and agreed by two other independent doctors.
4 That, generally, the wishes of the patient's immediate family had been given great weight.

Brazier and Cave (2007) note that these conditions did not survive the test of time, and point to three cases which have eroded these limitations:

Box 10.6 *Frenchay Healthcare NHS Trust v S [1994]*

A patient had taken a drug overdose and had apparently been in PVS for two and a half years. When his feeding tube became disconnected, the hospital sought court authorisation not to re-insert it. The declaration was granted by the Court of Appeal, but they did not insist upon a confirmation of the diagnosis of PVS by independent doctors, even though there were some doubts about this diagnosis.

Thus, the third of Lord Goff's conditions had not lasted one year. Perhaps a more logical approach to this case would have been to order the re-insertion of the feeding tube, seek confirmation of the diagnosis by two independent doctors, and then ask the Trust to return to court. The fact that the court did not do this suggests that it felt much more comfortable in ordering that the tube should not be re-inserted than in ordering its withdrawal. In other words, it remained unconvinced by the House of Lords' contention in *Bland* that withdrawal of ANH constituted an Omission rather than an Act.

Box 10.7   *Re D [1998]*

A patient had sustained severe brain damage following a road traffic accident, and her feeding tube became disconnected (as in *S*). This patient did not completely satisfy all of the criteria of PVS (as suggested by the Royal College of Physicians), but the judge was satisfied that there was 'no evidence of any meaningful life whatsoever' (per Stephen Brown P. at 420).

Quite what the judge meant by this is open to interpretation, but it certainly suggests that the courts are prepared to break free from the constraints laid down in *Bland*. Thus, a diagnosis of PVS was not absolutely necessary for ANH to be withheld; and nor, as can be seen in the next case, was it necessary for ANH to be withdrawn.

Box 10.8   *Re H [1998]*

As in *Re D*, the patient had sustained brain damage following a road traffic accident. Although severely disabled, she could not have been said to be in PVS (in the accepted sense of the term), for she displayed some awareness of her surroundings. For example, her eyes followed the movement of people across her room. Nevertheless, the High Court allowed the withdrawal of ANH.

Does all of this suggest that *Bland* initiated a slippery slope, albeit unwittingly? The concept of a slippery slope dictates that, once we get on it, we cannot remove ourselves, and we slide inexorably and ever more quickly until we reach rock bottom. The Abortion Act 1967 is occasionally cited as an example of this, for it is inconceivable that the architects of this legislation could have imagined that it would lead to the thousands of terminations carried out every year in the UK. A difficulty with this interpretation is that the Act coincided with changes in cultural philosophy, which led to a greater sense of personal freedom (sexually and otherwise). Had it not done so, it is not inevitable that the slippery slope would have occurred.

Despite this, the slippery slope remains a powerful argument for those who oppose the decision in *Bland*, and it is frequently resurrected when considering the issues of

Voluntary Active Euthanasia and Physician-Assisted Suicide (to which we shall return later). For now, we can end the discussion on the implications of *Bland* by drawing two main conclusions. The *first* is that the courts' default position of upholding the sanctity of life principle will be sacrificed if it is considered that the patient's life no longer has any value, meaning or quality. This must explain why the criteria for withdrawing ANH in *Bland* have been eroded so quickly in later cases, and why the concept of medical futility was so enthusiastically embraced. In other words, if treatment served no useful purpose, it could (and even should) be withdrawn. McLean (2006), however, has noted the inherent contradiction in this position:

> irrespective of the quality or length of the life ANH can sustain, its provision is certainly not futile as it achieves precisely what it is intended to: that is, it keeps the patient alive.

Nevertheless, where there is any indication that the patient derives some meaning from life, the court will quickly revert to its default position. In *W (by her litigation friend, B) v M (by her litigation friend, the Official Solicitor) and others [2012]*, for example, a patient was in a minimally conscious state (MCS), but there was evidence that she gained pleasure from company and from music. The court, adopting a balance-sheet approach, concluded that the preservation of M's life outweighed all other considerations, and therefore refused the withdrawal of ANH.

The *second* conclusion is closely allied to the first, stating that the courts will be heavily influenced by the evidence of the medical profession when making their judgments. This can, perhaps, be best seen in the following extract from the speech of Lord Browne-Wilkinson (at 882–3) in *Bland*:

> where the responsible doctor comes to the reasonable conclusion (which accords with the views of a responsible body of medical opinion) that further continuance of an intrusive life system is not in the best interests of the patient, he can no longer lawfully continue that life support system.

We have already suggested that the concept of 'best interests' may not have application in this scenario; and we can probably discount Lord Browne-Wilkinson's suggestion that a doctor might be guilty of battery if s/he continued to provide life-sustaining measures. What is of particular interest here is the phrase in brackets, for this is a definition of the *Bolam* test (from *Bolam v Friern Hospital Management Committee [1957]* – see Chapter 3). To put it another way, the judge is saying that withdrawal of ANH is a *clinical* decision, and doctors are therefore best placed to make this judgement. It could also be argued, though, that this is more of an *ethical* decision than a clinical one; and, if so, there is no reason why the views of doctors should be decisive.

It is with this thought in mind that a number of hospitals have created Clinical Ethics Committees (CECs). The Ethox website (www.ethox.org.uk) suggests that there are at least 60 such Committees across the country, and that their numbers are increasing. They are much more common in the USA (Slowther and Hope, 2000; McLean, 2007a), which is where they originated; and this probably reflects the increased risks of litigation in that country. Nevertheless, a Clinical Ethics Committee generally has three main functions:

1   It provides advisory support for clinicians when faced with a moral dilemma.
2   It develops policies and guidelines pertaining to legal and ethical issues.
3   It raises awareness of ethical issues among the hospital staff by means of education (Montgomery, 2003; Gillon, 1997).

The first of these may hold the most significance, but it is important to note that individual clinicians retain ultimate responsibility for any decision taken, and are therefore at liberty to reject advice from the CEC. Hendrick (2001) notes that this absence of binding authority essentially absolves the CEC from legal liability if a patient or relative was to seek redress for any decision made.

Membership of such Committees is variable, but inevitably will include doctors, nurses, and members of the Trust Board. Equally, it is expected that the CEC will include several lay members: for example, a lawyer, an ethicist, a chaplain, and possibly a service user. A CEC does, however, face a number of difficulties, most especially inter-disciplinary tensions and the concern among doctors that their autonomy is being eroded (Gillon, 1997). Despite these problems, though, such Committees represent an attempt to ease the pressure of ethical decision-making upon clinicians and to ensure that a variety of perspectives are considered when analysing complex moral dilemmas. Moreover, they represent an attempt to move away from Lord Browne-Wilkinson's implied contention that 'doctor knows best'.

We have seen that the decision in *Bland* has been subjected to heavy criticism, and that each statement of the judges presiding over this case can be disputed. We should not, however, be too critical, for they were faced with a terribly difficult decision. To their credit, they approached the issues conscientiously and rigorously, recognising that they alone were charged with determining Tony Bland's fate. The plaintive cries of their Lordships for legislation on this matter were destined for disappointment, for a Government is unlikely to tackle something that could lose votes so easily. Moreover, although the judicial reasoning may have been flawed, the decision accorded with most people's intuitions: namely, that Tony Bland no longer had a life that any of us would recognise as being meaningful. Perhaps there are two lessons to be learnt from this case (neither of which, incidentally, has shown any signs of being adopted):

1   Much confusion and hand-wringing could be avoided if everybody (especially the judges) was open and honest about what was happening when ANH was withdrawn (Mason and Laurie, 2011). The patient does not die of his/her original injuries or of PVS – s/he dies of dehydration, caused by removal of the life-support system.
2   The current definition of death relates to cessation of function of the brain stem (Conference of Medical Royal Colleges and their Faculties in the UK, 1976), and this created most of the problems in *Bland*, for it did not apply in this case. Therefore, technically, Tony Bland was not dead in the accepted sense of the term, and an intervention was required to make this a reality. Lord Browne-Wilkinson (at 878) suggested

that a re-definition of death (to include those in PVS) would avoid all of these difficulties, but felt that Parliament should be the ones to make this decision.

Adoption of these measures would not bring an end to the controversy surrounding the withdrawal of ANH from patients in PVS, for there will always be those who are bitterly opposed to the idea. It might, though, add a greater degree of stability to the law.

3 THE COMPETENT PATIENT

A REFUSAL OF TREATMENT

We start with the premise that an adult competent patient has the right to refuse treatment, even if this refusal will result in certain death; and that the right 'exists notwithstanding that the reasons for making the choice are rational, or irrational, unknown or even non-existent' (*Re T [1992]*, per Lord Donaldson at 653). This has not, however, always been the legal position, as the following case illustrates:

Box 10.9   *Leigh v Gladstone [1909]*

A suffragette was imprisoned and went on hunger strike in protest at her incarceration. She was fed against her wishes, and brought an action against the prison doctor, alleging that she was the victim of a battery. The court, however, held that the prison doctor had a duty to preserve the lives of prisoners, and that force-feeding was therefore justified.

In this case, the court's natural predisposition to preserve life was supported by the fact that both suicide and attempted suicide were criminal offences. In consequence, the prison doctor who allowed the suffragette to starve herself to death would be aiding and abetting this crime. The passing of the Suicide Act 1961 rendered the court's position in *Leigh* invalid, for it decriminalised suicide and attempted suicide. As Jackson (2010) notes, this Act had two fundamental purposes:

1   Prior to 1961, if a person committed suicide, his/her property was confiscated, imposing additional and unnecessary suffering on the relatives. The Suicide Act 1961 therefore removed this iniquity.
2   When a person *attempted* suicide before this time, s/he would be prosecuted and possibly imprisoned. The Suicide Act 1961 was an acknowledgement that such people need help, rather than chastisement. Moreover, they would be more likely to seek medical assistance before making an attempt if the fear of prosecution was removed.

Therefore, the case of *Secretary of State for the Home Department v Robb [1995]*, in which a prisoner's right to refuse food was upheld by the court, represents a good contrast with *Leigh*, and is a much closer approximation to current law. Note, however, that the individual must be assessed as competent before his/her refusal can be accepted as being legally valid. In *R v Collins, ex parte Brady [2000]*, it was held that the force-feeding of the Moors murderer Ian Brady was justified, because his mental illness rendered his decision to starve himself to death invalid.

Robb, of course, was not a medical case in the strictest sense of the term, but the principle enunciated there can be seen at work in the following:

Box 10.10   *B v An NHS Trust [2002]*

Ms B sustained a spinal haemorrhage, and within two years was paralysed from the neck down. She was only able to breathe with the assistance of a ventilator, but was fully conscious and alert. She was insistent that she had no wish to carry on living like this, and asked the doctors to switch off the ventilator. When they refused, she brought a court action against the Trust. The court was satisfied that Ms B was competent and that her decision was not the result of clinical depression. Therefore, continued ventilation constituted a battery, and the court ordered it to be switched off so that Ms B could be allowed to die.

This case mirrors the Canadian case of *Nancy B v Hotel-Dieu de Quebec [1992]* and the New Zealand case of *Auckland Area Health Board v A-G [1993]*, both of which involved patients with Guillain-Barré syndrome and whose continued survival depended upon artificial ventilation. It also has similarities with a slightly earlier English case:

Box 10.11   *Re AK [2001]*

A patient suffering from motor neurone disease was being ventilated and fed by means of ANH. He was able to communicate only by moving one eyelid, but even this movement was destined to stop shortly. He asked that, when this position had been reached, all life-sustaining measures should be withdrawn.

The difference with *B* is that *AK* was making an Advance Decision – such decisions had legal authority at the time under the common law (from *Re T [1992]*), but now have statutory authority under the Mental Capacity Act 2005 (sections 24–26), provided that certain criteria are met. Despite this difference, the two cases exemplify the court's willingness to uphold the principle of self-determination, even where this may lead to the death of a patient. The principle, however, is not absolute, and the following case illustrates an important distinction:

Box 10.12 *R v Director of Public Prosecutions, ex parte Pretty [2001]*

Mrs Pretty had advanced motor neurone disease, which left her with severe muscular weakness and the necessity to be fed by means of ANH. Her debilitated condition meant that she would not be able to take her own life, but she asked the Director of Public Prosecutions (DPP) for assurances that her husband would not be prosecuted for helping her to die. The DPP refused, and the High Court (2001), House of Lords (2002), and the European Court (2003) all agreed that his refusal was correct.

Her primary argument was that the DPP was in breach of the Human Rights Act 1998, but the courts refused to accept that either Article 2 (the right to life) or Article 3 (the right to protection from inhuman or degrading treatment) conferred a right to be helped to end her life. In retrospect, it is inevitable that this decision would be reached, given the position of the law in the UK as it currently stands. Ms B was asking for medical treatment (i.e. ventilation) to be *withdrawn*, whereas Mrs Pretty was asking that her husband be granted immunity from committing murder. Jackson (2006) argues that the distinction may not be as clear-cut as has been made out, for the doctors had to *act* to end Ms B's life (i.e. by switching off the ventilator). However, she also acknowledges that Ms B had withdrawn her consent to continued treatment and that the doctors were thereby absolved from their duty to rescue her. Mrs Pretty, on the other hand, was seeking a much more active intervention, and the law does not sanction such activity at present.

There was, nevertheless, an enormous wave of public sympathy for Mrs Pretty's predicament, which was made all the more poignant when she died 12 days after the European ruling, in much the same manner as she had most dreaded (and which she had sought to avoid). It is interesting to speculate upon what would have happened if her husband had helped her to die without seeking the DPP's approval. Almost inevitably, this would have been classified a 'mercy killing', and the courts have tended to be lenient in such cases in the past (Montgomery, 2003). It was not, however, a risk that Mr Pretty was prepared to take, even though 'playing by the rules' worked to his wife's disadvantage.

B THE DOCTRINE OF DOUBLE EFFECT

Just as the refusal of a competent adult will serve as a defence if life-sustaining treatment is withdrawn, so too can the administration of life-*shortening* treatment in certain situations. The doctrine of double effect can be stated thus: 'A good primary motive is seen to outweigh an undesirable, but known, secondary result' (Montgomery, 2003: 465). What this means, in essence, is that it is permissible to administer strong analgesia (e.g. Diamorphine) to the terminally ill – the *primary* motive here is to alleviate pain, even though it is known that such drugs depress respiratory function and thereby hasten death. The *secondary* result (i.e. death), therefore, may be undesirable and known, but it is outweighed by the over-riding wish to ensure that the patient's last days are as comfortable as possible.

There have been a number of criticisms of this doctrine, particularly in its application to Abortion (Beauchamp and Childress, 2001); but its application to the administration of drugs which hasten death has remained comparatively uncontentious and has been accepted as a principle of law (see *Airedale NHS Trust v Bland [1993]*). In order for it to be legal, however, Montgomery (2003) notes that three conditions need to be satisfied:

> i The patient must have a terminal illness, so that it can be argued that it was the *illness* that caused his disease, rather than the drugs alone. It has been suggested that the evidence for claiming that strong opioids hasten death is not entirely convincing, and that they may actually be life-prolonging (Sykes and Thorne, 2003). Certainly, it seems reasonable to assume that continuous agonising pain would be much more effective at shortening a person's life than strong analgesia. If this is true, then it would seem that the doctrine of double effect is somewhat overplayed. It will serve as a defence, however, even if the doctor's diagnosis of terminal illness is incorrect, as the following case illustrates:

Box 10.13   *R v Moor [1999]*

A patient (George Liddell) was 85 years old and had bowel cancer. He underwent a bowel resection and was discharged to the care of his daughter. However, he quickly became immobile, depressed, and in severe pain. Dr Moor (his GP) assumed that Mr Liddell's pain was caused by the return of his cancer, and he prescribed Diamorphine via a syringe driver. When the syringe driver ran out, however, he gave a bolus injection of Diamorphine and Largactyl, and the patient died within 20 minutes. At post mortem, it was discovered that Mr Liddell was not terminally ill from the cancer, although he did have a heart condition, which probably accounted for his appearance and level of debilitation.

The court was satisfied that Dr Moor's primary intention was to relieve pain in a patient whom he believed was in the terminal stages of cancer. Thus, even though his diagnosis was incorrect, he did not intend to kill the patient. Given the difficulties of securing a conviction in these cases, an acquittal was almost inevitable. There were, however, one or two aspects of this case that suggested that the court had acted generously, most notably that Dr Moor openly admitted in a TV debate that he had helped some of his patients to die (Arlidge, 2000). Perhaps, though, the judge's sympathetic direction to the jury reflected the fact that the alternative to acquittal was life imprisonment.

ii Prescribing the drugs must satisfy the *Bolam* test, i.e. it must be accepted as the proper thing to do by a respectable body of medical opinion. The following case illustrates this principle perfectly:

Box 10.14   *R v Cox [1992]*

Mrs Boyes was an elderly lady, who had rheumatoid arthritis (among other conditions) and who was in severe and intractable pain. Dr Cox had given her increasing doses of Diamorphine, but to no effect, and she begged him to end her misery. In desperation, he gave her an injection of potassium chloride, and she died shortly afterwards.

Dr Cox's closest friend (and certainly not a respectable body of medical opinion) could not have argued that potassium chloride served any therapeutic purpose. Its sole purpose, given in the concentration that it was in this instance, was to kill the patient, and it did this very effectively. The fact that Mrs. Boyes's body was cremated shortly after death proved fortuitous for Dr Cox, since it meant that a post mortem could not be conducted. In consequence, it could not be established 'beyond all reasonable doubt' that it was the potassium chloride that had killed Mrs Boyes. Dr Cox was therefore charged with the lesser offence of attempted murder, for which he was convicted and given a suspended prison sentence of one year. Moreover, he retained both his job and his registration.

iii The primary purpose of prescribing the drugs must not be to shorten the patient's life, but rather to ease his/her suffering. In other words, the doctor must always act in good faith. The assumption that this is always true, however, was called into question in the following case:

Box 10.15   *R v Adams [1957]*

Dr Adams was charged with the murder of an elderly lady after he administered large doses of opioids to her. She was incurably, but not terminally, ill, and Dr Adams had been named as a beneficiary in her will.

He was subsequently acquitted, for the court found it impossible to determine what level of opioid would constitute a lethal dose in this case. The opioids were medically indicated in her condition, and Dr Adams could not therefore be said to have been acting unreasonably. The fact that he stood to gain by his patient's death, however, added an uncomfortable complication to proceedings.

If we suspect that doctors Moor, Cox and Adams were all fortunate to escape the full consequences of their actions, we should acknowledge the dilemma faced by the courts. Legally, there is no distinction to be drawn between the cold-blooded killer and the doctor who administers large doses of opioids with the express intention of bringing a patient's suffering to an end: both are guilty of murder, for which the only penalty is life imprisonment. There is, though, a clear *moral* distinction, and this is reflected in judicial directions to the jury:

> You may consider it a great irony that a doctor who goes out of his way to care for [the patient] ends up facing the charge that he does. You may also consider it another great irony that the doctor who takes time on his day off to tend to a dying patient ends up on this charge (*R v Moor [1999]*, per Hooper, J.).

Therefore, the evidence suggests that the healthcare professional who acts in his/her patient's best interests will derive some protection from the law, although it remains a risky enterprise. Some would argue that there is an alternative strategy, which would achieve the desired effect and yet avoid the possibility of criminal charges. *Terminal sedation* is where the patient is heavily sedated so that s/he remains comatose until dead (Tännsjö, 2000). It was the favoured option of Kelly Taylor, a 30-year-old woman who had heart, lung, and spinal conditions, and less than one year to live (BBC News, 2007). She did not, however, have the support of the British Medical Association, who argued that terminal sedation was tantamount to euthanasia, and who were prepared to challenge her in court. Kelly later dropped the case (Care Not Killing, 2007), but it is interesting to speculate upon how the court would have addressed the issue. Is this euthanasia, or is it simply good palliative care?

Tännsjö (2000) argues that those who uphold the sanctity of life principle should be able to accept terminal sedation – it is not active killing, but it ensures that the terminally ill patient dies without suffering. Williams (2001), on the other hand, acknowledges that it satisfies all the requirements of the doctrine of double effect, except for one. Terminal sedation has to be accompanied by withdrawal of ANH if it is to achieve the desired result. However, withdrawal of ANH does not relieve suffering, and its intention is to bring about the death of the patient – the doctrine of double effect cannot therefore apply.

Kelly Taylor was in an interesting (albeit tragic) position. She had the right to refuse life-sustaining treatment (for example, ANH), but she did not have the right to demand treatment (i.e. terminal sedation) – see *R (on the application of Burke) v General Medical Council [2005]*. This rule suggests, therefore, that she would have lost the case, although the court would need to be satisfied that her symptoms could be controlled without the necessity for terminal sedation.

C PHYSICIAN-ASSISTED SUICIDE

For those who have a fundamental opposition to the premature ending of life, terminal sedation may represent the end-point of acceptability. In other words, they may just about tolerate this, but anything beyond this point will be anathema to them. They could not, therefore, accept physician-assisted suicide (PAS), in which the clinician provides the means to enable the patient to take his/her own life (Butcher, 2007). This may be by means of prescribing a lethal cocktail of drugs or setting up an intravenous system so that the patient can administer the medication themselves.

The American state of Oregon has passed legislation authorising the use of PAS in certain circumstances (Oregon Death with Dignity Act 1994). The patient must be terminally ill and competent to consent to PAS. In addition, the doctor's role is limited only to prescribing the oral medication (Brazier and Cave, 2007), and any form of direct assistance is prohibited. Mason and Laurie (2011) note that Oregon's Medicaid Plan funds PAS, but not certain other treatments (e.g. anti-retroviral treatment for HIV-positive patients), suggesting that resource issues may have played a part in this legislation (i.e. that it is cheaper to allow someone to die quickly than it is to maintain them in a state of chronic dependency). There is, however, a more fundamental problem with PAS, which was the reason why The Netherlands rejected it in favour of voluntary active euthanasia: namely, that it relies upon the patient being competent to do what is required (Campbell et al., 2006). The fact that the doctor is prohibited from assisting the patient means that s/he cannot even be present when the medication is administered, and there is clearly potential for the patient getting into serious difficulties here.

Therefore, if PAS were to be adopted in this country, the service provided by Dignitas in Switzerland would seem to represent a safer alternative. Note that the patient must still be competent, not only to consent to PAS, but also to administer the medication him/herself; and this would consequently have disbarred Mrs Pretty from availing herself of this service (for her muscular degeneration rendered her incapable of performing this act). Note also that it remains technically illegal to help anybody to travel abroad to obtain access to PAS, even though at least 100 UK citizens have done so since October 2002 and no prosecutions have resulted (Pattinson, 2009; Jackson, 2010).

The fact that nobody has been prosecuted so far is encouraging to those in favour of PAS, but the potential for criminal charges has not disappeared, since aiding and abetting a suicide remains an offence under the Suicide Act 1961 (section 2 [1]). In *Re Z [2004]*, the court acknowledged that a woman with a degenerative brain condition had the right to travel to Switzerland so that she could commit suicide, but the judge did not grant her husband immunity from prosecution by the DPP. The DPP did not prosecute, however; and nor were charges laid upon the parents of Daniel James, when they assisted their severely disabled son to travel abroad. He was not terminally ill, but the decision to take his own life was clearly his. Moreover, the DPP was satisfied that the parents had nothing to gain from their son's death.

Prosecution, therefore, is likely to be reserved for those who assist the suicide of another for selfish motives. That the DPP had not hitherto been open and honest about this left the law in a state of limbo and uncertainty, and the following case sought to clarify the position:

Box 10.16   *R v Director of Public Prosecutions, ex parte Purdy [2008]*

Mrs Purdy had progressive multiple sclerosis, and she foresaw that the time would soon come when she wanted to end her own life. She would therefore go to Switzerland, but wanted to postpone this until her condition had deteriorated further. At this point, she would probably need some assistance, and she asked the DPP for assurances that her husband would not be prosecuted. When the DPP refused to comment, she sought judicial review of this refusal.

Both the High Court (2008) and the Court of Appeal (2009) dismissed her claim, but the House of Lords (2010) held that the DPP was under a duty to be more transparent. His subsequent guidelines fell short of granting immunity to those who assisted the suicide of another, but they gave the clearest indication to date that those who act out of compassion and who report the suicide to the police will be afforded protection from prosecution (Laville, 2010). Some, of course, will see this as a major stride towards the legalisation of euthanasia, but the DPP was at pains to point out that he was not changing the law. If PAS were to be made legal, it would require Parliament to enact specific legislation, and there are no immediate signs that this is likely. Indeed, Lord Joffe has tried on numerous occasions to introduce an Assisted Dying for the Terminally Ill Bill (most recently, in 2006), but it has been defeated on each occasion. However, as Griffiths (1999) notes, the absence of legislation is likely to mean that PAS will continue 'without control or sanction and so is liable to true violation' (p. 116).

D VOLUNTARY ACTIVE EUTHANASIA

Proponents of the slippery slope argument will have detected a pattern in the foregoing. The courts' early acceptance of the doctrine of double effect has been followed by the legal withdrawal of ANH from those in a permanent vegetative state. In turn, the acknowledgement of terminal sedation as accepted medical practice has been succeeded by the DPP's tacit approval of PAS. Admittedly, this is a simplistic assessment of the situation, and each of these retain a number of safeguards to prevent abuse. Nevertheless, in combination, they represent a slow but steady erosion of one of the cornerstones of healthcare – namely, the moral prohibition on the premature termination of life. In other words, there has been a gradual desensitisation to the concept of hastening (or even causing) death. If we leave aside for the moment the idea that this is not necessarily a bad thing, the logical next step to take is that of Voluntary Active Euthanasia (VAE).

This stage has indeed been reached in The Netherlands, and the catalyst for change occurred in the following case:

Box 10.17 *The Postma Case [1973]*

A woman had a cerebral haemorrhage and was left severely disabled. She repeatedly expressed her wish to die, and her son (a doctor) gave her a fatal dose of morphine.

The doctor was prosecuted for murder, but the case excited a wave of public sympathy, and the court merely imposed a suspended sentence of one week's imprisonment. The importance of this case is that the court's judgment suggested that euthanasia could be acceptable in certain conditions. As a result, a number of subsequent similar cases all resulted in acquittal (or no punishment), until the Dutch Parliament eventually passed the Termination of Life on Request and Assisted Suicide (Review Procedures) Act in 2000. Essentially, this law was a recognition that euthanasia was already being practised on a large scale, and that there was a need to ensure that there were proper safeguards in place (de Haan, 2002). It is also an acknowledgement that the prevailing public mood was in favour of euthanasia. No doubt there were (and still are) voices of protest in The Netherlands, but they represent a minority.

Under the terms of the Act, any doctor wishing to terminate the life of a patient must satisfy the appropriate committee of the following things (section 2 [1]):

1 The patient has made a voluntary and well considered request for euthanasia. Thus, the decision can only be made by the patient him/herself; it can only be made by someone who is mentally competent; the patient must have been given sufficient information in order to make the decision (including the alternative options available); and the decision must be made in the absence of duress or undue influence from others. Moreover, the patient must have a durable preference for death, so that the wish remains consistent over a period of several weeks.
2 The patient must be in intractable and intolerable pain and/or have a terminal illness. Note that terminal illness is not necessarily a precondition for euthanasia to take place, but both doctor and patient must be in agreement that the situation is hopeless. For this decision to be made, of course, there must be an ongoing doctor-patient relationship.
3 The doctor must consult with an independent doctor, and the latter must be prepared to testify that VAE is an appropriate course of action to take.

Good practice within The Netherlands suggests that the doctor should also consult a nurse before making a final decision. This is not a legal requirement, but the doctor would be asked to justify why s/he has not availed him/herself of this option. Nurses are not permitted to administer the lethal injection, but they may be heavily involved in preparing the equipment and counselling the patient and relatives (Sheldon, 2001). A study by van Bruchem-van de Scheur et al. (2008), however, suggested that two-thirds of a sample of 1,172 Dutch nurses were opposed to assisting with this procedure, and they are allowed to withdraw on conscientious grounds.

Evidence to support or refute the contention that VAE in The Netherlands has initiated a slippery slope is frequently contradictory. Partly, this is because there is no statistical data of the number of patients who were euthanased prior to the passing of legislation, and comparisons are therefore impossible (Pattinson, 2009). But also, it is because the issue polarises opinion into two very distinct camps, and the 'evidence' may therefore be distorted to support a particular viewpoint. As Brazier and Cave (2007) state, 'dispassionate analysis of how voluntary euthanasia "works" in the Netherlands is hard to find' (p. 515).

Jackson (2010) cites evidence to suggest that the relatives of those patients who die as a result of euthanasia manage to cope better with bereavement. But perhaps the main argument of those who oppose VAE in principle is that the Dutch criteria are vague and lack precision (Keown, 1992). In other words, what exactly is meant by 'intractable and intolerable pain'? Wright (2000) notes that Dutch case law has extended the criteria to include patients with psychological distress and chronic illness, and may even have sanctioned involuntary euthanasia. But he goes on to argue that the movement towards the position found in Nazi Germany is by no means inevitable. Fundamentally, the question of *motive* is of crucial importance here: if euthanasia is carried out for reasons of social utility (i.e. removal of the so-called 'useless eaters'), it is clear that compassion does not feature highly, and a slide down the slippery slope becomes much more likely. If, on the other hand, euthanasia is motivated by compassion for others and a genuine desire to ease another human being's suffering, it is more difficult to see how this could be corrupted.

Smith (2005a; 2005b) contends that the arguments for the slippery slope are unpersuasive, but this fails to satisfy a number of commentators. Mason and Laurie (2011), for example, note that there has been no rush from other countries to copy the Dutch example (although, equally, there is no suggestion that the Dutch law will be overturned); and Herring (2008) expresses surprise that more has not been done to correct some of the weaknesses of the system so that a number of the criticisms can be defeated.

We have already seen that Oregon allows PAS, but criminalises euthanasia. Belgium, on the other hand, allows euthanasia, but criminalises PAS. The Northern Territory of Australia allowed both when it passed The Rights of the Terminally Ill Act 1995, but this was revoked one year later. Thus, the evidence that would allow for the generation of useful data and the production of meaningful comparisons is limited in both quantity and quality, and any arguments inevitably have to be largely theoretical.

So, is the Dutch system open to abuse, and is it likely to 'open the floodgates', so that large numbers of patients are put to death whether or not they have agreed with the decision? Some might argue that the dangers of abuse should not be allowed to deny people the right to choose when and how to end their lives. Such arguments cite the supremacy of respect for an individual's right of autonomy, but others would argue that the concept is never truly possible in a patient who is terminally ill (Pattinson, 2009). In other words, a degree of depression is almost inevitable, and the pain and medication will all combine to ensure that the patient's decision is rarely a well-considered one. Moreover, it could be argued that the inherent vulnerability of the terminally ill person renders them particularly susceptible to the entreaties of relatives who are keen to get their hands on the inheritance. McLean (2007b), though, suggests that requesting VAE because one no longer wishes to be a burden to one's family is not necessarily the result of duress or undue influence, and nor is it necessarily a bad thing. If, for example, one perceives the major purpose of one's life is to ensure a comfortable existence for one's offspring, why should a person be prevented from doing this?

A frequently cited argument in opposition to VAE is that palliative care has made significant advances in recent years, and that it should therefore no longer be necessary for euthanasia to be the only answer to relief of suffering (House of Lords Select Committee on Medical Ethics, 1994). In answer to this, Jackson (2010) acknowledges that palliative care may be able to alleviate pain, but it is unable to remove loss of dignity. VAE therefore offers patients an opportunity to die while they are still mentally competent and in control of their physical faculties.

One of the main arguments in favour of legalising VAE is that it would bring it out into the open so that proper checks and safeguards could be put in place (Herring, 2008). The same argument could, of course, be used for the legalisation of prostitution, and there are few signs that this is likely within the UK. Nevertheless, there is evidence to support the contention, most notably in America, where the practices of Jack Kevorkian achieved notoriety. He had admitted assisting several people to die, and he was prepared to challenge the legal system in order to pursue his firm belief that PAS and VAE were morally permissible. The fact that he never developed a close relationship with any of his 'patients' has led to the suspicion that they may have been mis-diagnosed (Beauchamp and Childress, 2001); and he lacked the expertise to make a proper assessment of them anyway. However, although his actions have been universally condemned, it is clear that he offered a service and level of support that was being denied to patients by legitimate means. Thus, for as long as the law prohibits euthanasia, it is logical to assume that there will always be people like Kevorkian prepared to ignore it, and there will always be people who are keen to avail themselves of their services.

CONCLUSION

The foregoing discussion has been designed to illustrate that there are strong arguments on both sides of the euthanasia debate. Harris (2003) gives expression to those who are in favour of the concept:

> I suggest that there is only one thing wrong with dying and that is doing it when you don't want to ... There is nothing wrong with doing it when you do want to.

Wright (2000), on the other hand, voices serious concerns that acceptance of VAE will swiftly lead to involuntary euthanasia, where judgements are made about the quality of another person's life, and decisions made about whether s/he should be allowed to continue to live. Quite evidently, anybody seeking to legalise euthanasia must be mindful of this possibility, and have clear and effective strategies to prevent its occurrence.

Jackson (2010) argues that the supporters of euthanasia may be able to claim a certain moral superiority over their opponents, for they have never contended that it should be mandatory. They are simply saying that people should have a choice, whereas those opposing euthanasia deny that the right to a choice exists. The latter, of course, may be citing a higher authority for their beliefs (i.e. the Scriptures), which allow for no compromise; but the increasingly secular nature of modern society has tended to weaken the impact of such guidance.

McCall Smith (1999) suggests that the current law on euthanasia represents an effective compromise, and should not therefore be disturbed. However, it continues to create difficulties for healthcare practitioners, and the *Cox* case (see Box 10.14) is a good illustration of how nurses can become embroiled in legal and ethical wrangling. When Dr Cox administered potassium chloride to his patient, it is clear that he was acting out of compassion. When the nurse (Ms Hart) reported his actions to the authorities, she was fulfilling her legal and professional duty. It would be a mistake to assume that Ms Hart lacked compassion, but this was the interpretation made of her actions by many. Both she and her family were subjected to verbal abuse and threats of physical violence, while her professional body did nothing to support her. Thus, the appalling dilemma faced by the doctor and the nurse, and the consequences to both of them, could all have been avoided if VAE had been legalised (Begley, 2008).

REFERENCES

TEXTS

Arlidge, A. (2000) 'The trial of Dr. David Moor', *Criminal Law Review*, 31.

Beauchamp, T.L. and Childress, J.F. (2001) *Principles of Bio-medical Ethics*, 5th edn. New York: Oxford University Press.

Begley, A.M. (2008) 'Guilty but good: defending voluntary active euthanasia from a virtue perspective', *Nursing Ethics*, 15 (4): 434–45.

Brazier, M. and Cave, E. (2007) *Medicine, Patients and the Law*, 4th edn. London: Penguin Books.

BBC News (2007) Legal battle over 'right to die'. Retrieved from: http://news.bbc.co.uk/1/hi/ health/6353339.stm. Accessed: 12/8/10.

Butcher, D. (2007) 'The experiences of illness and loss', in G. Hawley (ed.), *Ethics in Clinical Practice: An Interprofessional Approach*. Harlow: Pearson Education.

Campbell, A., Gillett, G. and Jones, G. (2006) *Medical Ethics*. Oxford: Oxford University Press.

Care Not Killing (2007) Kelly Taylor drops case. Retrieved from: www.carenotkilling.org. uk/?show=412. Accessed: 12/8/10.

Conference of Medical Royal Colleges and their Faculties in the UK (1976) 'Diagnosis of brain death', *British Medical Journal*, 2: 1187–8.

De Haan, J. (2002) 'The new Dutch law on euthanasia', *Medical Law Review*, 10, Spring: 55–75.

Ethox. www.ethox.org.uk. Accessed: 26/9/10.

Foster, C. (2005) 'The end of intolerability: the Charlotte Wyatt case in the Court of Appeal', *Solicitor's Journal*, 149 (40), 21 October.

Gillon, R. (1997) 'Clinical ethics committees – pros and cons', *Journal of Medical Ethics*, 23: 203–4.

Griffiths, P. (1999) 'Physician-assisted suicide and voluntary euthanasia: is it time the UK law caught up?', *Nursing Ethics*, 6 (2): 107–16.

Harris, J. (2003) 'Consent and end of life decisions', *Journal of Medical Ethics*, 29 (1): 10–15.

Hendrick, J. (2001) 'Legal aspects of clinical ethics committees', *Journal of Medical Ethics*, 27: 50–3.

Herring, J. (2008) *Medical Law and Ethics*, 2nd edn. Oxford: Oxford University Press.

House of Lords Select Committee on Medical Ethics (1994) *Report of the Select Committee on Medical Ethics*, Vol. 1. London: HMSO.

Jackson, E. (2010) *Medical Law: Text, Cases and Materials*, 2nd edn. Oxford: Oxford University Press.

Jackson, J. (2006) *Ethics in Medicine*. Cambridge: Polity Press.

Kennedy, I. (1991) *Treat Me Right*. Oxford: Oxford University Press.

Keown, J. (1992) 'The law and practice of euthanasia in the Netherlands', *Law Quarterly Review*, 108 (Jan.), 51–78.

Kinnell, H.G. (2000) 'Serial homicide by doctors: Shipman in perspective', *British Medical Journal*, 321 (7276) (Dec. 23–30), 1594–7.

Kumar, M. (2009) *Quantum: Einstein, Bohr and the Great Debate About the Nature of Reality*. London: Icon Books.

Laville, S. (2010) 'People who assist suicide will face test of motives, says DPP', *The Guardian*, 25 February 2010.

Mason, J.K. and Laurie, G.T. (2011) *Mason and McCall Smith's Law and Medical Ethics*, 8th edn. Oxford: Oxford University Press.

McCall Smith, A. (1999) 'Euthanasia: the strengths of the middle ground', *Medical Law Review*, 7, Summer: 194–207.

McLean, S.A.M. (2006) 'From Bland to Burke: the law and politics of assisted nutrition and hydration'. in S.A.M. McLean (ed.), *First Do No Harm*. Dartmouth: Ashgate.

McLean, S.A.M. (2007a) 'What and who are clinical ethics committees for?', *Journal of Medical Ethics*, 33: 497–500.

McLean, S.A.M. (2007b) *Assisted Dying: Reflections on the Need for Law Reform*. Abingdon: Routledge-Cavendish.

Medicinenet. www.medicinenet.com/diabetic_neuropathy/article.htm. Diabetic neuropathy: symptoms, treatment and care. Accessed: 8/9/10.

Mental Capacity Act (2005) Code of Practice (2007). London: HMSO.

Montgomery, J. (2003) *Health Care Law*, 2nd edn. Oxford: Oxford University Press.

Pattinson, S.D. (2009) *Medical law and ethics*, 2nd edn. London: Sweet & Maxwell.

Rachels, J. (1975) 'Active and passive euthanasia', *New England Journal of Medicine*, 292: 78–80.

Royal College of Physicians and British Society of Gastroenterology (2010) *Oral Feeding Difficulties and Dilemmas: A Guide to Practical Care, Particularly Towards the End of Life*. London: RCP.

Sheldon, T. (2001) 'Showing a little mercy', *Nursing Times*, 97 (17), Apr. 26: 1–11.

Slobokan. www.slobokan.com/archives/2005/10/03/terri-schiavo-6-months-later/. Accessed: 28/9/10.

Slowther, A-M. and Hope, T. (2000) 'Clinical ethics committees: they can change practice but need evaluation', *British Medical Journal*, 321 (7262), Sept. 16: 649–50.

Smith, S.W. (2005a) 'Evidence for the practical slippery slope in the debate on physician-assisted suicide and euthanasia', *Medical Law Review*, 13, Spring: 17–44.

Smith, S.W. (2005b) 'Fallacies of the logical slippery slope in the debate on physician-assisted suicide and euthanasia', *Medical Law Review*, 13, Summer: 224–53.

Sykes, N. and Thorne, A. (2003) 'The use of opioids and sedatives at the end of life', *Lancet Oncology*, 4 (5): 312–18.

Tännsjö, T. (2000) 'Terminal sedation – a possible compromise in the euthanasia debate?', *Bulletin of Medical Ethics*, November: 13–22.

Van Bruchem-van de Scheur, A., van der Arend, A., van Wymen, F., Abu-Saad, H.H. and ter Meulen, R. (2008) 'Dutch nurses' attitudes towards euthanasia and physician-assisted suicide', *Nursing Ethics*, 15 (2): 186–98.

Williams, G. (2001) 'The principle of double effect and terminal sedation', *Medical Law Review*, 9, Spring: 41–53.

Wright, W. (2000) 'Historical analogies, slippery slopes, and the question of euthanasia', *Journal of Law, Medicine and Ethics*, 28: 176.

CASES

A, Re [2001] Fam. 147 CA.

AK, Re [2001] 1 FLR 129.

Airedale NHS Trust v Bland [1993] AC 789 HL.

Auckland Area Health Board v A-G [1993] 1 NZLR 235.

B (a minor) (wardship: medical treatment), Re [1981] 1 WLR 1421.

B v An NHS Trust [2002] EWHC 429.

Bolam v Friern Hospital Management Committee [1957] 2 All ER 118.

D, Re [1998] 1 FLR 411.

Frenchay Healthcare NHS Trust v S [1994] 2 All ER 403.

H, Re [1998] 2 FLR 36.

In the matter of Claire Conroy [1985] 486 A 2d 1209.

J (a minor) (wardship: medical treatment), Re [1991] Fam. 33.

Leigh v Gladstone [1909] 26 TLR 139.

Nancy B v Hotel-Dieu de Quebec [1992] 86 DLR (4th.) 385.

Postma Case [1973] Nederlandse Jurisprudentie, No. 183 District Court, Leeuwarden, 21 Feb.

Pretty v UK [2002] 35 EHHR 1.

R v Adams [1957] Criminal Law Review, 365.

R v Collins, ex parte Brady [2000] 58 BMLR 173.

R v Cox [1992] 12 BMLR 38.

R v Director of Public Prosecutions, ex parte Pretty [2001] EWHC Admin. 788.

R v Director of Public Prosecutions, ex parte Pretty [2002] 1 All ER 1 HL.

R v Director of Public Prosecutions, ex parte Purdy [2008] EWHC 2565.

R v Director of Public Prosecutions, ex parte Purdy [2009] EWCA Civ. 92.

R v Director of Public Prosecutions, ex parte Purdy [2010] 1 AC 345 (HL).

R (on the application of Burke) v General Medical Council [2005] EWCA Civ. 1003.

R v Moor [1999] 318 BMJ 1306.

T, Re [1992] 4 All ER 649 (CA).
Schindler v Schiavo [2003] 851 So 2d 182.
Secretary of State for the Home Department v Robb [1995] 1 All ER 677.
W Healthcare NHS Trust and another v H and another [2004] EWCA Civ. 1324.
Wyatt v Portsmouth Hospitals NHS Trust [2005] EWCA Civ. 1181.
Z, Re [2004] EWHC 2817.

LEGISLATION

Abortion Act 1967
Human Rights Act 1998
Mental Capacity Act 2005
Oregon Death with Dignity Act 1994
Termination of Life on Request and Assisted Suicide (Review Procedures) Act 2000
The Rights of the Terminally Ill Act 1995
Suicide Act 1961.

Scenarios (answers at back of book)

1   A 70-year-old patient has breast cancer with multiple metastases, and it is clear that she is terminally ill. She has therefore been commenced on a syringe driver containing Diamorphine, and her family have been told that she is not expected to survive for more than a few days. However, although the Diamorphine appears to be controlling her pain, she is still alive two weeks later. The doctor subsequently modifies the treatment chart so that, when the syringe driver next becomes empty, it should be replaced with one containing double the dose.

What should the nurse do in this situation?

2   A 65-year-old man is currently being nursed in the High Dependency Unit with severe pancreatitis. He also has chronic obstructive pulmonary disease and is being administered nasal intermittent ventilation (NIPPV). It is clear, however, that it is not working as well as it might, and he becomes increasingly hypoxic with subsequent bouts of confusion. In between these bouts, he states categorically that he has no wish to be intubated and ventilated, and wants to die. His family, on the other hand, insist that ventilation is initiated and become very confrontational when it is suggested to them that he should be allowed to die in accordance with his wishes.

What should be done in this situation?

3   An 80-year-old male patient is being nursed on the ward and has multiple physical problems. He has end-stage heart failure, which has made him acutely breathless

(Continued)

(Continued)

and hypoxic (with consequent confusion), and he has now developed renal failure. In addition, he has severe rheumatoid arthritis, which causes him severe pain whenever he is moved. It is clear that he has only a short time to live, and the healthcare professionals wish to make his remaining days as comfortable as possible. They therefore initiate and administer Diamorphine via a syringe driver. However, it is known that he has had a strong religious background throughout his life, and has been a lay preacher. He has always adopted a Vitalist position (where it is believed that life should be preserved at all costs), and his family are insistent that all measures necessary should be taken to prolong his life. Knowing that the Diamorphine depresses respiration (and thereby hastens death), they subsequently remove the syringe driver and threaten the staff with violence if they seek to replace it.

What should be done in this situation?

APPENDIX
SUGGESTED ANSWERS
TO SCENARIOS

The following is an attempt to provide answers to the questions set at the end of the chapters. Constraints of space prevent detailed responses and the reader should bear this in mind. Moreover, a definitive solution will be rare, for each case has unique characteristics that may sway the outcome one way or the other. Nevertheless, the hope is that the key issues will be highlighted and that the relevant legal and ethical principles will be applied.

CHAPTER 3

1   The key to answering this question is to analyse it according to the three elements of Negligence. Thus, do you have a duty of care to your neighbour? Unless you have set yourself up as a telephone advisory service, there is no duty of care here and you would be perfectly at liberty to decline to give advice. The human and professional approach, of course, would be to advise him to seek medical attention if he is concerned, but your responsibilities do not extend beyond this. Once you begin to give advice, however, you have automatically established a duty of care. Moreover, the neighbour is entitled to rely upon your advice in the knowledge that you are a health-care professional (see *Hedley Byrne & Co. Ltd v Heller & Partners Ltd.* [1964]).

Once a duty of care is established, we must now move on to a consideration of the standard of care, and ask whether or not it is reasonable to make a diagnosis over the telephone. We might be able to argue that this is precisely the situation with NHS Direct, but the staff there work to clearly defined protocols. In the absence of such assistance, you cannot be confident that your diagnosis of indigestion is correct without taking a full history from the neighbour and conducting a thorough physical examination. On the face of it, 'indigestion' is not an unreasonable hypothesis, but you need to ensure the safety of the neighbour (and yourself from the threat of litigation). Thus, the sensible approach would be to advise the neighbour to seek medical attention if his pain does not subside within ten minutes of taking the antacid.

Finally, we must consider the issue of causation. Certainly, the neighbour can point to harm that he has sustained: he has a life-threatening illness, which will require major abdominal surgery and prolonged hospitalisation if he is to survive. The problem for the neighbour, though, is that he must establish (on the balance of probabilities) that it was the *delay* in seeking appropriate treatment as a direct result of your advice that caused him to have a perforated gastric ulcer. In other words, could this situation have been avoided if your advice had been more appropriate? This, one suspects, would be extremely difficult to prove, for it is at least equally likely that the perforation would have occurred even if he had been advised correctly. Failure to establish this element will destroy his claim for negligence, although it would still provide a salutary lesson for all healthcare professionals.

2   As a Community Nurse, you clearly have a duty of care to this patient, and this duty cannot be avoided. The diagnosis of candidiasis is not unreasonable in the circumstances, but it should not be made unless you are able to distinguish it from leukoplakia. Informing the doctor, however, largely shifts the burden of responsibility, although you would have an ongoing duty to monitor the effectiveness of the therapy. Thus, if the Nystatin has failed to effect an improvement within ten days, the doctor should be made aware of this. We might argue that the doctor has acted unreasonably by accepting a diagnosis without question and without examining the patient, but s/he may have a long-standing working relationship with you and s/he has faith in your judgement. Nevertheless, in terms of causation, the patient has clearly come to harm, and it should not be too difficult to establish that the unreasonable delay in diagnosis has created the situation where extensive surgery is required. None of the healthcare professionals are responsible for the patient's cancer, but a more appropriate response could almost certainly have avoided the magnitude of the subsequent treatment, and this will be worthy of compensation. (See *Manning v King's College Hospital NHS Trust [2008]*, upon which this scenario is very loosely based.)

3   As with the vast majority of healthcare interactions, the duty of care will be the easiest hurdle for a claimant to overcome, and there is no question that the dental practice has such a duty to this woman. More problematic, however, is whether or not there has been a breach in the standard of care. For example, is the treatment with these particular sealants reasonable, and is it common practice for them to be used on such a regular basis? In other words, would this practice be accepted as proper by a responsible body of professional opinion (see *Bolam v Friern HMC [1957]*)? An answer to this question in the negative would not necessarily be evidence of negligence, but the practitioner would need to be able to justify why s/he has departed from official protocol. The hygienist might also have a defence by arguing that s/he could not reasonably have known about the research linking breast cancer to exposure to bisphenol-A (see *Crawford v Board of Governors of Charing Cross Hospital [1953]*). Again, though, this defence will turn upon the facts: the hygienist could not reasonably be expected to read every research article, but equally, s/he has a responsibility to remain up-to-date. If, therefore, the study was widely known and reported, the defence will falter.

Finally, the claimant must establish causation, and this can be notoriously difficult. The results of the research would need to identify a clear causal link between bisphenol-A and breast cancer, and it is doubtful that one study alone could do this. Moreover, even if the link is conclusive, the woman would still need to show that *her* breast cancer was caused by exposure to the chemical. If, for example, there is a genetic trait for breast cancer within her family, her case loses a lot of strength, because this is an intervening factor. Thus, she would have to demonstrate that *but for* exposure to the chemical, she would not have developed breast cancer.

4   In analysing this scenario, we would have to say that the Trust not only has a common law duty of care to its employees, but also a statutory obligation under the Health and Safety at Work Act 1974 (section 2). This obligation clearly includes the provision and maintenance of a safe system of work, and we might argue that they have failed in their duty on this occasion. Much depends, however, on when the bed was broken, and whether or not it was reported. If the Trust managers had not been made aware, it would be unreasonable to have expected them to act to correct the situation. If, on the other hand, they were fully aware, but simply expected their employees to carry on regardless, the strength of their defence begins to waver. They cannot claim that such practices are 'unavoidable requirements' of the job, for all measures should be taken to maximise the safety of employees, patients and visitors.

On the assumption that the Trust has been remiss in this instance, we would have to say that the harm sustained by the physiotherapist is reasonably foreseeable. Her claim, however, may be weakened if there are other intervening factors (for example, a pre-existing back problem); but the fact that she can pinpoint the exact time when she sustained the injury will enable her to establish a direct causal link with the faulty bed. Having said that, there is a responsibility upon her to mitigate her losses as much as possible. In other words, the Health and Safety at Work Act 1974 also imposes upon employees an obligation to protect themselves and others (section 7). Thus, if she did not request assistance and/or her lifting technique did not conform to accepted practice, the Trust might be able to argue that she has contributed to her own injuries. This does not absolve the Trust from all responsibility, but it might result in a reduction of the damages payable to the physiotherapist (see *Egan v Central Manchester & Manchester Children's University Hospitals NHS Trust [2008]*).

CHAPTER 4

1   This is not an unfamiliar scenario for healthcare professionals, but it poses a number of difficult problems. The fact that the patient has a short-term memory does not excuse practitioners from seeking to enhance her understanding. She has a right to be informed of what is going to happen to her body, and the healthcare team have a legal, moral and professional obligation to both give her this information and endeavour to enhance her understanding. But does she have a right *not* to know? On the one hand, we could argue that she is exercising her Autonomous right not to be given

information; but on the other hand, this is a major abdominal operation, which will significantly alter her body image and will affect her future lifestyle. In such circumstances, it is difficult to make a case for withholding information, although the situation might be different if the surgery was less invasive and life-changing.

How much information she should be given, though, is another issue. Certainly, too much information is likely to induce confusion, fear and possible depression. It must, therefore, be kept as concise and as simple as possible, while ensuring that the patient has a grasp of the key aspects of the surgery and how it is going to affect her afterwards. In short, the healthcare professional should always examine the *purpose* of giving information: is it to avoid litigation, or is it to enhance understanding? Perhaps it is both, but the latter can only be achieved if information is tailored to the individual needs of each patient.

The final issue is whether or not this surgery is being done in the best interests of the patient. Clearly, her only hope of cure lies with surgical excision of her rectal tumour, and we might therefore be able to argue that it is in her best *physical* interests. It is conceivable, though, that major trauma of this nature may actually shorten her life, in which case the physical interests argument is weakened. We also need to ask whether the treatment is going to be in her best *psychological* interests. If she enters a spiral of depression following the surgery, it is difficult to see how her best interests have been served. Thus, this is a conflict between Beneficence and Non-maleficence. The default position is the preservation of life, and medicine has developed techniques to prolong it wherever possible; but there will be occasions when this position appears to do more harm than good.

2   A careful reading of Chapter 4 should have been enough to convince you that this situation does not pose a dilemma in the strictest sense of the term. The card stating that the patient is not prepared to accept a blood transfusion in *any* circumstances, even if his life is put at risk as a result, constitutes a valid Advance Decision to refuse treatment (see Mental Capacity Act 2005, sections 24–6). Any action that ignores this Decision constitutes a battery, and the surgeon exposes himself to the risk of legal and professional sanctions (see *Malette v Shulman [1991]*). In this classic conflict between Autonomy and Beneficence, the former will almost invariably prevail. We are assuming, though, that the patient is 18 or over; if he is younger than this, it could be argued that he is unable to exercise full Autonomy and that it would therefore be permissible to over-ride his refusal (see *Re E [1993]*; *Re S [1994]*). Even if the patient is 18 or above, the healthcare team would be justified in seeking to ascertain whether or not he was a committed Jehovah's Witness. If there are any intervening factors that would cast some doubt upon this, the surgeon may have a defence if s/he administers the blood transfusion (see *HE v A Hospital NHS Trust [2003]*), although it might be advisable to seek court approval beforehand. The surgeon might also consider that the patient is unlikely to discover that he has had a blood transfusion, and that this deception is justifiable in the circumstances. However, although undoubtedly done with the best of intentions, it assumes that the rest of the healthcare team are prepared to play along with the deception. This would impose an unfair burden upon them, and is not to be recommended.

3   In answering this question, there is a two-stage process that must be followed. Thus, we must first establish whether or not the patient is competent, and this is achieved by applying the C-test (from *Re C [1994]* and the Mental Capacity Act 2005, section 3). The facts of our scenario would strongly suggest that this lady is unable to understand the information given to her, retain it, or weigh it in the balance to arrive at a choice. In short, her toxic confusional state (and possible dementia) has rendered her incompetent to make a decision, and we can move on to the next stage. We must now be able to justify that any intervention that the nursing staff perform on this lady is in her best interests (from *Re F [1990]* and the Mental Capacity Act 2005, section 4). Once again, this should not be too difficult to establish, for she will become very sore if her hygiene needs are neglected. We might argue that enforced care would not necessarily be in her best psychological interests (at least in the short term), but it would be fair to assume that successful treatment of her medical condition is likely to improve her mental state.

Having established that her refusal to accept care can be over-ridden, the nursing staff are permitted to use reasonable force. 'Reasonable force' may be defined as the minimum required to achieve the desired objective; but such patients are clearly going to be challenging. The key to managing such patients is to try and establish a relationship of trust. It seems trite to say that this is not going to be easy, but it is worth the effort and calls upon skills that enable us to identify those who achieve excellence in nursing. Suffice it to say here that each patient will have individual needs and may require unique strategies before trust is established.

CHAPTER 5

1   This is a difficult and awkward situation and is one that will be familiar to many practitioners. Different people are likely to handle this in different ways, and the advice that I give may be at variance with that of others. The dilemma could have been avoided by asking the patient *on admission* whether or not he would be happy to have his medical details divulged, and to whom. However, in this scenario, we cannot be sure that the 'sister' is who she says she is: she could, for example, be a member of the press or a nosy neighbour. Even if she is the patient's sister, it is conceivable that the relationship is a strained one and that he never had any intention of giving her information about his condition.

In such circumstances, the *context* of the situation is largely determinative of the course of action. Thus, in an Intensive Care Unit, where a patient may be comatosed for a prolonged period of time, it might be reasonable to assume that the patient would want his/her relatives to be kept informed. It is neither wise nor reasonable to make such an assumption in our scenario, however. The practitioner must therefore consider the likely consequences of each action/inaction and determine which is the easiest to bear. My personal feeling is that the discomfort caused by not giving information is less distressing to all than the potential consequences of a breach of confidentiality. In other, words, the former can be repaired, whereas the latter may result in a fundamental loss of trust between patient and practitioner (not to mention the possible disciplinary repercussions).

Having said that, it would be unkind and unprofessional to ignore the sister's anxiety completely. Therefore, the reasons for not giving information should be explained clearly and sensitively. Moreover, she could be told that the patient will be asked when he wakens whether he is happy for her to know what is happening, and a promise can be made to call her back. It is not inevitable that she will be satisfied with this position, but you can take comfort from the fact that the patient's interests have been safeguarded, as have those of yourself and your employing organisation.

2   The Police and Criminal Evidence Act 1984 makes it clear that the police are entitled to search the records of all those admitted to Accident and Emergency, but *only if* they have obtained a warrant. A Justice of the Peace can issue such a warrant if 'there is material on premises which is likely to be of substantial value ... to the investigation of the offence' (s8 (1) (b)). However, medical records constitute 'excluded material' (as defined by s11), in which case the warrant must be provided by a judge (Schedule 1). In the absence of such a warrant, the healthcare team would be at liberty to refuse access to the patients' medical notes, and professional guidance suggests that they should (DH, 2003; British Medical Association, 2004). Different circumstances arise if the patient is suspected of terrorism, in which case the healthcare professionals are obliged to report their suspicions, even if not specifically asked to do so (Terrorism Act 2000, sections 19 and 20). Moreover, once a warrant has been issued, the staff are under an obligation to release the medical records, and continued refusal would be considered a contempt of court (Police and Criminal Evidence Act 1984, Schedule 1 (15) (1)).

No doubt there will be some practitioners who feel that a duty of confidentiality is not owed to this patient. There is, after all, 'no confidence in iniquity' (*Gartside v Outram [1856]*), and the patient cannot therefore claim a right to demand confidentiality in these circumstances. Moreover, as Dimond (2011) suggests, the staff frequently rely upon the police for protection when faced with aggressive patients. For the relationship between the two professions to remain mutually beneficial, it could be argued that a little 'give and take' is required from both. The other possible consequence of a breach of confidentiality, however, is that the patient will lose trust in healthcare professionals and may refuse to seek necessary medical attention in the future. Whatever decision is made, it would be advisable to involve senior management beforehand – in this way, the individual practitioner will be protected from possible disciplinary measures.

3   Those seeking to defend the actions of the staff in this scenario would be hard-pressed to develop a logical argument. For one thing, these actions impinge upon the Autonomy of those personnel whose clinical details are being accessed. Everybody has a right to expect that this information is being held on a strict 'need to know' basis, and the ward staff cannot claim such a need. Their actions clearly have the potential to do enormous harm, and it is difficult to see what good can come from them. In addition, this activity is unprofessional and represents a misuse of time – time that could better be spent by looking after the patients in their care.

But is it illegal? The Computer Misuse Act 1990 suggests that it might be, for section 1 states that a person is guilty of an offence if s/he 'causes a computer to perform any function with intent to secure access to any program or data held in any computer ... [and] ... the access he intends to secure is unauthorised'. The penalties for being in breach of this Act can potentially be a term of imprisonment for up to two years and/or a fine (s3), although such measures would be reserved for those who seek to create maximum damage from illegal access to computer material. Needless to say, though, the victims of the breach of confidentiality outlined in our scenario need only to raise their concerns to the authorities; having done so, they should feel confident that disciplinary measures will be invoked against the staff.

CHAPTER 6

These decisions are never going to be easy, and perhaps the fairest method of choosing would be by means of a lottery (i.e. the first name to be pulled out of the hat receives the organ). Certainly this would conform to our concept of Justice, where everybody has an equal chance. It is not, however, the method favoured by transplant units. A heart, when it becomes available, is a valuable and scarce resource; the unit will therefore feel an obligation to ensure that it goes to the person who will receive the most benefit from it. Inevitably, histo-compatibility and the severity of the patient's illness are going to be the primary considerations; but let us assume that this has still left us with four candidates. We must therefore look for other factors.

We might argue that Joseph and James have contributed to their illness by virtue of the fact that they are both smokers and one is overweight, whereas neither Anna nor Jennifer can justifiably be said to be at fault. This presupposes, of course, that the two men would *not* have developed heart failure if they had refrained from smoking and had eaten properly; and it also ignores the hereditary, social and psychological conditions that have guided this behaviour. The fact that both are still smoking, however, would count against them, for this may adversely affect the chances of success of the transplant.

Joseph and James might have stronger claims if we looked at the candidates' contribution and value to society. Both Anna and Jennifer have the potential to be of great value to society, but the two men can at least state that their potential has been realised. The less charitable among us might argue that Anna has even greater potential to be a burden upon society, but this would be to ignore the impact that her illness has had upon her education. It is conceivable (although not certain) that James will develop a treatment that will save the lives of countless women, in which case the Utilitarian principle of the action that produces 'the greatest happiness of the greatest number' will come to the fore.

Age is another factor that one would expect to be considered. Although neither Joseph nor James can be said to be old, they at least have had a chance of life, whereas this chance has been denied to Anna and Jennifer. This 'fair innings' argument also has clinical support, in that it might reasonably be expected that the youngest recipient of the heart might get to make the best use of it (in terms of longevity). In opposition to this, we might consider how many other people will be affected if any of the candidates were to die. None of them have dependents, and James does not even have a family, but we can safely assume that all will be missed. A headcount of each candidate's friends and family is one way of resolving this dilemma, but seems an unsatisfactory justification for rejecting three people's chances of receiving the organ. Needless to say, the fact that James is gay should not influence the decision, unless there are good clinical grounds for rejecting him on this basis.

Perhaps the key consideration here, though, is going to be the mental state of each of the potential recipients. It is inevitable that severe heart failure is going to have a deep psychological impact upon a person, and some degree of mental instability is to be expected. But for Harris (1985), the most important question is how much value an individual places on his/her life. Moreover, for clinicians, experience suggests that a positive mental attitude and a strong desire to go on living are powerful predictors of the success of a major procedure such as this. With the information at our disposal, it would appear that James fulfils these criteria the most. The refusal of Jennifer could potentially be over-ridden on the grounds that a 14-year-old is unable to make a competent decision when the consequences of such a refusal are so grave (see *Re M [1999]*); but the success of an operation as major as this requires the full cooperation of the patient.

Different people will come to different conclusions, and will consider other criteria for selection. Certainly, any decision made would require more supporting information about the candidates than is given here. We might, however, console ourselves with the fact that rejection of a candidate on this occasion does not necessarily represent their last chance of an organ. Another may come along at any moment, and we could argue that Anna and Jennifer need more psychological preparation before undergoing this procedure.

CHAPTER 7

1 There are at least three possible responses to this dilemma, none of which is entirely satisfactory. The first is that the patient could be sectioned under the Mental Health Act 1983 and thereby be compelled to receive treatment in hospital. There are a number of precedents to suggest that non-psychiatric care can be given under s63 of the Act in a variety of circumstances: for example, *Re KB [1994]* and *B v Croydon Health Authority [1995]* (both of which involved the force-feeding of patients refusing to eat), and *Tameside & Glossop Acute Services Trust v CH [1996]* (which authorised a Caesarean section on a pregnant schizophrenic woman). Nevertheless, *Re C [1994]*, where the court refused authorisation to amputate the gangrenous leg of a schizophrenic patient, illustrates that there are limits to the scope of the Mental Health Act. If it can be argued that the patient's mental state and physical illness are intimately connected, there might be a case for sectioning him; but, with respect to psychiatric institutions, it must be questionable whether his *physical* needs will be met most appropriately in such an environment.

The second option is to invoke the Mental Capacity Act 2005. We need, therefore, to assess his competence (from *Re C [1994]* and Mental Capacity Act 2005, section 3), and need to be certain that he fails this test before moving on. From the information at our disposal, however, there is no guarantee that this is the case. If we make the assumption that he is assessed as incompetent, we now need to justify that hospitalisation is in his best interests. There may be an argument that it would serve his best *physical* interests, but not necessarily his psychological interests. Moreover, with respect to general hospitals, it is doubtful that he will receive optimum psychiatric support in such an environment, and he is likely to be very difficult to manage.

A similar situation arose in *GJ v Foundation Trust, PCT and the Secretary of State for Health [2010]*, where a patient with vascular dementia and Korsakoff's psychosis also had insulin-dependent diabetes. His mental condition meant that he frequently forgot to give himself his insulin or that he would give it twice within ten minutes. Inevitably, he suffered a series of hypoglycaemic attacks, and he was initially sectioned under the Mental Health Act 1983, and then detained under the Deprivation of Liberty procedures (DOLS) set out in the Mental Capacity Act 2005 (as amended by the Mental Health Act 2007). The court ruled that the Mental Health Act did not apply in this instance because it 'does not extend to the medical or surgical treatment of unrelated physical conditions where giving that treatment will not impact upon the pre-existing mental disorder' (per Charles, J. at para. 54 (b)). Moreover, it was held that healthcare professionals should not 'pick and choose between the two statutory regimes [i.e. the Mental Health Act 1983 and the Mental Capacity Act 2005] as they think fit' (para. 59). The judge did not provide his own solution to the problem, but the clear implication is that there was no legal justification for the detention of this patient against his will. Thus, it would seem that he could only be admitted whenever he became comatosed from his diabetes; as soon as he recovered following appropriate treatment, he had to be discharged, whereupon the cycle would inevitably repeat itself. This goes somewhat against the grain of what we perceive to be best practice, but it represents recognition of a more fundamental principle: namely, the liberty of an individual to refuse medical treatment.

If we extrapolate these principles to our scenario, we are left with the third option, which is to allow him to remain in his own home. However, this is not exactly the same as 'leaving him alone' and condemning him to die a painful and undignified death. Essentially, he has lost trust in all healthcare professionals and is probably highly suspicious of their motives and intentions. It is the task of the healthcare professional, therefore, to endeavour to re-establish this trust so that he will eventually accept appropriate treatment in his own home. Although it may not be possible to provide optimum care in these circumstances, it would at least be respectful of his autonomy and his psychological needs.

2   This case is heavily modelled on that of *Re R [1992]*, in which the question of whether or not a child has the right to refuse treatment was considered. In that case, as in our scenario, the child was admitted informally, but the consent for admission was given by her parents. As her mental state began to recover, she demanded to be released and found support from some of the healthcare professionals looking

after her. Her doctor, however, disagreed; and it was left to the court to resolve this dilemma.

The court's task was to determine whether or not this child was Gillick competent (from *Gillick v West Norfolk and Wisbech Area Health Authority [1985]*): in other words, was she able to make a rational and considered decision regarding her welfare? To all intents and purposes, it appeared that she was competent, but Lord Donaldson acknowledged that this was not a permanent state:

> 'Gillick competence' is a developmental concept and will not be lost or acquired on a day-to-day or week-to-week basis. In the case of mental disability, that disability must also be taken into account, particularly where it is fluctuating in its effect (at 26).

Had she been above the age of 16 (and if the case had been heard after enactment of the Mental Capacity Act 2005), it is conceivable that the decision may have been reversed, for s3 (2) states:

> The fact that a person is able to retain the information relevant to a decision for a short period only does not prevent him from being regarded as able to make the decision.

However, the case of *Re R [1992]* illustrates two fundamental principles. First, a competent child can consent to treatment, but his/her refusal can be over-ridden by the doctors and the parents. Second, when assessing the suitability of a mentally ill patient for discharge, the court will give consideration to the wider interests of society. This helps to explain the decision in *R v Mental Health Review Tribunal for the South Thames Region, ex parte Smith [1998]*, where a schizophrenic patient was responding well to treatment, but his continued detention was justified by arguing that he would stop taking his medication if released and would subsequently relapse very rapidly.

The situation in our scenario could be managed by sectioning the patient under the Mental Health Act 1983 (as amended by the Mental Health Act 2007). She could therefore be released under a Community Treatment Order (s17A-G), in which her concordance with medication and her mental state could be regularly monitored by the mental health team. In one view, this represents the best option in that it allows the patient a degree of autonomy, while ensuring that she remains properly supervised. There is, however, an understandable reluctance to section young people: not only is it stigmatising, but it may create problems for them in later life (in terms of employment opportunities, life insurance, travel, etc.). It is not, therefore, a decision to be taken lightly, and a careful balance of the strengths and weaknesses of the respective options must be undertaken.

CHAPTER 8

1   This scenario has echoes of 'The Ashley Treatment' and Katie Thorpe, both of which have been discussed in the chapter. There were certainly a number of ethical

concerns raised about both cases, although it is possible to mount an argument in favour of such treatment. We also noted that, although the interests of the child should be paramount, these interests can be inextricably bound up with those of the parents (especially when the child is severely disabled). There are, however, at least a couple of distinctions to be drawn between the two cases and our scenario here. First, the parents' decision to reduce James's feeds has been done on their own initiative and without medical approval or supervision. On the assumption that neither is medically trained, it goes without saying that neither is in a position to make these kinds of judgements safely, and James is therefore at risk of harm. Second, the treatment given to Ashley and Katie was certainly more drastic than a reduction of feeding volumes, but they were single episodes, from which both would be expected to recover fully. James, by contrast, is being condemned to permanent discomfort through hunger, the dangers of malnutrition, and a subsequently increased predisposition to infection.

For these reasons, we could argue that James is a victim of abuse (physical and neglect), even though this was never the intention of the parents. Given that they appear to be a loving family, it would be unwise to adopt a heavy-handed approach in this instance, for the break-up of the family would serve nobody's interests. Social Services need to work closely with this family and in collaboration with expert paediatric services to develop a plan that will be an appropriate solution. Only if the parents ignore this plan will more draconian action be needed; in such circumstances, it would be clear that James's interests are no longer being served by remaining within this family (and, in fact, are being damaged), and he would be taken into care. The final thing to note about this scenario is that James has cerebral palsy and has a number of serious physical disabilities: this does not automatically imply that he is *mentally* disabled, and he should be fully involved in any decision that is taken about his welfare.

2   This scenario is modelled on a couple of cases, although the judicial reasoning was different in both. In *R v Lowe [1973]*, a man of low intelligence failed to call a doctor to the aid of his ill nine-week-old baby, who subsequently died of dehydration and malnutrition. He was charged and convicted of manslaughter and wilful neglect, although the manslaughter conviction was subsequently quashed on appeal. The facts in *R v Sheppard and another [1980]* were very similar: another man of low intelligence allowed his one-month-old son to die of hypothermia and malnutrition and he was convicted of wilful neglect contrary to s1 (1) of the Children and Young Persons Act 1933. The conviction was upheld in the Court of Appeal, but subsequently overturned in the House of Lords (although only by a majority of three to two).

Both the Crown Court and the Court of Appeal had applied the civil law concept of Negligence, in which it was held that the father had failed to reach the standard expected of a 'reasonable parent'. The majority of the House of Lords, however, held that the civil law had no application here. Instead, the offence of wilful neglect, as specified by the 1933 Act, could only be committed if the parent had *deliberately* failed to provide care. In other words, the neglect of one's child 'through stupidity or ignorance' (per Lord Keith at p. 914) are valid defences.

Sheppard effectively over-ruled the decision in *R v Lowe [1973]*, although one feels that the situation in both could be avoided. There may be an argument for removing children from families where the parents are of low intelligence; but, once the decision has been made to allow a child to remain there, the parents need as much support as Social Services can provide. If, on the other hand, Social Services are simply trying to accumulate evidence that will enable them to withdraw the child, it is inevitable that the parents will be reluctant to seek help whenever the child becomes unwell. In short, the child's interests are best served by the cultivation of a relationship of trust between the parents and Social Services; and the relationship should only change when the parents no longer have the best interests of their child at heart.

3   There are a number of issues with this scenario, the first of which is unquestionably that of Consent. There are ways in which the stepfather can claim parental responsibility, and thereby the authority to make decisions on behalf of Joanne, but he would need some form of documentary evidence to prove this (e.g. court order; written agreement of the mother; etc.). In the absence of such evidence, the nurse is entitled (and obliged) to assume that he does not have the authority to consent for his step-daughter. Joanne could consent to the treatment herself, but *only if* she was assessed as competent following application of the Fraser guidelines. Such an assessment could only be satisfactorily performed if the stepfather left the room; and the information at our disposal seems to suggest that she is likely to fail it anyway. Thus, if neither stepfather nor child can give consent to this treatment, it should not be prescribed. Careful explanation of the legal position should be given to the couple in an attempt to offset any ill-feeling; and they should be told that the mother's attendance is required before treatment can be initiated. Only if the treatment was an emergency would such considerations be waived; but in such circumstances it would be given out of necessity, and consent would not be required.

The second major issue in this scenario is that of the suspicion of child sexual abuse. In the absence of hard evidence, it would be unwise to throw around accusations, but the nurse has a professional obligation to report her concerns to the appropriate authorities. The suspicion may be completely unfounded, but the first and over-riding principle of the Children Act 1989 is that the welfare of the child is paramount (s1). This being the case, it would seem that the sensibilities of the stepfather are dispensable if the interests of Joanne are to be protected. A gentle approach needs to be taken here, though, for it is going to be very easy to cause irreparable damage to the trust between the family and healthcare professionals (which, in the long term, may be detrimental to Joanne's interests).

Inevitably, concerns should be expressed to Social Services, who are obliged to conduct an investigation. Their first action will probably be to search the database (established by the Children Act 2004) to see if the family and/or the stepfather have been under scrutiny before. Ultimately, however, evidence of abuse can only be confirmed if Joanne undergoes a proper assessment. For this purpose, it may be necessary to seek a Child Assessment Order (Children Act 1989, s43), which would compel Joanne to undergo physical and psychological assessment. This may seem a little heavy-handed, but the alternative may be to condemn a young girl to several years of intolerable suffering.

CHAPTER 9

1   The primary consideration for a qualified nurse must be the welfare of his/her patients (Nursing and Midwifery Council, 2008), and Jackie's actions have fallen far short of this. In addition to the verbal abuse she has directed to the residents and the physical abuse that she has inflicted on one resident in particular, she has set an appalling example to the Healthcare Assistants who are under her direction. Clearly, she is under immense pressure, and this has now transformed into genuine stress. Her inability to recognise the signs of this transformation, however, have made the current situation inevitable.

When faced with such a case, the Professional Conduct Committee cannot ignore the fact that Jackie has abandoned the fundamental principles of good nursing: she has inflicted physical and psychological damage when she should have been trying to create a safe and therapeutic environment, and she has helped to bring the reputation of the profession into disrepute. These alone would generally be enough to convince the Committee that she is no longer a suitable registrant. In her defence, though, she may be able to point to her previous record: if she has served many years without blemish and is able to secure favourable character references, the Committee may feel disposed to look upon this incident as a solitary aberration. She might even be able to argue that her response to the physically aggressive patient was an appropriate form of self-defence and that his cracked rib was an unfortunate accident.

Clearly, she has been placed in an extremely difficult situation, and there is an argument to be made that this is a system failure, rather than an individual problem. In other words, the low level of support that she has received from her employer has placed her in an intolerable position, which has ultimately led to a loss of personal control. Such a defence requires evidence that management have been made aware of the problem and have subsequently made no efforts to rectify it. However appealing this defence might be, though, it can never be used as an excuse for the abuse of patients. When faced with a shortage of resources, the practitioner must establish clear priorities and ensure that these are met, even though it might mean a decline in the standards that one has set for oneself.

Finally, the Committee will need to know whether or not Jackie admits her guilt and if she has genuine contrition for her actions. In addition, they are more likely to be impressed if she has taken measures on her own initiative to handle her stress (for example, by attending stress management classes). If she can convince the Committee that she is genuinely sorry and that she understands how this situation arose, they may feel that there is hope for her. In the absence of such contrition, there seems little doubt that her name will be erased from the register.

2   There is a case to be made for arguing that this is a *health* issue, and that the most appropriate response would be to refer the paramedic to the Health Committee. They

may then issue him with an Interim Suspension Order, so that he is able to access the necessary treatment and support for his depression. In practice, however, the Professional Conduct Committee is much more likely to see this as a *character* issue. The paramedic might claim that selling illegal substances is not directly impinging upon his work, but the Committee is entitled to question whether this activity is suitable for a healthcare professional. He has, in short, damaged the reputation of the profession.

Perhaps we may be inclined to take a sympathetic view of his desperate situation, and perhaps he can point to a previous unblemished record. He may also express genuine regret for his actions, and he may be able to demonstrate that he is taking measures to deal with his issues. For the Committee, however, there are higher principles at stake: not only has he brought the reputation of the profession into disrepute, but also he has betrayed the trust that was placed in him. If he can no longer be trusted by his profession, his employers and the general public, it is difficult to see how he can remain on the register. Inevitably, each case will turn on its facts and the strength or weakness of the defence; but there is one further factor that is likely to influence the Committee. Any display of undue lenience by them is open to challenge in the courts by the Council for Healthcare Regulatory Excellence, and reversal of the decision is both humiliating and even more damaging to the reputation of the profession.

3   Within this scenario, there are two issues at stake, the first of which is that of sexual harassment. We probably all know what *should* happen here: the dentist is taking advantage of his position to compel the hygienist to respond favourably to his advances, he is being extremely unprofessional, and the hygienist has been put in a very uncomfortable position. In consequence, he should be reported to the Primary Care Trust and possibly the General Dental Council, who will impose the appropriate sanctions. Anybody who has been in this situation, however, will know that the reality is much more complicated. It is all very well to have a Whistleblowers' Charter and a policy on the prevention of harassment, but their effectiveness is open to question when there is such an inequality of power between accused and accuser. The sad truth, therefore, is that the dental hygienist may end up doing herself more harm by facing this situation head on.

This is not to say, though, that she should be prepared to accept his unwelcome advances. In the first instance, she should report her concerns to the practice manager, who may be able to have some influence over the dentist. Above all, she should ensure that she is never alone in the same room as the dentist. Any complaints that she makes about his conduct while they are alone together will simply be his word against hers, and this is an argument that she is likely to lose. If he continues harassing her in the presence of witnesses, her case automatically becomes much stronger.

The second issue is the fact that the dentist often arrives for duty smelling of alcohol. Not only is this unprofessional, but also there is a clear fitness to practise concern here. In other words, his ability to function may be compromised, which is potentially endangering his patients. This is not something that can be ignored, for the possible consequences are too serious. Moreover, those who do not report their concerns automatically become implicated if and when an untoward incident occurs.

There is, of course, strength in numbers, and it would be unwise to tackle this situation alone. It is possible that the practice manager or a dental colleague might have more influence over him; and the ideal solution would be to address the problem at its source. If the dentist does not respond appropriately to this assistance, his colleagues will be left with little option but to report him to the Primary Care Trust (who may then go on to report him to the General Dental Council).

CHAPTER 10

1   A defence to murder in this scenario requires application of the doctrine of double effect, of which there are three criteria that must be established. First, the patient must be terminally ill, so that it can be argued that it was the disease that killed her, rather than the drugs. Given that this patient has breast cancer with multiple metastases, this is going to be a relatively easy hurdle to overcome for the doctor. Second, any treatment given to this woman must be 'proper and reasonable'. In other words, it should conform to the actions of a reasonable and competent practitioner, and should be accepted as such by a responsible body of medical opinion (see *Bolam v Friern HMC [1957]*). There may be a case for increasing the dose of Diamorphine, and terminally ill patients are frequently receiving very high dosages. Doubling it, rather than titrating it by increments, may not necessarily find favour with those practitioners who are experts in palliative care, however. The final criterion is that the primary purpose of the medication must be to relieve pain, rather than to shorten life. The facts of our scenario suggest that this patient is not currently in pain, and the doctor's purpose in increasing the dosage of Diamorphine is to hasten her demise.

If this is the case, a court may be disposed to consider this a case of euthanasia, and the doctor would be guilty of murder. Moreover, the nurse who administered this medication would also be implicated in the crime. Past experience suggests, however, that the courts are extremely reluctant to convict in such instances, for the penalty is life imprisonment. This is not something that one would wish to test, though, and the nurse would be well advised to report his/her concerns to the doctor. If the doctor is unable to provide a satisfactory rationale for his decision or simply ignores all protests, the nurse must then check with his/her managers and the consultant in charge of the case. If it is the consultant who has made this decision, the nurse could always approach the Medical Director.

Ultimately, however, the nurse should not feel compelled to give this medication unless s/he receives a satisfactory response to concerns raised. Thus, in the absence of support from managers and other medical colleagues, the doctor should be asked to administer the medication himself, for he has no right to implicate others in criminal activity. Needless to say, all of this should be clearly documented in case an investigation subsequently takes place.

2   The first thing to consider in this scenario is whether or not the patient is competent to make a decision regarding his welfare. It is conceivable that his refusal to accept ongoing treatment is a manifestation of his hypoxia; or, alternatively, he may be very depressed. If extensive assessment reveals that neither of these is present, it

is clear that continued treatment in the face of a competent refusal will constitute a battery (see *Re B [2002]*).

If, conversely, there is reason to doubt the patient's competence, the healthcare team must then determine whether or not continued treatment serves any useful purpose. While there is potential for recovery, the purpose is clear; but an absence of realistic hope for this patient renders such treatment futile. Once its futility is established, the healthcare team would be justified in withdrawing it (see *Airedale NHS Trust v Bland [1993]*). The wishes of the family should, of course, be taken into consideration, but they have no legal authority to insist upon treatment. In the face of their vociferous objections, it may be advisable to seek a court ruling on the matter; but the healthcare team also have an obligation to try and maintain a good relationship with the family and to explain the situation as clearly as possible. Where there are serious disagreements between healthcare professionals and family members, the atmosphere can be very tense (see *Glass v United Kingdom [2004]*); and, in such circumstances, it is going to be easier to take the pragmatic approach and accede to the wishes of the patient's relatives. This would, however, involve a sacrifice of one's integrity and may run counter to the best interests of the patient. Doing the 'right thing' may consequently require courage, but this should not deflect the healthcare team from their primary objective.

3   Whether or not this patient has a written Advance Decision to refuse treatment, we are in the fortunate position of knowing his wishes when he was competent. An Advance Decision does not give an individual the right to *demand* treatment (see *R (on the application of Burke) v General Medical Council [2005]*), and he cannot therefore insist upon measures that may prolong his life. It does, however, authorise refusal of treatment that may have this effect. Whether Diamorphine shortens life or prolongs it is a matter of some debate. Its respiratory depressive effects are well-known, but there is a strong case to be made that severe and intractable pain will exhaust the patient and ensure that his demise will come sooner rather than later.

The family's legal status in this situation has been outlined in the response to the previous question, but their threats of violence render this a police matter. The tragedy of this position, though, is that both sides want what is best for the patient, but there is no meeting of minds here. In consequence, the healthcare professionals will be called upon to exercise excellent communication skills if a complete breakdown of trust is to be avoided.

REFERENCES

TEXTS

British Medical Association (2004) *Medical Ethics Today: The BMA's Handbook of Ethics and Law*, 2nd edn. London: BMJ Books.

Department of Health (2003) *Confidentiality: NHS Code of Practice*. London: Department of Health (November).

Dimond, B. (2011) *Legal Aspects of Nursing*, 6th edn. Harlow: Pearson Education.

Harris, J. (1985) *The Value of Life*. London: Routledge.

Nursing and Midwifery Council (2008) *Code of Professional Conduct: Standards for Performance, Conduct and Ethics.* London: NMC.

CASES

Airedale NHS Trust v Bland [1993] 1 All ER 821.
B (consent to treatment: capacity), Re [2002] 2 All ER 449.
B v Croydon Health Authority [1995] 1 All ER 683.
Bolam v Friern Hospital Management Committee [1957] 2 All ER 118.
C (an adult: refusal of treatment), Re [1994] 1 All ER 819 (FD).
Crawford v Board of Governors of Charing Cross Hospital [1953] *The Times*, 8 December, CA.
E (a minor: wardship: medical treatment), Re [1993] 1 FLR 386.
Egan v Central Manchester & Manchester Children's University Hospitals NHS Trust [2008] EWCA Civ. 1424.
F (mental patient: sterilisation), Re [1990] 2 AC 1, sub nom F v West Berkshire HA [1989] 2 All ER 545.
Gartside v Outram [1856] 26 LJ Ch. 113.
Gillick v West Norfolk and Wisbech Area Health Authority [1985] 3 All ER 402 (HL).
Glass v United Kingdom [2004] TLR 11 March (ECHR).
GJ v Foundation Trust, PCT and the Secretary of State for Health [2010] 1 FLR 1251.
HE v A Hospital NHS Trust [2003] EWHC 1017.
Hedley Byrne & Co. Ltd.v Heller & Partners Ltd. [1964] 2 All ER 575.
KB, Re [1994] 19 BMLR 144.
M (child: refusal of medical treatment), Re [1999] 2 FLR 1097.
Malette v Shulman [1991] 2 MD. LR 162.
Manning v King's College Hospital NHS Trust [2008] EWHC 1838 (QB).
R (a minor) (wardship: consent to treatment), Re [1992] Fam. 11 CA.
R (on the application of Burke) v General Medical Council [2005] EWCA Civ. 1003.
R v Lowe [1973] 1 All ER 805 (CA).
R v Mental Health Review Tribunal for the South Thames Region, ex parte Smith [1998] 47 BMLR 104 (QBD).
R v Sheppard and another [1980] 3 All ER 899 (HL).
S (a minor) (consent to medical treatment), Re [1994] 2 FLR 1065.
Tameside & Glossop Acute Services Trust v CH [1996] 1 FLR 762.

LEGISLATION

Children Act 1989
Children Act 2004
Children and Young Persons Act 1933
Computer Misuse Act 1990
Health and Safety at Work Act 1974
Mental Capacity Act 2005
Mental Health Act 1983
Mental Health Act 2007
Police and Criminal Evidence Act 1984
Terrorism Act 2000

INDEX